Captain's
DIARY 2009

Captain's

DIARY 2009

HarperSports
An imprint of HarperCollinsPublishers

Harper*Sports*

An imprint of HarperCollins*Publishers* Australia

First published in Australia in 2009
by HarperCollins*Publishers* Australia Pty Limited
ABN 36 009 913 517
harpercollins.com.au

HarperCollins*Publishers*

25 Ryde Road, Pymble, Sydney, NSW 2073, Australia
31 View Road, Glenfield, Auckland 0627, New Zealand
A 53, Sector 57, Noida, UP, India
77–85 Fulham Palace Road, London, W6 8JB, United Kingdom
2 Bloor Street East, 20th floor, Toronto, Ontario M4W 1A8, Canada
10 East 53rd Street, New York NY 10022, USA

National Library of Australia Cataloguing-in-Publication data:

Ponting, Ricky.
  Captain's diary 2009 / Ricky Ponting and Geoff Armstrong.
  ISBN: 978 0 7322 8957 7 (pbk.)
  Ponting, Ricky – Diaries.
  Cricket captains – Australia – Diaries.
  Cricket players – Australia – Diaries.
  Test matches (Cricket) – Australia – History.
  Cricket – England – Tournaments.
  Other Authors/Contributors: Armstrong, Geoff.
796.35865

Cover design by Matt Stanton
Front cover photograph by Hamish Blair/Getty Images
Back cover photograph by Colleen Petch/Newspix
Typeset in 11/17 Sabon by Kirby Jones
Printed and bound in Australia by Griffin Press
70gsm Classic used by HarperCollins*Publishers* is a natural, recyclable product made from wood
grown in sustainable forests. The manufacturing processes conform to the environmental
regulations in the country of origin, Finland.

5 4 3 2 1   09 10 11 12

For all my supporters … in the team, in the crowd and especially in my family. In a year of ups and downs, the backing I received from Rianna, Emmy and those closest to me was unwavering, for which I am extremely grateful.

One of my favourite memories of the Ashes tour is from Headingley, straight after our win there, when Rianna and Emmy joined me on the ground. The victory was brilliant, one of the most decisive I've been involved in, and having them there to share the experience with me made it even better.

GEOFF ARMSTRONG

Ricky Ponting's co-author on *Captain's Diary 2009*, Geoff Armstrong, has worked — as writer, editor or publisher — on more than 80 books on sport, more than 30 of them on cricket. Between 1993 and 2005, he collaborated with Steve Waugh on each of Steve's 12 best-selling books, including all of his diaries and his autobiography *Out of My Comfort Zone*, and has worked with Ricky on the current Australian captain's annual cricket diary since 2006. Geoff is the author of *A Century of Summers*, the centenary history of the Sheffield Shield (featuring an epilogue by Sir Donald Bradman), *ESPN's Legends of Cricket*, which profiles 25 of the game's greatest players, *The 100 Greatest Cricketers*, and is the co-author, with Mark Gately, of *The People's Game*, a history of Australia in one-day international cricket. He has worked as co-author on books by David Boon, Ian Healy, Mike Whitney, Bob Simpson and Michael Bevan, and with Ian Russell produced *Top 10s of Australian Test Cricket*, a study of Australian cricket statistics.

Geoff is also the co-author, with Peter Thompson, of *Phar Lap*, the definitive biography of the legendary racehorse, and *Melbourne Cup 1930*, the story of the most remarkable of Phar Lap's many big-race victories.

CONTENTS

CO-AUTHOR'S NOTE

As he has done in previous years, Ricky Ponting kept notes pertaining to all the significant events and issues that occurred in Australian cricket from the time he gave the Bradman Oration in August 2008 to the final ODI on the 2009 Ashes tour. During that time and immediately afterwards, he and I went through that material, and also considered a number of radio interviews and countless internet and newspaper reports, including columns he wrote for the *Australian* and the London *Telegraph*, to produce in a diary format — not a day-by-day account; rather, a few days at a time — his take on another remarkable year of cricket. The result is this book.

Ricky and I are very grateful that in a year in which he won his first Formula One Grand Prix, Mark Webber was able to take the time to write the foreword for this diary. We also appreciate the support given to us by some notable people at Cricket Australia: Peter Young, Philip Pope and Lachy Patterson. We are grateful for the constant backing we received from Ricky's manager James Henderson and the entire team at DSEG, and from everyone at HarperCollins.

The statistics, scores and averages that appear through the diary and at the end of the book were derived from a variety of sources, including three excellent websites — *cricinfo.com*, *howstat.com: the cricket statisticians* and *cricketarchive.com*.

Geoff Armstrong
September 2009

Foreword

BY MARK WEBBER

IT WAS LATE IN 2008, a few days after I had been discharged from hospital having broken my leg, when a friend of mine got in touch with me and said that Ricky Ponting would like to come and say hello to me in Melbourne. This was the first time I had met Ricky, although because I'm sports-mad I have followed him and the side for years. In our discussions we not surprisingly talked sport, the beloved media and the most prized possession in cricket: the Ashes. After he left, I thought to myself, *that is a real Australian*. Just how I like them: not a huge amount of small talk, a very down-to-earth bloke.

Although our sports are very different, the same qualities are needed to be successful — the extended levels of concentration, ability to perform under changing pressures and the gift of being able to anticipate your rivals' tactics.

I'm a very passionate supporter of the 'Baggy Green', but I'm in no position at all to say that we should have taken a spinner into the last Test at The Oval for the Ashes in 2009. However, I certainly box my corner, sticking up for our Australian cricket side, especially at Red Bull Racing F1 where unfortunately more than 400 Poms work. And, no surprise, they now all automatically love cricket!

I was in Australia last summer when we got rolled over by the 'Saffers', but was stoked with the reply of the Aussies in the return series in South Africa a few weeks later. It was great to see the smile off Dale Steyn's face, who for some reason I took a strong dislike to, but who could well be a good bloke. Having travelled so well in South Africa, I thought we would be in great nick to do very well on the lush pitches of the UK, but unfortunately the Ashes series didn't quite go the way I expected. In total, we scored more runs and took more wickets but still lost. As always, there are key stages in top sporting events where that blade needs to go deep into the jugular. The last hour of the first Test at Cardiff is a prime example of how, during this series, the Aussies were unable to do that.

One of my greatest highlights was attending the Lord's Test match, where Ricky invited me into the Aussie dressing room. To be able to see one of my favourite teams at the 'Home of Cricket' is something I'll never forget. It was when I was in the room, seeing all the guys from this team together, that it really hit home to me just how huge the transformation our national team has gone through in the last few years has been. I felt young with the 2005 Ashes squad when I visited them; this time I felt old.

I wish Ricky and the team all the success possible in the future and I'll continue to be totally one-eyed when it comes to our boys competing. See you at the Boxing Day Test at the G!

Mark Webber
September 2009

Introduction

BY RICKY PONTING

IF I EVER NEEDED a reminder that the Ashes is the biggest thing for an Australian cricketer, the year of cricket from September 2008 to September 2009 provided it. In the space of 12 months we played a sequence of Test series and tournaments where, in different circumstances, any one of those series or tournaments could have been rated the major event of the cricket year. First, we went to India, where cricket inspires so much passion, for a four-match Test series. Then we had Test series home and away against South Africa, who as I write this in late September 2009 are the No. 1 ranked team in both Test and one-day international cricket. In June, we played in the second ICC World Twenty20 tournament. Right now, we are just hours away from the start of the Champions Trophy, the second biggest limited-overs competition in our sport.

However, for me and my team-mates, the Ashes series, played between June 8 and August 23, stands out so clearly. We knew from day one that in most people's eyes it was the measuring stick as to whether our year would be a success or not. It represented the chance for me and my team to make history, to establish our own Ashes legend. The interest these Test matches generated, in England and Australia, was phenomenal and we knew, though we were a long way from home, that our fans desperately wanted us to reverse the loss we suffered in 2005.

Our team four years ago featured some of the biggest names in the game, such as Shane Warne, Glenn McGrath, Matthew Hayden, Justin Langer, Jason Gillespie and Damien Martyn; this time, we were much younger but the pressure and the expectations were the same …

Captain's Diary 2009 is the story of this year in the life of the Australian cricket team. Strictly in terms of wins and losses, it wasn't a great 12 months but regardless of where we played or whom we played, we gave ourselves strong opportunities to claim every series. We played 17 Tests in all, but only at Mohali, Delhi, Cape Town and Lord's were we never in a position to force a win. Too often, though, we would put in a really bad session or blow the big moment, and a game might be lost. It became a year of 'what might have been'.

At Bangalore, in the first Test of the India series, we needed to bowl the home team out on the final day but couldn't, and the game ended in a draw. One more wicket at Nagpur and we might have been a chance, but instead MS Dhoni and Harbhajan Singh batted us out of the game. In Perth, we set South Africa more than 400 for victory, but they got them. At the MCG, South Africa were 7–184 in reply to our 394 but recovered to win. We were a wicket away from nailing the first Ashes Test by an innings. When we needed a fighting performance at The Oval, less than two weeks after our pace bowlers had blown England away at Headingley, we lost eight wickets in a session. In each instance, we just couldn't sustain our best form when the pressure was really on, even though every time we had played really well in the previous session or (in the case of The Oval) the previous Test to get ourselves in a position to prevail.

We had the same opportunities the great Australian teams of the past 10 years had to win matches, but unlike them we couldn't get the job done.

Why? My first reflex was to blame our inexperience. Now, though, with the benefit of just a few days' post-Ashes to think about our performances, I think we've been suffering not so much from a lack of experience and know-how as a lack of 'belief'. Simply put, there are a number of players in the current Australian squad who as yet have not consistently 'been there and done it'.

It was actually a quote from England captain Andrew Strauss during the one-dayers that followed the Ashes Tests that underlined this point for me. He was talking about Tim Paine, the young Tasmanian wicketkeeper who came into the Aussie team because regular keeper Brad Haddin was out with a broken finger and made his maiden ODI century at Trent Bridge, when we won to take a 6–nil lead in the series.

'He played very well,' Andrew said. 'He's playing in a confident side, which helps. It's easy to come into a side that's full of confidence and winning and show your true calibre. I think it's a bit harder when the side is low on confidence.'

The irony of Andrew's statement, of course, is that it came less than three weeks after we lost the Ashes. It's amazing what a few consecutive wins can do! Back in the mid '90s, I came into an Australian team that was winning, and so did every other Australian player to make his debut between 1995 (the year we beat the West Indies in the West Indies) and 2007. But the guys who established themselves in the team after that — and that's the bulk of those who wore the baggy green during the 2009 Ashes series — are not used to winning all the time.

Winning is a habit, it's contagious. I remember Matt Hayden making a comment that blew my mind after he scored his first Test hundred, against the West Indies in Adelaide on the Australia Day weekend in 1997, three years after he made his Test debut. Matt had scored more than 20 first-class hundreds by then, but soon after he made that first Test ton he said to me, 'You know, Punter, I didn't know if I was good enough to ever make a hundred at Test level.'

'What are you talking about?' I responded. 'You've done it over and over and over.'

I must confess that such a thought had never occurred to me, even though I wasn't even in the Test team at that point and was still six months away from making my first Test century. It just goes to show how different people think differently about the task at hand. You can tell a gifted young player that he has the goods, but if he doesn't truly believe it himself then he might be intimidated when the pressure goes on. Only when that player breaks through, by making a hundred or taking a five-for, will he become the star he's always promised to be. Matty Hayden went on to make 30 Test-match hundreds, and to be regarded as one of the greatest opening batsmen of all time. I think there are young players in the current Australian side who one day will be thought of in a similar light.

***

WE WENT TO SOUTH Africa in February, halfway through the year covered in this book, with a game plan to which we were all fully committed. For the first few days of this tour, while we were in camp in Potchefstroom, we worked as hard as we could to get ourselves up for the first Test. You could really sense, during that series, that we were a committed, passionate unit and the South Africans didn't quite know what hit them.

We set out to duplicate that feeling in England but there were times, especially at Lord's and maybe at The Oval, when maybe we built the occasion up into something so great that a few of the boys 'tightened up' as a result. I felt in 2005 we got a little lax at times in our preparation; this time, though, because of all the mystique and legend and scrutiny that surrounds the Ashes, maybe we went a little too much the other way. Since all of us were kids, whenever we dreamt about playing for Australia, we dreamt about beating England before anyone else, about going on an Ashes tour, playing a Test match at the 'Home of Cricket'. Again, if the self-belief had been there we would have been okay, but it's a bit like if you give some players a game plan that's too complicated, building a moment up too much can just confuse things, put too much pressure on. That's what I believe happened in 2009. Things can unravel a little as a result.

I've said many times that one of the most important skills a captain needs is to know how to manage different individuals within a team set-up. One guy might need a serve to prod him into doing his best, while the bloke next to him might retreat if you treat him the same way. Similarly, you have to be careful how you rev up the team as a whole, because what might be good for some of the group might have a reverse effect on others.

I know some people outside our group have misinterpreted the way we have responded to the big occasions by concluding that we don't have much fun anymore, but they're wrong. Sure, professional sport now is a different animal to how it was 30, even 10 years ago, but we haven't forgotten that it's a sport we're playing and a fantastic life we've earned for ourselves. Sure, our schedules are packed but there is still time for a laugh, whether it be on a golf course, at a charity event, watching a soccer game, listening to the Melbourne Cup thousands of miles from home. Our coaches see it as a challenge to vary our training to make sure it never becomes a grind. And while we mightn't party as hard as they did in the 'good old days', and we don't get out as much because the scrutiny the team is under is so much tougher, there are still plenty of opportunities available to enjoy each other's company. Furthermore, our families travel with us much more now than in the past, and I for one am much happier than I otherwise would be because that is happening.

I emphasise this point about my cricket life being fun quite deliberately here, because I know there is some speculation about my future, especially now that I have given up the Australian Twenty20 captaincy (the reasons for which I outline in the epilogue of this book). Aside from feeling the same anguish over the same result, I enjoyed the 2009 England tour more than four years ago. As I look back on my career to this point, the Ashes in '05 was the hardest series of cricket I've played — we were under so much pressure throughout that memorable English summer, there just never seemed to be a moment's rest. We were under the same sort of scrutiny, but I expected it this time. I was vigorously booed at every opportunity during the first four Tests, but that didn't really bug me; it was all part of it. In '05, there were times when it just felt really hard; this time, while it was just as competitive, I wanted to win just as badly and the media was always there, waiting for me to make a mistake, but I never felt consumed by it. I let a few runs slip away, and after the first Test I didn't make the really big score I yearned for, but there was a spirit about the series I really enjoyed, perhaps as much as any series I have been involved in.

I'll leave it to others to worry about whether I should be captain. As I've always said, I will keep playing (whether I've got a 'c' next to my name or not) as long as I feel like I can keep improving and adding something to the team and as long as I am enjoying it. I have been encouraged by the support I received after the Ashes series from Cricket Australia, and I also sense that the feeling this time is different to 2005, when there were a number of people, including some high-profile former Australian players, who were calling for my head. This time, there is a general acknowledgement that the team is still in transition, but on the right track.

However, that doesn't change the reality that in three of the four major Test series we played from September '08 to September '09, we weren't quite good enough. The only consolation I have is that I know I gave myself and the team every possible opportunity that we could to succeed. I've got no regrets about the way we prepared for these series. In England, I took any little opportunity I could find to provide support for my team-mates. I didn't play the game in Northampton between the second and third Tests, but I stayed with the boys and was at the ground for all but an hour (when I had a quick party with my wife Rianna and daughter Emmy, who was celebrating her first birthday). Same at Canterbury between the fourth and fifth Tests — it would have been easy for me to leave the team on the basis that a short break would leave me as mentally fresh as possible before the Ashes decider, but I didn't want to have any regrets about how the team approached what was for all of us just about the most important match of our lives. I'm sure our coaches would say exactly the same thing about their efforts and I'd agree with them.

Unfortunately, though, the coaches can't help us through difficult situations out on the field. Out there, we have to help ourselves. That's the lesson that keeps coming through in the pages that follow. If the young blokes in our team can just get a handle on how good they can be, and can truly convince themselves that they belong at the highest level, then the road ahead is a genuinely exciting one.

I really believe that.

Ricky Ponting
September 2009

PART ONE

THE AUSTRALIANS
IN INDIA, 2008

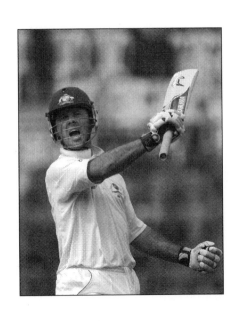

Sunday, September 14

First ODI, Australia v Bangladesh, at Darwin (August 30): Australia
8–254 (50 overs: SE Marsh 76, MEK Hussey 85) defeated **Bangladesh** 74
(27.4 overs: CL White 3–5) by 180 runs

Second ODI, Australia v Bangladesh, at Darwin (September 3):
Bangladesh 117 (36.1 overs: MG Johnson 3–17) lost to **Australia** 1–118
(22.4 overs: SE Marsh 69*) by nine wickets

Third ODI, Australia v Bangladesh, at Darwin (September 6): Australia
5–191 (50 overs: MEK Hussey 57*) defeated **Bangladesh** 125 (29.5 overs:
Tamim Iqbal 63; JR Hopes 3–30) by 66 runs

***

For me, the past six weeks have flown by. I've been recovering
from the wrist surgery that ended my West Indies tour early,
watched the Beijing Olympics (I hope one day Twenty20 cricket
can become an Olympic sport), delivered the annual Bradman
Oration, and missed the three one-dayers played in Darwin
against Bangladesh in late August and early September. Most
importantly, Rianna and I experienced the joys of parenthood,
as beautiful little Emmy Ponting (born on July 26, 2008)
enjoyed the first few weeks of her life. The perspective Emmy
has brought me has been fantastic, and while I'd never wish my
wrist injury on anyone, the fact that it has allowed me to spend
time at home during this wonderful period in our lives has been
a real blessing.

As I type this, my wrist isn't quite right, but it's close. I didn't pick up a bat until the pre-tour camp in Brisbane late last month, and have gradually increased my net-time from there, to the point where I feel that right now I'm hitting the ball okay. Matt Hayden, who's coming back from an Achilles tendon problem that curtailed his Caribbean adventure before the first Test against the Windies, is in a similar boat. Of course, it won't be until we get out in the middle that we'll know exactly how rusty we are, but I must say I'm confident we'll be right.

I delivered my tribute to Sir Donald Bradman on August 27, exactly 100 years after the great man was born in Cootamundra. I was extremely nervous in the lead-up, worried that I wouldn't do his memory justice, and I raced through what was supposed to be a 30-minute address ahead of time. But the reaction was positive, for which I am grateful. The main point I wanted to make was that Sir Donald's extraordinary influence lives on in the minds of all Aussie cricketers, young and old, from Test players to those who have fun every week in the park and in backyard games. Thousands of kids have grown up and will continue to grow up wanting to reach the same enormous heights so uniquely scaled by the greatest cricketer who ever lived.

I love the fact that we all know his Test batting average, and how that statistic — essentially a hundred per innings — demonstrates his clear superiority to all other batsmen. After he won eight gold medals in Beijing, some are saying the amazing American swimmer Michael Phelps might be the greatest athlete of all time. With due respect to Phelps, I don't put him in Sir Donald's class.

The reason for this is crystal clear. Of the 2519 batsmen to date who have taken the crease in 131 years of Test cricket, The Don stands alone. Olympic records come and go, but that 99.94 batting average is unassailable. Yet his impact on the game went

Delhi Bomb Blast

As I write this diary entry, news has just come through of a number of bomb blasts in New Delhi that have killed at least 20 people, maybe more. New Delhi is where the third Test is scheduled to be played. After the stance we and other teams took with travelling to Pakistan, which led to the Champions Trophy being postponed, I know there will be speculation as to the fate of the upcoming India tour.

Once again, I will listen to and accept the advice of the Australian Government, Cricket Australia and our players' association as to what we as cricketers should do. And once again, a terrorist attack has me thinking about my life as a professional cricketer, how as part of that job I am obliged to journey to places that are from time to time considered dangerous. I always come to the conclusion that it's worth it, that my family understands and agrees with me, and that the security measures put in place are sufficient. Occasionally, though, I wonder if I'll always feel this way.

far beyond his runs, as he was also a great captain and administrator, and an astute analyst on the game, too, a man who never lived in the past. I met him when I was a 15-year-old rookie at the Cricket Academy in Adelaide, something I'll never forget, and was struck by the fact that while he was short in stature and quietly spoken, everyone was clearly in awe of him, taking in every word he said.

In the lead-up to the Oration, I did plenty of research on his life and have come to realise that part of his continuing celebrity status is a result of the times in which he played. The memories of World War I were still vivid when he made his Test debut and by the time he made his first tour of England the world was in the grips of the

Great Depression. Bradman's prodigious achievements came during a time of despair. He lifted and energised a nation.

Sir Donald was a batsman capable of scoring 300 runs in a day's play. None of us today can do that, but we still aim to be entertainers, to try our best to keep the Bradman spirit alive. Really, when you think about all he did for the game and his country, that is the very least we can do.

***

THE SERIES IN DARWIN went well for us — three solid wins, with Shaun Marsh and Mike Hussey impressing with the bat, Mitchell Johnson and Stuart Clark with the ball, and Shane Watson doing some nice things as an all-rounder in games two and three. We might be in a rebuilding phase at the moment, after the retirements of a number of famous players in the past two years, but with the exception of the Commonwealth Bank Series last season, which was played during a turbulent time, Australia has been playing some outstanding one-day cricket of late. These games against Bangladesh were just an extension of that form.

The one negative to come out of the games up north was the decision to omit Andrew Symonds from the squad after he skipped a team meeting for a fishing trip immediately before the series. Michael Clarke, who was captain in my absence, copped a bit of heat over that decision, as if it was all his own doing, but the truth was that it was a judgment made by the team leadership group: me, coach Tim Nielsen, the team manager Steve Bernard and Pup.

We'd been a little concerned about Symmo for a while — nothing major, just a run of things that suggested he wasn't as focused as he could have been — and hoped that this jolt would get him back on track. No doubt, he'd been shaken by the events of the previous summer, when none of us felt he got all the support he deserved, but where the rest of us had done our best to move on, he was still cranky and anxious to prove he is his own man. That's okay, so long as it doesn't damage the game or the team fabric, but there have been times lately when Symmo has seemed to be missing that point. This certainly wasn't an easy decision, leaving out a bloke who in Tests in 2007–08 averaged 77 with the bat (one century and seven fifties) and took 12 wickets at 21. However, the decision to leave him out of the Bangladesh ODIs and then the one announced two days ago that he wouldn't be going to India for our four-Test tour that begins in less than a fortnight were both made, we strongly believe, in the best interests of the team and also of a bloke who has been and continues to be a good mate.

Chairman of Selectors Andrew Hilditch had this to say after the team for India was chosen: 'Andrew Symonds was stood down for disciplinary reasons in Darwin and is now going through a process designed to give him time to assess whether he is fully committed to all of the things needed for a cricketer to be a member of the world's No. 1 team.' Coach Tim Nielsen talked publicly about how we need to provide 'as much support as we possibly can' for Symmo, and we all agree with that, but as Tim emphasised, we don't need him back under any circumstances — only if he's 100 per cent devoted to the group. Right now, that ambition doesn't seem to be there, so we have to build our plans for India knowing we'll be without our first-choice No. 6 batsman and all-rounder.

Our squad for India contains a few surprises. No Symmo was obviously the main talking point but there is also no Beau Casson, who'd played in the final Test in the West Indies but who apparently had a tough time during the recent tour of India by an Australia A side. Instead, the spin spots had gone to a leggie, Bryce McGain, from Victoria, and an offie, Jason Krejza, now playing for Tasmania after moving south from New South Wales. Another Victorian, Peter Siddle, a quick about whom I'd received some good reports and who had bowled with great vigour in the 2007–08 Pura Cup final, also made the squad, while Shane Watson looks likely to fill the all-rounder's spot. The full squad is Ricky Ponting (captain), Michael Clarke (vice-captain), Doug Bollinger, Stuart Clark, Brad Haddin, Matthew Hayden, Michael Hussey, Phil Jaques, Mitchell Johnson, Simon Katich, Jason Krejza, Brett Lee, Bryce McGain, Peter Siddle and Shane Watson.

If Symmo is the big loss for this tour, a nice counterpoint is the return of Brett Lee, who also missed the games against Bangladesh for personal reasons. Bing was clearly our best bowler in 2008–09, taking 105 wickets in Tests, ODIs and Twenty20 Internationals, including 58 in nine Tests (by way of comparison, Glenn McGrath's most productive result from nine straight Tests was 54 wickets), and with the departure of Glenn, Shane Warne, Jason Gillespie and Stuart MacGill (among other outstanding bowlers) in the past couple of years, his top form is crucial to our prospects for success. A bit surprisingly, given that he's been a Test bowler for almost nine years, these will be Brett's first Tests in India. He missed the 2001 tour because of injury and was 12th man in all four Tests in 2004, when Glenn, Jason and Michael Kasprowicz bowled us to a famous victory.

Originally, we were scheduled to play in the Champions Trophy in Pakistan between the end of the Bangladesh one-dayers and the start of the Indian tour. However, the postponement of that tournament because of continuing security concerns has left us with no international cricket as part of our preparation for our time in India. This is unfortunate, but I don't think it will hurt us much so far as the Tests against India are concerned, as we've become used to playing series after a variety of preparations. My understanding is that a second warm-up game has been added to our itinerary.

Saturday, September 27

It happened at the media conference at Sydney Airport before we left for India and it happened again after we arrived a few days back in Jaipur. The reporters were very keen to remind me that my batting average for Tests in India is a mere 12.28. As if I didn't know.

I've had a couple of disappointing Test series in India. I didn't go too well in 1998, hardly scored a run in 2001, and in 2004 I missed the first three Tests of a four-match series because of a broken thumb; the only Test I played was the one we lost. The one they are always quickest to bring up is 2001, when I went 0, 6, 0, 0, 11 and Harbhajan Singh dismissed me every time. That experience was all about me not having enough faith in my technique, which all came back to the way Harbhajan got me in the first innings of the first Test. I actually felt I was in good touch going into that game, but straightaway I played forward to an off-break that bounced and spun a bit, took the inside edge, and I inside-edged a catch to bat-pad. From that moment, I was fearful of getting out that way again; I tried sweeping, using my feet, anything other than trusting my technique, and I ended up facing just 57 balls in the series. It wasn't until late in the following series — an Ashes series in England — that I finally found my confidence again.

Maybe during that testing time I was also fazed by the chronic negativity about playing in India that used to cloud the

Another Setback

Having lost Symmo before the tour started, we are now also without Bryce McGain, who we'd pencilled in to be our spinner in the first Test. Bryce hurt his shoulder on the recent Australia A tour of India and originally thought he'd be resting the ailment for a few days, but now we've learned that the 'niggle' is actually much worse and he headed home last weekend so he can get it right. At the moment, we don't know exactly when he'll be right to play again; it could be weeks, could be longer.

All our physio, Alex Kountouris, can say is that he is definitely gone for at least a month. Bryce thought he'd be okay when he landed in India, but when he tried to push things at training last week he felt what he called 'a bit of a pop' and knew pretty much straightaway he was in trouble. At first, we hoped he'd just be out for the opening Test, but it's much worse than that.

Less serious, but still a concern, is Michael Clarke's stomach bug, which has caused him to miss some time in the nets. On a brighter note, Matt Hayden is looking all right, if a little rusty, after his long break due to his damaged Achilles tendon.

One of the things I liked about our warm-up game in Hyderabad was that it was played on a slow wicket, the kind of track I'm fairly sure we'll be seeing during the Test series. Not so good was our batting effort in the first innings, when only Mike Hussey made a substantial score, and we needed a big last-wicket stand between Huss and Stuart Clark to avoid the follow-on. Our opponents were a competitive outfit, I was reasonably happy with my double of 41 and 58 not out, and it all added up to an okay dress rehearsal for the first Test.

Australian touring team's thinking. 'I think we made too much of the conditions in India a lot of the times before we got there,' I commented in Sydney before we boarded our plane. 'Quite often, the less you talk about it and the more you get to understand it, the people and the conditions, the better off you are.' Only four members of our squad this time (all batsmen — Michael Clarke, Matt Hayden, Simon Katich and me) have played Test cricket in India, but many of the guys have played over here and we 'veterans' have been keen to let the less experienced blokes know that they are in for an exciting and unique Test-match touring experience.

The greeting we have received here in Jaipur, where the local administrators and the staff at the Rajasthan Cricket Association (RCA) academy have been very kind to us, has underlined this modern reality. It was as close to perfect as we could ask for, as we were able to practise on different types of wickets and against a wide variety of good-class bowlers. I did have to laugh, though, when I read a comment from one senior Indian official. 'RCA is being a little too obliging to the Australian team,' this bloke complained. I guess this kind of chat all adds to the hype over this series that just keeps building. All I know is that when we last came here, in 2004, we played some outstanding cricket, and India did the same when they toured Australia last season. Expectations are naturally high and I think it will be a terrific series.

Tuesday, October 7

Tour game, Australians v Rajasthan Cricket Association Centre of Excellence, at Jaipur (September 27–28): Australians 218 (ML Hayden 73; G Singh 5–58) drew with **RCA Centre of Excellence** 122 (JJ Krejza 3–35, DE Bollinger 3–9)

Tour game, Australians v Indian Board President's XI, at Hyderabad (October 2–5): Indian Board President's XI 455 (RG Sharma 105, V Kohli 105, PA Patel 62, IK Pathan 56; MG Johnson 4–75) and 4–292 dec (W Jaffer 93, Yuvraj Singh 113) drew with the **Australians** 314 (MEK Hussey 126; PP Chawla 5–89) and 2–127 (RT Ponting 58*)

***

Ever since we arrived here in India we have been aware that there is plenty of conjecture about how long Sourav Ganguly can continue to hold onto his place in the Indian Test line-up. Yuvraj Singh's impressive hundred against us at Hyderabad only fuelled the debate. But it seems Sourav has put an abrupt end to such chatter by the way he concluded his pre-Test media conference. As I understand it, after pretty blandly patting back all the tricky questions, the former Indian captain (and my skipper at the Kolkata Knight Riders) flatly stated, 'Just one last thing lads … before I leave … I just want to say that this is going to be my last series. I've decided to quit. I told my team-mates before coming here. These four Test matches are going to be my last and hopefully we'll go on a winning note.'

Ganguly had only been chosen for the first two Tests against us, but now, I guess, he's locked in for the entire series. We'd heard whispers that he might not even make their team for the first Test, and maybe he felt a bit lucky to be included, but it would be a brave selector who dropped him now, given his career record and his popularity in many parts over here. He's been a tough opponent, a good, competitive cricketer, and I hope he enjoys some success (but not too much) during his 'farewell' series.

Much has been made of the turnover in our squad, but the Indians will soon be facing a similar conundrum. Ganguly is just the first of a number of famous names — Dravid … Kumble … Tendulkar … Laxman — who will have to be replaced in the next two or three seasons. Of these, I reckon only Sachin will have the luxury of deciding when he is going to retire, so if we start the series well the Indian media will inevitably begin asking questions and in doing so put pressure on them that could work to our advantage. For example, if we can make their fielding look old through some attacking running between wickets then straightaway there'll be headlines saying 'Ganguly can't field' or 'Dravid looks slow'. In all the time I've been in the Australian set-up we've prided ourselves on being ahead of the game when it comes to fundamentals such as fielding and running between wickets; now it's time to take our skills in these areas to a new level. That's what I was getting at when I said during today's media interviews that I want us to play a 'new-age' type of Test cricket. It might take a while to achieve this, but that's one of our objectives.

***

SOMETHING THE AUSTRALIAN CRICKET team has always managed to do over the past decade, even longer, is quickly yet effectively replace our departing champions. Allan Border retired just as Steve Waugh was beginning the best years of his cricket life. Craig McDermott and Merv Hughes left, and along came Glenn McGrath and Jason Gillespie. Ian Healy was the best wicketkeeper Australia has ever had until Adam Gilchrist came along. We kept winning despite losing batsmen of the calibre of Mark Taylor, Michael Slater and the Waugh twins because of the efforts of blokes such as Matthew Hayden, Justin Langer, Damien Martyn and Michael Clarke. Maybe we haven't convinced everyone that we can handle the loss of Lang, Marto, Pigeon and then Gilly, but I reckon the way Phil Jaques, Simon Katich, Stuart Clark and Brad Haddin have taken to Test cricket has been very encouraging.

The one big cloud for us is how to replace Shane Warne. We all knew the day would come when the great leg-spinner would retire, but we thought we had the short term covered with Stuart MacGill. In addition, we'd given young slow bowlers such as Nathan Hauritz, Dan Cullen and Beau Casson a taste of Test cricket. But now, with Stuey having retired ahead of schedule and no one else having really put their hand up as the natural long-term successor, we find ourselves with, potentially at least, a real problem. Beau went pretty well when he made his Test debut last June in the West Indies but missed selection for this trip. I must confess that I'm not the greatest fan of 'Chinaman' bowlers as a bowling style — at the top level I reckon they've got to be absolutely top-class to be successful, especially in India where the pitches are often slow turners — and while this is not necessarily a knock on Beau, it does underline the fact that he needs to keep improving to cement a place in the Test XI.

Our two spinners for this tour are Jason Krejza and now, with Bryce McGain out, Cameron White. Jason's first-class stats aren't impressive, but he gives the ball as good a rip as any offie I've seen and he could be suited over here. I've rated him from the first time I saw him, at our Centre of Excellence in Brisbane a few years back, when it seemed that for a young slow bowler he had all the skills: good flight, drift and drop, plenty of overspin, lots of turn. His problem has been his consistency — a few too many four balls mixed in with the good ones — but if he can get that right I still think he's got a real future. My feeling is we have to handle him carefully; if we pick him at the wrong time we might do him, and us, more harm than good. Cameron is something of a reluctant leggie, but very capable of bowling an unplayable ball, and he's proved in the Sheffield Shield and in ODI and Twenty20 cricket that he's a good hitter and a tough, smart cricketer who brings a lot to the group. It wouldn't surprise me if we played both of them in a Test match before this tour is through.

But not straight away. With Jason having taken 0–199 from 31 overs against the Indian Board President's XI in Hyderabad, Cameron now has the inside running to win his first Test cap in Bangalore. Still, while Jason's bowling figures might not have been too flash in that game, and there were times when the local batsmen (especially Yuvraj Singh in their second innings) really took to him, there was still a bit to like about the way he went about things. The guy wants to succeed and is prepared to back himself, and at the same time he's willing to learn. When the Board President's XI closed their second innings, I could hear all this yelling and screaming coming from somewhere. It was Jason on the boundary, expressing his disappointment at the fact that he wasn't going to get another over. For me, that was a good sign. Then at training yesterday, he bowled better than he had at any previous stage on this tour. He has all the skills he needs to become a very good off-spinner but at the same time Cameron is much more experienced, and he performed very well on the A tour here, albeit mainly in one-dayers.

The name of our first-choice spinner might have changed a few times in the past 12 months, but there has been one constant. Inevitably, whenever the subject of Australian spin bowling comes up, I am asked if there was any chance of Warney making a sudden return to the Aussie Test team. Apparently Shane raised the possibility himself during a recent interview.

'I'm not sure how much bowling he's done,' was my response.

'A few balls,' a reporter suggested straight-faced.

'That's good preparation for four Tests in India,' I replied.

The difference between our spin-bowling and fast-bowling stocks is substantial. It is true that our spinners are inexperienced and we could have problems if Cameron or Jason struggle, but while our quicks are similarly untried in Test cricket in India I have enormous faith in them. All three of Brett Lee, Mitchell Johnson and Stuart Clark have shown their class many times, while Peter Siddle has really impressed me in the nets and Doug Bollinger, who took three quick wickets when he got a bowl in Jaipur, is coming off a terrific 2007–08 season with NSW. I see no reason why our fast bowlers alone can't win us this Test series.

We do have a very different team here to the one that triumphed in 2004, and at times I'm sure I will have to come up with different tactics to get the job done than the way guys such as Adam Gilchrist, Damien Martyn, Glenn McGrath, Shane Warne, Michael Kasprowicz and Jason Gillespie succeeded four years ago. But I have always believed that anyone who plays for Australia is capable of getting the job done.

Wednesday, October 8

So now Virender Sehwag has come out and said we cheated during the Test at the Sydney Cricket Ground last January. Apparently this came about after he was asked if there would be any agreement between the two teams over ground-level catches during the upcoming series. Sehwag said there was no point in having such a pact because we hadn't stuck to it when it mattered.

'We'd have won the Sydney Test match if they hadn't claimed catches taken off half-volleys in that game,' Sehwag was quoted as saying. I would love to have said what I really thought when I heard what he'd said: that his comments were ridiculous and provocative. Maybe that's what he wanted me to say, but I know I have to be careful and not add fuel to unnecessary confrontations. In cases like this, playing the diplomat can be tiring, but that's the way it's got to be.

'That's fairly insulting,' was my measured reply when I was asked to respond, before I tried to steer the discussion away from Sehwag and towards the Indian team as a group. 'In the first innings [in Sydney] I didn't claim a catch because I wasn't 100 per cent sure. It's amazing how they've picked out a lot of negatives from that game and don't seem to be speaking about the Perth Test [the next game in last season's series), where we probably had the same things happen to us. Not one member of the Australian team has spoken about it. We go about our cricket in different ways.'

Maybe the fact they're still talking about last time is a good sign for us. I'm not sure what they are trying to achieve by constantly referring to what happened nine months ago. When the media pressed me on that Sydney Test, I didn't bite on the controversies. 'It was a Test we won,' I said, 'a crucial Test for the overall series. As I said at the time, it was one of the best moments I've had on a cricket field. To win the way we did was an outstanding effort by the team.'

Then, finally, we began to look to the future. Bangalore was one of the more bowler-friendly venues during the IPL last season — relatively quick with some bounce and seam. This pitch looks pretty hard, even though it was watered fairly heavily yesterday afternoon. Greg Chappell, who's travelling with the Aussie team at the moment, says it's the best track he's seen here. My expectation is that it will be a very good batting surface, at least for the first two or three days. The weather forecast is for overcast skies and fairly high humidity, so it might swing a bit more than usual. I know some people have suggested it will turn from day one, but I think it will probably take until very late in the game before it starts to spin too much or suffer from variable bounce.

Tuesday, October 14

First Test, India v Australia, at Bangalore (October 9–13): Australia 430 (SM Katich 66, RT Ponting 123, MEK Hussey 146; Zaheer Khan 5–91, Ishant Sharma 4–77) and 6–228 dec drew with **India** 360 (R Dravid 51, Harbhajan Singh 54, Zaheer Khan 57*; MG Johnson 4–70) and 4–177

✱✱✱

This was a pretty good Test match for us — one of those games where we did a few things wrong and a number of things right, but not enough to get over the line. The most frustrating part is that we were the team that clearly had the best chance to win the game, but we couldn't press home our advantage. Test matches are never easy, especially when you're playing a good team away from home, so the thing we have to work hardest on coming out of this match is regaining that ruthless streak that was once our trademark.

I know that's not as simple as just flicking a switch back on. Confidence is part of it; we also need all of our most important players to rediscover their best form. Our bowling attack lacked penetration at different times, and maybe we have to look at different ways of using our attack. With hindsight, there were times when it seemed we had our match-ups wrong, and while it's not always easy to have the right blokes bowling at the right times, it's something we have to think about. I'm especially keen to get more out of our No. 1 strike bowler, Brett Lee, who didn't have the impact we needed. Their fast bowlers were more dangerous with the old ball than ours were, though I would have liked to have seen Bing and Mitchell Johnson bowling late on the fifth day. Unfortunately, the fading light put a stop to that.

Still, I think the way this Test played out could hardly have pleased the Indians. I know the expectations of our fans and many in the Australian media remain high, but no one over here expects us to win, and that has created a pressure on the home-team players that might be handcuffing a few of them, particularly their more senior guys who are coming to the end of their careers. Ganguly was terrible in the field and cautious with the bat, Rahul Dravid seemed out of sorts at the crease, while Anil Kumble was clearly frustrated by his inability to break through. At the same time, it must be said, some of their other blokes — Zaheer Khan and Ishant Sharma, for example — are clearly relishing the challenge.

Similarly, I was most impressed by the way some of our less experienced guys went about their work. Brad Haddin didn't enjoy keeping on this wicket, which turned out to be much slower than we expected, but he batted well, being involved in important partnerships in both innings, while Shane Watson showed in our second innings how valuable a batter he can be. Watto also bowled well; in fact, over the five days he was probably the most consistent of our faster bowlers and it was good that his body stood up to the demands of this Test match given the problems he has had with injuries over the past few years.

***

THE GAME STARTED WELL for me. I won the toss and then managed to complete my first Test century in India, in my 15th Test innings in India, 12 years after I first played a Test here.

Given my abbreviated preparation for the series, because of the bad wrist, and because I was in during the first over (after Matthew Hayden copped a poor umpiring decision) I felt it was one of my better innings, even if there were times when it seemed I couldn't find the sweet spot of my bat. It was a grind at times, as the ball got soft and was hard to get away, but I was pre-occupied with setting an example and not letting our opponents' containment strategy prevent us from building a decent first-innings score. It was my 16th century as Australia's

Bump Ball?

There was one note of controversy late on the first day of this opening Test, when I was given not out after the Indians appealed for a possible caught-and-bowled by Anil Kumble. I was 110 at the time, when I drove at a full-pitched delivery and hit the ball straight back to the bowler. Umpire Rudi Koertzen saw it as a bump ball, but with the Indians insisting it was out, he checked with the square-leg umpire, Asad Rauf, who supported Koertzen's original verdict. They never went to the third umpire, but the TV replays weren't helpful anyway — at first view, it was a bump ball; then, looking more closely, it might have been out, it might not.

When it happened, I was positive I hit the ball on the full, right on the bottom of the bat. Most times, in such situations, the ball dribbles back to the bowler or a close-in fieldsman. But when I looked up, Kumble was catching the ball in front of his face. I don't know what happened for sure. I still think I hit it into the ground and with the video of the moment being inconclusive, it's hard to argue that the umpires made anything other than the right decision.

Test captain, putting me one clear of Allan Border and Steve Waugh, a record to remember.

I've always felt that I'm good enough to score Test runs in India, but my past performances and all the reminders about them had definitely got to me and I was more nervous than usual from the moment I woke on that first morning. I had a point to prove to a few people, as well as myself. When I reached three figures I was very excited and I think that showed in my celebration. Still, this hundred is just one step in the right direction. One innings doesn't make a tour.

Two late wickets on the first day curtailed our momentum, but largely through Michael Hussey's ninth Test century we ended up with a 70-run first innings lead. However, it should have been more, because Harbhajan Singh and Zaheer Khan put together an 80-run eighth-wicket stand. The last three Indian wickets totalled 128 frustrating runs, negating a clear advantage we had earned through some excellent running between the wickets on the second day (when, just as we expected, some of the Indian fieldsmen were found wanting) and then some excellent bowling from Mitchell Johnson on day three.

We should have been more patient in our approach when we couldn't get those crucial late wickets in India's first innings. Our quicks tried to blast Harbhajan and Zaheer out, but on such a slow wicket that strategy was inappropriate and all it did was give these two experienced cricketers — both of whom thrive on a bit of success but who in the past have gone missing when times were tough — a chance to swing themselves into some form. Soon, they were strutting around like a pair of pro wrestlers, the crowd went along with them, and on this occasion we weren't good enough or smart enough to arrest the change in momentum. It's amazing how once a tail starts wagging it keeps wagging; giving late-order batsmen a bit of confidence is always a dangerous thing to do.

By day four, the wicket was very slow and the ball got very soft, one of those situations where if the bowling team wants to slow the game right down they can. Too often, the ball bounced twice on its way through to the wicketkeeper. For the batsmen, survival wasn't too difficult (especially, in our case, because Kumble was hampered by a shoulder injury which will probably keep him out of the second Test), but forcing the pace certainly was, which made the sixth-wicket partnership between Hadds and Watto (75 in 18-and-a-half overs) even more impressive than it looks in the scorebook. We were pleased with the way we put ourselves in a position where India faced a tough fourth innings, but on the last day — when we weren't helped by Stuart Clark's elbow injury — we just couldn't break through. It seemed to me that the pitch played better on the last day than it had for the previous two or three, something that seems to happen more and more these days.

A definite highlight for us on that last day was the dismissal of Sachin Tendulkar, caught by Michael Clarke at cover, a notable first Test wicket for Cameron White. Surrounded by happy team-mates, Cameron was a bit teary straight afterwards, reflecting just how much playing at this level means to him, means to all of us. No one can ever take this moment away from him. All in all, I thought Cameron did a pretty fair job for us, convincing me that he has the talent to not just be economical (he conceded less than three runs per over from his 31 overs) but also to take Test wickets. Whether he's convinced himself yet, I'm not so sure.

Thursday, October 16

It's a bit hard to reconcile the fact that during Steve Waugh's time as Test captain, seven Australians made their Test debut, while tomorrow Peter Siddle will become the 16th man to wear the baggy green for the first time while I've been in charge. Peter, who comes into the team to replace the injured Stuart Clark, will be our sixth Test debutant in the past 12 months (after Mitchell Johnson, Chris Rogers, Brad Haddin, Beau Casson and Cameron White). Of course, such changeover of players in a Test team is not unprecedented — Mark Taylor welcomed 21 new Test caps during his time at the helm, including seven (the last of whom was me) in his first 15 months — but it does reflect the fact that we are very much in a time of transition.

I think Peter will go well. The word about him on the cricket grapevine late last season was all positive, and I like the way he goes about things — he's a bloke who just keeps going, hits the

Another Hussey Hundred

Before the first Test, Mike Hussey hadn't scored a fifty in any of his past five Test innings — the worst 'streak' of his remarkable first three years in Test cricket. The match in Bangalore also turned out to be the first Test of Huss's career in which he scored a century but we didn't win the game.

bat hard and can do a bit off the wicket. I think the selectors were keen to pick him for this tour because they thought the wickets would suit him but I reckon he's the sort of relentless, no-nonsense bowler who'll be effective on any surface. He's got a presence about him and bowled beautifully in the nets yesterday, as if he sensed an opportunity was opening up and he was determined to grab it. My impression is that any captain would love to have him, because every time you throw him the ball you know you'll get the maximum effort. He's willing to learn, too; our bowling coach, Troy Cooley, has enjoyed working with him.

Peter wasn't the only bloke to impress at training. Matthew Hayden stayed in the nets for an hour and a half, working on a variety of things, as if he had to make up for the time he lost in the middle in Bangalore (where he was the victim of two incorrect umpiring decisions). Michael Clarke was the same, and I'll be surprised if these two blokes don't cash in at some stage over the first couple of days of the Mohali Test.

The Test strip was under covers the whole time we were at the ground today, because of the threat of some light rain, and I'll be surprised if any of that moisture gets onto it. Even with Anil Kumble out (MS Dhoni will be their captain), I think it will be a track that offers very little to the faster men. I saw the groundsman interviewed on TV and he certainly expects the wicket to suit their spinners. It could be a tough slog for us in the field, a battle of attrition if you like, but that style of Test cricket has never scared us in the past and I don't think it will here.

Wednesday, October 22

Second Test, India v Australia, at Mohali (October 17–21): India 469
(G Gambhir 67, SR Tendulkar 88, SC Ganguly 102, MS Dhoni 92) and 3–314
dec (G Gambhir 104, V Sehwag 90, MS Dhoni 68*) defeated **Australia** 268
(MEK Hussey 54, SR Watson 78; A Mishra 5–71) and 195 (MJ Clarke 69) by
320 runs

***

I don't like losing. I never liked it when I was a kid, didn't like it
when I first started playing for Tasmania, or when it's happened
during my Test career — such as India in 1996, 1998 and 2001
or England in 2005. The fact the Australian cricket team has
been successful for so long or that we're without many recently
retired champions doesn't make losing any less or more hard to
take. I just don't like it. I want to turn things around here as
quickly as we can.

If anything could make a loss worse, it would be if it had
resulted, even in part, because of a split in the ranks or a lack of
spirit. Some observers have suggested that is what happened
here, after Brett Lee and I were seen 'arguing' with each other on
the fourth day. But what people thought they saw was not what
happened. There is no problem between Bing and me. Yes, we
did have a discussion before lunch on day four and yes, it was a
bit animated. But to tag it a major argument or proof of
dissension is way over the top.

More Injury Woes

We went into the Test knowing that Phil Jaques would be heading home because he has failed to overcome a back complaint that has been bugging him for a while. The decision that Jaquesy was done for this tour was made on the eve of the game, and it's such a shame, considering how he went last season, when he was in the Australian team from the first Test to the last. My understanding is that Western Australia's Shaun Marsh, who did so well in the IPL here last April and in the one-dayers in the West Indies after that, will be his replacement. Some have been suggesting this might have been an opportunity for Andrew Symonds to be recalled, but that won't be happening.

Our debate, which occurred just before lunch on the fourth day, was caused by over-rates and our struggle to maintain them. Brett was upset that he hadn't bowled in the first session and couldn't understand why he hadn't been called upon. But we had resolved before play started that he wasn't going to be used immediately, because we wanted to take the pace off the ball and try to frustrate the Indian batsmen. Maybe I didn't communicate that fact adequately in the dressing room, though to be honest, I thought I had. So we used Shane Watson and Cameron White first up. Then I turned to Mitchell Johnson and Peter Siddle, who'd each taken three wickets in our first innings. In normal circumstances, Brett would have got a bowl too, but during play I was informed we'd fallen five overs behind on our required over-rate. If this had deteriorated further I would have been facing a suspension for the next Test and we all know that isn't in the best interests of the team. So Brett missed out. When he

Sachin's Record

I know the reporting of this alleged rift between Brett Lee and me is big news in Australia, but over here the home fans are much more concerned with their huge victory. Adding to their joy, their great hero, Sachin Tendulkar, is now the leading run-scorer in Test-match history, a feat he achieved on the first day of the Test, when he glided Peter Siddle down to third man for the three runs he needed to go past Brian Lara's old record. Later in the afternoon, Sachin reached his 50th Test half-century and became the first Test batsman to reach the 12,000-run mark.

The crowd was very disappointing on that first day, considering he was such a big chance to get the runs he needed, but those who were there — many of them schoolkids — made a lot of noise, while on the field we were all quick to congratulate the new record holder. I think I might have been the first to shake his hand. I've always had the highest regard for Sachin as a cricketer and a person, even if in one way I don't have too many great memories of him, because he tends to score so heavily against us. He is a true champion, one of the all-time greats, and reaching this milestone is a fantastic reward for all he has done for the game.

raised the matter on the field his disappointment was clear, but I set him straight and that was the end of the matter.

At the lunch break, he explained his attitude this way: 'I'm a bowler, I want to bowl; you're a batter, you want to bat.' I understand what he meant. The bloke's a no-holds-barred competitor, part of the reason he has been such a great cricketer, but in the circumstances I'm sure we did the right thing. With the over-rate improved, Bing came on straight after lunch and bowled pretty well.

It can't be easy for a front-line bowler to see someone like Mike Hussey operating when you think you should have been called upon. But as I said, I needed the over-rate sped up and I thought Huss could do it without the game situation changing too much. Cameron White had already had a fair spell and I didn't want to see a part-time spinner being carted all over the place any more than I wanted our over-rate to get any worse. Furthermore, Huss's slow-mediums sort of fitted in with our initial strategy of keeping the pace off the ball and he did a pretty fair job for us, before and after the lunch break. Bing and I are sweet now; to suggest there's any sort rift between us is pure rubbish.

I think part of Brett's frustration is that he knows he is performing below his best, and we've reached a stage of the tour where we have to admit that he is not alone there. Matthew Hayden and Michael Clarke are still looking for a big score, I missed out in both innings and we also need Stuart Clark not just back but back to his best after he missed this Test because of his elbow problem. When the experienced guys aren't contributing, it adds to the pressure on the new blokes, who are naturally keen to learn from the good examples of the established players. In the circumstances, I thought Peter Siddle, Cameron White, Shane Watson and Brad Haddin (none of whom have played more than six Tests) all went pretty well. But the rest of us let them down. If we're going to get back into this series, the experienced men have to lead the way.

***

INDIA FINISHED THE FIRST day at 5–311, with Gautam Gambhir, Sachin Tendulkar and Sourav Ganguly all going past 50, and if we could have started day two well we might have been a chance. Instead, Ganguly went on to his century, MS Dhoni almost marked his second Test as captain (and first against Australia) with a hundred of his own, and they went all the way to 469. We needed a positive start in our reply; instead, Matty Hayden was bowled by Zaheer Khan for a duck and I was lbw to Ishant Sharma for five. We never recovered.

It was an impressive display by the Indians. Ganguly and Dhoni played the sort of tough cricket for which we've become renowned and their pacemen, especially Sharma, found something in the wicket that had eluded our quicks. Adding to their excitement, their new leggie, Amit Mishra, had a dream start to Test cricket, dismissing Simon Katich in his third over and then Michael Clarke in the last over of the second day. The following morning, Mishra continued to impress, and finished his first Test innings with five wickets. He looks a natural successor to Anil Kumble.

Dhoni could have enforced the follow-on but instead he did the logical thing and batted again. After that, all we could do was defend as best we could and prepare to bat for at least a day and a half if we wanted to save the game, but that task proved well beyond us. Simply put, we batted very poorly, showing a dreadful lack of discipline as we lost five wickets for nine runs to crash to 5–58, and then three more for two runs to go from 5–142 to 8–144. Pup and Hadds were the only Aussie batsmen to show any fight and the end came late in the first session of the fifth day. We wanted to be positive but instead some inept shot selections just made us look silly and against a pumped-up opponent we were thrashed. This was as bad a loss as I've been involved in with the Australian team.

It's certainly not a time for us to panic, but over the next three days, when we have some time off to recover from the exertions of the first two Tests, we've got a lot to think about. It's only a

Over-rates

I've said before that over-rates really do my head in. In 21st-century Test cricket, you can't afford to slip behind as often as we've been doing lately, but I've found that the problem has a way of sneaking up on you. One minute, things are fine, but an hour later we're in trouble. Some of our bowlers have long run-ups and long follow-throughs, and they are pre-occupied with getting every ball right. Because of all the analysis we do, we have different fields for different batsmen, which means there are more field changes than there were in the old days. Furthermore, I'm keen to get my fields exactly right, and often feel compelled to talk to a bowler. We spoke to match referee Chris Broad during the first Test in Bangalore about the problems we were having, and he pinpointed my discussions with the bowlers as being a major cause, but if I don't talk to them when I feel it's necessary then I fear a chance to change the game might slip by.

Of course, there are a variety of things that can slow the game down and not all of them can be controlled by the bowling side. Somehow the batsmen always seem to escape scrutiny when a tardy over-rate is highlighted, and there are often issues with things such as getting the sightscreen moved or getting the crowd to settle between deliveries. Drinks breaks can take forever.

Still, unless we work the problem out, I know as captain that sooner or later I'm going to miss a Test because of a tardy Australian over-rate. It's bad enough that I always seem to be shelling out a couple of thousand bucks in fines because we're two or three overs behind. As bowlers and fieldsmen, we have to be aware of the matter all the time; as captain, every time I change the field or talk to a bowler, I have to ask myself, Is it worth it? and when the team is chosen, I guess the selectors have to consider the speed at which guys get through their overs. If a bowler concedes too many runs per over or takes too long to get back to his mark, maybe that has to count against him.

week since we played pretty well in Bangalore, but this second Test has shown very clearly that there are a number of areas where we have to sharpen up. When you're five per cent off in these conditions, deficiencies get highlighted very quickly. Suddenly, you're under big-time pressure and the fall can be dramatic.

In part because of our dust-up on day four, critics want to focus on Brett Lee's poor return from the first two Tests (four wickets at 59.25) but the truth is there are a number of us who are not performing well enough. Take my hundred in the first Test out and I'm struggling. How we react over the next few weeks to our current predicament could help shape how our Test careers are remembered. We might not be going too well at the moment, but if we can get our fightback right then this experience here in India could become one of the most important of our cricketing lives.

Tuesday, October 28

The time we've had off since the second Test has been very welcome, but ever since we got back together we've been working extra hard — in the nets and also in a series of team meetings where we've put plenty of thought into how we're going to approach the third Test, which starts in Delhi tomorrow.

Essentially, these meetings have revolved around the following themes: what we're going to start doing, what we're going to stop doing and what we're going to keep doing. I feel like we've now got a clear plan about how we're going to confront the Indians, though I've been quick to hammer the point that it's all very well to write these things on a piece of paper and talk enthusiastically about then, putting words into action is what really matters. None of us are going to be judged on the quality of our team meetings.

As captain, I've made a point of grabbing some time with every member of the squad during the past two days, to see how they're travelling. If one conversation stood out, it was with Matthew Hayden, where we focused on the manner in which he batted in the second innings in Mohali, when he took on Zaheer Khan. It looked pre-meditated and a bit reckless, too good to last, as our openers added 49 in 7.2 overs before Haydos was dismissed for 29. That has left our great opener with a run tally of just 42 for the series, at 10.50.

I've always thought Haydos is at his best when he's locked into a one-on-one battle with an opponent. The sense of confrontation fires him up. Whenever I see him staring back at the bowler, almost daring his rival to stare back, I feel like he's on top of things and likely to set us up for a big total. But he went beyond that in Mohali, to the point that he looked desperate rather than determined, as if he was trying to convince *himself* that he was in charge, rather than sending a message to Zaheer and Ishant Sharma. It didn't work. Even though he saw Zaheer off he was still not thinking right when the new bowler, Harbhajan Singh, came on and Matty was soon dismissed. He conceded he'd made a mistake, but I was able to reassure him that he remains the batsmen the Indians most fear — you can see by the way they react when he gets out and also by the way Zaheer has been so quick to give him some lip that they rate Haydos as the key wicket.

Matt's a bit down on confidence not ability; there is nothing about his technique that has changed, as far as I can see. Both he and Brett Lee seem to be paying the price for their interrupted winters, but both have responded in absolutely the right way. Bing has been working hard since the second Test, spending a lot of time with our fitness advisor, Stuart Karppinen, as he searches for the spark that was a feature of his bowling last season. Their thinking is that because Bing had such a stop-start off-season he's lost a bit of speed and condition. Because he's a bit underdone, he's been bowling at half-pace and three-quarter pace at training, concentrating on his technique, trying to get that right. But by doing that maybe he's conditioned himself to bowling slower than usual in games too. So in the past few days, he's reverted to bowling off his long run at training, trying to replicate the dynamic stuff that sets him apart from other bowlers. If he can get his rhythm back, he can still have a big influence on this tour.

We need him bowling very well. He's the guy everyone in our attack looks up to.

As I talked to Brett I sensed he's got a lot out of the work he's done in the past few days, and that beyond that he's gradually feeling more at ease with himself. Most times, these informal chats I have with the guys are about little things away from cricket, how they're going, mutual interests, is there anything happening off the field I can help them with.

For example, when I spoke to Brad Haddin we spent little time talking cricket and plenty of time comparing notes on what it's like to be missing our babies — Zac Haddin was born in September, not long after Emmy Ponting came into this world. I miss my little girl more than I'd imagined and she makes me more determined to succeed. The last thing I want to do is waste the times when we're apart.

Monday, November 3

Third Test, India v Australia, at Delhi (October 29–November 2): India 7–613 dec (G Gambhir 206, SR Tendulkar 68, VVS Laxman 200*) and 5–208 dec (VVS Laxman 59*) drew with **Australia** 577 (ML Hayden 83, SM Katich 64, RT Ponting 87, MEK Hussey 53, MJ Clarke 112; V Sehwag 5–104) and 0–31

***

In the lead-up to the third Test, the curator in Delhi reputedly promised that his pitch would be a 'present' for Anil Kumble, who has had some success here in the past. As it turned out, it was a going-away gift for the Indian captain, who announced his retirement during the final day's play, but it wasn't enough to give the home team the series win they crave. The final result was a high-scoring draw; we now head to Nagpur to decide who will claim the Border-Gavaskar Trophy.

The fact the pitch in Delhi was tailored for the spinners hardly worked to our advantage. In the lead-up, we were tempted to play both Cameron White and Jason Krejza and probably would have if Stuart Clark had pulled out, but when Sarf passed his fitness test we decided to go with the status quo. Sticking with Cameron over Jason was a hard call, but Bear had bowled pretty well in the first two Tests and we felt an obligation to stick with him. As it turned out, it wouldn't have mattered who we picked, the wicket was always going to win in the end.

It's not a Test I'll remember overly fondly. Our work in the two days before the game was the best I'd seen for a long time (Steve

On The Defensive

Following on from Gautam Gambhir's clashes with Simon Katich and Shane Watson during India's first innings of the third Test (which has led to Gambhir being suspended for the fourth Test, though an appeal is pending), there was a further confrontation on Sunday, as the match faded out to a draw. This time it involved two blokes you don't always associate with this sort of thing — Mitchell Johnson and VVS Laxman.

I was nearby when it happened, and I can tell you there was no real malice in anything Mitchell had to say. Their discussion related back to some comments Laxman had made at his media interview after his double hundred, when he sledged us for being too defensive and tried to spin the yarn that India were the only team on the attack. We thought that was a bit rich, especially when there was an opportunity on the fifth day for the home team to try to create a big finish, but they preferred to let the game fizzle out. I know they're on top in this series, so I guess they can say what they like, but some of the stuff a few of them have been coming up with in the press has been ridiculous. Interestingly, you don't see their great players mouthing off; instead, they let their cricket do the talking.

Overall, I thought we had the better of this Test from about tea on the second day. Proof of this was the way India batted in their second innings, when they were content to defend their series lead. To me, this exposed a defensive mindset that we'll be seeking to exploit.

Waugh, who is in India, came to practice on the Monday before the game and said afterwards he'd never seen a team train as well as we did) but the Delhi smog, a leftover from the *Diwali* festivities of the past few days, created a slightly weird atmosphere and while we got a couple of early wickets on the first morning, Gautam

Gambhir, Sachin Tendulkar and VVS Laxman then batted us out of the match. Gambhir and Laxman scored double hundreds, the first time two batsmen have reached 200 in the same Test innings against Australia, and all our blokes could do was keep toiling away. There was nothing wrong with the effort we put in, and all I kept thinking was that it would have been a very nice toss to win. There were a couple of incidents, one involving Gambhir and Simon Katich and the other featuring Gambhir and Shane Watson, but from our perspective there didn't appear to be a lot in them, a case of the batter getting cocky and the bowler and fieldsman getting frustrated. The Indian opener is a very well-organised player, but he was in a provocative mood and in the end he earned himself an appointment with the match referee.

In reply, the top five in our order all passed 50, with Matthew Hayden getting to 83 and Michael Clarke going on to his eighth Test century. It can be intimidating having to reply to such a colossal first innings by your opponent, but we handled the assignment with a maturity I found encouraging. Our final total of 577 was the highest ever achieved by an Australian Test team in India. I scored 87 but was filthy that I didn't make a big hundred when it was there for the taking. I was proud of the way I kept battling and then I was bowled by a Virender Sehwag off-break that spun more than I expected. With Harbhajan not playing and Anil Kumble off the field with a finger injury, Sehwag was pushed into the frontline and responded by achieving the first five-for of his Test career. He bowled well, too, the one slow bowler in the Test to consistently get anything out of the placid pitch.

Two late Indian wickets on the fourth evening meant we went in to the final day as the only team that could win, but deep down we knew that there'd be no magical victory like the one Shane Warne conjured up against England in Adelaide a couple of years ago. We actually managed to reduce them to 4–93, but

Tendulkar, Laxman and Ganguly had little trouble batting through towards the end of the match, when Kumble declared so he could have one last bowl in Test cricket.

So we are left needing a win in Nagpur if we want to get anything out of the series. I feel like we're still a chance, not least because India spent a lot of time in the field from late on the second day to late on the fourth, and they might still be feeling that when the fourth Test starts on Thursday. I've always believed that our fitness levels are better than India's and that could be a real factor with there only being three days between the third and fourth Tests. I saw signs in the way they batted yesterday that suggested they might be starting to fade.

If we bat first and Haydos gets going like I really think he's going to, then we'll finally get the chance to set a Test up and dictate how we want the game to be played. Such a start would be great, of course, but we need to fix facets of our play that are letting us down. I know the Delhi pitch was too flat but the fact is we're struggling to take wickets. For this reason, we've got to look long and hard at the guys on the sidelines — Jason Krejza, Peter Siddle and Doug Bollinger — and determine if they can add anything to our bowling group.

Jason was in the twelve for this Test and came very close to playing, reflecting the fact that he's kept improving in the nets throughout our time in India. I've spent plenty of time with him at training, talking about his pace and varying the amount of spin he generates and the angle of his deliveries (for example, when a batter starts sweeping he needs to bowl more stump to stump), and I think all the work is beginning to pay off. All the senior guys who have faced him in the nets have commented on how he is a different bowler to the bloke who landed in Jaipur in September. It would have been too big a gamble to pick him for the opening Test of the series but not now.

Wednesday, November 5

Melbourne Cup Day is an institution back home in Australia and I can't remember a year with the Australian team when we haven't had a sweep, no matter how far away from Flemington we might have been. So it was this year in Nagpur, when the Cup didn't stop us from training in the morning but it did delay a team meeting that someone had inadvertently scheduled to clash with the big race.

We'd watched a replay of the 100–1 shot Rebel Raider's win in the Victoria Derby on the Australian Television Network during the Test in Delhi last Saturday, but there was a stage when we weren't sure if we'd be able to see the Cup live, because we have access to a much narrower range of stations here. For a while, it seemed we'd have to just call home and get someone to put a radio near their receiver so we could hear renowned commentator Greg Miles' call on speaker phone, but then Cameron White, who has been known to have a punt, managed to get the races up on the internet in his hotel room. So we all gathered in there. The picture was a bit wonky but good enough.

Shane Watson was put in charge of the sweep, Stuart Clark was considered honest enough to draw the horse names out of a hat, and Mike Hussey was handed what proved to be the winning ticket, Viewed, ridden by Blake Shinn and trained by the master, Bart Cummings. You never underestimate a champion and when it comes to Melbourne Cups there is no greater legend than Bart.

Verbal Abuse

So Gautam Gambhir gets suspended for elbowing Shane Watson, his appeal is knocked back, and I have to answer questions about the way we're abusing our opponents. That sounds about right.

This came about after the judge at the Gambhir appeal fined Watto 10 per cent of his match fee for 'verbally engaging' Gambhir in the lead-up to the incident and also made a number of references to the manner in which we Australians talked to Gambhir at different stages during his double century. I was very surprised to read these comments, because if we had overstepped the mark I'm sure we would have heard about it from the umpires on the field and from the match referee, Chris Broad, straight after play.

Before the series, Chris made it very clear to players from both teams that there was an acceptable level of 'banter' that could occur on the field. Such talk is part and parcel of international sport, not just cricket. And Chris also pointed out during the original hearing in which Gambhir was suspended that the Indian opener gave as good as he got on the field. Things did get a bit heated for a few moments, but our belief is that the match officials handled the matter appropriately. All our attention now is on the upcoming fourth Test.

This was his 12th Cup win and maybe it could be a bit of an omen for us. Plenty of people over here think we're all washed up; it would be nice, Cummings-like, to prove them wrong.

I placed a few bob on the imported horses Profound Beauty and Mad Rush, who both finished out of the places, but I also backed the Kiwi, C'est La Guerre, for a place and he ran third, which provided a big enough return to cover my bets. It was a reasonable result but not my biggest collect of the tour. That had come back in Hyderabad, when I found a number of team-mates who didn't think Manly could win the NRL Grand Final. The Sea Eagles won 40–0 and I cleaned up big-time.

I just wish my luck would extend to the all-important Test-match tosses. We had the better of the Test in Bangalore after I won the toss but my failure to call right at Mohali and Delhi cost us dearly. Steve Waugh used to always reckon that it didn't matter all that much who batted first and his results as captain seemed to confirm that, but I reckon this is only true in certain conditions. It also helps if you have a balanced bowling attack that can adapt to a wide range of circumstances. Right now, we're very keen to bat first in Nagpur (the pitch is bare and concrete hard) and with that in mind the lads started a coin-tossing competition — a bit like two-up on Anzac Day — during a quiet moment at practice today. Sure enough, I was perfect, heads every time. It's always easy when there's nothing riding on the result.

***

THE CUP WAS GOOD, a nice reminder of home, but it was really just a brief diversion from the task that is dominating our thinking: how do we win in Nagpur to level the series to retain the Border-Gavaskar Trophy? In my view, our best chance lies in finding the right balance — in our approach and our team line-up. Sure, we have to push hard to win the Test, and we must never let the game stagnate if we can prevent it, but it's not as simple as just going on an all-out attacking blitz. On the slow but batsmen-friendly decks we've seen during this series, the one thing that can destroy you is a lack of patience, especially if the bowling team's policy is to sit back and wait for the batsmen to make the mistake. Go too hard and the game can easily get away from you.

So balance is important, but our greatest challenge is to find a way to take 20 wickets, because quite frankly we have not looked like doing so in the first three Tests. I was encouraged by the way we bowled early on in India's second innings in Delhi, but as had been the case earlier in the series we couldn't follow-up after getting a couple of quick wickets. Nor could we break the vital partnership when we desperately needed to. We've come to the conclusion that right at the moment, given the pitch conditions, Jason Krejza is the bloke in our squad most likely to get wickets, so we're now firmly of the view that we should pick him and back him, give him every chance to spin people out. With Sarf still troubled by his bung elbow, we'll probably stick with Cameron White as a second slowie and use Shane Watson as our third seamer.

One thing I keep hearing when I talk to the boys is that to a man they've learnt a helluva lot about playing five-day cricket in India over the course of this series. I've learnt plenty, too. This is probably as big a Test match as many of the guys have ever been involved in; after all, being 1–nil down in a series with a game to play is a situation we've rarely experienced over the past 15 years. We pride ourselves on playing well in important games and the position we're in provides a terrific opportunity for us to stand up and show we're still entitled to think of ourselves as the No. 1 team in the game.

Saturday, November 15

Fourth Test, India v Australia, at Nagpur (November 6–10): India 441
(V Sehwag 66, SR Tendulkar 109, VVS Laxman 64, SC Ganguly 85,
MS Dhoni 56; JJ Krejza 8–215) and 295 (V Sehwag 92, MS Dhoni 55,
Harbhajan Singh 52; JJ Krejza 4–143) defeated **Australia** 355 (SM Katich
102, MEK Hussey 90) and 209 (ML Hayden 77; Harbhajan Singh 4–64) by
172 runs

***

There was a stage during this fourth Test, at stumps on day two,
when things didn't look too bad for us. We were 2–189 after 49
overs in reply to India's 441. Sachin Tendulkar had made his 40th
Test hundred (and 10th against Australia) on the opening day,
VVS Laxman had marked his 100th Test with a slow but stylish
64, but for us the main story of the home team's first innings was
Jason Krejza's stunning first Test appearance: 8–215 from 43.5
overs. It was the second best Test debut by an Australian in
history, after Bob Massie's 8–84 and 8–53 double at Lord's in
1972. The last five Indian wickets fell for just 19, all to Krejza,
and then Simon Katich and Mike Hussey batted beautifully,
putting together an unbroken stand of 115 in 31.5 overs to get us
to stumps on that second evening thinking we were a real chance
of getting something out of the series. But then it all went wrong.

There'd hardly been anyone in the ground when the game
started, a sad contrast to the huge crowds who had flocked to the

IPL games six months ago (there are a number of theories put forward for the poor crowd; most seem to think that the cost of the tickets was the chief culprit), so it was a bit weird the way our excitement echoed across the ground on the opening morning when Jason broke through for the first time: Dravid, caught at short leg by Simon Katich for a duck. Earlier in the series, Cameron White and Peter Siddle had both made Tendulkar their first Test wicket; this time, ironically, Sachin was one of the two wickets to fall elsewhere — he was lbw to Mitch Johnson just before stumps on day one.

Jason liked the fact that another Aussie with an Eastern European background was involved in his first Test wicket, and he found it hard to contain his excitement. He was very nervous early, but I kept talking to him, Matty Hayden was great with his encouragement and the end result was very encouraging. There were times when he was a bit costly, especially when Virender Sehwag went after him at the start, but I knew I had to stick with him. I think any captain would have done the same. When we batted, we were committed to being positive though we were also aware that we couldn't overdo the aggression, because India, one-up in the series, always had the option of slowing the game down.

MS Dhoni exploited this advantage to the extreme, starting day three by setting an 8–1 field (eight fieldsmen on the offside, plus a man at mid-on) and instructing his quicker bowlers to aim well wide of the off-stump. Then Harbhajan bowled his off-breaks with six men on the legside. The result was one of the most tedious days I've witnessed in Test cricket, as we scored just 166 runs in 85.4 overs, including a miserable 42 in the first session. I guess they were perfectly within their rights to slow the game down in this way and in effect say to us, *If you want to win the Test and keep the trophy you have to take all the risks.*

But it still didn't sit well with me. It was a dreadful advertisement for Test cricket. Maybe it was lucky the crowd at the ground was so poor. I hate to think what it looked like to TV viewers in Australia.

With hindsight, maybe we should have risked all, but then had we faltered — and the bowling was so skewed to the defensive that is almost certainly what would have happened — then inevitably we would have been slaughtered for our recklessness. Instead, we chose to meet grind with grind and aim to build a first-innings lead, in the hope we could bowl them out on the last day, but this strategy came unstuck when Kato was dismissed just before lunch and then three wickets fell in quick succession after the main break. The thing that is most ridiculous about all this was that throughout this series Ishant Sharma has provided plenty of evidence that he is already one of the two or three best quicks in world cricket, yet his captain here asked him to bowl like a hack medium-pacer. I can't help thinking that a team that is so quick to use such negativity when they are leading will eventually lose their way; you can't survive for long in this world unless you truly believe in yourself.

I guess Indian fans will read this and think it's just sour grapes on my part, but I don't care about that. It was a terrible day's cricket. I know from speaking to some of the Australian journalists covering the tour that they were very critical of the Indian tactics, but the local writers all seem to think Dhoni is a genius. This was the context of Kato's sharp response to his interrogators when he was told at the media conference after his excellent hundred that *Australia* had been too defensive. 'You're kidding me, aren't you?' Kato shot back. 'We were defensive with an 8–1 field?' The one thing I guess I had to admire about India's strategy was that they came up with a plan and stuck to it, something Kato conceded. 'It's a good strategy if you can execute it,' he said. 'If you don't get it right you can pay the price. They executed it well.'

On day four, even though Jason Krejza took another four wickets and Shane Watson and Brett Lee bowled extremely well, they eventually batted us out of the series, leaving us 382 to get in a bit more than a day on a wearing wicket. We created a major problem for ourselves with the over-rate during this innings, which led to a major controversy, but more of that in a moment. Reaching such a big fourth-innings target on a flat deck is possible at many venues in 21st-century Test cricket, but this new Nagpur wicket was deteriorating towards the back end of the game. Gee, I wish I'd called tails. We decided to be aggressive from the jump on the final day, but Kato took that to extremes and then I ran myself out. Haydos batted well, gallantly fighting a losing cause, but after he was dismissed the end came quickly. India only bowled 21.3 overs in the first session, when we scored 98 runs but lost three wickets, and they only picked up their over-rate when the game was safe. The final wicket — Mitchell Johnson, lbw Harbhajan 11 — fell in the 51st over, when we still needed 173 to win.

***

SO THE SERIES WAS lost, but as far as the Australian media was concerned that wasn't the big story. They seemed totally focused on the events of that fourth afternoon, which led to my captaincy being scrutinised more brutally than at any other stage of my career, even more closely than it had been in the aftermath to the 2005 Ashes series.

The scene was set in the overs before tea, when we suddenly and dramatically found ourselves right back in the game. Shane Watson started our revival with a heroic 11-over spell where he

Everyone Up

No bowler had conceded as many runs in his first Test innings as Jason Krejza did in Nagpur, but that didn't stop me setting an ultra-attacking field when India's No. 11 Ishant Sharma came to the middle.

Jason was on a hat-trick after dismissing Zaheer Khan and Amit Mishra with consecutive deliveries, and knowing that Ishant — a team-mate of mine at the Knight Riders in the IPL — is not the greatest batsmen in the world I brought in a short mid-off, silly point, first slip, leg slip, leg gully, forward short leg and short mid-wicket. Given the way Jason's debut was going, anything was possible, but the batsman kept his nerve and pushed the hat-trick ball away. But I kept the ball up and in Jason's next over an inside edge went low to Simon Katich in close on the legside to end the innings.

Jason dismissed three Indian batsmen (Dravid, Mishra and Sharma) for ducks in this innings. There was only one home-team duck in the first three Tests: Laxman, caught Haddin bowled Johnson, in the first innings back in Bangalore.

got the ball to reverse swing and pinned the Indian top-order down. At the other end, Brett Lee bowled his best spell of the series — five overs for three runs and the wicket of Sehwag, caught behind. The fall of that wicket left India 3–142, a lead of 228. Twenty minutes before the break, we switched to Mitchell Johnson and Jason Krejza, and in the second over of his new spell our rookie offie turned the game on its head. First, he bowled Laxman through the gap with a beauty that spun almost square; then he ended Ganguly's last Test innings at the first opportunity. Two overs later, second-last ball before tea, in a bizarre piece of play that stunned the small crowd, Tendulkar ran himself out. India were 6–166. Four sessions to go. We were buzzing in the rooms at tea, as if we'd been given this huge surge of adrenalin after weeks in the desert. But amid the excitement, we had to have a talk about the over-rate. I had been told, not long before the tea interval, that we could be as many as six overs down. During the break, I let our support staff know what the situation was, and we agreed that while we didn't want it to get any worse, as it stood things were manageable. However, straight after the tea, I was told that we were now *nine* overs down, and that, I knew, was trouble. I dashed off the field to confirm that if we didn't fix the over-rate, and fix it fast, we were facing pretty severe penalties, including a suspension for the captain. When I returned to the field, first thing I did was speak to my vice-captain, Michael Clarke, and we went through the problem and the consequences of not getting things right. 'Mate, we've got to get the spinners on,' he said to me. 'Let's keep attacking with our best spinner from one end and try to get through the overs as quickly as possible from the other.'

In effect, we had caused ourselves a lot of grief by taking wickets in the half hour before tea. Since the drinks break, an hour into the middle session, we had taken 3–18 in only 10.5 overs, when you're supposed to average 15 overs per hour.

A maze of conflicting thoughts was buzzing through my head. An hour earlier, I thought the series was gone but the over-rate was sweet. Now, we were a real chance but the over-rate was stuffed. *Is winning worth me missing a Test?* Having already taken 10 wickets in his debut Test, Jason was a natural to keep going, but Watto, the guy who had got us back in the Test, was spent; someone else would have to bowl from the other end. *What will they think if I just ignore the match referee?* If Mitch or Bing could get the ball to reverse like Watto had, maybe we could run through their lower order. But as well as the pair had bowled before tea, it was still a fact that they'd taken only two wickets between them to this point in the match. *It's not like they are sure things to take the wickets we need.*

In the end it came down to a simple fact: rules are rules. *We've always said if we get into trouble with the over-rate we'll fix it with the spinners.* But I couldn't worry about that now, part of my brain kept nagging, because Test cricket is all about winning.

Isn't it?

Mitch had bowled the first over after tea, but now I went with my gut instinct, something I'll never regret. Cameron White had been our first-choice spinner for the first three Tests, and though he hadn't taken many wickets in those games he is a guy who can bowl the occasional near-unplayable delivery. Dhoni and Harbhajan wouldn't be expecting him. Something different. A contrast to Krejza. *It might just work.* And it wouldn't hurt the over-rate. So I made the change.

I'm happy for people to disagree with this move, but it was not illogical. If we didn't have the problem with over-rates I might still have brought him on, because I was pretty keen on the White v Harbhajan match-up. The Indian No. 8 (who averaged more than 40 with the bat for this series) tends to go after the spinners, an approach that can cost him early in his innings. If it had worked I imagine I would have been lauded for my enterprise, but unfortunately, at a time when we needed something special, Bear proceeded to bowl just about the worst six balls of his life, conceding 12 runs including five from an ugly legside wide. India scored 21 runs in four overs, and the mood changed. All the while, I was dwelling on our predicament: because of the runs that were scored in these four overs, the spinners weren't fixing the over-rate and now the scoreboard was getting away from us. And we couldn't just ignore the match conditions and the match referee. Earlier in the series, I'd used

Mike Hussey's slow-mediums to move things along, and it had worked okay, so we decided to have a bet 'each way': keep things tight at one end by continuing to attack with our main wicket-taking weapon, hope that when it was sweet to bring the quicks back, the chance to win the Test would still be there.

Ironically, Huss did a good job for us this time, sending down four overs in ultra-quick time for three runs. Then Michael Clarke, the same bloke who had spun us to victory in Sydney 10 months ago, came on and bowled five overs for 18. (I actually would have bowled Pup before Huss, but he had been off the field because of a stomach upset and couldn't bowl until 3.10pm.) At the other end, though, Jason was too expensive — at a time when we needed him to keep taking wickets or at least keep things very tight he conceded 0–51 in eight overs. Our resurgence was over, the Dhoni–Harbhajan stand added 108 runs, our fourth-innings target was more than was possible on this Nagpur pitch, and I knew I was going to be questioned for my actions. But I wasn't expecting such a vitriolic, unforgiving response from critics whom I sensed had been waiting for another chance to bash me. If only I'd bowled the quicks straight after tea, I was angrily told, things would have been very different.

'To an almost bizarre degree, Ponting lost the plot,' wrote Peter Roebuck in the *Sydney Morning Herald* and the *Age*. 'It was the most incomprehensible spell seen from an Australian team for a quarter of a century.'

'Over 131 years, 404 men have been accorded the honour of wearing the Baggy Green cap, arguably the most significant and recognisable symbol in Australian team sport,' ABC Radio's Glenn Mitchell grieved. 'Many today would have hung their head in sadness while others would have turned in their grave. What happened today in Nagpur was at odds with what team sport is all about. May it never be allowed to happen again.'

'I don't know what to make of all this,' Allan Border, a Cricket Australia board member, had said while commentating for Fox Sports. 'They go into the tea break on a high and come out worrying about over-rates. I am glad Ricky can't read my mind right now because he is not going to like it.'

This was the call that riled me the most. AB is a terrific bloke who has often helped me during my career. But he is also a member of Cricket Australia, who ever since that controversial Sydney Test at the start of this year have been on to us about how we have to do the right thing by the game. Now here he was very publicly telling the world that I should have just ignored the match referee and worried only about winning. For him to say what he said was, in my view, unfair given his association with Cricket Australia. He, as well as anyone, should have been aware of the pressure we've been under.

In the News Limited tabloids, their reporter covering the tour, Jon Pierik, described my captaincy as a 'joke'. Malcolm Conn in the *Australian* wrote that it was my 'worst day as national captain'. The Indian papers had a field day, revelling in their own team's position and also hammering the point that we'd let them off the hook. Meanwhile, a large group of former players added to the uproar, and what got me about this was the eagerness with which some of them went about putting the boot in. The former Indian spinner Ravi Shastri was one of a number of commentators who claimed I had put myself ahead of the team, that I didn't care about winning, only about playing in the next Test. Shastri, like all of them, would know what a sinister and despicable accusation that is. I've never played that way and never will. Yes, I'd used our bowlers in a way to make up the overs, and yes, in the back of my mind was the fear that I'd be suspended, but we never stopped trying to win and I never believed that the tactics I was employing were turning victory into defeat. As we all know, things turned bad for us and I take full responsibility for that, but I wish people would accept that nothing in cricket is certain except the past. I could have bowled the quicks straight after tea without success, and then, I imagine, my critics would have been on my back because I didn't bowl the spinners on such a slow wicket. And they would have assailed us for not adhering to the spirit of the game. Sometimes, you can never win.

In my post-Test comments, I made the mistake of responding to some of the things that had been said. I wish I'd let it go, but I was cranky and we'd just lost the Border-Gavaskar Trophy ...

'To tell you the truth, I'm disappointed with some of the criticism, particularly from former Australian captains and Cricket Australia board members. As captain of the Australian cricket team, I feel I have a responsibility to play the game in the right spirit. I have an obligation to bowl 90 overs in a day's play and the way we were heading, if the quicks had continued we would have been maybe 12 overs down ...

'Everyone has an opinion on the way I captain the team or the way the team plays, but the thing I am most disappointed about is this inference out there that I put myself totally ahead of the team. Anybody who knows me or the way I play my cricket or how I operate around the Australian team would hopefully not say that is the case ...'

WHEN I CALMED DOWN I realised that the main lesson from all this is that we have to do something about our seemingly perpetual slow over-rate. The problem hurt us in Perth last season, again in Mohali, and now here. I've written previously

Harbhajaned Again

On day two of the fourth Test, I had the misfortune to fall to my old nemesis Harbhajan Singh once again, this time giving the Indian offie his 300th Test wicket. It was a good piece of bowling, but a terrible bit of batting, as I misread the line and length as I tried to cut a ball that was too full and too close to the stumps. It was the first time I'd been bowled by Harbhajan in a Test match, and all up the 10th time he'd got me in Test cricket.

There has probably been a worse example of me losing concentration while batting in a Test, but at the moment I can't think when that was. I'm not sure why it happened, but my guess is that while I don't think the constant cricket over the past month has had much of an effect on me physically, perhaps mentally I'm in need of a respite. Perhaps my abbreviated off-season, where I spent my time recovering from wrist surgery, left me more vulnerable than I expected. This is not an excuse, more something I have to learn from.

about what we need to do, and everyone in the team has responsibility in this, but the one I'm going to have to focus on, though I'm loath to change my ways too much, is the way I consult with our bowlers. I don't think I talk too much to the bowlers, except for this very significant fact that it's taking up too much time. If that's going to hurt us, things will have to change. But I hope as we talk about the problem from our perspective, others also have a look at the situation. Are batsmen also guilty? Are the drinks breaks too long? Do we see too much of the 12th and 13th men? Should the umpires be more proactive?

Perhaps our problems with over-rates have exposed a more general problem we've had for a few years, but have been accentuated in the two recent series against India: that while as a team we're good naturally aggressive 'frontrunners', we're not so good at turning things around once we've lost control. Certainly, the Indians have been much better and shrewder at slowing the game than we have, but I can think of other games from the past decade, such as Kolkata in 2001, Antigua in 2003, Adelaide in 2003–04 — when we couldn't respond when our opponents took the game to us. It's easier to build momentum when you've got your opponent pinned to the canvas than when you're down for the count. A bit like a golfer who starts missing greens, we have to learn to 'scramble' better.

And there is one other thing that has struck me during this debate about over-rates. It seems to me that our current problems have demonstrated yet another advantage Glenn McGrath and Shane Warne brought to the Australian team. Both kept the pressure on and the runs down, so there was little time wasted chasing balls to the boundary or changing fields because we'd conceded a single. Further, they were such superb operators, there was less need for the captain to talk to them in the middle of an over, or to change tack because plan A wasn't working. Warney, of course, was a leggie, which naturally kept things moving. No wonder over-rates were less of a concern when these great bowlers were in the side.

In the days that followed the Nagpur Test, the criticism continued, with more former stars having their say. Mostly, it was the cricketers who had been out of the game for a number of years who were quickest to denigrate, whereas guys who I played with — such as Shane, Steve Waugh, Justin Langer and Adam Gilchrist — were much more supportive. Cricket Australia CEO James Sutherland was another strong backer, for which I am grateful. In last year's diary I wrote how we players and Cricket Australia were working to rebuild our relationship after the stresses of last season and this was the first real test of that. There were press reports that James had issued us with a specific 'please explain' but that wasn't right — we always get together after a series and it was no different this time. He came out publicly after that chat and said he thought my actions were 'very reasonable'. Talking about me, he continued, 'Any suggestion that he put himself first ahead of the team last week in Nagpur is completely off beam and can only come from someone who does not know him or understand him.'

Warney did say that he didn't agree with what I'd done, but his criticism was constructive and he was keen to remind people that I've had a bit of success leading the side during the past few years. I saw where Steve Waugh wrote, 'In the end you only need to look into the mirror and be able to sleep easy at night knowing you captained to the best of your ability and gave it your all.' I'm definitely sleeping okay, though now I'm back home I've got to come to grips with sharing the house with a beautiful baby who's a little more than three months old. I don't think I've suddenly become a bad captain, or a less ruthless one, and I'm keen to prove that point in the upcoming Tests against New Zealand and South Africa.

***

THOUGH I DON'T LIKE to admit it, there's no doubt that the final result of this India series was a fair one. There's no escaping the fact that this was a bad loss for us, a time for some real soul-searching. It was the first time since we drew a three-game rubber 0–0 with New Zealand in 2001–02 that Australia has failed to win a Test during a series, and the first time since the

West Indies won 3–1 in 1988–89 that Australia has lost a series by two clear Tests. We played some good cricket in Bangalore but for much of the time after that we were chasing our tails. When we reflect on the series, I'm sure we will learn a lot — I feel like I've learnt a lot already — but too often we were slow to react as the games got away from us. When the big moments came up, when we needed to be outstanding, we couldn't raise our games; instead, we lost our way. Against a good team like this Indian team, that lack of adaptability proved fatal. The occasions when this reality was most evident was during what turned out to be crucial middle-order partnerships by the home team: Harbhajan and Zaheer at Bangalore; Ganguly and Dhoni at Mohali; Dhoni and Harbhajan here.

Still, there were some good things to come out of the series for us. The more I think about what has happened to us over the past seven weeks, the more confident I am about the future. Kato's continued good form, following up his efforts in the West Indies, was very encouraging. He handled the conditions better than any of his team-mates. Watto's bowling stood up as good as any of our quicks and his batting in Mohali demonstrated that he clearly has the talent to be a top-six batsman. His problem in the past has been his inability to stand up physically to the constant demands of modern Test cricket, but this time he finished off the tour as well as he started it. He and Andrew Symonds might have an interesting battle this summer, fighting over the all-rounder's spot. Maybe we can fit them both in, especially on a seamer's deck at the Gabba, but that would have to be at the expense of a specialist spinner. After Jason Krejza's stunning debut, that's an alternative I'm not too keen on.

Jason bowled a little slow during his second innings in Test cricket, when he failed to fully appreciate that if the bounce is uneven an offie should be firing the ball in a bit more, but he's demonstrated on this tour that, at age 25, he's got something about him that few finger spinners of his age can match. He's only the third Australian (after Bob Massie and Clarrie Grimmett) to take 10 wickets or more in his debut Test, though it is also true that his match figures of 12–358 are the second most expensive of all time. His improvement over the past month has been fantastic — I don't think there is any way he could have taken 12 wickets in the first three Tests of the series. I have no regrets with the way we managed our spin-bowling resources during this tour; we did the best we could.

One bloke who'll definitely enjoy bowling in Brisbane will be Mitchell Johnson, who ended up our leading wicket-taker for the India series. The wickets never suited him, but like Ishant Sharma for India (clearly the player of the series) he kept running in, bending his back, doing everything required. Mitch is getting better every day. I was also encouraged by Peter Siddle's debut, the way he persevered, his strength, that presence he has about him. Best of all, he's a fast learner. I sense over the next year or two we're going to need young blokes like that.

The final image I'm left with from our time in India is the look on the guys' faces in the plane on the flight home from India. There was a sense of determination about them, a keenness to prove that this difficult tour was an aberration. Obviously, we've got a lot to prove. The times are changing quicker than I expected. I've said many times in the recent past that I think this is a very exciting time to be captain of the Australian team, but I never expected it to be such a stern character test, too.

PART TWO

AUSTRALIA V
NEW ZEALAND TESTS,
2008–09

Monday, November 24

First Test, Australia v New Zealand, at Brisbane (November 20–23):
Australia 214 (MJ Clarke 98; TG Southee 4–63) and 268 (SM Katich 131*)
defeated **New Zealand** 156 (MG Johnson 4–30) and 177 (LRPL Taylor 75;
MG Johnson 5–39, SR Clark 4–43) by 149 runs

***

THE CRITICISM OF MY captaincy during the Nagpur Test
continued for what felt like an eternity (in fact, it went on until
the moment the first ball of this Brisbane Test against New
Zealand was delivered), and it wasn't until after the final ball of
this game was bowled that I felt as if I could take a deep breath
and really start to move on. Anything short of a clear victory in
this Test would have added to the furore, but fortunately we
produced some good cricket on a difficult wicket, so different to
anything we saw in India, and in the process reminded people
that we can still play. I sense that our supporters are prepared to
be patient; that they realise that we're in a rebuilding phase and
there will be a few bad days to go along with some good ones. If
you listen to a few commentators we haven't got a friend in the
world, but the reality is much different to that.

I sometimes wonder where some of the guys in the media get
their perception of public opinion. It's as if there's this little club
that sets the mood, and nothing beyond that matters. I
occasionally read about how we elite cricketers live in a cocoon
of sorts, as if we're shut off from the real world, but sometimes

Horses for Courses

The spicy Gabba wicket ('spicy' being Matthew Hayden's adjective, not mine) created an awkward selection conundrum for us, because purely in terms of this Test the most logical way for us to go was to pick three quicks — Brett Lee, Mitchell Johnson and Stuart Clark — plus Shane Watson, who bowls fast-medium, and rely on Michael Clarke and the recalled Andrew Symonds to provide the few overs of spin we'd require. The negative of that was that we'd be leaving out Jason Krejza, who took 12 wickets in our most recent Test, which also happened to be his first Test appearance.

A bloke shouldn't get dropped after enjoying such a productive debut, but at the same time it's wrong to pick a player who is most likely not going to get a chance to make a significant contribution. The alternatives were leaving out Watto, who went so well in India with both bat and ball, or Symmo, which would have been a bit silly after we'd gone to the trouble of bringing him back from his personal troubles.

After I saw the pitch the day before the Test, I was fairly sure it would play more like a lively day-one Sheffield Shield wicket than the day-one Test track we've become used to seeing for the past 10 years in Brisbane. In the end, we adopted a 'horses for courses' approach, left our offie out, and were vindicated by the final result.

I wonder if there are a few commentators and cricket writers who need to get out more. I'll read how the public is universally sick of the Australian team, how they're 'fed up' with our attitude, but then at a function or in a café or as I walk along the street or down a fairway I get a different feel. It was like that after the Sydney Test against India last season, in the lead-up to the first Test against New Zealand, and it's still like that now.

Sure, many people were disappointed by our performance in India and confused by the events on the field in Nagpur, but not everyone has given up on us.

All the negativity made for a slightly surreal atmosphere in the days before the Gabba Test. Despite the gloom and doom in the press, we were still expected to win the game and win it easily, which created a weird kind of pressure that intensified after we were all out for 214 on the first day. After days of rain and limited practice opportunities, the wicket was green, the Kiwis bowled well and we were lucky Michael Clarke batted superbly, but it wasn't until day two, when our quick bowlers restricted them to just 156, that we rediscovered that winning feeling that we haven't felt in a Test for nearly a year. In the end we won by 149 runs — a fair margin in a low-scoring game after we lost the toss.

For me, one of the most positive things to come out of the game was the return of Andrew Symonds. He might not have made a major contribution with the bat (26 and 20) or the ball (0–4 and 0–12), but there were good signs both times he batted, especially on the second afternoon when he and Simon Katich added an important 56-run partnership after we'd stumbled to 4–53 in our second innings. It's clear he's excited by the opportunity he's been given, and I just liked having him among the group — always a presence in the field and still a lively personality in the dressing room. Despite all the attention he's getting, it looks to me that he's starting to get back to being the Andrew Symonds of old. That's what Australian cricket needs.

It was typical that when something very unusual happened during the game, Symmo was at the centre of it. On the first day, he went to smash the Kiwi quick Iain O'Brien but only managed to hit a catch straight to Aaron Redmond, who kindly put the chance down. Undeterred, Symmo tried the same thing again and this time he managed to get the ball out towards the mid-wicket boundary.

It didn't make the rope, but he and Michael Clarke went for the all-run four, there was a shot at the stumps, and the ball speared off to the third-man boundary. An eight! Next ball, though, was a beauty and all Symmo could do was nick it through to the keeper.

Pup in our first innings and Kato in the second were our batting stars, each playing an innings of the highest quality. It was never easy, especially for the guys who'd been in India, where the ball was often hitting the toe of the bat rather than the splice. Pup's last-man-out 98 was better than many of his hundreds, and we would have been in dreadful trouble without it, but Kato's gallant effort was even better, as he batted right through the innings, an achievement only 10 other Australians have managed in Test cricket. It was a feature of the great Australian teams of the past 15 years that someone usually stood up when a big effort was needed, and it wasn't always the same person who dug us out of trouble. This was a reminder of that, as neither of the team's two most experienced batsmen — Haydos and me — did much, but we still scored more than enough runs to win the game. My two digs, just 4 and 17, were disappointing and from my perspective unexpected, as my previous 10 Test innings at the Gabba included four centuries and five fifties (123, 3, 54, 50, 51, 149, 104 not out, 196, 60 not out and 56). Maybe the stresses of the previous fortnight took a bigger toll than I thought.

Our bowlers were terrific. It's not easy adjusting from the slow decks in India to a seamer like this one, but they did so beautifully, never giving the Kiwi batsmen a chance to settle in. Stuey Clark was back to his best in the second innings, and while Brett Lee was not quite as lethal as he can be, he was still pretty good, giving every indication that he might soon be back to his best. The way he attacked their top-order on the second day was very impressive. Bing took his 298th and 299th Test wickets on the second day, and then his 300th when I caught Jamie How off

We're No Angels

Back in August, New Zealand captain Daniel Vettori released his autobiography, and in the lead-up to the first Test a few reporters from the other side of the Tasman seemed keen to get my response to a line from the book in which he described me as an aggressive character who is often 'spoiling for a fight' on the field, and tagged me, Matt Hayden and Andrew Symonds as 'the three most overtly aggressive players in world cricket'.

To tell you the truth, I've go no problem with Dan writing this if that's what he thinks. My only gripe is with the perception that goes with it — that we Australians are out there playing it hard while other teams are behaving like angels.

the third ball of the New Zealanders' second innings. This achievement puts Bing in pretty rarified air — the only other Australian bowlers to take 300 Test wickets are Shane Warne, Glenn McGrath and Dennis Lillee. No doubt, he'll be much better for the effort he put in here.

Mitchell Johnson's best work came with the old ball, a fact reflected by his efforts on the fourth morning, when he took three of the Kiwis' final four wickets, including their best bat, Ross Taylor, to complete the first five-for of his Test career and match figures of 9–69.

I enjoyed the way he knocked Taylor over. At the hotel after day three, and then before play the next morning, I put it to him, 'Taylor is their danger player ... I want you to bowl at him straight away. Attack his off-stump and I reckon we'll get him caught behind.' Sure enough, that's what happened.

Mitch has probably been our best bowler in the past nine months, often on slow wickets that haven't suited him. He is by nature an attacking bowler who can concede a few runs, and as captain I want to take advantage of his wicket-taking ability, but in India we didn't often have the chance to operate that way, so often he had to just toil, which he did brilliantly. Here he was able to focus on trying to get wickets, and especially against the right-handers he was outstanding. There are still some technical things he can improve that will help his control and boost his ability to keep the seam upright and swing the ball, and he and bowling coach Troy Cooley are working hard on those, but he's so fit and strong and hungry I believe the sky is the limit for him. At the moment, I'm not really thinking of him as a new-ball bowler, but that won't be far away.

***

AFTER THE GAME, IT was clear that Matt Hayden would be the focus for those in the media who like to speculate on which established star will be dropped during the season. It's almost a tradition. I've seen it happen quite a few times during my career, with champions such as David Boon, Mark Taylor, Steve and Mark Waugh, Justin Langer and Glenn McGrath. But my strong view is that, even after Kato's wonderful knock here, Matty is our best opener. Trust me, he still has the skills and that hunger that sets him apart. Sure, he failed twice in this Test but the conditions were such that anyone from the top order of either side can be excused for that. The perfectly pitched outswinger from Chris Martin that knocked him over first ball of the second innings would have dismissed just about anyone.

What impressed me was what happened the morning after that setback. Matty knew I was coming down to the ground early and, as he often does, he asked me to bring him a coffee from the hotel. Which I did, but when I got to the dressing room he wasn't there, so I just left it on his seat. Then I went to the indoor net at the Gabba, and there he was — he'd been there for an hour — trying to get things right. Over the years, I reckon I have got to know his game as well as anyone; at different times I have noticed things about the way he is thinking and the way he is batting, to which he'll reply, 'How do you know that?' But I'm usually right.

This time, I haven't seen anything to suggest he is not as good today as he was 12 months ago, when he was the best opening bat on the planet. A couple of poor decisions, an unplayable ball or two, and when you've had your 37th birthday, as Matt did last month, then inevitably the critics are going to be writing your cricket obituary. But he'll be playing his 100th Test in Adelaide in a few days time and then, if I have any say in it, he'll be a key figure in our upcoming South African and Ashes campaigns.

***

SO WHILE IT WASN'T a great win, it was a good one, something I'm sure we can build on. Afterwards, the selectors announced that Shane Watson had been dropped for the second Test, in Adelaide, a call I know was a tough one. Symmo might have been lucky to hold his spot, but when you look at the good things he did in Test cricket over the past 18 months it would have been counter-productive, surely, to leave him out so soon after bringing him back.

It seems to me that everyone has missed just what a good Test cricketer Symmo has been over the past two seasons. I think he has been our most consistent batter during that time. He averaged 58 in the 2006–07 Ashes series, scored 103 runs without being dismissed in two Tests against Sri Lanka in late 2007, averaged 68.33 in last season's home series against India, and 66 in the three Tests we played in the Caribbean just six months ago. In

300 Test Wickets

I'm not sure there's a better way to demonstrate just what an outstanding Test bowler Brett Lee has been than to simply list the players who have taken 300 Test-match wickets. It's an exclusive club. In my view, Bing is fully entitled to be one of them. All stats are correct as at the completion of the first Test of this current series against New Zealand.

Player	Tests	Wkts	Avg	Best	5w	10w
Muttiah Muralitharan (SL)	123	756	21.92	9–51	65	21
Shane Warne (Aust)	145	708	25.42	8–71	37	10
Anil Kumble (Ind)	132	619	29.65	10–74	35	8
Glenn McGrath (Aust)	124	563	21.64	8–24	29	3
Courtney Walsh (WI)	132	519	24.44	7–37	22	3
Kapil Dev (Ind)	131	434	29.65	9–83	23	2
Richard Hadlee (NZ)	86	431	22.30	9–52	36	9
Shaun Pollock (SA)	108	421	23.12	7–87	16	1
Wasim Akram (Pak)	104	414	23.62	7–119	25	5
Curtly Ambrose (WI)	98	405	20.99	8–45	22	3
Ian Botham (Eng)	102	383	28.40	8–34	27	4
Malcolm Marshall (WI)	81	376	20.95	7–22	22	4
Waqar Younis (Pak)	87	373	23.56	7–76	22	5
Makhaya Ntini (SA)	92	363	27.94	7–37	18	4
Imran Khan (Pak)	88	362	22.81	8–58	23	6
Dennis Lillee (Aust)	70	355	23.92	7–83	23	7
Chaminda Vaas (SL)	107	348	29.31	7–71	12	2
Allan Donald (SA)	72	330	22.25	8–71	20	3
Bob Willis (Eng)	90	325	25.20	8–43	16	0
Lance Gibbs (WI)	79	309	29.09	8–38	18	2
Fred Trueman (Eng)	67	307	21.58	8–31	17	3
Harbhajan Singh (Ind)	72	306	30.78	8–84	22	5
Brett Lee (Aust)	73	300	30.45	5–30	9	0

nine Tests in 2007–08 he totalled 777 runs at 77, with seven fifties and one hundred. He also took 12 wickets at 20.92. Symmo is more than handy and I'm happy to have him in the side.

At the same time, Watto was bitterly disappointed, not least because he went really well in India and losing your place on the back of one unproductive game always leaves a bad taste. Still, I can see the logic of the move. Like the decision to leave Jason Krejza out of the Test just gone, there is an element of 'horses for courses' about leaving Watto out. Jase will definitely play at the Adelaide Oval, which meant that if Watto was to stay in the XI he would have had to force one of the top six out. But after his double failure with the bat at the Gabba (1 and 5) that wasn't going to happen. Instead of keeping him in the 12-man squad, the selectors went for a fourth specialist quick, Peter Siddle, as cover for the three guys — Lee, Clark and Johnson — who barring injury will lead our attack. Of course, none of this will make Watto feel any better. Ask any player and he'll tell you that he'd much rather be in the squad as 12th man than out of it.

One thing I do know is that Watto still has the talent to score a lot of Test-match runs and take plenty of wickets, too. I don't think he will be out of the team for long.

This was one of those situations when I was more than happy with the bloke who had come into the side but still very disappointed to lose the bloke who'd been omitted. When I was asked about these decisions at the post-game media conference, I suggested that they might be a precursor for a new selection philosophy ...

'I just think we've got to be a bit more flexible in our selection for different places ... We've got South Africa (playing Test matches) here, at the WACA — which will be a good place for the swing and quick bowlers — and then we've got Melbourne and Sydney, which will be the other way.

'Then we take (South Africa) on over there on wickets which we saw last time seamed all over the place.

'We have to start looking at the guys that are going to be suited to those conditions and even look ahead to England as well. We're going to need people over there who can swing the ball and stand the seam up, and do that all the time.

'If we go to Adelaide on a wicket that's very flat and might offer a bit of reverse swing, we have to pick guys who can use those conditions better.

'We need to look at every way you can to have the most impact. They are some of the lessons we all learnt in India.'

This was all good and true. There were times in India when we clearly weren't as well equipped for the conditions as we could have been, which suggested to me that there will be occasions when we need to look further into the talent pool in Shield cricket to see if there are blokes who can do a particular job for us, maybe only for a single game or because of a specific set of circumstances. The decision to leave Jason Krejza out of the first Test here was in keeping with this kind of thinking. But then I was asked specifically about the selection of Pete Siddle … *Would he play in Adelaide?* I did Stuart Clark a disservice in the way I responded.

What I did was describe Stuey as a bowler who is at his most dangerous on a seaming deck, such as the one on which the just-completed Test was played, but who might not be so lethal in Adelaide, where having the ability to swing the new ball and reverse-swing the old one can be very useful. The implication was that Siddle might be a better bet.

It is a fact that Stuey has never been a big swinger of the ball; his modus operandi is to present the seam and he can usually produce significant sideways movement by doing so. This doesn't mean he can't get wickets at a ground such as Adelaide, or that he can't do an important job for us there, but the reality is that, like just about every bowler who's ever lived, some conditions suit him more than others. Shane Warne averaged 20 with the ball in Test cricket at the Gabba, but 36 in Perth.

Of course, no one ever considered leaving out Warney at the WACA, and as far as I know Stuey will definitely be playing in Adelaide. Understandably, though, some reporters ran the story that despite taking 4–43 in the Kiwis' second innings, Stuey's place in the side is in jeopardy. I sometimes get dirty when I see comments I've made get misinterpreted in the media but this time I have no one to blame but myself.

Over-rated Again!

I couldn't believe it when I was told on the third afternoon that we'd fallen behind in our over-rates again. For a while, I had to bowl Andrew Symonds and Michael Clarke in tandem to get us back on track a bit but even so I was still fined 30 per cent of my match fee because we finished three overs down.

Part of the problem was that we didn't have a specialist spinner in the side, but I am still very disappointed that some lessons are still to be learned. For this Test, we had guys on the sidelines monitoring our movements on the field, to see where we can make up time. As well, Mike Hussey was big on getting the bowler's cap to the umpire between overs and at times you could see some bowlers making a concerted effort to hurry back to the top of their run-ups between deliveries.

I didn't talk to players individually about over-rates before the Test, on the basis that if they didn't know about the problem, after all the debate that had been in the papers, then they never will. Maybe that was wrong. But at least we were a little better in this game, and I think we will continue to improve as the season goes on. I guess when people stop talking about the issue — that's when we'll know we've got it beat.

Thursday, November 27

My time as Australian captain these days seems to be a life of one step forward, two steps back. The first Test win was satisfactory, but a couple of days back the story broke that Andrew Symonds was involved in an incident at a Brisbane pub in the aftermath of our win at the Gabba.

I'm not sure of the exact circumstances of what went on. I do know Symmo was at the pub with a few team-mates and that some members of the Australian rugby league World Cup squad were also there. Most of us had gone back to our team hotel at the end of the cricket Test.

Symmo has released a statement in which he explained that 'a member of the public acted unreasonably towards me while I was with friends, at which time I took steps to remove myself from the situation'. The manager of the pub says Symmo wasn't drunk, and had been drinking light beer. James Sutherland has cleared him of any wrong-doing. 'Whilst Andrew agrees that he should have thought twice about actually going to the hotel, his response when subsequently provoked was restrained and mature,' James said.

Given all this, it seems hard to be too critical of the bloke, though my view is that he shouldn't have gone to the pub, which we knew would be busy on the Sunday night. But surely we haven't reached the stage where high-profile sportsmen can't spend some time 'in public' with their mates? Yes, we have to be

Spun Out

At the same time Andrew Symonds, James Sutherland and I were fronting a media conference where I had to answer questions about whether we were going to 'stick' with Symmo — 'If he wasn't worth it, he wouldn't be sitting here right now,' I said — I also had to come to grips with the news that Jason Krejza has rolled an ankle and is in big doubt for the second Test.

This is a terrible blow for Jason, who after his effort in Nagpur is in a position to establish himself as Australia's No. 1 spinner for the next few years. There's no doubt he has the talent; all he needs is consistency. If he's out, his replacement will be NSW's Nathan Hauritz, a bloke I have plenty of time for but who wasn't even in the Blues' XI for their most recent Sheffield Shield match. The fact we're even considering Nathan when he couldn't make his state team reflects the paucity of top-class spin-bowling talent in Australia at the moment, but the Test selectors believe he's bowled pretty well whenever he's had the chance. You would have thought Shane Warne would have inspired a generation of young Aussie spinners, as Greg Norman inspired a group of outstanding Aussie golfers, but for some strange reason that just hasn't happened.

If Nathan plays here in Adelaide he will be the seventh specialist spinner to play for or tour with the Australian Test team since Warney retired in January 2007, after Stuart MacGill, Brad Hogg, Beau Casson, Bryce McGain, Cameron White and Jason Krejza.

smart and careful when we go out, but we shouldn't be confined to our quarters. Having said this, whenever people ask why more and more we tend to stay in our dressing room to celebrate a win, part of the answer lies in episodes such as this one.

✳✳✳

ONE OF THE QUESTIONS I was asked by the journos implied that having Symmo in the team is causing more harm than good. I don't agree. 'Andrew Symonds is definitely worth having around and he knows what commitment is required for him to stay around,' I replied. 'It's as simple as that.'

But quickly the question of whether Symmo was good for the team or bad, partly to blame, just because he went to the pub in the first place, or blameless because it appeared he actually didn't do anything wrong, was off the radar, as news of the terrorist attacks currently playing out in Mumbai emerged. From what we can gather, terrorists have attacked a number of sites, including two luxury hotels that we Australian cricketers are very familiar with — the Taj Mahal and the Oberoi. Many innocent people have died, and many more have either been taken hostage or are imprisoned in hotel rooms that we might once have stayed in. I reckoned I've stayed at the Taj maybe 15 times; there'd be very few parts of the hotel that I haven't walked through.

One of the things about Indian hotels is that every time you go there the staff are always the same — it's genuinely chilling to think that some of the men and women who have always greeted us so warmly have now been caught up in the catastrophe.

The attacks began in the evening of November 26, Indian time. This morning, over breakfast in Adelaide, it was all we talked about, partly because it was, naturally, the main news story, but also because many of us are so familiar with the city, the area, the hotels, the people. It was the same at training — the chatter was all about Mumbai and at times I struggled to get some ghastly images out of my head. More than once we had to make a real effort to refocus, to try as best we could to concentrate on the task at hand.

Tonight, as I write this with the cable news on my television, I keep thinking about how sad it is that something like that has happened in India. It is a country I have always enjoyed visiting,

Hayden's Hundred

In my view, playing 100 Tests is the most significant thing you can do in cricket. I certainly rate reaching that landmark as my greatest achievement in the game.

To play 100 Tests proves you were good enough and durable enough to sustain a high level of performance over a number of seasons, a difficult feat in the take-no-prisoners world of modern international cricket. Matthew Hayden made his Test debut back in 1993–94, but didn't establish himself in the Australian side until 2000 but since then he has been a constant, scoring centuries at a rate of one every three Tests, averaging better than 50 and building a platform that we latter batsmen in the order have been happy to exploit.

As captain, I have always valued Matty's input, but perhaps never more than now, as the team is rebuilding. The trait I admire most is his extraordinary determination, which has always seemed to become even more pronounced when he finds himself under pressure. I think about the hundred he made in the fifth Ashes Test of 2005, when anything less would probably have seen him dropped from the side, or his effort in the 2007 World Cup, when he was clearly the best batsman in the tournament just a few months after he'd been written off as a one-day cricketer.

Tomorrow, we get the chance to salute one of Australian cricket's great careers. My hope is that there are still plenty more big days to come for Haydos before his time is through.

even when the results haven't gone our way and I've been struggling for runs. Further, India has established itself as the centre of world cricket, and it would be bad for the game, in my opinion, if this evolution was stifled. And being selfish, I'm struggling with the fact that these attacks appear to have been aimed at foreigners. Some people still like to say that cricketers won't be in danger when they visit some of the world's trouble spots, purely because they are not personally involved in what is driving the conflict, but less and less do I believe this to be the case.

Cricket Australia has stopped travel by Australian teams to India until further notice. At this stage, it seems the Twenty20 Champions League scheduled for next month, which was to feature Victoria and Western Australia and a few other Australians playing with Indian sides, will be cancelled. I was asked about the tragedy when Matthew Hayden and I met the media this afternoon, an interview that had been arranged so Matt and I could talk about his 100th Test match. Straightaway, I was able to point out that Matt had been due to fly out for India straight after the game that starts tomorrow. He won't be going now.

TOP: A great honour came at the start of the 2008–09 season, when I was invited to give the annual Bradman Oration.

MIDDLE: Arriving in Jaipur at the start of our Test tour of India.

BOTTOM: The series in India started well for us. We made 430 in our first innings and then, when Mitchell Johnson (leaping in the air) dismissed VVS Laxman, India in reply were 4–106.

I was at the striker's end, batting with Matthew Hayden, when almost all of us had to quickly take cover as a swarm of bees buzzed over the field during the third Test at New Delhi. Umpire Billy Bowden, however, had to be different.

My run out in our second innings at Nagpur — I knew as soon as I took off that I'd made a mistake and was in serious trouble. The fielder is Amit Mishra.

Two centurions from our series against New Zealand — Simon Katich (left), who batted through our second innings at the Gabba, and Brad Haddin (right), who made his first Test century in Adelaide.

Matt Hayden with his oldest two kids, Joshua and Grace, at the Adelaide Oval after a presentation staged to celebrate his 100th Test appearance.

ABOVE LEFT: Mitchell Johnson at the WACA, on his way to 8–61 in South Africa's first innings and 11 wickets for the Test.

ABOVE RIGHT: A Boxing Day hundred.

BELOW: Andrew Symonds leaves the MCG after being dismissed by Dale Steyn during our disappointing second innings of the second Test.

Mitchell Johnson
has just bowled
injured South
African captain
Graeme Smith to
end the third Test.
For Matt Hayden
(middle photo, far
left), it was the
final big moment
of his wonderful
career in
international
cricket.

Top: Dave Warner made an immediate impact when he was called into our Twenty20 line-up.

Middle: Mixing with the locals at Whittlesea in the aftermath of the Victorian bushfires.

Bottom: Ben Hilfenhaus takes a wicket with his second ball in Test cricket — Hashim Amla, caught by the captain — on the second day of the first Test at Johannesburg.

TOP: **At Durban, we stopped before play to remember the victims of the terrorist attack in Pakistan. From left: me, Michael Clarke, Phillip Hughes, Simon Katich and Mitchell Johnson.**

MIDDLE: With Graeme Smith after the Test series in South Africa, at the presentation of the Test Championship Mace and the ODI Championship Shield for 2008–09.

BELOW: **With Rianna and Emmy during our pre-Ashes tour visit to the Sacred Heart Primary School at Mosman in Sydney for the launch of the Run Ricky Run initiative.**

During the year, I found myself acknowledging some of the game's greatest players.

ABOVE: **Anil Kumble's** outstanding Test career came to an end in New Delhi.

LEFT: **Sachin Tendulkar** became Test cricket's leading run-scorer in Mohali.

BELOW LEFT: **Jacques Kallis** scored his 10,000th Test run in Johannesburg.

BELOW RIGHT: **Andrew Flintoff** played his final Test at The Oval.

Wednesday, December 3

Second Test, Australia v New Zealand, at Adelaide (November 28–December 1): New Zealand 270 (AJ Redmond 83; B Lee 4–66) and 203 (BB McCullum 84*; B Lee 5–105) lost to **Australia** 535 (RT Ponting 79, MEK Hussey 70, MJ Clarke 110, BJ Haddin 169) by an innings and 62 runs

***

THIS GAME STARTED WITH me losing my fifth toss in a row but still ended in an Australian victory by an innings, and it was a good effort for a number of reasons — not least because of Brett Lee's nine wickets for the match and Brad Haddin's first Test-match century. It was great to see Brett bowling with some real rhythm and at a pace that was faster than it has been for a while. Hadds' effort was the 14th highest ever made by a wicketkeeper in Tests and the second best ever by an Australian keeper, after the 204 Adam Gilchrist made against South Africa at Durban in 2002.

It is true that the final winning margin flattered us a little, given we were 5–247 before Pup and Hadds added 181 for the sixth wicket and then, except for Brendon McCullum, the Kiwis' batting was mediocre in their second innings. Still, Bing was the sharpest he's been since his off-season and I was happy with the efforts of all our bowlers, including Nathan Hauritz, who came in when Jason Krejza was ruled out, rolled his own ankle on the first day, but fought back to take a tidy 2–32 from 24 overs in New Zealand's second innings. I think Jase will be right for our next Test match, and if he is he'll be our first-choice spinner, but if we had to call on Nathan again I wouldn't be disappointed.

I must confess I was really pleased with the way I batted and then filthy with the way I got myself out straight after tea, when a dominant hundred and more was there for the taking. I couldn't believe it when I hit an Iain O'Brien long hop straight to Peter Fulton at short mid-wicket and then was astonished when O'Brien gave me a gobful as I began the walk back to the dressing room. It was one of the worst deliveries I've ever been dismissed by in my life, and for the bowler to carry on as though he'd just bowled a beauty was embarrassing for all of us. Later he reckoned he'd just reminded me that 'I'd missed out on a big one' and I guess it might have been something like that, but most worrying for me was the gross concentration failure that cost me my wicket. A few times in India — such as the two innings in Nagpur when I was bowled by Harbhajan Singh trying to cut a well-pitched delivery and then run out attempting a suicidal single — I got myself out unnecessarily. Making it worse this time, I was in excellent touch; you never want to waste days like that.

Earlier on day two, the big crowd was stunned when what turned out to be Matthew Hayden's only innings of his 100th Test match ended when the big man was run out for 24. Ironically, Haydos looked to be in good form before a mix-up with Simon Katich cost him his wicket, and I could sense his mix of anger, disappointment and frustration when we crossed as he walked away from the centre. I remember how keen I'd been to make a century when I played my 100th game and I knew Matt was just as ambitious. At least he didn't get clobbered by the only ball he faced, which is what happened to his great mate Justin Langer when Lang played his 100th Test at Johannesburg in 2006.

Even though he missed out on the century he craved, I'm sure Haydos will still remember this game fondly. For the rest of us,

Tails Again

As everyone knows, I'm a bit of a punter. I know a little about odds and the concept of value on the racetrack and the so-called laws of probability — the idea is to get the odds in your favour and then bet accordingly. This was my 50th Test as captain, but in the previous 49 I'd only won the toss 19 times, a success rate of just 38.78 per cent. So going into the Adelaide Test I was due for a win ... called heads as I always do ... and watched as the coin landed the wrong way yet again.

'Surprise, surprise,' I muttered when I saw that it was tails.

I'm not going to change what I call, because I still believe things will even out in the long run. However, I have no doubt that losing the toss three times out of four didn't help us in India. I guess the impact of the toss all depends on the subsequent circumstances of the game, and the strength and balance of the two teams' bowling attacks. Here, losing the toss might have been to our advantage, as Daniel Vettori decided to bat and as it turned out that meant we had the best of the batting conditions on days two and three.

though, I won't be surprised if a few years from now we'll look at this game chiefly for the way it re-established Brad Haddin in the Australian team. I thought his glovework was first-class in this match, and his hundred was magnificent, reached in just 133 balls. Test cricket is a much easier game if your No. 7 is averaging 40-plus and scoring quickly while doing so — Adam Gilchrist proved that time and again — and Hadds certainly has the ability and cricket sense to do that. Such a player can turn an innings score of 5–250 into 450 or 500 rather than 300 all out, and in the process he can initiate a crucial change of momentum that makes a team seem close to invincible. Gilly was the master at this. It has to be soul-destroying for bowlers and fieldsmen to work hard to get themselves in a winning position, only to see the mood change in a session, maybe even an hour.

Brad has been under pressure ever since he conceded 39 byes in the first Test in India. His batting was okay in India, but he never played a match-turning innings and there were whispers about before this New Zealand series that the selectors were looking at Western Australia's Luke Ronchi as an alternative. I don't think that was true, but even so Hadds knew he needed a big score, if only for his own peace of mind. It was about more than just fulfilling a long-held dream when he reached three figures, so understandably he was very animated, and then he set out to get as many as he could. You've always got to cash in on the good days. He wasn't dismissed until late on the third afternoon, when his job was done and we were pondering a late-in-the-day declaration, and then afterwards he was asked what he felt when he swung his bat and thrust his arms in the air when he achieved the century. 'Relief,' he said with a smile.

Anyone who has ever been under pressure to keep their place in the team knew exactly what he meant. 'I just trusted my game,' Hadds added. 'I can only trust what I do is going to be successful in Test cricket and not try to be anyone else.'

***

SO NOW IT'S TIME to look forward towards the South Africa series, which begins in two weeks time in Perth. As I conceded two days back, during the media conference straight after the second New Zealand Test, we were 'a fair way below our absolute best' in India but I believe we've 'taken a step closer here to being at our best'.

What a Catch!

It's amazing how the most spectacular catches you take just happen — it's not like you have time to think, *I'm going to make this great catch*. I guess they're the result of a lot of hard work at practice, natural athleticism, sharp hand-eye co-ordination and being in the right place at the right time.

The slip catch I took that dismissed Jamie How in New Zealand's second innings was certainly one of my better ones, mainly because I had to cover a fair bit of ground to reach it. What made it possible was that I saw it clearly off the bat, and it came hard (which often makes these type of catches easier, because if they hit the right part of the hand they stick) and at a nice height, though well to my right.

Initially, I thought it was passed me but I caught up to it and snared it between the thumb and forefinger of my right hand. Afterwards, when I saw the TV replay, I was surprised by the way I extended my body so that at one moment, just after the ball hit my hand, I was actually parallel to the ground. There are few worse feelings in cricket than dropping an easy catch, because you can't shake that thought that you've embarrassed yourself and let all your mates down, but when you grab a good one, the buzz it gives you and the team is terrific and contagious — one of the best feelings you can get in sport. That's true of Test cricket and I'm sure it's true of park cricket and beach and backyard cricket, too.

'We know the South Africans are a well-balanced side,' I continued. 'They have a really good fast-bowling attack and I think four or five of their batsmen are in the top 10 run-scorers for 2008.

'They are a good side and we are not kidding ourselves. We've got a long way to go yet if we want to stay the No. 1 team in the world.'

With Brett Lee running into form and Mitchell Johnson also bowling well, my hope is that this year the authorities in Perth will give us a typically bouncy WACA wicket. Even though they've got a good pace attack themselves, that would be my ideal way to welcome the South Africans to Australia. Last year, we were disappointed when we played India in Perth on what turned out to be a pretty tame deck (making our decision to go into the game with four quicks look a little ridiculous) and it would be a shame from our perspective if we were given something similar this season. By all accounts, the newer pitches at the WACA have been very lively (Pete Siddle told us the wicket for last week's Western Australia-Victoria Sheffield Shield encounter was pretty frightening), but not all the square had been re-laid so it is possible we will be playing the Test on an older, friendlier surface.

For me, the next week will be a quiet time. I was hoping to play for Tasmania in their next two one-day games — against New South Wales on Sunday in Hobart and South Australia in Adelaide next Wednesday — but after a brief chat with our medical team I've decided to give my right wrist (the one that was operated on last July) a rest. The wrist hasn't been hampering me since I've come back, I haven't missed a game or a training session because of it, but at different times it has ached a bit and I think a week off will do it a lot of good. I'm going to go to Melbourne tomorrow, for a pre-arranged routine follow-up with Dr Greg Hoy, who performed the surgery, and I'll be astonished if there is anything major wrong with it. The doc might recommend a cortisone injection to reduce some inflammation in the joint, and if he does I'll follow his orders, but despite what's been written in today's tabloids my career is certainly not 'under threat'.

PART THREE

AUSTRALIA V SOUTH AFRICA TESTS, 2008–09

Saturday, December 13

IT WAS NICE TO have last weekend off, to spend some time with Rianna and Emmy and also to mull over how the Australian team has performed during the past couple of months. I also couldn't help but continue to ponder the terrorist attack in Mumbai ... the hostage drama itself lasted until the morning of November 29, Indian time, but I'm sure the implications for life in India will linger for many more days than that. My main thoughts continue to be for the people who were physically caught up in the drama — the hotel staff, the tourists, all innocent bystanders. Of course, cricket has been impacted, with the Twenty20 Champions League cancelled and England's tour of India delayed. I can only imagine what the security will be like next time we travel to the subcontinent. What effect will it have on the IPL?

As far as our cricket in Australia is concerned, I'm pretty happy with the way we have managed ourselves since we lost the Test series in India. I feel like we're well positioned for what is going to be some very tough Test-match cricket against the South Africans over the next three months. The talk among the lads after the Adelaide Test was about what a great challenge the two series — here and then in South Africa — will be, so if it is right that we're getting back to our best then our timing is pretty good. A key for me is that we need Brett Lee and Andrew Symonds fit and firing, and the signs are, especially with Bing, that this could

A Question of Time

It's amazing to think that we've been playing almost constantly for the past 10 weeks, and I was feeling pretty exhausted by the end of the New Zealand series, and yet we've only just started what will be an intense 18 months worth of cricket. I know that when Cricket Australia and the Australian Cricketers' Association are negotiating the next Memorandum of Understanding next year programming will be high on the agenda, and that ACA Chief Executive Paul Marsh is very aware of the players' thoughts on this issue.

In recent times, my concerns have not been so much with the amount of cricket we play but the scheduling — that we have to be careful not to program games too close together and there needs to be an acknowledgement that travelling between venues can be exhausting. You can't land in a new city or country one day and play at your best the next.

Now, with the boom in Twenty20 cricket and the financial appeal of the IPL, I'm not sure it's going to be possible for any of us to play every game any more. I saw that someone estimated that I could be 'on the road' for 318 days next year, playing 140 days of cricket in at least six countries. We'll probably see more 'specialists' in the future — guys who play one or two forms of the game but not all three — and we're also going to have to see players being rested from certain games, maybe even some tours or tournaments, to make sure they are at their peak when the really big matches and series come along.

Paul Marsh puts it this way: 'We need to look at better management of players or prioritisation of games, not only so that players are performing the best they can on the field but so they are keeping their personal lives together off the field.'

happen. People have forgotten how good these blokes were just last season; we can't afford to carry them, but if they get back to their best then I'll be more than happy to compare our line-up to anyone else's. I'm as keen to help Bing and Symmo as I am excited to be working with the younger blokes to ensure we survive this transitional stage the team is currently going through.

People might wonder why I haven't included Matthew Hayden in that last paragraph, but the truth is that while I concede there is some question about whether Bing and Symmo can rediscover their finest form, I have no doubt Haydos will be scoring plenty of runs during the next few months. You only have to see how hard the bloke is working to believe this. I have found it inspiring watching the man as he fights so hard to get his timing back.

One guy who won't be part of team for the South Africa Tests in Australia is Stuart Clark, who in the next few days will be undergoing surgery to remove bone spurs from the elbow of his bowling arm. This will keep him out for at least a month, probably longer. Stuey has been carrying this injury for three or four months, but after being selected in the squad for the first Test against Graeme Smith's men he found the pain was too nagging to bowl through, and booked an appointment to go under the knife. Peter Siddle, who was originally left out of the squad for Perth after being 12th man in Adelaide, is a natural replacement and will almost certainly play.

As good a bowler as Pete undoubtedly is, I can't help thinking what a big loss Stuey will be. Our opponents must be delighted, as they would surely remember the impact he had on our last series, in South Africa in 2006 when he took 20 wickets in what were his first three Tests. I can only imagine how disappointed Sarf must feel — you always like facing teams against whom you've had success in the past, and he'll be missing a real heavyweight clash, the No. 1 and No. 2 rated teams in Test cricket going head to head. Add to that the fact that he's only 10 wickets short of 100 in his career and he'll be missing the Melbourne and Sydney Tests, the two biggest occasions of the Australian summer, and it's a cruel blow ... for him and the Aussie team.

His absence means we'll be relying even more on Brett, but I'm OK with that. The South African press all want to talk about how good their Dale Steyn is, but as good a bowler as Steyn undoubtedly is, Binga is quicker and has proven his ability at the top level over a long period of time. Steyn is still to do that. I'll back our bloke every day of the week.

The talk has been about what a fine bowling side South Africa is, but to tell you the truth I think their batting could prove to be their strength. It says a lot about the depth in their batting resources that their best batter of the last decade, Jacques Kallis, has been in moderate run-scoring form lately but they've still been winning.

Tuesday, December 16

TEST-MATCH EVE. THERE'S BEEN a good build-up to this first Test, with a sense of expectation at least the equal of any home series against South Africa I have been involved in (and that's all of them bar the first since the Proteas came back into Test cricket in the early '90s).

I realise part of this is about the fact that many see us as vulnerable after our bad loss in India and given that South Africa have won 16 of their 23 Tests since Christmas 2006. There is also that the ratings have us as the best two teams in the world at the moment, and the natural rivalry that has developed in the past 15 years. They haven't been able to beat us when it has mattered and we've enjoyed casting and keeping that spell over them.

Yesterday, I found myself at a pre-Test lunch where I took a fairly low-key approach when I was asked about the battles ahead.

'I know the feeling around the team is really good at the moment, our work over the last couple of days has been great.

'I think we improved in the second Test match against New Zealand compared to the first one, so there are some good signs there for us.

'We are heading in the right direction. We are still in that transitional phase as a team, but we are ranked

No. 1 in the world and I expect the guys to go and play a brand of cricket that will keep us at No. 1 for a while to come ...'

At today's media conference, however, I decided to be a little more assertive. I'm not quite sure why — as I've said in the past, I'm not a believer in making big predictions or playing what some people like to call 'mind games' in the lead-up to a game or series — mostly, it was a bit of a reaction to all the people who have been trying to talk us down over the past few days. There are a number of commentators who clearly expect us to fail, and at least one or two, I sense, who are primed to write stories calling for mass sackings and big changes in our leadership group, if we give them half a chance.

'It is very fair to say that we have had the wood on them for a long time in both forms of the game,' was how I began my response, after I was asked if the results of past Tests would have a bearing on this one ...

'There's no doubt that a lot of those guys in that South African side have played a lot of cricket against us and would be carrying some of the scars from previous series. It's up to us to make sure we start the series and the game well enough to reopen some of those scars again.

'The first hour of the first game is so important for a number of reasons. One, it gives you some momentum. Two, it can put some pressure back on the opposition, and if we do bowl first hopefully we can do some damage early on, and some of the batters — if we knock them over early — will start having all those doubts back in their minds again, about competing with Australia in Australia ...'

***

I HEARD TONIGHT THAT the News Limited papers are going to be running a story by Graeme Smith tomorrow, in which the South African captain will claim that Shane Warne tipped him off on how to bowl to Matthew Hayden and me while Smith and Shane were playing for the Rajasthan Royals in the IPL last season.

Good luck to him if that happened, though I can't imagine Warney telling him anything that he couldn't have worked out for himself. If I could have got into their conversation, I would have told Smith that their problem has been that when the pressure has been on they've been too conservative, that they've seemed reluctant to back themselves. In the big moments, they've been found wanting.

Have a look at many of their players' records against Australia compared to how they go against other teams. I reckon just about every player in world cricket knows what his record is like against different opponents, whether it's specific batsmen or bowlers or a team. All their batsmen will be aware that their records against us aren't as good as they are against other countries, and that could be weighing on their minds.

Maybe they'll be different this time. If they are, they'll be hard to beat. If they aren't, a lot of the pressure we've been feeling after India will quickly revert to them.

Monday, December 22

First Test, Australia v South Africa, at Perth (December 17–21):
Australia 375 (SM Katich 83, MJ Clarke 62, A Symonds 57; M Ntini 4–72)
and 319 (BJ Haddin 94) lost to **South Africa** 281 (JH Kallis 63, AB de
Villiers 63; MG Johnson 8–61) and 4–414 (GC Smith 108, HM Amla 53,
JH Kallis 57, AB de Villiers 106*, JP Duminy 50*) by six wickets

∗∗∗

I FIELDED THROUGH THE famous partnership between VVS
Laxman and Rahul Dravid in Kolkata in 2001, when they batted
for more than a day and set up a win for India after we'd enforced
the follow-on. I was crook and didn't play in the fourth Test in
the West Indies in 2003, when the home team set a new record for
the highest winning fourth-innings score in Test history, but I was
there and felt our pain at conceding such a total. There have been
a few other occasions when we've managed to lose games we
should have won. But none have hurt as much as this one.
Somehow, we managed to play plenty of quality cricket for the
first three innings of the Test, but then — through a mixture of
outstanding batting by South Africa and uninspired bowling and
fielding by us — we lost a game we had to win.

Not surprisingly, the South Africans are now on top of the
world — a lot of the demons that have pervaded their cricket
against Australia in the past might be things of the past. Graeme
Smith has gone from being a mediocre captain to being a genius,
when the truth is he's always been something in between.

Meanwhile, we're shattered. There's no other way to describe it. Our sense of invincibility is being eaten away. I keep thinking, *if we can't knock them over in these circumstances, when will we?* Getting 20 wickets in a Test was a big problem for us in India, and it seems nothing has changed. This loss will be a tough one for morale, and I'll be looking out for any blokes in the team who aren't prepared to work bloody hard to get things right. As far as I'm concerned, anyone who isn't prepared to dedicate themselves to returning Australian cricket back to No. 1 has to be cast aside. We'll find our form soon enough, I can guarantee you that, but there's a general malaise in the set-up at the moment that's come about because of a lot of things all happening in a short period of time: retirements, controversy, injuries, personal issues, an all-round loss of confidence. We're still putting in at training, our tactics aren't the problem, the talent is still there. We've got to get our attitude back.

***

THE TEST STARTED IN unusual fashion — I won the toss. I thought it was a good one to win and had no hesitation in batting first, not least because we'd included Jason Krejza ahead of Shane Watson in our line-up, and though we lost three wickets in the first session, at stumps on day one I was pretty comfortable with our position (by the end of the game, though, I was wondering out loud whether it would have been better to bat last). Simon Katich and Michael Clarke batted very well, producing a fourth-wicket stand of 149 that counteracted some fine early bowling from Dale Steyn and Makhaya Ntini.

I was one of two Australian wickets to fall before the first drinks break — out first ball, caught by AB de Villiers at third slip off Ntini. It was the second golden duck of my Test career, after Chennai in 2001, when I was stumped off Harbhajan Singh.

After Kat and Pup fell in quick succession, Andrew Symonds and Brad Haddin put together the second important partnership of the innings. Symmo was terrific, slamming 57 from 68 deliveries, but he was filthy when he got himself out to Paul Harris, South Africa's left-arm spinner. Then Hadds fell to the second new ball and it looked like we wouldn't get many more than 300, but a late-innings resurgence gave us a score I was very comfortable with. The pitch wasn't all that easy to bat on throughout the first day, and it wasn't much different on day two — the day Mitchell Johnson came of age as a Test-match bowler.

This was of the best spells I have ever seen. South Africa had been 1–16 and then 3–110, but while neither Jacques Kallis nor AB de Villiers looked totally comfortable they had taken the score to 3–225 with 10 overs left in the day when I called back our pace spearhead for one last spell before stumps. His first over was uneventful, Jason Krejza conceded six runs at the other end, and then everything changed. In 33 minutes, charging in with the wind behind him, Mitch took a phenomenal 5–2 from 21 deliveries as the visitors collapsed to 8–243 at stumps. He was quick and scary, getting the old ball to swing and bounce in a way I didn't think possible on this deck, which until this point I'd seen as a new-ball wicket — tough to bat on when the ball was new and hard, but easier once you'd settled in. None of de Villiers, Kallis, JP Duminy, Morne Morkel or Paul Harris could counter him, the two established batsmen both falling caught behind, the other three being beaten by sheer pace and sudden lift.

There haven't been too many great left-arm quicks in cricket history. Wasim Akram and Alan Davidson stand out, while Bruce Reid was outstanding for a year or two. I think we've found another.

A Run of Outs

Matthew Hayden's disappointing run continued on the first day of the Test when he was out for 12 — three fours — as the South Africans sought to take advantage of some genuine bounce and movement off the pitch in the first hour. Previously, I haven't been concerned that Haydos has been missing out, because his attitude has been great, he's been working very hard and I haven't seen anything different or technically wrong with the way he's been batting.

But this time was a little different. The early blows to the boundary suggested he was determined to be decisive, but then Makhaya Ntini went round the wicket and straightaway Haydos jabbed at a ball that pitched short of a length and bounced a bit, and the result was a catch to Graeme Smith at first slip. The right 'shot' was to let it go, but from where I was sitting he didn't appear to have the confidence to do that. Maybe his mindset hadn't adjusted to Ntini changing his line, which suggests his focus isn't as sharp as it used to be. It just didn't look right. Later in the day, as I sat in the dressing room and pondered my own first-ball dismissal, I looked over at him and wondered if the public debate about his future has begun to affect him.

What he needs is a change of luck. Instead, in the second innings, he copped another poor umpiring decision — one of those calls which will hasten the introduction of referrals to the video umpire. The replay clearly showed the ball hit only pad before it rebounded back to Dale Steyn, but by then he'd been given out caught and bowled. Haydos showed a lot of class the way he copped the ump's verdict, and all of us hope that fate will at least even things out in the remaining Tests.

One outcome of this pulsating spell was that it got the crowd right behind us, in a way I haven't felt since the final session of the Sydney Test last season. Three days later, after we'd made only 319 in our second innings and South Africa then produced one of the greatest batting efforts in their history, as the local fans slowly came to realise that we were going to lose, that passionate support seemed like a distant memory.

AFTER THE GAME, I upset a few people with my comments about the pitch, about how the track we played on was more like

---

Under Pressure

Jason Krejza bowled pretty well in our first innings, better than his bowling figures of 1–102 suggested. Sure, he went for a few runs but there was never a time when it didn't look like he could get a breakthrough. His dismissal of Hashim Amla, clean bowled with a beauty, which came at a time when it looked like Amla and Graeme Smith might be getting on top, was very important. He's an attacking bowler and as captain I love backing players of his style.

Unfortunately, on the last day, as Jacques Kallis, AB de Villiers and JP Duminy took control, Jase didn't bowl well and because he conceded runs so readily that put a lot of pressure on our other bowlers. He hasn't played a lot of cricket since the India tour, having been 12th man in Brisbane and then he turned his ankle in Adelaide, and I think that showed in the fourth innings. Of course, he is not the first spinner to struggle on the fourth and fifth days in Perth — it was only three years ago that Shane Warne couldn't dismiss Jacques Rudolph and Justin Kemp at the WACA when the first Test of the 2005–06 series was drawn. Back in 1995–96, in my debut Test match, a young Sri Lankan offie named Muttiah Muralitharan took 2–224 in his first Test in Australia. That certainly wasn't the end of Murali's career, and I doubt this'll be the last time we see Jason Krejza at the highest level either.

Adelaide than Perth, and maybe with hindsight it would have been smarter if I'd kept quiet. It wasn't the wicket's fault we lost, but some people saw my comments as suggesting precisely that. I am disappointed the Test was played on a pitch that was slower than the WACA wickets of old, and I still don't understand why this occurred, but it wasn't like last season, when we were led to believe the deck was going to be quick and lively but it played a lot slower than that.

It was a weird sort of wicket. For the first half of the Test, it was one of those pitches where the batsmen never seemed fully 'in'. South Africa's first innings collapse was simply the result of great bowling, but at other times the wicket played a few tricks and those who tried to play conventionally suffered as a result. No one made a hundred until the fourth day — when Brad Haddin was our last man out for 94 and then Graeme Smith scored his first Test century against Australia — by which time it had settled down into a really good batting wicket. There's no doubt Test wickets across the world have become more durable, it is no longer rare for teams to get 300 or more batting last, and in this instance I knew we'd have to work hard to chisel the South Africans out. But I never thought they'd get 4–414 rattling along at nearly three-and-a-half runs an over. It was superb batting and I admired the way they beat us, but we definitely let ourselves down.

Going into the last day, South Africa needed 187 to win with seven wickets in hand. I fully expected us to be fired up from the first ball, but instead Kallis and de Villiers settled in and then began their charge to victory. Maybe the fact the fourth day's play didn't finish until 8pm played a part in this, but if it did it shouldn't have. More significantly, it seemed to me that the fear of defeat was nagging at our psyche much more than any belief or hope we had of victory.

In contrast, our opponents played as if they expected to win and in the end it wasn't even close. When we finally got a breakthrough — Kallis, caught Hussey bowled Johnson, to make it 4–303 — I hoped it might be the start of a turnaround. This was Mitch's 11th wicket of the game. I thought back to Duminy's first-innings failure, when he made only 1 during Mitch's wonder spell, but this time, the young left-handed batter played magnificently, while de Villiers was in the middle of one of the best hundreds of his life. Often, it seems AB goes back to balls he should be playing forward to, but he is rarely found out and he has been in sensational form all year. In 2008 he has scored Test centuries against the West Indies, India, England and now Australia.

***

THE THING I WAS trying to do when I criticised the pitch after the Test was underline an issue that I see as very important. I really believe, based on our experiences over the past four years, that the uniqueness of the WACA as a Test-match venue is being lost and I think that is a bad thing.

I've said it many times: one of the joys of playing Test cricket in Australia used to be the vast array of conditions we'd see as we travelled from Perth to Sydney, Brisbane to Melbourne, Adelaide to Hobart. It's not like that any more, not to the same degree, and the worst example of it has been the WACA, where especially in the past two seasons the pitches for Sheffield Shield matches have been lightning fast but for the Tests they've been more placid, improving as the game goes on. Over the past four years, batsmen have averaged 27.64 in the first two innings of Tests at the WACA and 49.34 in the third and fourth innings.

Of course, the pitch you play on in a particular game is the same for both sides, so it's very hard to ever blame the wicket for a defeat. My complaint goes beyond the result of this Test; it goes to the sort of cricket and cricketers we want to see playing the game in this country in years to come.

***

AS WELL AS MAKING comment on the WACA pitch, I also went public with my concerns about the way some guys are playing. I said we had 'a lot of passengers in the team' for this Test, a comment I won't back away from. A few of our players

Body Language

One thing that did surprise me in the wash-up of the first Test was the extent of the criticism I copped for my allegedly ultra-negative body language on the final day, as the Test slipped away from us. My sins, according to one journo, included 'standing with his hands on hips' and 'generally looking downcast'. Another wrote that my body language was 'substandard when the side needs him most' and suggested I resembled a 'human teapot' while our young bowlers were under pressure.

I'm sure if I'd stood passively chewing my gum I would have been sledged for lacking emotion. I can remember Steve Waugh being bagged for this same poor body language crime when he first became captain, but then the team started winning and the criticism stopped. Similarly, Graeme Smith's body language was questioned when his team struggled against Australia, but it's not at the moment even though to my eye he is carrying himself on the field in a similar way now to how he handled himself in 2005–06, when we won five Tests out of six.

It's amazing how perceptions can change when you're not on top.

did some special things in this game, but we still lost, a reality that shows up the other guys who didn't make much of a contribution. Most people saw this comment as a direct dig at Brett Lee, and while it's true Bing was not the only Aussie down on form in this game, I'm sure he'd be the first to agree he wasn't at his best. A couple of times, most noticeably at the start of South Africa's second innings, he seemed close to full speed, but at other times he was more economical fast-medium than the express swing bowler we require. My understanding is that he will stay in the squad for the Boxing Day Test, and I know that it's never wise to write off a champion, but the days when Binga was a surefire selection for the Test XI seem to be gone.

Although Kato, Pup, Symmo and Hadds all played good innings here, as a batting group we should have done better. We had an opportunity to bat South Africa right out of the game in our second innings, but we failed to do that. They scored 4–414 in their second innings, while we were 7–162 in ours, and though the batting conditions might have improved as the game went along, the difference between the third day and the fifth was not that stark.

So I guess there'll be a few guys waiting nervously for the announcement of the team for Melbourne, but that should be natural after a defeat like the one we suffered here. 'We will have to think about the bowlers we have got in the side at the moment, with the conditions we are going to be confronted with in Melbourne and Sydney, whether we think they are the best guys to win us the next two games,' I said straight after the Test, following on from my 'passengers' quote. 'If they're not, we will have to make some changes.'

I feel let down, there's no other way to describe it. I know it's a bit hard for me to be putting too much blame on others, because it's not like I've been scoring heaps of runs myself, but this is the first time in my career when there have been guys wearing the baggy green who might not be able to do the job expected of them. I never thought I'd be part of an Australian team that didn't seem capable of bowling good batting sides out and I guess I've been so slow to adjust to the fact that some of the new guys in the side haven't got a real solid foundation of first-class cricket under their belts. These guys are learning as they go. That's okay for the long term but it's testing now. I guess it was the same back in the 1980s when future champions such as Steve Waugh, David Boon, Craig McDermott, Merv Hughes, Dean Jones and Ian Healy all came into the team and had to survive some tough losses before they started to win.

Based on this game just gone, blokes like Peter Siddle and Jason Krejza aren't quite ready for Test cricket at the moment, but they will be one day and maybe the bitter experience of losing a Test like this will accelerate their development. At the same time, I'm still learning about these new players — what makes them tick, how best to communicate with them, how they react to stress, criticism, a pat on the back — and I realise my captaincy and man-management skills are under a lot of scrutiny. It will be interesting to see who can handle the pressure of the next few weeks and months, and who can't.

It's going to be hard for us to win this series now. Being one-nil down in a three-match rubber is a situation Australia hasn't been in since the series in Sri Lanka in 1999, Steve Waugh's second series as Test captain, when we lost the first Test and drew the final two. The only other time it has happened during my career was in India in 1998, when Mark Taylor was in charge. The experienced guys have to see our position as a challenge, the younger blokes as an opportunity; it's up to all of us to make sure we're doing everything right over the next few days so we can give ourselves the best chance of bouncing back.

Wednesday, December 24

I UNDERSTAND THE SELECTORS talked about a number of players before they picked the team for the second Test, but in the end they only made a couple of changes: Nathan Hauritz in for Jason Krejza and Ben Hilfenhaus added to give us a 13-man squad. I've long been a fan of 'Hilfy', a genuine new-ball bowler whose recent progress has been hampered somewhat by injuries. I'm not sure he'll play in Melbourne, because we have the option of retaining Peter Siddle so he can play in front of his home crowd (an idea I'm pretty keen about), or we could include Shane Watson to bowl first change and strengthen the batting. That latter option also has some appeal, but late today I was told that Watto is struggling with a stiff back and might not be able to play if we pick him.

Andrew Symonds is also battling injury — in his case a bung knee which troubled him during the Perth Test, and actually made it hard for him to bowl on the last day. It's one of those things that comes and goes a little bit. Trouble is, Symmo is one of those blokes who won't tell you if he's hurting. His leg could be hanging by a thread but the expression on his face wouldn't change. We're confident, but not certain, he'll be right to play on Friday, but if does play it will be as a batter who bowls a little bit of off-spin. He won't be bowling medium pace.

Symmo's ailment did get a run in the papers this morning, but most of the media talk is about the futures of Brett Lee and Matthew Hayden. Of course, neither is in flash form, but my view remains that both have done so many good things for us for so long that it would be unwise to cast them aside. It wasn't that long ago that Bing began his Test career with an explosive five-for against India in a Boxing Day Test, while Haydos has scored six Test centuries at the MCG. They deserve our support and I'll continue to back them. I saw that South African coach Mickey Arthur rated Haydos among the blokes they fear the most, because of his ability to dominate a bowling attack and in doing so set the tone for the match. I'm sure the South Africans are enjoying seeing our main man struggle — not because they like seeing a great player out of form, but because it means they're being spared some tough times in the field. One of the best morale boosts a team can get is to make a star opponent feel like he's more Bruce Wayne than Batman.

While Arthur was enjoying his time as coach of the team leading 1–0 in the series, our man, Tim Nielsen, received a nice boost with the news that he had signed a two-year contract extension that will take him to the end of the 2011 World Cup. There have been some whispers about that Vin's job was under threat, but none of that was coming from within the team set-up. In my view he's doing a terrific job in circumstances that would have tested any of his predecessors, and I hope we'll be working together for at least a few more years.

Tomorrow will be a special day for Rianna and me: our first Christmas with little Emmy. For the past couple of years I haven't been at the team Christmas party, mainly because it has become an event tailored more for the families with kids, but this year we will be there for a while, so Emmy can attack some gift boxes and have a few minutes with the big man in the red suit. I'm sure I'll be up early tomorrow, probably the earliest I've been up on Christmas Day for 30-odd years. And I also know that I'll be running a fair way back when it comes to presents; most of the gifts Rianna has brought down from Sydney don't seem suitable for a 34-year-old

In the Swing

I spent a bit of time reading the papers today and like any sports tragic most of my attention was taken by the back pages. In an article by Alex Brown in the *Age* I saw some quotes from our bowling coach Troy Cooley which mirrored some comments he made to me, concerning Mitchell Johnson.

The one thing that's been missing from Mitch's repertoire and it's the skill that sets great left-arm quicks apart from good ones, is the ability to swing the ball in from outside a right-hander's off-stump. Without that delivery, a right-hander can let a lot of balls go; with it, and the batsman can never be sure if he has to play at the delivery or not. Mitch has a sort of slinging action, and his arm has probably dropped a fraction so he's slightly round-arm, which has meant that he hasn't been as dangerous with the new ball as he was when he first made the Australian team. Troy acknowledged this, but he also revealed that Mitch is working hard to get his inswinger back.

male. But that's good — I've got the handycam ready and I'll be recording all those magic moments when Emmy rips at the wrapping paper.

I'm sure our fans must have felt let down by our effort in Perth, but I've still received a lot of pre-Christmas cheer over the past couple of days. Everyone I have bumped into since we arrived in Melbourne has seemed pretty keen to see us get out and turn what happened last week around. They want to see us play well. They want to see us win and it's our job and our responsibility to do that.

If I could have a couple of Christmas wishes this year, I think I'd ask first to win the toss — on what I've seen of the wicket that could be a real advantage — and two, I need us to play well for all five days, rather than just in patches like we did at the WACA.

Wednesday, December 31

Second Test, Australia v South Africa, at Melbourne (December 26–30):
Australia 394 (SM Katich 54, RT Ponting 101, MJ Clarke 88; DW Steyn
5–87) and 247 (RT Ponting 99; DW Steyn 5–67) lost to **South Africa** 459
(GC Smith 62, JP Duminy 166, DW Steyn 76; PM Siddle 4–81) and 1–183
(GC Smith 75, ND McKenzie 59*) by nine wickets

***

WELL, I DID WIN the toss. And we did play well ... for two
days, but not five. After that, it was a disaster, worse than Perth,
something I didn't think possible.

Late on day two, we had South Africa 7–184 in reply to our
394. Our fans were buzzing, we were excited, get the last three
wickets for 10 runs or less and we'd have the option of asking our
opponents to follow on. At the wicket was their No. 6, JP Duminy,
playing in just his second Test, and Paul Harris, who is a tough
cricketer but not a very good batter. To come were Dale Steyn, a
tailender with a Test batting average (from 28 Tests) of less than
10 and just two scores of more than 20, and Makhaya Ntini,
whose record is far inferior to Steyn's. Two-and-a-half days later,
we lost by nine wickets. The series is gone. We've taken all 20
wickets in a Test only six times out of 14 in 2008. Cricket-wise, it's
been a very ordinary year; 2009 can't come quick enough.

At stumps, they were 7–198. Duminy was on 34, Harris on 8.
On the first day, I'd made one of my better hundreds and with

strong support from Simon Katich and Michael Clarke, who both worked hard on a wicket that offered a bit to the bowlers. Day two was a special one for Peter Siddle, who had the Melbourne fans cheering for him as if he was Dennis Lillee or Merv Hughes. The quality of Pete's bowling wasn't too far from that level either, as he ran in hard and hit the bat harder, justifying the high hopes we've had in him since he was picked for India. The roar when he knocked back Neil McKenzie's off-stump during his first over in Test cricket at the MCG was one of the most memorable I've heard. But on day three we were listless, uninspired and pretty dreadful. Duminy, in contrast, was superb, producing one of the best innings played against us in the past decade. At the same time, we couldn't put any pressure on Harris and especially on Steyn, who somehow came up with the innings of his life.

Late-order partnerships often have a habit of sneaking up on you. Harris was determined to swing the bat, as if that was his best chance of scoring 20 or 30 that would have got South Africa towards 300. That was the mood out on the field at the start of play. He finished with 39, outscoring Duminy in the process. We were a bowler down because Brett Lee was off the field with a foot problem, which the doctors are describing as a 'hot spot' (the forerunner of a stress fracture), so our plan was to bowl Johnson and Siddle for a little while at the start of the day and then use Nathan Hauritz and Michael Clarke and maybe Mike Hussey until the second new ball was due. Ideally, the two quicks would have cleaned up their tail immediately, but they didn't bowl well — one short ball made Harris look silly, but at other times there was too much short of a length stuff that landed in his hitting zone. Subconsciously, I think we just expected him to get himself out, while Duminy would end up 70 or 80 not out at the end of the innings. That would do. But the spinners hardly

When We Were Kids

Boxing Day was special when I was a boy. We'd head for our holiday house on the coast in north-east Tasmania, and with Christmas out of the way I could bounce up early to count the minutes until Nine's coverage of the first day's play commenced. Great players such as Dennis Lillee, Rod Marsh and Greg Chappell, then Allan Border, Kim Hughes and Tassie's own David Boon were my heroes, and I'd spend the first session praying they'd succeed and then head outside during the lunch break to play in our family matches.

There might have been 40 or 50 members of our extended family involved in these Boxing Day Tests. The games were very, very competitive, often featuring a flash new cricket bat that someone had got from Santa, taped-up tennis balls and plenty of fieldsmen, all stationed in a ring. Everyone got a bowl; all I wanted to do was bat ... until 20-to-2, when someone shouted, 'They're back on!' and I'd run inside to watch the middle session. Then during the tea interval we were outside again, as our Test resumed.

Most of the guys in the team have similar stories about family matches over the Christmas holiday, and about watching the Boxing Day Test on the TV. And with it comes a sense of responsibility now we're playing for Australia. We know we're carrying on a tradition and we want to inspire the next generation so they can enjoy the same fun we had with our cricket when we were kids.

threatened, and it was Huss who finally got the breakthrough. Eight for 251; we were still looking at a lead of more than 100.

Two overs into the Duminy-Steyn partnership, we took the second new ball and I don't think there was anyone in the ground who didn't believe that would do the trick. But Duminy was almost Lara-like, extremely comfortable and composed, and Steyn seemed to appreciate his confidence. With hindsight, we didn't attack the stumps enough but the biggest problem was our energy level, which was just down on what is required. Every time Mitch pitched short and at the body, Steyn looked terrible and likely to pop up a catch, but he kept fighting and it was when we were walking off for lunch that I knew we were in trouble. Last ball before the break, he'd driven Mitch clean as you like past mid-off for four, and there he was striding off like a batter, clearly fancying the idea of a long stay at the crease. Duminy, meanwhile, was on 78 and impregnable. They were 8–304, trailling by 90. Psychologically, they were probably already in front.

Afterwards, the critics were into me about not trying different things. *Why not Katich's left-arm wrist spin?* In fact, I got Pup to ask Kato how he was feeling, but the response I got was that he wasn't too keen — he'd been battling a sore shoulder and has hardly bowled in the nets. *What about Andrew Symonds?* We all knew Symmo's knee has been crook, so I was hoping to get away without using him. In the end, though, I had to bowl him, which made the excuse that he was too sore to bowl look pretty silly. The main problem was that we just couldn't believe that Steyn could bat as well as he did. By the time we came to realise he wasn't going to get himself out, we were spent, mentally more than physically, and couldn't recover. Worse still for me personally, I dropped Steyn when he was 32, a slips catch I should have swallowed, while Mike Hussey had a horror moment when he lost a skied catch in the sun and the ball landed harmlessly beside him. The partnership went all the way to 180, the third-highest ninth-wicket partnership in Test history, and then Duminy and Ntini rubbed it right in by adding another 28 for the last wicket. I left the field downhearted, angry and embarrassed, determined to bat my very best in the second innings but knowing deep down that our best chance to square the series was long gone.

Three days later, as I write this, I'm a little more philosophical. But sitting in that dressing room after stumps, trying to come to grips with what had happened — that'll be the lowpoint in our fall from grace and what I hope will be our rise back to the top of Test cricket. The No. 1 team in the world doesn't let Dale Steyn score 76, not when so much — the series, reputations, pride — is on the line. For the second Test in a row we'd played so well to get in a winning position, and then we'd chucked it all away with a poor performance. I took a little comfort from the fact that we'd got ourselves into those winning positions before throwing it all away, but not too much.

My captaincy hadn't been great — in their second innings in Perth and then again here I should have been more adaptable, more proactive, have recognised sooner that the mood was changing. I feared that switching too quickly to the unorthodox might have been self-defeating, because I was determined to show faith in guys who are new to the team, but instead I went the other way and let the games get away from me. I don't think we've been too bad at building strategies for our inexperienced bowlers, but where we have fallen down is that we haven't thought enough about what to do if the tide turns. In the past, when the flow of the game turned against us, champions like Warne and McGrath usually made the right adjustments quickly, to regain the momentum. That is a rare skill that takes time to learn. We have to learn it quickly, because I don't want any more days like day three of the 2008 Boxing Day Test.

That was probably the hardest day of my cricketing life.

***

I WAS VERY PLEASED with my first-day hundred, even if I was a bit lucky in that I was dropped by Neil McKenzie at third slip just before lunch. I've always said that the 'lucky' batsmen are the blokes who take advantage of their good fortune, so in that regard I was really happy with the way I took control in the middle session.

The dropped catch was a weird one. I was thinking too much about the lunch break, and got caught in two minds ... do I play, do I not. At the very last moment I tried to drag the bat out of the way but the ball from Dale Steyn caught the bat on the way through. When I looked around and saw it going as slow as it was, I didn't think there was any way McKenzie would put it down but that's what happens in this game sometimes.

There was a real vibe around the MCG at the start, as I sensed everyone desperately wanted Matt Hayden to make a big score. However, it wasn't to be, as he sliced Makhaya Ntini to backward point after he'd made only 8. But Simon Katich was in excellent form, and he reached his fifty before we went to lunch. First ball after the break, I drove Ntini down the ground for four and from that moment my aim was to be as aggressive as possible, to try to put the bowlers on the back foot a bit. The pitch was definitely harder from this point on, and I could really feel the ball coming onto the bat. I hit three fours in a row off Ntini to go from 48 to 60, and then another 37 balls to get to my hundred. It turned into a terrific afternoon for me.

Afterwards, one of the press boys asked me if my daughter had enjoyed her first day at the cricket. 'She got to see a good one,' I replied.

My reaction when I reached three figures was a mixture of joy and relief, reflecting the reality that it had been a stressful time deflecting all the scrutiny after the first Test defeat. I made a point of seeking out Rianna and Emmy and then acknowledging

Caught or Not? (Part One)

In last year's *Captain's Diary 2008*, on pages 168–169, I discussed in some detail the question of whether a ball caught at grass level — where the fingers get under the ball but the speed at which the ball is travelling probably means that it forced its way partially through the fingers and grazed the turf — has been grounded or not. So I won't go over the territory again here.

However, another example occurred in our first innings, when Nathan Hauritz was caught at slip by Graeme Smith, and this time there was an added edge because the South African captain said he wasn't sure if it was out or not, and asked if it could be referred to the video umpire. Technically, he was out of order when he did this, because players aren't allowed to influence umps to 'go upstairs', but I saw no harm in it. Except that, as has been shown many times, the video often can't separate fingers and grass and ball.

To my eye, the video suggested, but didn't confirm conclusively, that a catch had been taken. That information was relayed back to the on-field umpires, who then gave Nathan out and I was fine with that process. However, as I've said many times, if I was in charge, in cases like this it would have been up to the catcher — if he thought he'd caught it, it was out; otherwise, the benefit if the doubt goes to the batsman. If a replay later exposes a fielder as dishonest, then he should be suitably punished. Such a system mightn't be perfect, but it would be close and that would be good enough for me.

the big crowd, who I felt were with me throughout, but then I went and wrecked everything by getting out almost immediately. I was the one bloke who had worked out the real pace of the wicket, so I really needed to go on and get a big score. Instead, Paul Harris did me through the air and I was out for 101.

Three days later, I played another long innings, though this one was more of a mental battle as I fought to save the game while — bar for a 96-run fourth-wicket partnership with Michael Clarke — wickets fell at regular intervals at the other end. Steyn bowled beautifully throughout the game, delivering some superb outswingers at pace and taking five wickets in both innings and showing why so many people rate him the best fast bowler in the game. When he was bowling I could never relax,

Bold Siddle

Test cricket is not supposed to be funny, but there was one moment of humour on the second afternoon, which came about as South Africa lost 3–15 and it seemed we were getting right on top.

Peter Siddle had told us he was going to go out and 'show 'em I can bowl quick'. And on this occasion he did, especially late in the day when he had Graeme Smith caught behind and then beat AB de Villiers for pace ...

Pete had charged in, pitched the ball on a good length, from where it cut back and hit the top of de Villiers' back pad. Then the ball disappeared from his view, as he turned around and began a fabulously animated appeal. We catchers behind the wicket knew that a bail had been dislodged and the batsman was out, but Pete had no idea as he continued to shout his hardest. Then he spun around and looked at us, bewildered that he hadn't got the decision and wondering why he wasn't getting our support.

It was only when he noticed Brad Haddin pointing at de Villiers' broken wicket that our rookie paceman's face broke into a big grin. Pete might have been a gear or two down in South Africa's second innings, but in the first he did enough to suggest he's got a long Test career ahead of him.

and Ntini and Morne Morkel offered admirable support. Still, playing against top-class opponents is what Test cricket should be all about, and having spent most of the previous day in the field watching Duminy, Harris and Steyn take the game away from us, I was determined to bat for as long as I could ... and I couldn't quite manage that. I'm not sure anyone will ever realise just how much I wanted to put together a really big score.

With this as my ambition, but with seven wickets having fallen for 180, the pressure magnified as I approached another century. By this time there was a little bit of irregular bounce in the wicket, and the reality of our position meant that the individual milestone meant little to me, and I kept reminding myself that getting out at this time, whether it was just before or just after I reached three figures, would severely diminish the value of my effort, because I had to make 150 or 170 if we were going to set South Africa a decent target. *If you're going to get out*, I kept saying to myself, *you've got to be last man out.*

The result, unfortunately, despite my best efforts to stay 'in the moment', was that I got ahead of myself — Morkel bowled a slower ball and I pushed half-heartedly at it and spooned a catch to Graeme Smith at short cover. I was out for 99, missed a century in both innings by a solitary run, but it wouldn't have made any difference to me if I'd made the extra run for the hundred. I knew with my dismissal that we were almost certainly going to lose. That's what hurt.

***

IN THE END, WE set South Africa just 183 to win, and the six overs before stumps only added to our anguish. Brett Lee gallantly took the new ball, even though he knew the pain in his front landing foot could turn into a stress fracture at any moment, and promptly bowled Neil McKenzie, only for the wicket to be stolen by the umpire's 'no-ball' call. Graeme Smith then set about the bowling, slamming 25 from 19 balls before the close, when the score was 0–30.

'We have to get out there tomorrow with an attitude that there is a game on the line, and we have to do everything as well as we can for the remainder of the game to give ourselves the best chance of winning,' I said hopefully at the media conference after the fourth day's play, but deep down I knew we were going to struggle. Maybe if we'd got a couple of wickets straightaway the next morning we might have been a chance, if only because this series to date has been about unexpected turnarounds. But Smith is in excellent form, McKenzie and then Hashim Amla both played sensibly, and the end came soon after lunch. All I could do was glumly concede that over the course of the two Test matches we've been outplayed.

Matt Hayden's struggles had continued in our second innings, when he scratched his way to 23 but then chipped a catch to JP Duminy at short cover. The South Africans are attacking the area on or just outside his off-stump, and Haydos appears to have lost his decisiveness, pushing too hard or too cautiously at balls he used to let go or hit for four. I really feel for my mate at the moment, and at the same time I have to respect the way in which our opponents have come up with a plan to attack our key batter, and have then stuck to it.

'We're all feeling for him a bit at the moment,' I said after the fourth day's play. 'He's going through a pretty rough trot, which all of us as batsmen have probably been through at some stage in our careers. We'll help him along the way as much as we can and expect him to be upbeat and giving us as much as he can in the field tomorrow.'

'Will he play in Sydney?' I was asked.

'We'll leave that up to the selectors to decide,' I replied. 'We haven't spoken about any selections for next week just yet. That will be done at the end of the game.'

'Do you expect changes to be made?'

'If we lose,' I said, remembering that there was still a day to play, 'we might be thinking along those lines a little bit more. I am really not sure exactly what is going through the selectors' minds. There will be time to talk about that for me and the selectors at the end of this game. As you know, changes tend to be made more when you're losing games. When you're winning games, they don't tend to be made. The selectors, I am sure, will have had their thinking caps on over the last couple of days of this game already. We will wait until the end of the game and see what comes of it.'

Yes, these responses were pretty nondescript, but there was

A Hundred and a 99

I must confess I figured I'd be on my own as a batter who scored a century and a 99 in the same Test match. But it has been done before, by England's Geoff Boycott at Port-of-Spain in 1974. One difference between me and Boycott is that he made his 99 in the first innings, so he wasn't dismissed when he was one run short of scoring a century in each innings of a Test.

Another is that Boycott's double led to a victory. In fact, looking at the scorecard of that Test against the West Indies — the fifth and final Test of a series that ended tied at one-all — his effort was quite superb. No other Englishman scored more than 45 in either of their innings during the Test, and Boycott's second innings 112 meant that the Windies had to score 225 to win the series. They fell 26 runs short.

little else I could say. I knew that Brett Lee (foot), Shane Watson (back) and Andrew Symonds (knee) would be unavailable for the third Test at the SCG, so two or three new faces would be coming in, but my view at the end of the Test, even though we could snare only one wicket in South Africa's second innings, was that it would have been wrong to suddenly revert to mass sackings. There's a real sense of embarrassment in our ranks right now, and my hope is that this feeling in itself will help initiate a revival. I still have a lot of faith in the blokes in the current squad, who without exception are excellent people and very good cricketers, and while we've had a couple of terrible

Time for Reflection

New Year's Eve was a quiet one for me. I just needed to 'get away', have a little time at home with Rianna and Emmy. So while most of the lads watched the fireworks on Sydney Harbour, I was at our new home, which we moved into only a few weeks back.

Unfortunately, given I've spent most of my time since September away playing cricket, I didn't contribute much to the moving process. But we set ourselves the task of making the house liveable by Christmas, and Rianna worked every chance she could to make that happen. So it was that we were able to spend some quality time as a threesome and then my wife and I could sit out the back and enjoy a glass of wine while the clock meandered to midnight. It was just what I wanted and needed, a reminder that while the Test team mightn't be firing at the moment, I've got a fabulous wife and daughter and I'm getting very well paid for playing a game I love. I'm very lucky. In just about every way, my life is pretty much perfect.

days we've had some good ones, too. But the gap between our best cricket and our worst cricket has been way too big. We have to improve, especially when the big moments are upon us, and we have to learn, but we can do all that. That the selectors eventually decided to keep the changes for Sydney to a minimum — bringing in New South Wales left-arm quick Doug Bollinger and Victorian all-rounder Andrew McDonald to join the 10 fit guys from Melbourne (the nine who played plus Ben Hilfenhaus) — indicates their thinking is similar to mine.

This is the first time Australia has lost a series at home since 1992–93, when Allan Border's side was unlucky to lose to the West Indies. It is also the first time Australia has lost a series to South Africa since the Proteas returned to Test cricket in 1992.

These were proud records we have been trying to defend, and though it is inevitable that winning streaks will end one day, like losing the Ashes in 2005 it still hurts a great deal that this has happened on my watch. To be honest, the fact we've been beaten isn't so bad — sometimes you just have to tip your baggy green to your opponent, and this South African team is a very good one. Guys like Smith, Steyn, De Villiers and Duminy have played really well. We've let ourselves down; we have to get relentless like the Aussie teams of old and we have to do it quickly. I really think we can.

I know a lot of our supporters are dismayed by the way we capitulated in the second Test, but I don't feel that the glass is even close to half-empty. An Australian fightback is a lot more likely than many people think.

Thursday, January 1

I KNOW DOUG BOLLINGER reasonably well, having toured with him to the West Indies and India in the past few months, but I have to confess I hardly know anything about Andrew McDonald. I have been told he goes by the nickname of 'Ronnie' (thanks to his surname and red hair), and blokes whose opinions I respect tell me he is a very sensible cricketer who has had some success with both bat and ball in this season's Sheffield Shield and the Ford Ranger Cup.

Both men are 27 years old. Andrew is certain to make his Test debut in Sydney on Saturday, taking the all-rounder's spot at No. 6 that was filled by Shane Watson in India and more recently by Andrew Symonds. Dougie will be a big chance to play, too, given his excellent SCG record; the alternative, of course, is Ben Hilfenhaus, but we're leaning the local man's way.

Picking Doug would be in keeping with the 'horses for courses' selection strategy we used earlier in the Australian season.

I did like what both new blokes were doing when they were informed of their promotions. There was something very Aussie about the fact that Doug was mowing the lawn and Andrew was getting his boards ready for a few days surfing on the Victorian coast when the call came from Cricket Australia.

It will be the first time since November 1999, when Adam Gilchrist and Scott Muller came into the team, that two

Australians will make their first Test appearance in the same match. It will also mean that no less than eight Aussies have debuted in the 12 months since the end of last season's SCG Test: Chris Rogers, Brad Haddin, Beau Casson, Cameron White, Peter Siddle, Jason Krezja, McDonald and one of Bollinger or Hilfenhaus. All but Rogers are bowlers, which underlines one of the difficulties we've faced in recent months — the inexperience of our bowling attack. Backing up over after over is a skill that has to be learnt, as is the ability to fight back when a batting line-up starts to get on top. Our bowlers are getting a top-level cricket education on the run; how quickly they learn could well determine how long it is before we start winning Test matches again.

Thursday, January 8

Third Test, Australia v South Africa, at Sydney (January 3–7): Australia 445 (MJ Clarke 138, MG Johnson 64) and 4–257 dec (SM Katich 61, RT Ponting 53) defeated **South Africa** 327 (HM Amla 51, MV Boucher 89; PM Siddle 5–59) and 272 (HM Amla 59, AB de Villiers 56) by 103 runs

***

WE SENSED THERE WAS a lot of goodwill in the Sydney crowd when this Test match started. It was as if our losses in the first two Tests, plus the fact that there were so many new faces in our team (only four of us had played in the fifth Ashes Test of 2006–07), had finally forced the realisation that we are a young team that needs support. Added to this, it seemed everyone wanted Matthew Hayden to score a truckload of runs. Whether that would mean his Test career would continue or he'd go out on a high note didn't really matter — they just wanted to see him back to his best.

As it turned Haydos couldn't quite come through, making 31 and 39, but at least he had the pleasure of being involved in another memorable tight finish at the SCG, the second in two years. I'm not sure what the future holds for him now; the impression I have is that he is now going to go away and have a good think about his future. I've seen it before, how champions lose that crucial fraction of desire and it all too quickly results in their retirement. Is that where Haydos is now? If it is, I think it's only happened in the past two or three weeks, when the pressure on him has been relentless, but it might mean we'll have to go to South Africa and England without him.

The Test started with me winning my third straight toss, but any joy I felt at that break was negated when I got another first-ball duck — second in three Tests — after Hayden and Simon Katich had added 62 in the first 13 overs. Kato was in outstanding touch, scoring 47 from 52 balls, but for the rest of the day the boys had to battle for every run. Michael Clarke, who on day two went to one of his most important hundreds, took 115 balls to reach his fifty and copped a few nasty blows along the way. At 5–162, we were in serious trouble, but Pup and Brad Haddin then added 75 for the sixth wicket and after that our lower order was magnificent. On day two, we went all the way to 445, with Mitchell Johnson demonstrating that if he is not a genuine all-rounder yet, he's not far away. Mitch (64), Nathan Hauritz (41) and Peter Siddle (23) all posted their highest Test scores, as our last four wickets added 208 runs.

The pitch was playing beautifully, and we were only able to get one wicket before stumps on day two, but Mitch was able to land one major blow. With the score on 0–35, he managed to get a ball to rear from just short of a length outside Graeme Smith's off-stump and struck the South African captain a fearful blow on his left hand. Smith had to leave the field and later we learned that he had a break just above the little finger on his left hand. Indications were that he wouldn't be picking up a bat for six weeks.

Day three belonged to Peter Siddle, who took his first Test five-for, including a late spell of 4–7 from 22 balls, an excellent follow-up to his terrific first-innings bowling in Melbourne. Despite a seventh-wicket stand of 115 between Mark Boucher and Morne Morkel, we managed to gain a first-innings lead of

In The Pink

For all the excellent cricket played in this Test, I reckon the thing this game will be most remembered for is how the crowd became a sea of pink on each of the five days' play and especially on day three, which was officially designated 'Jane McGrath Day'.

Jane died last June after a long fight with cancer, but from not long after she was first diagnosed with the illness she established a foundation to raise funds for cancer research and to support the families of cancer patients, and the colour pink became synonymous with her charity.

For this Test, Cricket Australia and the SCG Trust came up with the brilliant idea of asking the fans to wear something pink, and it looked as if everyone got into the spirit of things. There were pink stumps, caps, ties, tops, batting grips, hats, flags, ribbons, T-shirts, shorts, bandannas, shoes, thongs. Shane Warne, commentating for Nine, wore a delightful pink suit, while the groundstaff were clad in pink shirts. Umpires Bowden and De Silva wore pink wrist bands.

Over in the area that was once the Hill, in front of the new Victor Trumper Stand, the statue of Yabba, the legendary fan from between the wars, had a hot pink bandanna tied around his neck. So, when it was unveiled behind the Members Stand on Jane McGrath Day, did the new statue of the Demon Spofforth. Richie Benaud's statue behind the Ladies Stand was daubed with pink zinc.

The South Africans also got into the spirit of things, many of them wearing pink bandannas at training, while we did all we could to help as Glenn and the other good people from the Foundation raise awareness for their magnificent work and as much money as they could.

118, and we built on that steadily on day four. Haydos batted okay for 39, before Morkel knocked him over, Kato had to battle for his 61, a marked contrast to his first-day aggression, while I was excited with the way I batted. I went out there determined to be assertive, and after being very lucky to survive my first delivery (an inside edge ran away for four, when it could just as easily have deflected back on to the stumps) I scored at nearly a run a ball. The pitch was cracking up and there was always that fear that a ball might jump or skid, but it didn't bother me — this was one of those days when my feet and hands and instincts were in sync, and I was as surprised as anyone when I edged a Morkel delivery back on to my stumps just after I reached my half-century.

The timing of our declaration was awkward. It was one of those times when I wanted to be aggressive, yet in the back of my mind was the thought that successful fourth-innings run chases are more prevalent these days. It seems I've developed a bit of a reputation for making conservative declarations, though I'm not sure why because I can't think of too many instances when I've cost us a win. So when I called us in after Pup was dismissed in our second innings — leaving South Africa to get 376 in more than three-and-a-half sessions — many people were surprised, even wondering if I'd let them back into the game. Perth is still strong in the memory. But my logic was pretty simple: as the cracks on the pitch widened, scoring runs at speed was getting tougher and tougher, though simply defending was not that hard. Even though they were a batter down, I thought we'd need plenty of overs to get them out, and the only way we'd lose was if we bowled badly. And you can't go making decisions based on the premise that you're going to play badly. I wanted to win, and what others considered a slightly sporting declaration gave us our best chance of that. South Africa were 1–62 from 26 overs at stumps, the only man out being makeshift opener Morne Morkel, who became Doug Bollinger's first Test wicket.

***

MAYBE, YEARS FROM NOW, we'll look back on this last day as a turning point. It was so important we came out of this match with a win; for me, an 'honourable' draw would have been akin to a loss. All day, it looked like we'd get the result we were after, but first the weather turned threatening, and it seemed the game might get washed away, and then Dale Steyn and Makhaya Ntini, batting nine and 10 because Graeme Smith was nursing his broken hand, refused to yield. Their 105-ball partnership went for an eternity. It set up a dramatic finish.

The South Africans had been 4–139 at lunch, 7–193 at tea. There were dark clouds about, and stories of torrential rain on Sydney outskirts. As we walked back on the field, I saw that the groundstaff had the pitch covers ready. Six overs into the final session, Siddle trapped Harris plumb lbw with one that kept low, bringing Ntini out to join Steyn and the tension began to grow. I tried all five of our frontline bowlers, switched around the field, put in three close-in legside fieldsmen for the quicks, eventually had eight men around the bat. The weather started to clear a little. Finally, after 74 minutes, Andrew McDonald got the breakthrough, two balls after he spilt a difficult caught-and-bowled chance. I was impressed by what Ronnie did in this game, and he's got a sense of humour, too. With the overs running out, he chased a ball all the way to the mid-off boundary, turning a four into a one, but this meant last man Ntini would be off strike for the first ball of the next over.

'Why didn't you kick it into the boundary?' I asked him, a stern look on my face.

He knew that would have been the wrong thing to do, but he didn't say anything, just looked at me like a schoolkid worried he's about to get into trouble even though he was sure he hadn't done anything wrong.

Then I laughed, he laughed ... and we got on with trying to win the game.

Graeme Smith earned a lot of the headlines, through his act of coming out to bat after Steyn was finally dismissed, when South Africa were 50 balls from a draw, and I couldn't help but be impressed by his tenacity. Though, to be frank, I think most cricketers in a similar situation would have done exactly the same thing. We expect each other to get out and do the job no matter how sore or tired you are. It was certainly courageous in cricket terms — I said that straight after the game — but as people tried to outdo each other with superlatives to describe his actions I think it was important a little bit of perspective was added to the story. Because, when you think about the circumstances some special people across the world find themselves in, there's really nothing brave about cricket. We're playing a game. Sure, Graeme risked further damage to a nasty and painful injury, and in terms of the sport he deserves our total admiration and respect. He showed a lot of character. But that's all. The real heroes are found in other fields — war zones, third-world slums, hospitals.

This said, there was a genuine sense of theatre when he emerged from the away dressing room to try to save the game, and the way he got behind the line had me thinking that we'd finish a wicket short. Ntini played very well, even swinging Hauritz away for two fours in the third-last over, and it reached the stage where I wasn't sure who I wanted on strike — the proven No. 11 or the injured captain. Fortunately, Mitchell Johnson produced a beauty with the second ball of

What Doubt?

I thought the controversy about an lbw decision that went Matthew Hayden's way late on the third day was a classic beat-up. Of course, with all the conjecture about Matt's future, this not-out call by umpire Asoka De Silva received plenty of attention, but I was surprised by the tone of much of it. The clear implication was that the ump had made a grievous error, as if he'd ruled not out on a run out when the batsman was three or four metres from safety. It was nothing like that.

Sure it was close. When I saw the TV replay for the first time that night, my initial reaction was that it was tight, but it probably wasn't out. In the commentary box, Richie Benaud said immediately that he thought it was going down the legside. Soon after, 'Hawkeye' suggested it was going to hit the stumps, and maybe it was, but the point is that it was one of those decisions that have been going each way (if anything more in the batsman's favour because we're supposed to get the benefit of the doubt) ever since the lbw law was invented.

However, that didn't stop one writer the next morning claiming categorically that the ball 'would have smashed the base of middle stump', while another bluntly described the verdict as an 'incorrect umpiring decision'. A third claimed Mr De Silva 'must have been asleep'. All I can say is that if I was playing for my Test career, I wouldn't want any of these people wearing the umpire's coat.

the second-last possible over, a fierce in-cutter that shattered Smith's stumps. I think it would have been too good for either of them.

***

AT HIS MEDIA CONFERENCE after the Test, Smith explained that at the start of the day he had no intention of trying to bat, to the point that he didn't even bother bringing his cricket gear to the ground.

'I arrived here without any kit,' he said. 'I had some pants that I shoved in my cricket bag to protect my bats, and I managed to borrow a shirt from Jacques [Kallis] and a pullover from "Harry" [Paul Harris] that still had a hamburger stain on the front left side of it. I had Morne [Morkel] dressing me and putting my shoes on and pads on ...'

This all sounds good, but I was surprised that the best jumper he could find was one with a big hamburger stain down the front of it. One assumes there were other jumpers in the room, and a few of the South Africans are Graeme's size, so either no one else was prepared to lend the skipper any gear, or maybe they're all sloppy eaters.

I did like Graeme's tribute to Makhaya Ntini, who went into the innings with a Test career batting average of 9.43 but survived 75 balls for 28 not out. 'I thought Makhaya should have protected me a little bit more,' he said, 'being the senior batsman out there.'

***

IT WAS GOOD TO win. There is a sense of satisfaction in our camp that we've managed to come back from the Perth and Melbourne defeats; relief, too, that for a little while at least we'll have the critics off our back. I was so happy for our young blokes, who were tested on the last day but still came through, but a little sad for Haydos, who dropped a catch off Ntini with seven overs left and is clearly wrestling conflicting emotions about what he should do with his cricket life. 'I'd love Matty to keep playing,' I said when pressed again on the subject after the Test. 'He is great for our team ... I'd take him into battle every time.'

I also couldn't help but ponder how different the atmosphere of this game was compared to the angst and anguish of the India Test here last season, even though both games ended in thrilling Australian victories. This series has been played in excellent spirit, tough and hard-fought but always fair and sporting. This time, there was no sense of suspicion or antagonism in the air, no late-night disciplinary hearing to attend; instead, we were able to stay in the dressing room until late in the night, sharing drinks with team-mates, friends and rivals. In the old days, we might have headed out into the city for a few beers, but we enjoy the privacy our room offers and the knowledge that if we stay there no one is going to cause us any trouble and we're not going to get into any trouble ourselves.

On this occasion, though, there was a bit of a dust-up late in the evening, because Michael Clarke, who's from Sydney, wanted to get away to spend a little time with some old friends. But we'd settled in and Mike Hussey was in no hurry to sing the team song. Pup tried to hurry Huss up, Simon Katich suggested he be patient, and the two got into a bit an argument. Neither man was drunk; it was over and done with in about 30 seconds. There was nothing to it really, it doesn't happen often, but I have seen a couple of similar minor confrontations in my 14 years with the Australian team. I'm sure the two will sort out any differences pretty quickly, but there were a fair few people in the room when it happened, so I guess we'll be reading about it in the papers soon enough.

Earlier, Pete Siddle had been named man of the match, Smith man of the series, and to my mind they were both clear calls. I guess JP Duminy and Dale Steyn would have been the other main contenders for the series award, while our best over the three Tests was definitely Mitchell Johnson, who continues to grow as a Test cricketer.

I liked Smith's comments about Mitch, when he talked about the final minutes of the Test: 'He probably would have got me if I had both arms available. It cut back off the crack there,' he

---

Caught or Not? (Part Two)

As had occurred in Melbourne, there was a turf-level catch in this game that was 'sent upstairs' for a decision. This one happened on the last day — Jacques Kallis, always a key wicket, this time caught-and-bowled by Andrew McDonald — and as had been the case with the Nathan Hauritz dismissal at the MCG it was settled amicably, with none of the bitterness that surrounded a couple of decisions involving Indian batsmen in Sydney in 2007–08.

Andrew was sure the ball hadn't touched the pitch as he grabbed it, and I had a good close view and was also certain it was a fair catch. Umpire Billy Bowden's first instinct was that it was out, but he still asked the TV Umpire Rod Tucker to study the replays. Just as with the Smith catch of Hauritz, it looked out on the television, though maybe the ball did fractionally scrape the deck, which I believe is what Tucker relayed back to Bowden. The ump on the field then went with what his eyes had told him and ruled in our favour, Kallis left the crease without any fuss, and after the Test Smith said the decision was fair.

I like the fact that it's now up to the on-field umpires to make the decision. I've always been against the replays being the judge because they are so rarely conclusive. In my view, Smith's catch in Melbourne and McDonald's here in Sydney were both good decisions.

---

said. 'Mitchell has bowled superbly throughout the series, finishing with 17 wickets. I saw them having a little group meeting before that over, and I was hoping they would throw the ball to someone else.'

In this Test, I bowled Mitch first change in both innings, after Siddle and Bollinger. Now he has to become a new-ball bowler, which will come when he and Troy Cooley nail that inswinger to the right-handers they've been working on.

So we've lost the series here in Australia 2–1, but soon we'll be in South Africa trying to square the ledger. In the old days, of course, Test series were usually over five Tests and that number of games is still, I think, the benchmark as to what the perfect length of a series should be — if you really want to determine who is the superior side. I understand that in this modern era of crowded schedules it is rarely possible to program a five-Test series in one country, but maybe we have to re-think things just a little. Air travel is not as arduous as it used to be and the concept of warm-up games before a series is fading away. Rather than these two back-to-back Test series — here in Australia and then in South Africa — being considered as two separate entities maybe they should just be one six-game series.

I really believe that it won't be until the end of the three matches in South Africa that we'll have a true idea as to which of us is the better team.

PART FOUR

HAYDOS

Thursday, January 15

ON JANUARY 8, MATTHEW Hayden was left out of Australia's squad for the two Twenty20 internationals and first two one-day internationals against South Africa. He'd actually been told he was dropped in the dressing room after the third Test, and I'd been told about the decision too, but typical of the bloke he kept the news to himself, so he wouldn't sully the mood. Chairman of selectors Andrew Hilditch explained that the move was a 'strategic' one, made with an eye to the ICC World Twenty20 to be played in England later this year and especially to the 2011 World Cup.

Five days later, Matt announced his retirement from first-class cricket. At this point, the selectors had not revealed their hand in regards to our Test tour of South Africa or the Ashes Tests later this year, but my best guess was that had he been available he would have been chosen. Whether his omission from the one-day squad was a factor in his decision to quit now, I don't know — maybe it hastened his retirement a bit, but Matt was left out of the one-day squad in 2005 and came back to be the batting star of the 2007 World Cup. If the fire was still in his belly, I'm sure he would have kept fighting.

I'm not surprised that the tributes Haydos received were fantastic. Steve Waugh claimed he 'had changed the face of Test match batting forever'. Jason Gillespie revealed that he sometimes thought about wearing a helmet when he bowled to him. Adam Gilchrist talked about Matt's 'extraordinary mental strength', how his greatest assets were 'his faith and belief in himself, coupled with his amazing work ethic'. Glenn McGrath described him as a 'legend of the game', and spoke of how important he had been to establishing the Australian team's aura.

'It was an absolute honour and a privilege to play with him and even more so to call him a mate,' Glenn said.

'Matthew's legacy across Queensland club cricket, state cricket and Australian cricket will be one of someone who got the absolute most out of his ability and being someone who left no stone unturned in terms of his preparation,' I commented. 'His work ethic, his pride in the baggy green, his presence in the dressing-room as someone who enjoyed everyone's and especially the team's successes ... no matter what he had done or how well he played, Matt always wanted to be better. That will be the legacy he leaves.'

As he tells the story, Matt made his mind up while he was in the backyard after the Sydney Test, doing the gardening with his six-year-old daughter Grace. 'I was picking this crazy bush of wild tomatoes that we had and I was with Grace at the time,' he said at his retirement media conference, which was held at the Gabba on the morning of the second Twenty20 game against South Africa. The entire Aussie team was in attendance. 'I was just talking with her and I said, "Darling, I think I've had enough. I want to be here."

'She said, "Daddy, one more Christmas." Because she loves the Boxing Day Test match.

'I said, "No, that's it, love. It's time."'

***

MATT HAD PHONED ME last Monday night to tell me what he'd decided and as I listened to him explaining how he felt he didn't have it in him to fight his way back to top form again, I couldn't help thinking, *I've had a bit of practice at this lately*. It was impossible not to think back to the conversations I'd had with Shane Warne, Glenn McGrath, Justin Langer, Adam Gilchrist …

'I suppose there's no chance of me changing your mind,' I said, knowing there was no chance of me changing his mind.

'What do you reckon?' he replied.

So that was that.

'I'd love you to be at my press conference,' he asked.

'Of course, mate, I want to be there,' I answered. Sure, we had a game to prepare for that night, but I wanted to be there for the big fella.

We had a few more chats on the phone that evening, trying to work out the best way to handle the announcement. Matt wanted to make sure it fitted in with what the team was doing. *The bloke has retired*, I thought, *but he was still more worried about the team than about himself.* At one point during our conversation, he apologised for giving it away while the team was evolving; he said he felt he'd 'left me hanging a bit'. He also expressed disappointment that now he wouldn't be able to see close-up how the young blokes in the team grow as men and cricketers. In fact, it's the new guys who'll miss out. The example Haydos set — through his hard work, persistence, dedication, the way he got every last little bit out of his ability — was such a bonus for new guys trying to find their way at the elite level. But he's earned the right to spend more time with his family.

Quickly, plans were put in place for Matthew to do a lap of honour at the Gabba during the break between innings in the T20 international. At the same time, a mutual friend had contacted me with an idea that I thought would be a beauty, if only Matt would agree to it. A couple of hours before his media conference, I rang him with the suggestion — that he play in my place in the T20 game, so the Gabba crowd could give him the ultimate send-off.

But Haydos declined. 'Thanks mate,' he said. 'But I can't do it. I don't want to announce my retirement and then go out and play for Australia again.'

I don't know what Cricket Australia would have made of the move, because it never got that far. I respect Matty for knocking it back, but I still wish it would have happened. The fans would have loved it and so would have every single person in the Australian set-up.

***

MATT'S FINAL CAREER RECORD is imposing. He scored 8625 runs in 103 Tests, averaged 50.73, having made his Test debut in 1994 but then only playing seven Tests in the next six years. His 30 Test hundreds, one more than The Don, ranks third among all Australian players and sixth among all cricketers. His highest Test score, 380 against Zimbabwe at the WACA in 2003, has been beaten only once, by Brian Lara six months later. He scored hundreds in four consecutive Tests twice, and 1000 runs in a calendar year five times. A two-time World Cup winner, Haydos hit 6133 runs (seventh all-time for Australia) in 161 ODIs at an average of 44.10, with his highest one-day score, 181 not out from 166 balls against New Zealand in Hamilton in 2007, being an Australian record. The stats are amazing, but for me it was about even more than that — it was about the way he took on opposition attacks and dominated them. He could set the mood for a day's play, for a match, even a series.

I'll never forget how, against Pakistan in Sharjah in 2002, he was struck on the helmet by a fierce bouncer from Shoaib Akhtar. Immediately back on his feet, he stared down the pitch and muttered, 'Is that the best you've got.' Then he went on to make a hundred, in heat so oppressive I thought we were going to melt. No other batter in the Test made more than 44; Pakistan were bowled out for 59 and 53 in their two innings, which meant Haydos beat them by an innings. More generally, an image that stays with me is how, the day before a Test, he'd sit on the turf at one end of the pitch and visualise how he was going to dominate the next day. This level of preparation was taking the game to a new level. No opening batter has hit powerfully through the line to greater effect, or better demonstrated that charging a bowler can be ruthless rather than reckless.

Matt never backed away from an on-field exchange, and as a result he wasn't universally popular in opposition dressing rooms. Once you got to know him, you couldn't help but love the bloke, but I could understand how rivals who only engaged him in battle, when his competitive streak was red-hot, might struggle to warm to him. To me, he was a hero on and off the field, the rock on which many an Australian victory was built.

Ask me to name a standout performance and I think immediately of one of our sport's biggest events: the 2007 World Cup in the West Indies. During the one-day games in Australia that preceded that tournament, Matt wasn't in fantastic form and there was some talk outside the team that his place in the squad might be in jeopardy. Then he made a hundred against New Zealand at the WACA after he was dropped early on, and it was as if he'd reinvented himself as a batter during that innings. Suddenly, he was in devastating form.

He was the leading run-scorer at that World Cup, smashing three hundreds, including two in consecutive games. The best of them was the 101 he scored against South Africa in St Kitts, which came about after he told us at a team meeting that he and Adam Gilchrist were going to take Shaun Pollock down in the first few overs of the match. Most people rated Pollock as one of one-day cricket's best ever bowlers, and most batsmen were happy just to nudge the South African around, but Haydos reckoned that on a flat wicket there was a better way. He argued that Pollock's strength, his consistency of line and length, could also be a weakness, because it was predictable. At training the day before the contest, he and Gilly set up a bowling machine to mimic Pollock's delivery and then carted balls all over the place. On game day, we were 0–50 after five overs and Haydos reached his century in 66 balls, the fastest hundred in World Cup history. We made 6–377 from our 50 overs and Pollock's final bowling figures were 0–83.

Six years earlier, on the eve of our tour of India, at a time when he had just fought his way back into the Test XI, Matt organised for a pitch at the Allan Border Field in Brisbane to be well-worn so it would resemble the conditions he'd be seeing on the subcontinent. Then he worked and worked to refine his technique against the spinners, especially the way he used the sweep shot, which he saw as a potential weapon. Haydos went on to score 549 runs in the three Tests, including a crucial 119 in the first Test at Mumbai and 203 in the third Test at Chennai, the start of a magnificent run of scoring that continued, pretty much unabated for seven years.

In those same three Tests in India I accumulated the grand total of 17 runs. He averaged 109.80 for the series; I averaged 3.40. Little wonder then that on the day of Haydos' retirement announcement, I said, 'You can even look through the history books of the game and try and see if there has ever been a better opening batsman in the game, let alone Australia.'

A few people wanted to sledge my knowledge of cricket history after I made that remark, and I'm happy for them to have their views. Of course, there have some legendary opening bats over the decades — such as WG Grace, Jack Hobbs, Victor Trumper, Len Hutton, Sunil Gavaskar, Herbert Sutcliffe, Barry Richards, Bob Simpson and Geoff Boycott — and I know I'm biased, but I still wouldn't swap any of them for my man. I batted No. 3, straight after him, so I know how comforting it felt to see him go in ahead of me, and I also saw first-hand the sort of devastating impact he could have on opposition bowlers. There are few bigger confidence boosters for a player waiting to bat than to see a comrade out in the middle flaying the bowlers to all parts of the ground. Often, I'd go out to the middle and be genuinely surprised to discover how tough it was. Matty had made it look too easy. Only the truly great players can do that.

***

A FEW WEEKS AGO, I read an article in the *Courier-Mail* by Robert Craddock, in which he quoted Haydos as saying the best piece of advice he ever got was from the great rugby league coach Wayne Bennett.

'Don't get bitter,' Bennett says. 'Get better.'

More than once during his career, Matt had to go away and reshape his game, to take it to a new level. He did it before he forced his way into the team in 2000, before he went to India in 2001 and he did it again when he lost his place in the one-day team in 2005. Few players have so clearly kept improving the longer their careers have gone. Similarly, our friendship has got better and better the longer we've known each other, though I have to confess that my first impressions weren't too flash because when we first faced each other in Sheffield Shield cricket there was usually a bit of niggle between us. It was the same when I took on Justin Langer and Damien Martyn when Tasmania played Western Australia. We were young blokes fighting for a place in the Australian XI so little wonder things were competitive. Looking back, it was good grounding for when we eventually earned our places in the Test side.

Matt and I celebrated many birthdays together while away from family — his in the days before the Melbourne Cup; mine a week before the start of the Boxing Day Test. We've had the joy of seeing each other become a husband and a parent. He's a well-grounded bloke who was always there when I needed someone to talk to. If I had a problem, whether it was about my cricket or away from cricket, he was one of the first people I turned to. He's also built a well-deserved reputation as a chef, and many was the time on tour when he'd garner all the necessary ingredients and cook the lads a quality meal. It might have been something simple like steak sandwiches on the bus between games in England, or a seafood extravaganza on the beach in the West Indies, or a curry in the team room in India. He loved doing it, and I loved being there, chatting with him as he got things exactly right. In this last testing season he and I were as close as we've ever been, and I was so grateful for the way he kept trying to rev up the boys even as his own form deserted him.

I know that in a few days I'm going to get excited again about the journey the Australian cricket team is currently on, but right now I feel just a little bit lonely. I'm going to miss not having Matthew Hayden in the Australian dressing room, we all will. But the memories and our friendship will last forever.

PART FIVE

LIMITED-OVER MATCHES V SOUTH AFRICA AND NEW ZEALAND

Saturday, January 31

THE REST OF THE South Africa tour flew by. Last year, we played Test cricket throughout January, but before that the first month of the calendar year was always hectic, as we were usually involved in the three-team one-day tournament that followed the Test matches. This season, Cricket Australia introduced a new concept — two Twenty20 games and then a five-ODI series against the same team — but January still seemed as busy as ever. This time, though, there was no happy ending.

Ideally, I would have been able to take a game or two off, but there just never seemed to be an appropriate time for this to happen. We handled the two T20 games well, but then lost form in the one-dayers and I knew it would have been wrong for me, as captain, to leave the ship. This means I'll have to take a break during the Chappell-Hadlee Trophy matches we'll be playing through February. There is so much cricket ahead, I have to take a few days off at some point but right now there just doesn't seem to be a best time to do that.

After our win in the Sydney Test, I felt we'd go into the shorter games with a bit of momentum and what transpired in the two T20 games seemed to indicate that was true. Not even the loss of Peter Siddle, who discovered he had a stress fracture in his left foot, could stop us winning the two T20 games comfortably — by 52 runs at the MCG and by six wickets at the Gabba.

Australia v South Africa Twenty20 Internationals 2008–09

First T20 International, at Melbourne (January 11): Australia 9–182 (20 overs: DA Warner 89; DW Steyn 3–38) defeated South Africa 130 (18 overs: JP Duminy 78; DJ Hussey 3–25) by 52 runs

Second T20 International, at Brisbane (January 13): South Africa 5–157 (20 overs: JP Duminy 69) lost to Australia 4–161 (18.5 overs: RT Ponting 38, MEK Hussey 53*, CL White 40*) by four wickets

The game in Melbourne was especially notable for the debut of Dave Warner, who went into the contest having never played a Sheffield Shield game for NSW (he had played 10 one-day and 10 T20 matches for the Blues), but started with a bang, smashing 89 from 43 balls (including his first 50 from 19 deliveries) and being named man of the match. I immediately saw a bit of me in Dave, in that he's a young bloke from the working-class suburb of Matraville, which is a few kilometres due south of the SCG, who's committed to pursuing a career in cricket. He was also a little Adam Gilchrist-like in the way he swung his bat. He hit some huge sixes when I was batting with him; it was some of the sweetest hitting I've ever seen.

Quickly, Dave became a media star, with stories about of how his game evolved in tough backyard matches and how his parents had sacrificed plenty to give their son his sporting chance, and again I saw a parallel with my early cricket life. Of course, a big difference between his situation and mine 15 years ago lies in the opportunities cricket now offers. Already, Dave has signed an IPL contract, and he can make plenty of money even if he never plays a Test. But from talking to him, I know Test cricket is his primary ambition. A challenge for him, me, the selectors and the coaching staff will be to get his development right, so he gets the chance to shine in all forms of the game. He struggled a little in the one-dayers against South Africa, but I'm sure he's got the talent to be much more than just a power hitter. He might find a role in Test matches that sets him apart from other players of his generation.

I'll also remember this MCG game for a remark made by one of the umpires while we were fielding. Rod Tucker used to be a team-mate of mine in Tasmania before he became a first-class umpire, and now here he was out in the middle for a T20 international and asking me how it felt to be the oldest member of the Australian side.

'You know you are the old boy around the team,' he said with a smile.

No I am not, I thought to myself. *Surely there's got to be someone around older than me.* But I looked around and discovered Rod was right. Mike Hussey was closest, five months younger than me. It's a weird feeling, being the senior player, something I've never experienced at any level of cricket. Even in the juniors, I was always playing at least a year or two above myself.

These two T20 games were similar to the matches we've played in the past couple of years — in that they were very enjoyable to play and attracted big crowds and huge TV ratings, yet as I write this about three weeks later it is hard to recall too many things from the games. Yet I know at the time I was as competitive as ever. I was 'wired up' in both games, so I could chat with the TV commentators, and I remember how Ian Healy in Brisbane asked me to pre-mediate a shot. It was the last ball of an over, after Mike Hussey had hit three fours, a two, then a one ...

'C'mon mate, you're on television,' Heals said.

'Sorry mate, we've got a game to win,' I replied.

***

I WAS VERY COMFORTABLE with the change of format from a three-team ODI tournament to a two-team series. We players — and I think the public, too — had been keen to see this type of five-match rubber against one opponent; that the 'triangular series' had reached its use-by date. At a team meeting before the first game, we talked about the fact that it was time to start looking ahead to the 2011 World Cup, and it was a point I kept thinking about, even as our form fell away at the end of the series. Someone had worked out that Australia is scheduled to play about 80 ODIs between the start of this series and the first game of the World Cup, and my view is that every one of those games had to be looked upon as an opportunity for players to develop their skills and experience. It's less than two years since we won the 2007 World Cup, but because of retirement and injuries only five guys — me, Mike Hussey, Nathan Bracken, Michael Clarke and Shaun Tait — appeared in that competition and in these one-dayers against South Africa.

We should have won the series opener, at the MCG, but their excellent all-rounder Albie Morkel and stand-in captain Johan Botha hit 51 runs from 35 balls to give the Proteas a win with three deliveries to spare. We had them 7–221 in the 44th over, chasing 272, but some terrific hitting from Morkel and a couple of untidy misfields proved crucial.

Also important was the new innovation for this series: the batting powerplay. I must confess it took me a little while to get my head around it, and I still think it's one of those things — like backing wide runners from an inside draw — where you can do everything right and still end up a loser. Before the series, I spoke to a few of the guys in our squad who had some experience with the concept in the Ford Ranger Cup, but they were divided as to when was the best time to use it. The South Africans kept their powerplay up their sleeve until the death, and then Morkel swung away with the boundaries unprotected and smashed them to victory.

I had actually been thinking of taking ours early in our innings, straight after their bowling powerplay, when Shaun Marsh and I were going along pretty well, and there was also a temptation to use it after over No. 34, immediately after the white ball was changed, on the basis that the harder ball might be easier to get away. But then we lost a wicket, so we delayed until the 42nd over, when David Hussey and Cameron White were at the wicket. In the end, we scored 43 runs from our five overs with the field in, compared to the 49 Morkel and Botha hit, but the advantage they had — chasing a target with the field in at the death — was very significant.

***

GAME TWO WAS ANOTHER thriller, but this time an Aussie victory. The final margin was five runs, and we had to withstand another late South African charge — this time from Albie Morkel and Mark Boucher — to seal the win.

I was happy with the way we stood up to a pressure situation on this occasion, though the tight finish only came about because we didn't get as many runs as we could have. We were 1–152 in the 30th over (after Dave Warner, making his ODI debut, was caught Boucher bowled Steyn for 5), which should have guaranteed a total of 280, even 300, especially as we had our batting powerplay to come, but instead we only made 9–249. That proved enough, not least because Nathan Bracken was very good, especially during the South Africans' batting powerplay, and Ben Hilfenhaus kept his nerve pretty well at the end, but it was a lot tighter than it needed to be.

***

MITCHELL JOHNSON CAME BACK for game three, having enjoyed a decent break after the Test matches, and he returned at a time when the debate over the workloads of the top players was getting plenty of attention. For me, it's an issue that demands a reasoned debate, though I fear that once again it will get hijacked by people who reckon we're just whingers who don't realise how good we've got it. This happened in the lead-up to the Sydney one-dayer, after I made some comments about team rotation at a pre-match promotion. 'How can you complain about the international program,' these critics responded, 'when at the same time you want to play county cricket and in the IPL?'

The problem, as I see it (and a lot of people agree with me), is that we must recognise that the human body needs time to rest and recuperate, so the key is *managing* the top players' workloads. It's not that we play too much cricket; rather, that at times we're asked to squeeze too much into a short period of time. And it's not just the playing; it can also be a combination of the travel, the time zones, the training, the off-field commitments, the scrutiny, the days and weeks away from family. We actually want to play plenty of cricket — and this is the best time of our sporting lives and we can't waste it — but we also need to be fit and sharp so we can show the world what we can do. However, from the start of our tour of India last October to the World Twenty20 tournament in the West Indies in April 2010, we're projected to play as many as 26 Tests and more than 50 ODIs and at least 20 T20 internationals, all without a significant break. We're scheduled to play in eight different countries (if you count the nations of the Caribbean as one country) and have two typically packed home summers during that time.

I think it's too big an ask, but to me there is a solution and I'll keep arguing for it despite what some might say. The players, Cricket Australia and the players' association need to start identifying what are the series and tournaments where we need to have the team as strong and fit as possible. Fact is, some matches are more important than others. The important thing for us is to start prioritising, to do our best to ensure we have all our best players not just taking part in the big Test series and big one-day and T20 tournaments, but that we are as fit and ready to go for those games as we can be.

For the third ODI against South Africa, which we lost by three wickets, we had eight Cricket Australia-contracted players out injured (Stuart Clark, Michael Clarke, Phil Jaques, Brett Lee, Bryce McGain, Peter Siddle, Andrew Symonds and Shane Watson). We can't afford such a situation going into an Ashes series or a World Cup, but that could happen unless we address the problem. I reckon there are very, very few players who will participate in the IPL or county cricket if they believe it will impinge on their international performance — I know I'm looking at the 2009 IPL right now and thinking, *maybe I'd be better off giving it a miss* — and I hope the wider cricket community will acknowledge this. Other sports, such as Major League Baseball and elite European football, have flourished despite their top players not participating in every contest, and international cricket needs to head in the same direction.

***

IN SYDNEY, MUCH OF the attention leading into the third ODI was focused on Dave Warner, who after a couple of low scores was suddenly under pressure to meet all the hype that had surrounded his fantastic international T20 debut.

'I guess in a way he probably wishes he didn't make that 80-odd in that first Twenty20 game because it brought a bit of that pressure and spotlight on to him,' I said the day before the game.

'For David now, I guess it's a matter of working out a style that will work for him in the 50-over game and trusting himself.'

Of course, it's easy to say that, especially with the upcoming game being on familiar turf. 'Being in front of a home crowd can have a couple of different effects on you,' I said. 'I know when I play down in Tassie I probably try too hard to do well for the home crowd, but we'll see how Dave responds tomorrow.'

As it turned out, Dave did his bit, scoring 69 from 60 balls, but South Africa then came out and made 7–269, breaking the record for the highest successful run-chase in a ODI at the SCG. They achieved this on the back of a 96-run partnership between those two veterans, Herschelle Gibbs and Jacques Kallis, who showed you don't have to bludgeon a bowling attack to score quickly in one-day cricket. We'd dropped a couple at the start of the South African innings, and once Gibbs and Kallis settled in, I knew we were in trouble. Another late Albie Morkel cameo, this time 40 from 22 balls, sealed the deal.

'We did our homework on Morkel,' I explained helpfully after the game. 'We know what he's capable of, we know the areas that he hits to. Unfortunately, (this time) he hit them 30 or 40 rows back and not to our fielders.

'Maybe if a high ball goes up next time when Morkel is next in, maybe we will let it bounce and get on with things.'

Quite seriously, there have been times when talking about tactics for 50-over games that we've discussed the logic of trying to keep a guy who's struggling at the crease at the wicket, rather than dismissing him and seeing a more dangerous batter take his place. It makes some sense, though my cricket instinct tells me that if we did it would come back to bite us. Maybe it would work better in a Twenty20 game.

Earlier in this match, we'd had more problems with the powerplay, after I decided to use it while Dave was in full flow.

Australia v South Africa One-Day Internationals 2008–09

First ODI, at Melbourne (January 16): Australia 8–271 (50 overs: SE Marsh 79, RT Ponting 46, DJ Hussey 52) lost to South Africa 7–272 (49.3 overs: JH Kallis 41, JP Duminy 71, ND McKenzie 63, JA Morkel 40*) by three wickets

Second ODI, at Hobart (January 18): Australia 9–249 (50 overs: SE Marsh 78, RT Ponting 64; M Ntini 3–39) defeated South Africa 6–244 (50 overs: JH Kallis 72, AB de Villiers 44) by five runs

Third ODI, at Sydney (January 23): Australia 269 (49.2 overs: SE Marsh 43, DA Warner 69; J Botha 3–32) lost to South Africa 7–270 (46.3 overs: HH Gibbs 64, JH Kallis 60, JA Morkel 40) by three wickets

Fourth ODI, at Adelaide (January 26): Australia 222 (48 overs: RT Ponting 63, JR Hopes 42; DW Steyn 3–49, M Ntini 3–52) lost to South Africa 2–223 (38.1 overs: HM Amla 80*, AB de Villiers 82*) by eight wickets

Fifth ODI, at Perth (January 30): South Africa 6–288 (50 overs: HM Amla 97, AB de Villiers 60, JP Duminy 60*; JR Hopes 3–44) defeated Australia 249 (49 overs: MEK Hussey 78, BJ Haddin 63) by 39 runs

But he was bowled by Dale Steyn two overs later, we lost 5–75 in the next 14 overs, and the game's momentum changed. The South Africans, in contrast, kept theirs to the 40th over and Morkel immediately hit 14 from one Mitchell Johnson over. I like this batting powerplay concept because it adds something to the game — it can change a team's bowling tactics, and it certainly makes you think.

I'm just not sure it likes us.

***

MICHAEL CLARKE'S THUMB INJURY still wasn't right for game four, in Adelaide, and we also went into that encounter without Nathan Bracken, who had been our most effective bowler in the first three games. Bracks had a calf strain. His absence suggested it would be our bowlers under pressure, but I went into the game convinced it was the batting that needed to improve. I needed to look no further than my own efforts in the first three games, when I had scored 46, 64 and 29 — three decent efforts, but every time I had got out when I should have gone on to make the big score that would have put the game out of South Africa's reach. Getting out when you're set is often a bigger crime that making a low score. We made 13 individual scores of more than 20 in the first three games of this series, but nothing more than 79.

It's been demonstrated so many times — if someone at the top of the order makes a hundred then his team is generally going to make an innings total in the high 200s, maybe plenty more.

It was a must-win game for us, we knew that if we played our best cricket we'd be competitive … and we were hammered, losing by eight wickets after South Africa knocked us over for just 222 on a beautiful batting wicket. This time it was Hashim Amla and AB de Villiers who were too good for us, though long before that we were struggling, after we lost two wickets in the first three overs of the match. Once again, I made a good start but failed to go with it, and all I could do afterwards was shoulder the blame for what had been a pretty embarrassing loss. First, we'd lost two out of three in the Tests and now the one-day series with a game still remaining.

Another defeat in Perth, in the fifth and final game of the series, and we'd lose our official ranking as the No. 1 ODI team in the world.

***

IN THE LEAD-UP TO this game, Andrew Symonds managed to get his name back in the spotlight, even though he's out of the team recovering from the minor knee surgery he had after the Boxing Day Test.

This time, it involved a radio interview he did in which he criticised NSW's decision to include the New Zealand wicketkeeper Brendon McCullum in their team for the domestic Twenty20 final against Victoria. The fact Symmo had an opinion was one thing; the fact he said some pretty derogatory things about my Kolkata Knight Riders team-mate was the problem; the suggestion he might have had a drink or two before he went on air only made things worse.

The press was on to me on a few fronts. *Do you still want him in the Australian team?* 'Absolutely, in all three forms of the game,' I said. 'He has been great for us during the last three or four seasons in one-day cricket, and during the last two seasons in Test cricket he's been a vital cog in our side. No one can ever doubt his cricket talent and match-winning ability. Hopefully he keeps progressing really well with his fitness.'

What was your reaction to what he said about Brendon McCullum?

'If I was in that situation I wouldn't have done that. Andrew's obviously going to have a look at that radio interview and work out for himself if he thinks he's done anything wrong.'

What about the reports he was drinking before the interview?

'He's not part of our set-up at the moment and I don't think there's ever been anything in place at the moment to say he can't go out and have a drink. Does he need more rehab? That's up to him and his counsellor to work out.

'Hopefully everything's still on track for him and he continues to work with his counsellor as much as he can to make himself a better person and a better cricketer.'

I hated the questions and I hated having to answer them. I would have much preferred to stay right away from the subject, to say it's none of our business, but I know that's only partly true. I understand the reporters have a job to do, that they are entitled to ask me, as captain, for a response. And I know, as captain, that I have to make a statement that shows that we are taking the matter seriously (which we certainly are). But I also have to make sure I don't add any fuel to the story, for Symmo's sake, my sake, the team's sake and cricket's sake. It's close to politics, a juggler's act. It's probably the worst part of my job.

***

FOR GAME FIVE, WE welcomed back Nathan Bracken and Michael Clarke, but it wasn't enough as we slumped to another defeat. Whether it be in domestic cricket over the past couple of years or at different stages of the matches we've played against South Africa, the guys have shown they have the skill and talent to play international cricket and play it well, but as a team we couldn't sustain the quality of our cricket. We've been putting in — our training effort has been excellent — but the way we've faded at the back end of this one-day series is terribly disappointing.

It is true that we've had a few guys out, but the absence of some of our more experienced players provided opportunities for others, and it's been frustrating that these chances haven't been taken. It would have been good to have someone come in and make a couple of hundreds or produce a magic spell or two, and in the process announce themselves as a real star of the future. Of course, you don't see that very often — think of the way most of our great champions of the past 20 years began their international careers —

but it does happen and it would be handy if it could happen now. Making things worse, our opponents rested Dale Steyn, Makhaya Ntini and Jacques Kallis for the final game and still handled us comfortably. After the Sydney Test, I thought we were definitely on the improve, that we could look forward to South Africa and the Ashes tour with confidence. Now I'm not so sure. The rebuilding process might take longer than I first thought.

Yet I do remain optimistic, because I still believe we're a squad with plenty of talent and also because of the character of the guys. I was wondering what it would be like, playing without all those familiar faces with whom I played for so long, and I can honestly say that it's fun and exciting. We have used 26 different players in all three forms of the game in the past four months, including seven debutants, and we have to be a little patient with some of the younger players. Players like Shaun Marsh, Ben Hilfenhaus and David Warner have to be treated as long-term investments; they are learning on the job. There are going to be steps forward and steps backward, because these days very few players arrive at international level with their skills and temperament fully developed.

I know from years of watching AFL that teams in a rebuilding phase can be a cause for considerable satisfaction. The past few seasons at North Melbourne are a fair example of this. It can be fascinating and rewarding seeing young sportsmen play their early games. It's a journey for the player, his colleagues, coaches, fans and captain. Furthermore, when you get beaten you tend to examine everything you did more closely. I've always believed you learn more from a tough defeat than a comfortable victory.

No one likes losing, me as much as anyone, but I see a lot of spirit in my new and not-so-old team-mates, and eventually that will translate into victories. Hopefully, it can happen sooner rather than later.

Monday, February 16

IT WAS A LITTLE less than two years ago when I didn't go to New Zealand for a Chappell-Hadlee Trophy series. My back was playing up, vice-captain Adam Gilchrist also needed a rest, so Mike Hussey took over the captaincy. A group of young cricketers that included Mitchell Johnson, Phil Jaques, Brad Haddin, Shaun Tait and Shane Watson were given a chance to show what they had, while players like Huss and Michael Clarke were expected to take on more of a leadership role (unfortunately, Pup suffered a hip injury and had to return home before that series started).

Our results weren't flash. Just weeks before the start of the World Cup, we lost all three games. The criticism of the team was massive, while Gilly and I were slammed for having deserted a sinking ship. But we were working to a plan to ensure our more experienced players were ready for the tournament that really mattered, and at the same time providing an opportunity for our up-and-comers to grow as cricketers and men.

We're further out from the World Cup at the moment, but in a way we're in a similar situation. Again, I was heavily criticised for missing matches — this time, my intention was to miss the second and third games of a five-game series — but again the move was about the bigger picture, in this case trying to ensure that I am as fit, mentally and physically, as I can possibly be when the Tests start in South Africa next month. I actually questioned the move when it came time for me to depart for a few days, but team management insisted I put my bat in the locker. A lot of planning has gone into this decision, just as there was before we decided to rest Brad Haddin for the T20 games against South Africa and Mitchell Johnson for those two games and the start of the one-day series that followed.

It's never an easy thing missing games for Australia, but our hope was that it would end up being a positive thing for the team. I've never checked the stats, but I'd be astonished if my performances straight after a few days off haven't been better to those immediately before. I certainly know I've felt better, and I know Gilly used to say he always benefited from some time away from the team in the middle of a long season. Further, I like the idea of the young blokes getting a chance, especially now when there are genuine opportunities on offer. A batter like Callum Ferguson from South Australia, who replaced me in the Aussie line-up, was able to press his case for a trip to South Africa for the one-dayers over there, which probably wouldn't have happened if I'd been playing. Sure, you can take that sort of experimenting too far, but in this case I thought my break made a lot of sense.

However, after we lost the first two games to the Kiwis — the first in Perth, the second at the MCG — it seemed there were very few people outside the team who agreed with me ...

***

THE LOSS IN GAME one might have been a last-ball-of-the-match job, but it was still one of our worst efforts of the season. The wicket was doing a bit, but we still should have scored more

Australia v New Zealand One-Day Internationals 2008–09

First ODI, at Perth (February 1): Australia 181 (48.4 overs: MEK Hussey 49; KD Mills 4–35) lost to New Zealand 8–182 (50 overs: LRPL Taylor 64; NW Bracken 3–35) by two wickets

Second ODI, at Melbourne (February 6): Australia 5–225 (50 overs: MJ Clarke 98, MEK Hussey 75) lost to New Zealand 4–226 (48.5 overs: BB McCullum 43, LRPL Taylor 47, GD Elliott 61*) by six wickets

Third ODI, at Sydney (February 8): Australia 9–301 (50 overs: BJ Haddin 109, MJ Clarke 64, MEK Hussey 51; I O'Brien 3–68) defeated New Zealand 269 (47.3 overs: PG Fulton 40, GD Elliott 115) by 32 runs

Fourth ODI, at Adelaide (February 10): New Zealand 8–244 (50 overs: MJ Guptill 45, LRPL Taylor 76; MG Johnson 3–51) lost to Australia 4–247 (48.2 overs: BJ Haddin 43, DJ Hussey 79, MEK Hussey 75*) by six wickets

Fifth ODI, at Brisbane (February 13): Australia 4–168 (22 overs: BJ Haddin 88*, CJ Ferguson 55*) versus New Zealand 6–123 (14 overs: MJ Guptill 64). No result due to rain

than 181. As we'd done against South Africa, we seemed to make key mistakes at crucial times, so that rather than asserting some authority we continually stifled our own momentum. Seven of our top nine batters reached double figures, but no one made a 50, and the captain and vice-captain were run out. I thought our bowling effort was admirable, but we dropped a crucial catch when Ross Taylor, their best batter, was given a life, and we also gave them 11 wides, too many in a low-scoring game.

After the game, there was more controversy when New Zealand captain Daniel Vettori had a shot at Brad Haddin over the dismissal of Neil Broom, who was given out bowled during Michael Clarke's fifth over. It was one of those weird dismissals where — as Broom had given himself room to cut but missed — the bat, ball, stumps and keeper's gloves were all pretty close together, the bails were dislodged and the umpires gave the batsman out. Out in the middle, many of us weren't sure what had happened (though Brad said he was positive it was out), no replay was called for, and after the new batter took guard play continued. Meanwhile, the TV replay was showing that the ball had struck Hadds' gloves in front of the stumps, so it should have been a no-ball, and it was hard to tell whether it was the keeper or the ball that had broken the wicket.

'I think you saw from Haddin's reaction that he knew something was wrong,' Daniel said. 'He probably should have made more noise about it. It was disappointing.'

I thought that was rubbish. As I explained at my media conference, Brad was certain the ball had flicked the off-stump and he didn't realise his gloves were in front of the stumps, so he was entitled to believe it was out. We were disappointed Dan decided to question our integrity so publicly, and I must admit I expected him to apologise once he had time to think about what he'd said. If you're going to call someone a cheat, which is how we interpreted the New Zealand skipper's remarks, you want to be pretty sure you're 100 per cent right. Brad and Dan did exchange text messages, and Brad told me everything was sweet, so when a reporter asked me if Dan had said sorry I replied yes, he had. Turns out he hadn't; instead the Kiwi camp said he had merely explained that there was 'nothing personal' in his remarks, which left me looking a bit silly. He's a good bloke, Dan, and I should have talked to him as soon as possible after his initial remarks made the headlines. I really regret not doing that. By sniping at long range through the media we created a messy episode that didn't do anyone any favours.

✳✳✳

FROM PERTH WE FLEW to Melbourne for the Allan Border Medal presentation, but on the night much of the talk was about the Michael Clarke-Simon Katich confrontation that occurred on the night of the Sydney Test, which had finally made the papers. What amazed me most about the way this story developed was how the press seemed to split into pro-Pup and anti-Pup camps as they described what might have gone on. Here was proof, they claimed, of 'simmering tension' in the Australian set-up. There is no such 'tension', not by a long shot, but there was nothing I could say or do other than let the fire burn out, which I knew would take a day or two. And that's pretty much how it worked out.

I was pleasantly surprised to be up on stage at the end of the night, sharing the Border Medal with Pup after a tight vote that saw us finish just in front of Mike Hussey, Mitchell Johnson and Simon Katich. Another highlight of the night was the induction of Steve Waugh into Australian Cricket's Hall of Fame. Steve had really annoyed me with some comments he made about me taking a break — the usual stuff about how if we're playing IPL then we shouldn't complain, plus a line about how he never took a game off when he was captain and, worst of all, a reminder that 'every game you play for Australia should be a treasured opportunity' (as if I didn't know that) — but I was still very happy for him. I was always grateful for Steve's support when he was captain, and admired the way he backed his team-mates and himself no matter what situation we found ourselves in.

The Allan Border Medal

I spent most of the Border Medal night sitting back, enjoying myself, waiting for either Michael Clarke or Mitchell Johnson to be announced as the winner. So I was amazed when my name was read out as a joint medallist. The list of award winners for 2009 reads as follows:

Allan Border Medal: Michael Clarke and Ricky Ponting (shared)
Test cricketer of the year: Michael Clarke
ODI cricketer of the year: Nathan Bracken
State cricketer of the year: Michael Klinger
Women's international cricketer of the year: Shelley Nitschke
Bradman young cricketer of the year: Phillip Hughes

'As we all know it's been an up and down year for the team and everybody at the moment is writing us off,' I said on stage after Pup and I were given our medals. 'But I know in my heart we're not very far away at all. The last couple of months, it's been an amazing time with some of our greats leaving the team and some very young and exciting players coming into the team.

'It's an amazing challenge for me and certainly Michael to keep leading this team in the right direction, hopefully showing some direction and passing on some experience to the younger guys. It's something I'm looking forward to.'

***

ON FRIDAY, FEBRUARY 6, the same day we lost game two of the Chappell-Hadlee series, the Pakistan Cricket Board announced we'd be playing five ODIs between April 24 and May 7 at neutral venues — the first two in Dubai, then three in Abu

Dhabi — and then a T20 game back in Dubai. That cuts right across the IPL program, so I don't think I'll be playing in that competition this year.

Two days later, Cricket Australia announced that their captain was returning from his mid-season break early, to play in the third one-dayer against New Zealand at the SCG.

I knew from the moment we went 2–0 down that I had to come back early. As captain, I felt I had no choice — for the team's sake, but also for all the other major stakeholders in Australian cricket. I guess we could have been stubborn, could have stuck to our contention that in the long term we'd be better off, but I also had to acknowledge the team was going through its worst season, in terms of results, for 20 years. We knew sections of the media were prepared to get into us, and we risked putting our fan base offside if an impression was left that the skipper didn't seem to care. Of course, that was ridiculous; every loss cuts me deeply. But as I've learned many times during my career, perceptions do matter. So back I came.

The process worked this way. I first discussed the matter with people close to me on the Saturday, the day before the match, and then at 8am the next morning I rang my manager James Henderson again, to talk the matter over one more time. Then I called coach Tim Nielsen to confirm that I wanted to play, with my only fear being that he'd say, 'No mate, you've got to rest.' But Vin was sympathetic. Then I called Andrew Hilditch, and it didn't take much for me to talk him around.

After all the debate and discussions, I guess we would have looked pretty silly if we'd lost the game, especially if I'd failed with the bat. But while I only scored 16, Brad Haddin opened the batting and completed his maiden ODI century, Pup went in first with him and made 64, Mike Hussey continued a run of good form (scores of 78, 49, 75 and 51 in successive innings) and we totalled 9–301. That proved more than enough and I was left well satisfied with the way the guys performed. Sure, it wasn't a great win, but my main concern was simply with breaking our losing run — if you're in a deep hole, your only concern should be getting out, not how pretty you look as you try to escape.

Inevitably, given they're both keepers, the move to turn Brad into an opener brought comparisons with Adam Gilchrist, who Steve Waugh had pushed to the top of the Australian one-day team's batting order in early 1998 — a move that proved to be a masterstroke. If Hadds has anything like the success Gilly achieved as a one-day opener then we'll all be very happy. I know our current keeper is a good and sensible batsman, I was keen for some stability at the top of the innings and we felt he and Pup offered our best chance of finding that. Afterwards, I said he could open the batting 'for as long as he likes' if he kept batting the way he did in this game. The two of them looked like they were in control from the very first ball. Hadds' hundred was the first by an Australian in a ODI since Shane Watson made 126 in Grenada last June, the game in which I hurt my wrist. Boy, that seems like a long time ago.

***

MIKE HUSSEY MADE ANOTHER decent score in game four at the Adelaide Oval, his brother David also passed 50, and we won comfortably by six wickets to level the series. And when the final game of the series at the Gabba was interrupted and eventually ruined by rain we had managed to hang on to the Chappell-Hadlee Trophy. It was hardly a decisive victory, the Kiwis probably had their noses in front when the 'series decider' was abandoned, but having been down 2–0 there was still a sense of satisfaction that we'd managed to get something out of the one-day home season. Finally, the two teams played a Twenty20 game in Sydney — a game in which Brad Haddin captained Australia for the first time while Michael Clarke and I had the night off. I didn't watch the game, which the good guys won by one run.

For all the Husseys' good work, the clear standout from the Adelaide one-dayer had nothing to do with the on-field action. It was the way the cricket community came together to raise more than $6 million for the victims of the bushfires that devastated large parts of Victoria on the weekend of February 7–8. Further to this, on the morning of the match I received a phone call from Pup, who had come up with the idea of the team going to the affected area as soon as possible after the game, to lend our support. His concept was that the visit needed to be low-key, away from the media cameras if possible, but he really thought we could help. I spoke to the right people, and they contacted the office of the Victorian premier John Brumby to ask the key question: 'How would the people react?' They thought it would be a wonderful thing to do, and the next day we travelled from Adelaide to Brisbane via Whittlesea, which is located about 40 kilometres north of the MCG. There, at the town's main oval which has been converted into a firefighting staging area, we met bushfire victims. I hope we gave the people there a bit of relief from their dire positions, helped lift their spirits.

Ironically, Pup couldn't go because he had to get some urgent treatment for a back injury, but our visit was 100 per cent his idea and I tried my best to make sure everyone knew that. Some of the Victorian players in the Aussie squad have a personal connection with the area, because they grew up nearby or by knowing people who've been directly affected. Peter Siddle's brother was good mates with two blokes who passed away. I had no direct connection, but trying to come to grips with the extent

T20 International, at Sydney (February 15): Australia 7–150 (20 overs: DJ Hussey 41) defeated New Zealand 5–149 (20 overs: BB McCullum 61, NT Broom 36) by one run

of the tragedy, how many homes have been destroyed, lives and livelihoods shattered ... these are fellow Australians ... so my first instinct after Pup made that call was, *If there is anything we can do, let's do it.*

At the same time, you don't want to be seen as intruding, so I was apprehensive that our arrival might be seen as some sort of publicity stunt. I also didn't know how I'd respond when I met people who'd been through hell. But the media coverage was generous and sensitive, and we appreciated the way they left us alone when we first got there, to mingle with the locals and get a feel for the mood without having cameras and microphones in our faces. There was a lot of emotion and a lot of anguish in the air, and at the start, we kept ourselves in groups of two or three to make sure no one got themselves in a situation they couldn't handle. Of course, we signed plenty of autographs and got involved in some cricket matches, and I found myself facing the bowling of a kid named Koby, 10 years old and from nearby Kinglake, who looked a pretty fair cricketer. *I'll just play a few quietly and then get myself out,* I thought to myself, but he quickly knocked me over before I was set. Later, I learned that Koby's school, Middle Kinglake Primary, had been burned to the ground in the inferno, which is why he'd got the day off to come and meet the Aussie cricketers.

Being introduced to families who'd been cruelly victimised by the fires was very tough and very moving. A schoolteacher came up and thanked us for coming, said it was the first time since the blaze she's seen the kids from her class with smiles on their faces. I met one woman who was holding a baby boy who must be the same age as Emmy — they had lost all their possessions when the fire tore through their home. The minutes I spent with one woman at the local community centre were as confronting as anything I've been through in recent times. She kept saying I look exactly like her son, who she hasn't seen since the fires struck. It was awful for her, the not knowing. Huss spoke to her, too, and I hope we helped a little. The pain I saw in people's eyes was heartbreaking; yet amid the gloom and the sadness, there was a resolve among the locals we couldn't help but respect.

It was reassuring to see such courage and strength of character, and I came away with a renewed faith in the Aussie spirit. I was proud of my team, the way they were prepared to step outside their comfort zones, and I couldn't help thinking how lucky I am to be sharing a dressing room with them. I was also filled with admiration for all the volunteers and charity workers who were operating around the clock for none of the acclaim or income we elite sports people get for doing far, far less. And, of course, there were the firefighters, who'd risked life and limb in the cause of community, mateship and doing the right thing. I was genuinely in awe of all these good people, and privileged to be among them.

PART SIX

THE AUSTRALIANS IN
SOUTH AFRICA, 2009

Thursday, February 19

TOMORROW, I AM GOING to use my regular column in the *Australian* newspaper to confirm something I've been thinking about for a while now: that I won't be playing in the Indian Premier League this year.

I don't like letting people down, but to tell you the truth this isn't a difficult call. As far as cricket is concerned, my country comes first and it just wouldn't have been possible for me to give my all for Australia in the coming weeks and months if — during the only two-week break we have over the next seven months — I went and played for the Kolkata Knight Riders.

I have been discussing the matter with the Knight Riders for the past few weeks and they have been very understanding. Of course, I would only have been able to play in a couple of matches this year, so I don't think my absence will harm them too much but the fact they have been so good about it is one the reasons why, in my mind, I am already fired up about the idea of making a major contribution to their 2010 campaign.

When Lalit Modi, the IPL boss, first launched his new competition he made a commitment that 'traditional' international cricket would always take priority over the IPL franchise. I see my situation as a classic example of what he was getting at. As I've documented in these pages, there was never a good opportunity for me take a break through the Australian season. Immediately afterwards, we were on the

The Squad for South Africa

Because of a variety of ailments, Brett Lee, Andrew Symonds, Shane Watson, Stuart Clark or Phil Jaques were not considered for our tour of South Africa. This was the squad that selectors announced on February 5, two days after the Border Medal presentation: Ricky Ponting (captain), Michael Clarke (vice-captain), Doug Bollinger, Brad Haddin, Nathan Hauritz, Ben Hilfenhaus, Phillip Hughes, Michael Hussey, Mitchell Johnson, Simon Katich, Andrew McDonald, Bryce McGain, Marcus North, Peter Siddle.

plane to South Africa for three Tests, two T20 games and five ODIs. Then it's off to the Middle East to play Pakistan, then a two-week break, the World Twenty20, the Ashes Tests and one-dayers, a one-day series in India, another Australian summer. If I didn't take the two weeks during the IPL off, when could I have a holiday?

I am desperate for some time with my family — it is always hard to leave Rianna and I cherish every second I spend with Emmy. I also want to be as fresh as possible for all of the challenges the Aussie team has ahead of it in 2009 and beyond. At the same time, though, it is disappointing that I won't be involved in the IPL. Everyone who played in it last year enjoyed the experience and loved being involved in what is essentially a new and exciting frontier.

So when the 2009 competition starts I will definitely be sneaking out during the night to watch the Knight Riders' matches on TV.

***

I SHOULD ADD THAT this decision should not be taken to mean that I intend to ease myself out of Twenty20 cricket or that I'm thinking about cutting my overall workload. Maybe a few commentators will come to that conclusion after tomorrow's announcement, but they'll be wrong. I love captaining my country every time I can and will not let go easily while I believe I have a contribution to make. Indeed, one of the things that helped make my decision to pull out of the IPL a little simpler was my strong desire to be at my sharpest for the World Twenty20 in June. That's a competition I'd really like Australia to win, not least because it is the one major international trophy that has never been part of Cricket Australia's treasure trove.

Twenty20 is a demanding game, physically and mentally, and it'll find you out quicksmart if you're not at your best. I feel like I'm in really good physical shape at present, although it is true that at times during the summer I was a bit flat. This was especially true during the one-dayers against South Africa and at the start of the Chappell-Hadlee series, which came, of course, after a very intense and demanding Test series. The jet lag got me, too, when I landed here in South Africa, but after just a couple of days 'in camp' here in the small city of Potchefstroom (which is situated in North West Province about 120 kilometres south-west of Johannesburg) I'm starting to feel rejuvenated.

I sense quite a few of the boys feel exactly the same way.

Trial by Referral

One aspect of the upcoming series that will, I guess, be interesting is the 'umpire referral system' that will be in use for the three Tests. It's part of a trial that began in Test matches last year, with certain series being used, and now it's our turn. I'm definitely a little each-way on this one — the traditionalist in me wants to keep the video replay out of the game as much as possible, while the pragmatic side of me recognises that maybe the video can help.

Given this, I'd be mad not to keep an open mind. I note that the ICC has now reduced the number of challenges a team is allowed in any one innings from three to two, to reduce 'frivolous challenges' and I like the sound of that. Watching the recent Australian Open tennis, it was obvious that players were questioning calls simply because it was late in a set and they still had challenges left over, so why not use them. Apparently, that's been happening a bit in cricket, too, with teams disputing lbw decisions late in an innings, as if it's a crime not to use all your challenges.

Mike Hussey told us at a team barbecue in Potchefstroom that he was going to be questioning the decision every time he was given out. 'Huss, don't forget you bat at No. 4,' I laughed. 'There might not be any challenges left by the time you get out there!'

My understanding is that the upcoming series will be the last of the trials, before the ICC makes a decision on the system's long-term future later in the year. The thing we have to remember — now and when the final verdict on the system is handed down — is that there will always be mistakes. But hopefully the referrals can eliminate the blatantly bad decisions that frustrate players, fans and, I presume, umpires too.

Tuesday, February 24

Tour game, South African Board President's XI v the Australians at Potchefstroom (February 20–22): South African Board President's XI 7–403 dec (I Khan 100, HG Kuhn 99, D Wiese 50*) and 182 (MJ North 6–69) drew with **Australians** 5–360 dec (SM Katich 124, RT Ponting 93, MJ North 52*) and 4–171 (PJ Hughes 53, MJ North 50)

***

BACK IN THE EARLY '80s I used to revel in the fact that North Melbourne, my team in the VFL (now the AFL), was so dominant at their home ground, Arden Street. They went through a period when I was six to eight years old, 1981 to 1983, when they won 19 of the 25 games they played at the ground, even though they weren't a truly dominant team through that period, winning a total of 41 of 70 games in those seasons. It was a big advantage for the Kangaroos to play at home in those days.

With international cricket, it can often be the same. But not always. There's much to be gained by having your supporters so close, being familiar with the local conditions, where you train, your schedule, team hotels, the way the media works, occasionally getting to sleep in your own bed. However, playing at home can also be tough, because of the constant scrutiny and the standards you're expected to meet. If you don't win when you're supposed to, there can suddenly be a lot of negativity about, the critics turn against you and instead of believing or even hoping you're going to do well, there's a fear you're about to let everyone down. The great Australian golfer Peter Thomson once wrote, 'Hope builds, fear destroys.' He was on the money.

I wonder if we might have suffered from this a little during this season's Tests in Australia. In the few days we stayed at our 'base' in Potchefstroom (where we headed straight after landing in South Africa on February 16), I've felt like a change has come over us. Everyone seems more relaxed than we were back home, and we were able to focus on the job at hand — which is getting ready for the upcoming Test series. It's like we've been given a fresh start, and I can't help but think that, having won that Test in Sydney, if we can quickly put the South Africans under pressure here, then they might have some of the same problems we had in Australia. The home ground disadvantage might reappear, and this time we might be the team that benefits.

This is one reason why right now I'm feeling reasonably good about our chances over here. That wasn't exactly true a week ago, just before we boarded the plane to fly out of Sydney, when I was feeling a bit weary and was contemplating our mediocre form in the limited-over games against New Zealand, and also how we'd be taking on the South Africans without Brett Lee, Stuart Clark and Andrew Symonds. I did have the third Test win and my faith in the character of my team-mates to cheer me, but it wasn't until we arrived here, started training really well, and saw how unbelievably confident the locals were that I started thinking that we could surprise some people.

As we settled in and got to work, I really started believing that maybe we've turned a corner.

*** *

THE NEW GUYS IN the squad have played a significant part in this turnaround. Marcus North, captain of Western Australia in the Sheffield Shield, an experienced left-hand batter and right-hand off-spinner (who played his junior cricket in WA with Mike Hussey), is a quiet, sensible cricketer in the Andrew McDonald mould. The thing I like about what these guys potentially bring to the Test XI is the fact that they can bat in the top six or seven and bowl some more-than-useful overs too. I think the value of having a capable fifth bowler is often underrated in Test cricket, just as having a really good attacking batter at No. 7 wasn't appreciated enough until blokes like Ian Botham and Adam Gilchrist proved the point. If that fifth bowler can give the frontline bowlers a rest and threaten the batsmen while doing so, then the fielding team has a much better chance of maintaining its grip on the game or preparing itself for a counterattack.

Adding even further to Northy's value is the fact he's got great hands and would logically slot into the gap left at first slip by Matt Hayden's retirement. Even before he played well in our warm-up game at Potchefstroom, I could picture him playing in the Test team as either our No. 1 spinner or, if the pitch is a turner, as part of twin spinning attack with Bryce McGain or Nathan Hauritz.

If Northy is a likely starter for the Test that starts on Thursday in Johannesburg, Phillip Hughes is a certainty, given the fact that we've only got five specialist batsmen in our squad (I'm calling Northy an all-rounder when I write this). Phillip forced his way onto this tour through the sheer weight of runs he's scored in the Sheffield Shield. His style is a little unorthodox, so if he wasn't piling up the runs it would have been natural for people to think he needs more time to get his game in order. I heard that knock on him more than once whenever his name came up in conversations about Test stars of the future. But when you look at him closely with a bat in his hand, as I've done at practice here and again when he batted in the game just gone, you see that his balance is terrific and at the moment ball meets blade he's usually doing everything right.

Like Adam Gilchrist, who was born in Bellingen, he hails originally from the NSW north coast, from Macksville. The first time I really got to talk with him was at the Border Medal, when Justin Langer and I introduced ourselves and the three of us talked a bit of cricket. There was nothing too serious about our conversation — for me, it was a just a 'get to know you' sort of chat, and it was good to have my old mate Lang alongside me, because I figure short left-handed opening batsmen must have many things in common and Lang's never been a bloke short of a word in a cricket conversation. I could just listen, throw my two bob's worth in, and get a feel for what kind of bloke Phillip is.

It was funny, I knew then that he was in the touring team, but the side hadn't been officially announced so I had to keep quiet about that. Most people there that night assumed he'd make the team, especially because the news was about that Phil Jaques' back was playing up on him again. But you should never take these things for granted and Phillip certainly wasn't doing that. I followed up this first brief discussion with a much longer chat on the flight from Sydney to Johannesburg, and I discovered that while the jewels in each ear he wears off the field might suggest he's 'new age', in many ways he's 'old school'. He strikes me as a sensible, serious sort of bloke, with a strong desire to learn and improve, and a real ambition to succeed at the highest level. Simon Katich, his captain at NSW and soon-to-be opening partner for Australia, raves about his toughness and his temperament, two assets that'll take the young bloke a long way. Phillip Hughes is not overawed by the challenges ahead, but he's not oblivious to them either. That's a good place to be.

Youth v Experience

I was disappointed that some comments I made at the end of January were twisted by a few people to make it look as if I didn't want Phillip Hughes in the Aussie team. That was bunkum. I was asked if it was time for a new generation to come into the squad and I replied this way: 'I'm not sure if it's a time for us right now in Test cricket to really go all out looking for youth. We have to pick who we think are the most competent and best players around the country to embark on a couple of very big Test series that we've got coming up.'

The key part of that quote was 'all out'. Of course, if a gifted young player comes along we'd be mad not to take a real good look at him. But that's true whether the team is winning or losing. I was 20 when I made my Test debut and I went okay, so I'm hardly likely to be telling the selectors that young blokes are to be avoided. All I was trying to say is that there is value in experience; it's not something to be casually cast aside, especially during a rebuilding phase. There are some blokes in their 30s who have been down on form or struggling with injuries this season, but in previous years they have done some great things for the Australian cricket team, and they need to be respected, considered and looked after.

As an example, Phillip Hughes has done absolutely everything in his power to get the selectors' attention — his record for NSW over the past two years has been outstanding. But that doesn't mean we should have just ignored the fact that when Phil Jaques played Test cricket for Australia he did very well. He even made a hundred in his most recent Test, against the West Indies in Barbados last June. In the end, Jaquesy's ongoing injury worries meant he wasn't a contender for the South Africa tour, but if he had been he certainly deserved to be strongly considered.

Come Thursday, he'll become the youngest Australian Test cricketer since 19-year-old Craig McDermott made his debut in the Boxing Day Test against the West Indies in 1984–85.

***

SO PHILLIP IS SURE to make his Test debut, Marcus North will most likely join him, and we could have a third debutant if we go for Bryce McGain or if we pick Ben Hilfenhaus to be part of our pace attack, behind Mitchell Johnson and Peter Siddle. To tell you the truth, I think Bryce will only play if the pitch in Johannesburg looks like being extremely spinner-friendly (which it's never really been in the past), but Hilfenhaus is a big chance.

Ben was close to playing in Sydney in the New Year's Test, when we eventually decided to go with Doug Bollinger because of the NSW man's excellent record at the SCG, and I thought he looked a bit more dangerous than Dougie against the SA Board President's XI, especially on the first day. So it surprises me that just about everyone outside our camp is suggesting that the choice for the final place in our XI is between Ben and Andrew. I'm wondering, *why can't they both play?*

Apparently, the last time three Aussies made their Test debut in the same game was back in 1985–86, when a trio who all turned out to be quality Test cricketers — Merv Hughes, Geoff Marsh and Bruce Reid — made their first appearance against India in Adelaide. Outside the two seasons of World Series Cricket (1977–78 and 1978–79), when 23 Australians made the Test debut, the last time five Australians made their debut in a sequence of two successive Tests was back in 1964–65, when Ian Chappell and David Sincock came into the team for a Test against Pakistan at the MCG, and then in the next Test Australia played, against the West Indies at Kingston, Peter Philpott, Grahame Thomas and Laurie Mayne made their Test debuts.

Furthermore, if we do have three 'first gamers' in the first Test, there'll be more debutants (three) in our XI than there will be Australians who appeared in the last Test series we played in South Africa, just three seasons ago. Mike Hussey and I are the only two 'doubling up'. Michael Clarke was in our squad for that tour but didn't play in a Test.

I guess some would be discouraged by such a turnover of personnel, but I see it as a challenge. With some of the new blokes, I'm still learning about them, what makes them tick, if they need guidance or motivating so the time we've had together in this first week of the tour has been invaluable for me, as were the one-on-one chats I had with each of the guys. Having lost Brett Lee and Stuart Clark for this tour, I see genuine parallels between our situation now and what happened in the West Indies in 1995. Back then, the leaders of our pace attack going into the tour were Craig McDermott and Damien Fleming, but both 'Billy' and 'Flem' got injured and had to miss the Tests. Glenn McGrath, Paul Reiffel and Brendon Julian stepped up and the Windies were beaten at home for the first time in 22 years.

There's a real opportunity this time for one or more of Johnson, Siddle, Hilfenhaus or Bollinger to do the same, to really make a name for themselves and forge their own identity at international level.

I also see some similarities between where we are now and what happened after the 2005 Ashes series, when we regrouped after we returned to Australia, worked hard as a team and made sure that when the next Test came around we were in the best possible shape we could be. I sensed something similar happening through the past week, the kind of effort and enthusiasm that could really make a difference.

I've taken a real 'hands on' approach at training. I've told the senior players and the coaches that we have to get everything we do at training exactly right and that each player has to know what he is expected to be doing at any time during practice. No excuses, no short cuts. To ensure that happens, I am sitting down with the coaches before each session, to map out everything that is to be done and to go through what we are going to say. No confusion, no mixed messages. Often during net sessions I'd go and stand behind the stumps at the bowler's end, as if I was an umpire, to be at the centre of things. No no-balls, no avoiding the captain's gaze. It's finicky, it's time-consuming but I think it will work.

Away from the nets, we broke into small groups and came up

Endless Flight

I wasn't quite sure what to think when I learned that Bryce McGain had missed our flight to South Africa. Apparently, he was a few minutes late arriving at Melbourne Airport, and then the plane to Sydney he did get on was delayed, so he wasn't with us when we left for Jo'burg.

It must have been an ugly feeling knowing the team had left without him. We did discuss the matter at a meeting of our leadership group and resolved to talk to him when he finally joined us, which happened at breakfast last Tuesday, about 24 hours after the rest of us had settled in. But really, I reckon it was one of those situations when no one had to say anything — Bryce knew he'd made a blue and he would have had plenty of time to feel like a goose before and during his solo flight west. What he did was amateurish, but he isn't the first good cricketer to miss a flight and provided it doesn't happen again I'm prepared to forget about it.

with mission statements about how we want to go about our cricket. A strong theme was that the team needs to work as a well-oiled unit, everyone going in the same direction. We've had these sorts of sessions in the past, but these were the most productive I've been involved in. At least in part, this was because those new to the squad felt comfortable asking questions and those of us who played in the great Australian teams of the past were able to share our philosophies about what makes a successful team and talk about our experiences in a more relaxed environment, away from the constant hustle and bustle of a summer at home. So good were some of the statements we came up with, we're going to get them laminated and display them in our change rooms during the Test series, as a constant reminder of the things we discussed.

Near the end of these meetings, I said that I didn't want to hear any more about 'senior' guys and 'younger' guys in our squad. 'We are all playing in the same game,' I explained. 'I don't care if you've played no Tests or 100, we have to believe in ourselves and believe in our ability as a group to get through no matter what the situation.'

But this wasn't just a few days when we worked hard on and off the field. There was also time for a few coffees and beers, where senior blokes like me could sit down and chat to guys new to the squad with whom we haven't played much cricket — men like Marcus North, Phillip Hughes, Andrew McDonald, Bryce McGain. Again, there's been such a big turnover of talent over the past few months, and so little time to just relax and talk casually, it was fantastic to be able to actually get to know each other. Without any major social event or exercise being organised, our time in Potchefstroom evolved into a terrific six-day bonding session.

Back at those team meetings, another thing I hammered is that if we are going to win this series and the Ashes series, too, we need everyone to have a real go — no passengers — and for someone to always be there ready and able to do a job, under pressure, when those big moments I keep harping on come along. I sense that'll happen. You can feel it in our net sessions. One of the press boys described them as 'no-nonsense' and I think that's about right. A favourite mantra of mine when it comes to batting in the nets is that you practise like you play. I want the fast bowlers to try to knock my block off and there's been a bit of that here, even when the practice wickets have been a bit dodgy. There's been no letting up, which from my perspective is fantastic.

If we can carry that attitude on to the field, we're going to surprise a few people. Yes, we had a couple of bad losses in Australia but at other times we played really well. In fact, I reckon our best cricket during the Test series was better than their best. If we do everything as well as we can, then we're right in this series.

✳✳✳

THE ONUS IS ON us to get off to a great start, because that will shake the incredible optimism that has taken hold in South African cricket circles. As I've found to my cost at times, it is impossible to manage the public's expectations of your team and your players. As captain, I always want to talk my blokes up, either to get them the proper recognition or to maybe boost their confidence. I want my team-mates to hear the positive things I'm saying about them. But sometimes the public responds by expecting the subject of that praise to become a superstar. It's a tough one to get right.

Over here right now, a lot of very nice things are being said and written about the South African team. It's as if they're

Soweto

We headed to Jo'burg straight after our game in Potchefstroom, and the next morning we headed out to Bramfischerville Oval at Soweto, to have a hit with some young cricketers. The oval was a rare patch of grass in a landscape that is dominated by red, dusty streets and the makeshift shacks the locals call home. It was a rough'n'ready environment, but the cheerfulness of the people we met and the quality of cricketing and athletic talent on show made for an enjoyable day.

I have to say we were very impressed with the talent of the kids we met. It certainly wouldn't surprise me if a few years from now one of the bowlers on show emerges as the new Makhaya Ntini. A couple of them were genuinely sharp. And there was plenty of batting talent, too, plus the odd cheeky bloke quick to remind us how well their new hero, JP Duminy, had gone in Australia. Brad Haddin was happy to give some wicketkeeping advice, and also to participate in a hand-stand competition. He didn't win. Simon Katich donated his man-of-the match cheque from last weekend's game to buy some cricket gear for the township, while Phillip Hughes seemed a little bemused by all the attention he received. 'It's a long way from Macksville,' he said with a grin when a reporter asked him what he'd made of the experience.

invincible. It feels like everyone here has placed a huge level of importance on their boys achieving the No. 1 spot on the ICC Test rankings; their success in Australia has created a high level of expectation that they'll finally overtake us during this upcoming series. If the South Africans are too good for us over the next month they'll claim the No. 1 spot, and I sense there are very few people here who don't think they'll do it.

This was apparent when I fronted the South African media after we landed in Jo'burg. Just about the first question I was received was, 'Is the No. 1 ranking important?'

'I'd be lying if I said it's the reason we play the game,' I replied.

Next question: pretty much the same as the first one ...

'Anyone who plays a team sport or an individual sport, to be recognised as the best, that's what playing international sport is about,' I responded. 'We've held this trophy for a long time. It does mean a lot to us. It's something we've never, ever taken for granted.'

And so it continued. Once the last question had been asked, they all wanted photos of me holding the Test championship mace, staring at it, they probably would have liked me to kiss it but I wasn't going to do that. Next day, the part of my responses that got the most attention was this:

It does mean a lot to us.

But were not obsessed about it. A few South Africans might be.

***

THE GAME THAT FINISHED two days back was all right for us. In the scorebook, it mightn't look too flash because we were unable to win, but that didn't worry me. I was more excited by the way we started to come together as a group. I felt we were a better unit at the end of the contest than we were at the beginning, and what I like most is the way everyone is on the same wavelength — we're going to go into the first Test with a specific plan and we'll all be working our butts off to turn that strategy into a win.

The match didn't start that nicely, as our opponents managed to score 5–393 from 91 overs on the first day. As we went into the game with a team that included the seven blokes from whom we'll pick our bowling attack for the opening Test (Johnson, Siddle, Bollinger, Hilfenhaus, McDonald, McGain and North), this wasn't a great result, but it really wasn't that bad. As a first run after a let-up, it was an all-right workout — I won the toss and bowled first to give everyone a go, and the effort was terrific even if the wickets didn't tumble. Hilfenhaus got the ball to swing early, and took an early wicket with a classic outswinger, while Siddle, McDonald and North were all pretty economical on a day when the runs were often flowing.

On day two, we batted pretty well, with Simon Katich making an excellent hundred, I got myself out in the 90s and Marcus North did his Test chances no harm with an unbeaten fifty. Even the blokes who didn't get a score, like Phillip Hughes and Andrew McDonald, looked in fair nick during their time at the crease, but it was true that the deck was flat and full of runs. I especially enjoyed hitting their spinner, Imran Tahir, so far over the sightscreen that after a brief search they had to call for a ball change. As any cricketer knows, whether he or she is playing at a big ground or small, on the beach or in the backyard, there's something really good about leaning on your bat while the fielders are looking for a ball you've just smashed.

We were excellent on the final day, as first we knocked them over in their second innings for just 182 — despite having Pete Siddle and Bryce McGain laid low by a stomach bug — and then the rest of the day was spent getting some more valuable batting practice. Marcus North, who earlier in the day had taken six wickets (some of which I watched close-up from first slip, and I was impressed by his control and changes of pace), scored his second half-century of the match, while Phillip Hughes also got to 50 before he retired so Andrew McDonald could have another hit.

One funny thing to come out of the final day occurred when Doug Bollinger was bowling. For some reason, the fans on the hill were in to him for much of the innings, but Dougie responded by taking 3–29, a good response after Ben Hilfenhaus had been the pick of the pair on the first day. But during one over, he pushed one a little down the legside, and the barrackers wanted the delivery called a wide, as it would have been in a limited-over game. The ump was unmoved, which didn't impress the spectators, who were still heckling when our man reached the top of his run-up.

Dougie started … stopped … looked up at the blokes in the outer … and shouted, 'It's a four-day game fellas, there are no wides!'

There wasn't a big crowd in, so the remark echoed around the ground. We all had a chuckle — partly because of his cheek in shouting back rather than ignoring his tormentors and also because the wide is still part of the longer version of the game, even if it's not policed so strictly. Mostly, though, it was because we were playing the third day of three-day game.

Monday, March 2

First Test, South Africa v Australia at Johannesburg (February 26–March 2): **Australia** 466 (RT Ponting 83, MJ Clarke 68, MJ North 117, BJ Haddin 63, MG Johnson 96*; DW Steyn 4–113) and 207 (PJ Hughes 75) defeated **South Africa** 220 (AB de Villiers 104*; MG Johnson 4–25) and 291 (GC Smith 69, HM Amla 57; MG Johnson 4–112) by 162 runs

***

AS SOON AS I saw the Jo'burg wicket I knew we'd be going into the game with three debutants: Hughes, North and Hilfenhaus. It was a track that I really felt would suit Ben more than Doug Bollinger, but it wasn't a deck that was so green or potentially bouncy that we needed to take in four specialist fast men. The Wanderers is a ground where, over the past decade, a number of swing bowlers have done very well. Both Hilfy and Dougie can swing the ball, but I've always been a fan of Hilfy's outswinger, and he had it working well at Potchefstroom and I was confident he could do the same thing in a Jo'burg Test match. I loved the balance of our attack going into this game, which I thought was ideal for the conditions: Mitchell Johnson's left-arm swing and rare ability to knock any batsmen over; Peter Siddle, who hits the seam all the time; Andrew McDonald's steadiness and ability to block up an end; and Hilfy. Plus Marcus North's offies. I really thought they could come through for us ...

Demand for tickets was so high going into the match that the

A First-up Ton

I've always looked back on my first appearance in Test cricket with mixed feelings. I went into the game just hoping to make a good impression and score some runs, but after I passed 50 I started to think about the prospect of joining that exclusive club of batsmen who hit a century in their first Test. At that time, 16 Australians had scored a first-up ton (10 of those being in the first innings).

Unfortunately, I copped a poor lbw decision on 96, we didn't need a second innings, and my chance for the debut hundred was gone.

Between that Test, against Sri Lanka at the WACA in 1995–96, and this game only one more Aussie achieved the feat: Michael Clarke, who made 151 and 17 against India at Bangalore in 2004. Thus, Marcus North becomes the 18th baggy green wearer to do so, and he was very excited by the achievement. We all were — it's a sign of a tight unit when every member genuinely enjoys a mate's success. At age 29, he's the second oldest Australian to score a century in his maiden Test match, after Herbert Collins, who was 32 years old when he scored 70 and 104 in the first Test played after World War I. He's also the first to do so in a Test against South Africa.

Marcus is a naturally confident cricketer, which clearly helped him settle so smoothly into the atmosphere of Test cricket, and he was very patient and composed throughout his knock. The contrast with Phillip Hughes — who aimed a nervous slash at Dale Steyn's fourth ball, a fast riser well wide of the off-stump, and was caught behind for a duck — was stark. Fortunately, Huey still had the second innings to make a good impression, which he did by top-scoring with 75.

number of seats sold prior to the first ball was almost as high as the largest match attendance at a Test at the New Wanderers Stadium. The locals clearly liked the fact that their team had won 18 of their previous 25 Tests, going back to December 2006, including two of their past three in Australia. And after I won the toss and made the tough call to bat on what was clearly a wicket with plenty of juice in it, they had even more to get excited about when we crashed to 3–38 (Hughes 0, Katich 3, Hussey 4). When I was joined in the middle by Michael Clarke, I reminded him of something we'd emphasised before the game: the need for partnerships. It was vital that he and I, vice-captain and captain, came through with a big stand, and that was what we did.

Getting to lunch was an adventure, but we tried to ignore the conditions and trusted our natural games. I've always felt that one of the great strengths of the Australian cricket team over the years has been our ability to counter-punch when things have been difficult and that ability helped us big-time here. Having made it to the first interval on that wicket with only three wickets lost gave us a significant advantage, one that we retained for the rest of the Test. It was one of the most important innings of my career, and while I was dirty I didn't turn it into a big hundred it will still remain high on my list of favourite innings. Better still, Pup, Marcus North, Brad Haddin and Mitchell Johnson all followed up with tremendous efforts and we finished with an innings total way higher than anyone could have expected after the first hour's play. Just as I'd demanded the building blocks were a series of partnerships: 113 for the fourth wicket (Clarke-Ponting), 113 for the sixth wicket (North-Haddin), 117 for the eighth wicket (North-Johnson) and 53 for the ninth wicket (Johnson-Siddle).

Everyone knew 466 was a winning score, and though the memories of our bad bowling days in Perth and Melbourne remained in the back of my mind, after our week in

Potchefstroom I was supremely confident that we'd come through. As it turned out, South Africa couldn't get to 300 in either of their innings, and we ended up winning by a decisive 162 runs. If the two three-match series were combined into one rubber, we'd be two-all with two to play.

It was a game with many positives for us. If this Test is any guide, we've got all-rounders in every batting position from five to nine. Mitchell Johnson's batting was explosive (the highlight being the 26 runs he took from one Paul Harris over), and so controlled and dominant was he with the bat that the impression was left that the pitch had calmed right down. But then he, Ben Hilfenhaus and Peter Siddle came out and had the South Africans jumping all over the place. Graeme Smith was caught Haddin bowled Johnson off the fifth ball of their innings, then Hilfy got a wicket with his second ball in Test cricket, when Hashim Amla edged an outswinger to me at second slip. For the rest of the day, our cricket was consistent and relentless, a fact reflected in some of the bowling figures at stumps: Johnson 1–8 from nine overs; Hilfenhaus 1–14 from 10; McDonald 0–11 from seven. Hilfy's outswinger was working nicely; Mitch's quick, much-improved inswinger was fantastic. Pete Siddle had Jacques Kallis caught in the gully before the close, and the next day, though AB de Villiers batted beautifully, we earned a first-innings lead of 246 runs.

Even though there was some rain forecast, I was never going to enforce the follow-on. We've had so much success in recent times batting again that there won't be many occasions in the future when I'll be doing so, and I've noticed that most other teams in world cricket have adopted a similar philosophy. AB de Villiers admitted that after he made his hundred. 'If I was Ricky I would have done the same to try to get us totally out of the game,' he said. Johnson, Siddle and Hilfenhaus had each bowled about 20 overs in their first innings, and we ended up setting South

A Sort-of 'Hat Trick'

Mitchell Johnson missed out on his maiden Test century in somewhat bizarre circumstances. He'd gone from 57 to 96 in 13 balls, but was stuck at the non-striker's end when, third ball of the over, our No. 10 Peter Siddle was caught by Jacques Kallis at second slip off the bowling of Morne Morkel. Pete started walking to the dressing room, but it was a no-ball so back to the middle he went.

Next ball, exactly the same thing happened ... an edge to Kallis ... only this time it was a legal delivery and he was out. Nine down. Ben Hilfenhaus had been waiting a day and a half to get involved in his first Test innings and now he found himself trying to help Mitch to his hundred. It didn't happen. First ball, Morkel bowled the same line and length that had worked for Siddle, Hilfy sparred at it and the catch went straight to de Villiers at third slip. Now we could get on with the business of bowling out the South Africans.

Africa 454 to win, which was plenty, so I could hardly have any regrets about the move. Even though they batted very well on the fourth day, to the point that some locals were suggesting another historic run chase was about to occur, from the second session of day two we were always the team most likely to win.

***

THE 'DECISION REVIEW SYSTEM' we are trialling in this series turned out to be pretty much as I expected: a mixture of good and bad. A couple of incorrect decisions were put right, which has got to be good, but there were a couple of strange ones where it seemed that the umpire in the middle gave the benefit of

Lovin' It!

I was fairly sure Phillip Hughes has what it takes to be a Test cricketer after the week we spent in Potchefstroom. I liked his attitude, his self-belief. I'd never played a game against him, seen a little of him on TV, and I'd heard a lot of good things about him from his team-mates in the NSW team. When you hear positive character references from blokes like Simon Katich, Michael Clarke, Brad Haddin and Stuart Clark, you've got to figure the kid is all right.

He got out in the first innings here to a pretty ordinary shot, but I was fairly sure that was a one-off and he'd set the record straight soon enough. In the second innings, he was a bit lucky, but I was still taken by the way he went about his business. The South Africans were in to him and I made sure I was around him and the bowler when a few of the verbals were taking place, just to see how he was handling it all.

Every time they said something he would just look at me with a smile on his face, and then he'd tell me how much he was loving it. I've always enjoyed the contest of bat versus ball — it's one of the things that keeps me playing the game — and Huey clearly enjoys it too. Furthermore, I think he got a real kick out of the sledges he was receiving, on the basis that if they weren't worried about him, they would have kept their trash talk for somebody else.

the doubt one way and then the man upstairs went in the other direction, when the evidence didn't seem conclusive. If I was in charge, I'd leave those ones to the ump on the field and only allow the video official to change clear mistakes.

The weirdest moment came on day two, when we asked for a referral after Peter Siddle had an appeal for a caught-behind against JP Duminy turned down. This was one we were pretty confident about, but then the umpires had to inform me that one of the cameras — a key one in this case — wasn't working. I had no option but to withdraw the appeal and get on with the game.

At other times, it became a tactical decision: *do I use a referral now or keep it to later?* You haven't got a lot of time, and often the people directly involved — batter, bowler and fieldsman — aren't sure. I used one against Graeme Smith in the first over of South Africa's second innings and then I was left with only one for the rest of the innings. The South Africans had a couple, especially during Phillip Hughes' second knock, when they probably should have asked the question but didn't, and a couple more when they did refer the decision but shouldn't have.

***

I'LL ALWAYS LOOK BACK on day five of this Test as a special one. I knew if we played up to our maximum ability we'd win, but it's never as simple as just walking out and doing your best, especially at Test level, which can be such a strain on body and mind. Of course, there were plenty of people keen to remind us about what happened in Perth a couple of months ago, and I guess it is impossible to get that memory totally out of mind. But after the time we spent in 'camp' before this Test, when I felt the team really came together as a unit, I was as certain as I could be that the boys would respond to my plea for the maximum effort, to make sure everyone knew how hungry we were for this win. When they respond just the way we needed, the feeling, as their captain, was glorious.

There were no passengers. The intensity we brought to the contest was magnificent, and it was a real buzz to be on the field as we hunted as a pack and earned a clear victory. This was a real team win; when they announced Mitchell Johnson as the man of the match after the Test, after his double of 96 and eight wickets, I almost felt like running on to the stage and saying, *Look, I know Mitch was superb but, really, you've got to give 11 awards in this game.*

In fact, it should have been even more than 11. Everyone in the playing squad plus all the support staff from Tim Nielsen down worked as hard as they could to achieve this victory. But it was the young blokes I was happiest for, because they've copped a lot over the past few months about how they can't fill the shoes of the legends who've just retired. Straight after the last wicket fell, I grabbed all three stumps at the keeper's end and gave one each to the new guys who had played so well. For them, like me, it was a Test to remember.

At the start of the day, South Africa were 2–178, needing 276 more runs to win. Like a lot of modern wickets, this one seemed no worse on the fifth day than it was on the third. We started really well but couldn't get a breakthrough, and my fear was — like a football team that fails to turn field position into points — that if Amla and Kallis survived they might be around for a while. But finally, after 14-and-a-half overs, second over after drinks, Peter Siddle got what we were after when he got one onto Amla a bit quicker than the batter expected and Amla tamely flicked an easy catch to mid-wicket. If that was prize for hustle, a few minutes later Andrew McDonald was rewarded for his persistence when de Villiers, the first-innings century-maker, was plumb lbw. For some reason, de Villiers referred this decision upstairs but it did him no good. We were on our way.

About half an hour before lunch, Kallis was lbw to Johnson, but the video umpire this time ruled in the home team's favour, judging that the ball pitched outside leg. On the field, we thought this one was 100-per-cent out, which just goes to show you. It didn't really matter, though, because in Mitch's next over the

Geeves for Bollinger

We had a couple of setbacks on the fourth day of this Test. First, just as we were thinking about exactly what target we were going to set South Africa, we lost three wickets for none, four for five, and in the end needed a swashbuckling last-wicket stand of 33 between Hilfenhaus and Siddle to get us to a final total of 207. There was some ordinary batting — the first time in the game when we weren't at our best — but in the end we were able to extend our overall lead past 450, which was what we were after, so the batting collapse was hardly a catastrophe.

More serious was the news that Doug Bollinger had suffered an abdominal strain while bowling in the nets. It's one of those injuries where we're not sure how long Dougie might be out, so the decision was quickly made that Tasmania's Brett Geeves would be called up as his replacement. The doctors are also a bit concerned about Pete Siddle (left foot) and Ben Hilfenhaus (lower back pain), who came out of the Test feeling a little sore. So as a precaution another quick, Western Australia's Steve Magoffin, is also coming to join us.

I'll be surprised if either Pete or Hilf miss any cricket because of their ailments. But we have to be careful — with back-to-back games you have to be careful with niggling injuries, especially with blokes who are new to international matches. We're finding that one of the hardest things for new bowlers is to adapt to five-day Tests, as distinct from four-day cricket.

same batter aimed a big drive at a well-pitched-up delivery and only managed to drag the ball back into his stumps.

It took us nearly an hour after the main break to get the wicket we were looking for, and again it was that man Siddle who did the job. It was a straightforward catch from JP Duminy to second slip and I saw it all the way. From there, the end came fairly quickly and I loved every minute of it.

Rarely in all my time as an Australian cricketer has *Under the Southern Cross* been sung with more emotion. The Wanderers was just about empty, the fans had all gone home, the media commitments were done, and it was maybe three hours after the last wicket fell when we walked out of the dressing room and strolled slowly out to the middle. Doug Bollinger had an esky under his arm, while I made a point of being with Phillip Hughes so I could tell him that he should never forget this moment, how good it feels. Mike Hussey got in the middle of the group as we formed a tight circle and he quickly reminded us that while this was a great victory, it was only one win in a three-Test series …

> *Don't get carried away, boys …*
> *We haven't got two weeks between games to get ourselves ready again …*
> *We've gotta do it all again in Durban in a couple of days …*

Everyone had a beer in their hand, we sang our hearts out, and then the ale was poured unmercifully over the heads of our three debutants. It was beautiful.

Wednesday, March 4

WHEN I WROTE MY DIARY entry two nights ago, straight after the first Test, I was on top of the world. I couldn't wait to wake up and go down for breakfast the next morning, so I could be with my mates to talk some more about all we'd achieved. How could I have known that so quickly our mood would turn sombre, because of events from far away that are totally beyond our control?

No matter what happens in this world, no matter how many briefings I attend in connection with security matters and how threats of violence relate to international cricket, nothing could have prepared me for the news I received when I was woken earlier than I expected the morning after the Test: the Sri Lankan team has been targetted in a terrorist attack as they made their way to the stadium in Lahore, Pakistan, to play the third day of a Test match. None of the cricketers had been killed, and their support staff had also been spared (as were the umpires and match referee), but a number of policemen and the driver of the bus carrying the umpires died. Others were badly wounded, including the fourth umpire. This is such a terrible and frightening thing for the people involved, and a dire development for cricket and for Pakistan.

Last night, I issued this brief statement:

An act of violence like this is a terrible thing and when it involves those who are part of our cricketing family, players the world over are affected. The wider cricketing community has been shocked ... and our thoughts and full support is with those involved.

We have spoken with members of the Sri Lankan team this morning and made them aware we are extremely saddened by what has happened and that our best wishes are with them all.

I'm not sure if the events in Lahore will sway any of our guys to avoid the IPL in India in April or to think twice about our matches against Pakistan in April-May. It's too soon after the attack to think about that. With all security concerns, I'm still okay to trust the judgment of Cricket Australia, the ACA and the Australian Government. But not surprisingly, what has happened is dominating discussions among our group, not least because a number of us have direct links with people who were in the line of fire. This was a direct assault on our sport, on people we know and like, on blokes who share our love of the game. Our physio, Alex Kountouris, has worked with the Sri Lanka team, and he has called a few of their players to make sure they're all right. I asked him to send a message to the Sri Lankans on behalf of our players, to say we are thinking of them and feel for them. Brad Haddin has spoken to Trevor Bayliss, the former NSW coach who is now coaching Sri Lanka, while Tim Nielsen has been in contact with his fellow South Australian, umpire Steve Davis, who was in a mini-van behind the Sri Lankans' team bus when the attack occurred.

It's crazy the way we were celebrating after such a good win and then we woke up to learn about what has happened to our game. There was already a strong security presence around the Australian team on this tour but that security has certainly been amped up in the wake of the tragedy. In the past 24 hours, I've seen plenty of guards carrying machine guns in our hotel and at training, and I've been informed we'll be getting a police escort to and from the ground for every day of the upcoming Test.

There will also be a minute's silence before play on the first day, as a mark of respect for those who died. For both teams here, we just have to get on with the game, which we'll be able to do — it's not as if what happened in Lahore will impinge on our performance, but that doesn't mean we won't be thinking about it. The whole thing is just so bloody dreadful, so terribly sad.

Thursday, March 12

Second Test, South Africa v Australia at Durban (March 6–10): Australia 352 (PJ Hughes 115, SM Katich 108, MEK Hussey 50) and 5–331 dec (PJ Hughes 160, RT Ponting 81) defeated **South Africa** 138 (JP Duminy 73*) and 370 (JH Kallis 93, AB de Villiers 84) by 175 runs

***

THE FEAR I HAD, coming into this game, was that we might struggle to recapture the verve and intensity we had in Johannesburg. Returning to that level of performance is not as simple as just flicking the switch back on. But we did so, and for that I think we have youth to thank — or, specifically, Phillip Hughes' youth to thank. His effort, in scoring a hundred in each innings in just his second Test match and only 98 days after his 20th birthday (when he reached the second ton), was remarkable.

In the context of the game, the opening partnership put together by Phillip and Simon Katich on the first day was crucial. Same as what happened in Jo'burg, I won the toss (something I've got pretty good at lately) and again I decided to bat on a wicket that looked like it would have something in it for the bowlers. It turned out to not have anything like the devil the Wanderers deck had at the beginning of the first Test, but it was still tricky — a fact reflected in the way our first innings fell away and then South Africa's reply collapsed — so the importance of

Close but Not Close Enough

For this second Test (and the third Test, too), the ICC decided to use 'hot spot' technology to help the video umpire ruling on decisions referred to him from the field. I didn't have much of a problem with this, though I wondered if it was right to 'change the rules' in the middle of a series. As it turned out, some of the 'teething problems' from Jo'burg recurred here. Like anything connected with umpiring, any referral system is not going to be perfect, but I'm coming to the conclusion that there is more good than bad to the concept.

A funny one here came on the first day, after Mike Hussey was given out lbw to Morne Morkel. He decided to go, but as he walked off past Simon Katich, his batting partner, Kato, said, 'I reckon you might as well check it.'

Kato admitted later that he wasn't sure; from his angle it just looked close. So Huss did check it, and the replay showed the ball pitching just but clearly outside leg-stump. He was four at the time, and went on to a hard-fought 50.

Kat and Huey's achievement in adding 184 for the first wicket can't be underestimated.

Our openers set the platform by taking the bowlers on, catching the South Africans off-guard, and from there we won the game with a polished team effort. In all the excitement of Phillip's extraordinary performance, Kat's contribution has been largely overlooked but it shouldn't have been. This was his seventh Test century, and fifth in 14 Tests since he came back into the side in the West Indies last year as a replacement opener after Matt Hayden was injured. I know he worked very hard with Bob Simpson to get his game back in top order, and the fruits of that labour are there for all to see. He has become a very confident, very well-organised Test cricketer, who brings a real strength to our outlook and who has become a genuine mentor for his new opening partner. I think of him as a bit of a throwback to a previous era; the 'senior pro', the bloke you want next to you when times are tough.

Kat had the perfect viewing spot when Huey cut loose. Forty of the young bloke's first 52 runs in his first innings came in boundaries, including four in one over from Morne Morkel. He

Twin Tons

This victory was a great team performance — maybe even more satisfying than the win in Jo'burg because we had to back-up so quickly — but it is impossible not to single Phillip Hughes out.

Among Australians, only 19-year-olds Neil Harvey, Archie Jackson and Walters were younger than Huey is now when they scored their first Test centuries.

He became the 14th Australian to score twin hundreds in a Test and — at 20 years, 98 days — the youngest from any country to do so. The previous youngest was the West Indies' George Headley, who was 20 years and 271 days when he completed his second hundred of the game in his third Test, against England at Georgetown in 1929–30. The previous youngest Australian to manage this feat was Doug Walters, who was 23 years 59 days when he scored 242 and 103 against the West Indies at the SCG in 1968–69).

Huey is the first Aussie to manage the feat in any of his first three Tests. Arthur Morris, who scored 122 and 124 not out against England at the Adelaide Oval in 1946–47, and Jack Moroney, who scored 118 and 101 not out against South Africa at Ellis Park, Johannesburg, in 1949–50, did so in their fourth Tests.

had 17 fours on his way to 93 and then he reached his maiden Test hundred with two sixes off consecutive deliveries. So much for the 'nervous nineties'. He'd been good in the second innings in Jo'burg, but he was quite superb here, and because the South Africans had been a bit critical after the first Test, questioning his technique and even having a jab at his courage, he made them look a little silly. By the fourth day it looked as if they had no real plan for bowling to him.

At stumps on day one we were 4–303 and hoping to compile a total of 450 or beyond. But it was as if we were playing on a different pitch on the second day, as first we crashed to 352 all out, losing our last five wickets for four runs, and then South Africa collapsed completely — had it not been for JP Duminy, who scored an unbeaten 73 out of 138, they would have struggled to make three figures.

Once again, Mitchell Johnson was superb. He was quick and dangerous, and he had his inswinger working beautifully. That delivery, which he and Troy Cooley have been working on for many months, has turned him into a truly lethal bowler; in my view, he has to be close to the best paceman in the game right now. For the second time in two-and-a-bit months he broke one of Graeme Smith's fingers, and he forced Jacques Kallis to retire hurt after a riser got past the grille of his helmet and cut him under the chin. He also dismissed Neil McKenzie and Hashim Amla in his opening over, and was a threat whenever he had the ball in his hand. When Kallis returned to the middle, on the fall of the fifth wicket after getting some stitches in his chin, I immediately had Mitch warm up at mid-on, as if he was coming back on to bowl. I don't know if that had any impact on Kallis' mindset, but he lasted only two more balls and Mitch was able to enjoy a longer break before he came back for his next spell.

Ben Hilfenhaus also contributed, trapping AB de Villiers lbw to make the South Africans' first-innings score 3–6 (with Smith retired hurt), and late in the second day Andrew McDonald proved his worth again by taking three wickets in six balls (Paul Harris, Kallis and Morne Morkel) as they fell to 7–106. Duminy got them to 7–138 at stumps, but next morning Peter Siddle dismissed Dale Steyn and then Makhaya Ntini with the second and third balls of the day respectively and we were batting again.

There was probably more logic in enforcing the follow-on this time than there had been in the first Test, because our strike bowlers had not bowled quite as many overs this time as they had in Johannesburg. But I was still more than happy to bat again, and then thrilled to be able to bat with Huey as he progressed towards his second hundred. The wicket had settled right down — the locals blamed what happened on the second day on the tide, which if it comes in at the right time can apparently put some life into the square — and the South Africans seemed happy enough to wait for a declaration. My only disappointment was that I got myself out when Phillip was two runs short of his ton, which meant Huss was the man at the other end when the boy from Macksville made history.

When we closed on the fourth morning South Africa needed 546 to win, and while I didn't believe for a moment they could win I knew that they'd be tough to chisel out. Peter Siddle dismissed McKenzie and Amla reasonably quickly, but then Kallis and de Villiers settled in and batted for the best part of two sessions, into the last day. Finally, a bit out of the blue, Mitchell Johnson was too quick for Kallis, no mean feat with such a quality batter set, and after that wickets fell reasonably regularly. The longest delay came during an 80-minute stand between Morkel and Mark Boucher, which Marcus North eventually

As Happy as I've Ever Been

I've been a Test cricketer for more than 13 years and a Test captain for five, but I've never had a series win like this one. I came into the Australian team just after the historic win in the West Indies in 1995 and since then we've been expected to win just about every Test series we've played. Maybe a couple of times in India it's been an even-money bet going into the rubber, but this time we were long outsiders. But we came through.

Little wonder then that immediately after this Test I said that I was 'as happy as I've been in my whole career as an Australian player'. Then I continued ...

'I'm extremely proud of the players. We played some amazing Test cricket over the past couple of weeks. This is a great achievement from this team, and I'm sure there will be a lot of people back home in Australia really proud of what the team has done.

'To be able to bounce back and win the way we have here against a side that no one thought we could beat makes the achievement even more special for me. World Cups are great. Ashes '06–07 was an amazing achievement — to win that 5–0, bouncing back the same sort of way we have now.

'I'm not putting it above any of those but if you look at our group of players, and you all did I know very carefully, that we were bringing away on this tour, there'll be a lot of people around the world who didn't think this was achievable. So for us to have achieved what we have done over this week would make this win as special as any I've been a part of ...'

broke with a sharp caught-and bowled, and not long after the series was won with a couple of hours to spare.

It was good to be able to have the spinners, Katich and North, bowling at the end, to give our gallant posse of quicks a well-earned respite. The three of them — Johnson, Hilfenhaus and Siddle — had bowled 280 overs in 12 days and had every right to be exhausted. They mightn't be household names yet, like 'McGrath' or 'Gillespie' or 'McDermott' or 'Hughes' once were, but they might be soon. And we still have Brett Lee and Stuart Clark to come back from their injuries.

***

OUTSIDE OUR SQUAD, THERE seemed to be almost a sense of panic a few weeks ago over what was happening with the Australian side, but we realised we are a team in transition and that we had to stay true to the plan we had developed and we had to do that even though we knew there would be days when we'd struggle. As long as we kept faith in ourselves and our strategies, and didn't do anything silly or make changes just for the sake of it, then we were confident we would rediscover our winning ways. 'Back yourself' is a motto that has been quoted so

Still the One

I couldn't help but have a quiet chuckle to myself when one of the South African journos finally asked me about the No. 1 ranking and the mace that is held by the team that earns that status. They'd been so keen to talk about it when we landed in the country three-and-a-half weeks ago.

'I haven't mentioned the trophy once around this whole group because it's not the reason we play,' I replied. 'We play to win games of cricket for Australia and to do the best that we can for each other as a group of players. Whatever happens as a result of that happens. If silverware comes your way then great, but that's not the reason we play the game.'

often that some people think it's an easy thing to do, but after the experiences we've been through over the past 15 months I now know with great certainty that it is very difficult if the general feeling is that your ship is floundering. Motivators like to tell you that 'winning is contagious' but negativity can spread like a virus, too. We had to rebuild confidence, stay true to a set of core beliefs, and develop a positive vibe in this new group of Australian cricketers, and this has taken time. A key now is for us to sustain our current mindset through the rest of this tour and on to the World Twenty20 and Ashes Tests in England.

We lead this series two-nil with one to play. People said we couldn't win over here, but I knew we could. The selectors were criticised in Australia for choices they did and didn't make, but though it might not have always been apparent — especially on the last day of the Perth Test and the third day in Melbourne — we were heading in the right direction. The results of these latest two Tests are not as surprising as some people might think.

I'm not saying this with the benefit of hindsight. Those closest to the group saw the signs. I keep thinking about a moment on the second day of Durban Test, when Christian Binder, the Australian team's masseur, a bloke who has worked with some successful sporting sides (including the Australian team at the 2007 World Cup and the Melbourne Storm rugby league club) was sitting next to me. We were discussing how we were going as a group and he said something that I couldn't help but feel good about.

'I have been around a lot of very good and successful teams,' Christian said. 'I want you to know that I've never been around a group that has such a great feel about it and such a good buzz about where it's heading.'

Monday, March 23

***

THERE WAS A STAGE when I wasn't sure which South African
captain would be joining me for the toss before the third Test. With
Graeme Smith out with a broken finger, our first thought was that
Ashwell Prince would get the job. Prince had gone to Australia as
vice-captain, but injury kept him out of the side for that series and
his replacement, JP Duminy, went so well that there was no room
for him when our battles resumed over here. Prince was expected
to come back into the team for this Test in Cape Town.

If not Prince, we figured, maybe Mark Boucher, who led the
South Africans on the field in Durban after Mitchell Johnson
broke Smith's finger. We found this move a little strange, only
because in Australia, when Smith was injured during the third
Test, Neil McKenzie had taken over.

Pretty much straightaway after the second Test, the South
African selectors announced that Prince would return to the team
as an opening bat and captain. McKenzie had been dropped, as
had Morne Morkel. Next day, however, they changed their minds,

and announced that Jacques Kallis would be skipper, on a 'one-off' basis, so Prince could concentrate on being an opening bat, a position he's not used to. It was hard not to conclude that the old vice-captain wasn't happy being made to open up, and the captaincy switch was a reaction to that. Who motivated that switch we don't know — there were a few versions of events floating around — and to us it didn't really matter. Prince is a very

No Joy for the Poms

No sooner had we won the series over here and the news came from the Caribbean that England had lost a Test series to the West Indies for the first time since 2000. The Poms almost pulled off an unlikely victory on the last day of the fifth and final Test in Port-of-Spain, but the home team hung on to force a draw and thus win the series 1–0.

I'm not sure if this result will have any impact on England's preparations for the Ashes series (which starts on July 8). Their team has been through plenty of drama in the past few months, culminating in Kevin Pietersen's resignation as captain in early January and the departure of coach Peter Moores. Under new skipper Andrew Strauss, they seemed a little unlucky not to get something out of the series against the Windies, and it won't surprise me at all if they reverse this result when the two teams meet again in a two-match series in England a couple of months before the Ashes Tests.

Pietersen's form in the series that just ended was, by his high standards, okay but not brilliant. However, he remains their most dangerous player, a personality who seems best suited to the big occasion — and there is no bigger occasion for an Australian or English cricketer than an Ashes series. If they also have Andy Flintoff and Michael Vaughan back and firing, then in my view they'll be a pretty tough side to get past.

good player, capable of scoring plenty of runs wherever he bats, and Kallis has been around long enough to know how to captain a team, even if he has the sort of laidback character that usually isn't suited to leadership. We had to focus on our own preparation; we knew it would be difficult to sustain the momentum we'd built up, but we also realise it was important that we did so. A loss would leave us with three Test wins each over the two Test series in 2008–09, and we didn't want to give the South Africans the opportunity to say they'd finished the summer all square.

One thing I didn't want to talk about before the game or use as an alibi afterwards was the old 'dead-rubber syndrome' that many people like to refer to whenever a series is decided early. Newlands is a venue that has suited us in the past, and we always enjoy playing there. We went into this game desperately keen to win but we were outplayed by an opponent who over the course of the four days of the game was much better than we were. Guys were playing for places in the Ashes squad, and there was a chance for a clean sweep away from home against the team many were calling the best in the world before the series began. We might have won three Tests in a row (one in Sydney, two over here), but we still have plenty to prove and we want to keep improving all the time. I even scheduled short one-on-one meetings with each of the guys in our team to stress how important it was that we finish the series on a high. But it wasn't to be.

We'd had a few days off after the Durban Test, and a number of the guys were joined by their wives and partners for a bit of sightseeing in and around Cape Town. I don't think this relaxation took the edge off us; mentally, at least, I thought we went into the third Test as sharp as we had been for the first two, but maybe the big effort we put in throughout the first three weeks of the tour did take a toll, especially on our bowlers, and when the South African batsmen — led by Prince, Kallis and De

For Richer or Poorer

We were expecting Adam Voges to come over for the one-dayers and T20 games, but just before the third Test we learned that he had decided to stay in Australia — because he is getting married.

It must have been a tough call for Adam, because he is on the fringes of the national squad and by pulling out he has given someone else an opportunity. But as someone who has always argued that nothing is more important than family, there's no way I'm going to be criticising his decision. My understanding is that his fiancée told him to come over, and he asked the selectors if he could just miss a couple of games, but they decided that with all the changes we've had to the Aussie squads because of injuries over the past few months, it just wasn't practical for the squad to be short-handed even for just a few days.

Instead, Adam's WA team-mate Marcus North will now stay in South Africa as a member of our one-day team. When Adam heard this news, all he could say was, 'I guess that means there'll be one less guest at the reception.'

Villiers — took command on days two and three we weren't able to fight back.

When you're not quite at your best in Test cricket, the results can go against you really quickly. This was only the second time South Africa had ever beaten Australia by an innings in a Test match.

***

BEFORE THIS MATCH, MY most recent experience of Test cricket in Cape Town was in 2006, when Stuart Clark took nine wickets on debut. So before we arrived I had visions of us playing the same XI for the third Test in a row. But then we saw the pitch at Newlands being prepared for this game and saw there wasn't a lot of grass on it, nothing like Jo'burg, and there were bare patches at either end. It looked like a wicket that might suit the spinners more than the quicks, so we starting pondering the idea of playing leg-spinner Bryce McGain instead of Andrew McDonald.

That would have been a terribly tough call on Ronnie, whose contribution to our success in recent weeks has, I think, been underrated. In the first two Tests, he has taken five wickets for 125 runs from 60 overs, an economy rate of just a fraction more than two runs per over. In modern cricket, where there is always pressure on batsmen to get a move on, his ability to tie up an end and also threaten to get wickets at the same time, has been invaluable. His batting has been disappointing, but while he might not be a top-six batter, he's still got a good technique that can get him useful runs as a No. 7 or No. 8.

But for all that, there were also a lot of upsides to playing Bryce. It would be good to get a look at him before the Ashes Tests, and it would be good for him to get some experience at this level. It would also be a nice reward for him, after the disappointment he must have felt when his tour of India last October was cut short almost before it began. It was a hard call, but in the end the decision was made for us when Marcus North was cut down by a stomach virus so severe he spent some time in hospital. He was ruled out, Brad Haddin moved up to No. 6, Ronnie to No. 7, Mitch to No. 8 and Bryce, six days short of his 37th birthday, became the oldest Australian to make his Test debut since Bob Holland played his first game at the age of 38 years, 35 days, against the West Indies at the Gabba in 1984–85, Kim Hughes' last Test as captain.

Losing Northy upset the balance of the batting order a bit, which hurt us in the first innings when we went from 5–152 to

209 all out. It's amazing how rejigging the batting order like this, putting blokes one place higher than they're used to, can impact on everyone in the team, and I think a few of us struggled to adapt in this Test. The more I play this game, the more I believe that a key to a well-balanced XI is having six specialist batsmen, one of whom can bowl, a No. 7 who can average 40-plus and get those runs quickly, and four bowlers, one of whom is a spinner. That bowler in the top six doesn't have to be a champion, just someone like a Marcus North or an Andrew Symonds, who can tie up an end, give the frontline blokes a break, and pick up a few important wickets along the way.

I've been criticised for the way I handled Bryce and I'll have to cop that. Truth is, he never looked comfortable from the moment I gave him his first over late on the opening day and Prince hit him second ball for six over long-on. They had a pre-conceived plan to go after him and it worked for them, though I don't think he bowled as badly as his figures suggest. On the second day, I stuck with the quicks for what some would consider a long time, but I've done that often in the past, even when Shane Warne was our spinner. My logic is that you want the faster bowlers operating when the conditions best suit them. Eventually, I brought him on not long after Kallis came to the middle, but his first three balls went for four and his third, fourth and fifth overs cost 14, 19 and 14 runs respectively. After that, there just never seemed to be a good time to bring him back. Prince was in excellent form from the start, and Kallis has proved many times that he is the sort of batter who can slaughter loose bowling. I tried him from both ends, but to no avail. On the third day, when de Villiers and Albie Morkel were racing along at a run-a-ball, Bryce kept going for plenty. He finished with 0–149 from 18 overs, and I felt very sorry for him, because he's a better bowler than this game suggests.

Where to Turn?

There were suggestions about that I should have bowled Simon Katich more and earlier, but I don't agree with that. I know, after he picked up two cheap wickets at the end of South Africa's innings, that Kato has taken 5–54 with his left-arm wrist-spinners over the course of these last two Tests, but the fact is we had a specialist spinner in our line-up for this game and if I'd brought another slow bowler on earlier he would have been taking some of Bryce's overs.

We shouldn't forget that all five of Kat's wickets were tailenders or that he can get some pain in his lower back from bowling, which is why I'm always wary of bringing him on in the middle of a game. That actually happened here, when he seized up a little during warm-ups the next morning after bowling three overs at the end of their long innings. Fortunately, that didn't effect his batting this time — he had yet another good Test, scoring 50 in both innings and twice being involved in half-century opening stands with Phillip Hughes — but it is something we have to think about.

Back in the dressing room after getting our picture taken with the trophy awarded to the series winners, at the end of two intense back-to-back series, we much preferred to celebrate the series victory rather than ponder the match defeat. It was a bit weird thinking about what we've done — our cricket in the first two Test matches was as good as we've played for a long time, but some of the cricket we played on the first two days of this Test was as poor as we've played for a long time.

I'm sure it's best to think about some of the great steps forward we've made on this tour. I still know that I've taken more pleasure from this series than from any other I've been a part of, either as a player or a captain, and I'm also confident that — after all that I've been through over the past 15 months — I'm becoming a better captain, better equipped to lead a younger group of players. The next Test-match cricket we play will be the Ashes, and that will be another great challenge.

I bet there are a lot of people around the world looking forward to that one.

Sky's the Limit

I was proud of the way we didn't chuck it in during our second innings, happy to see Andrew McDonald get a few runs, and more than a little in awe of Mitchell Johnson's display as he hit his way to a superb century. His final score of 123 not out, scored off 103 balls and featuring 11 fours and five sixes, was the best score by an Australian No. 8 in Test cricket since 1884–85, when George Bonnor belted 128 against England at the SCG. He went from 95 to 101 with a six over deep mid-wicket off Dale Steyn, which is not a bad trick.

Mitch has worked hard on his batting, and while he has the potential to get even better he's already a potential match-winner in the lower order. He is more than capable of taking any bowler down at any time. That ability to consistently hit quick runs, and in the process turn an innings total of, say, six or seven for 280 or 300 into 400 or 450, can change the mood of a day's play, a match, even a series.

Interestingly, the highest score ever made by a No. 8 in Tests is 257 not out by Pakistan's Wasim Akram. Now I'm not suggesting Mitch is as good an all-rounder as Wasim, not yet, but when I think about how much he has improved in the past six months — he's taken 33 wickets and scored 401 runs in the past six Tests against South Africa — the sky really is the limit when you talk about where he might go as a cricketer.

Monday, April 20

IT'S BEEN A LONG MONTH. One thing the Australian team has prided itself on throughout my career has been that we have done our utmost to be up for every game — Test match, one-day international or, in the past couple of years, Twenty20 international. Rarely has that ambition been more tried than during the past four weeks, when we played two T20 games and then five ODIs. I think part of this was a result of all the cricket we have played since October; but part of it, too, was about the fact that we've seen a lot of the South Africans recently. We still put in, and I was extremely proud of the way we played in the final one-dayer, even though the series had already been decided. But in the middle of those games, sometimes it just felt like hard work.

South Africa played very, very well — in both the T20 games and the ODIs — and thoroughly deserved their victories. For us, the main positive came with the efforts of the new guys, most notably Callum Ferguson, who played a lone hand when we were thrashed in the one-dayer at Centurion and followed that up with good innings at Newlands and the Wanderers. Brett Geeves and Ben Laughlin made their T20 debuts for us, and Ben and Shane Harwood won their first ODI caps.

Ideally, the T20 games would have been important lead-up games to the World Twenty20 in June, but with so many guys out injured we'll probably have a very different line-up when that tournament comes along. Instead, it was good to give guys such as Brett, Ben and Shane a taste of international cricket, and none of them looked out of place. Ben was particularly impressive, especially when you consider that at the start of the 2008–09 season he'd only appeared in one first-class game and

On Top of the World

On March 26, on behalf of the Australian Test team and Cricket Australia, I was handed the ICC's gold-plated mace and a cheque for $US175,000 ($A252,500) because I am captain of the team that will finish at the top of the ICC's Test Championship table on the annual cut-off date of April 1.

At the presentation, I described our No. 1 ranking as 'a tribute to the hard work of the players and the back-room staff'. As well as the Test trophy, I also collected a $US75,000 cheque for coming second in the ODI Championship. South Africa are currently rated the top one-day team in the game.

ICC Test Championship

Rank	Team	Rating
1.	Australia	128
2.	South Africa	119
3.	India	118
4.	Sri Lanka	108
5.	Pakistan	100
6.	England	98
7.	West Indies	89
8.	New Zealand	81
9.	Bangladesh	0

Both tables as at March 25, 2009

ICC ODI Championship

Rank	Team	Rating
1.	South Africa	125
2.	Australia	124
3	India	122
4.	New Zealand	112
5.	Pakistan	111
6.	England	107
7.	Sri Lanka	105
8.	West Indies	92
9.	Bangladesh	46
10.	Zimbabwe	23
11.	Ireland	19
12.	Kenya	0

Australia v South Africa Twenty20 Internationals 2009

First T20 International, at Johannesburg (March 27): Australia 7–166 (20 overs: DA Warner 38, DJ Hussey 88*; RJ Peterson 3–30) lost to South Africa 6–168 (19.2 overs: MV Boucher 36*, JA Morkel 37) by four wickets

Second T20 International, at Centurion (March 29): South Africa 5–156 (20 overs: RE van der Merwe 48) defeated Australia 8–139 (20 overs) by 17 runs

never played a limited-over game for Queensland. Dave Warner also played in the T20s, and while he didn't go on to make a big score in either game he still managed to show the people over here that special gift he has for pure hitting.

The one-day series started well for us when we won easily at Durban, a venue that seems to suit us. We went into the game hoping our quicks, led by Mitchell Johnson, could make an impact on a pitch that has some pace and carry in it, and they did bowl well. However, it was Nathan Hauritz's off-breaks that did the damage, as he dismissed Graeme Smith, Mark Boucher and the two Morkels while conceding only 29 runs from his 8.1 overs after we made 7–286. Nathan hadn't played a game to this point during the tour, but he'd done plenty of work with our coaches during early-morning training sessions and it paid dividends for him in this game.

After that win, I really thought we could win the series, but the momentum changed dramatically after I decided to bat first on a green wicket at Centurion. I gambled on us getting through the early overs, but instead a series of poor shots allowed Dale

Steyn and the young left-armer Wayne Parnell to reduce us to 5–19. Callum batted very well to score 50 and get our innings total over 100, but in the afternoon the pitch flattened out and the home team cruised to victory.

For the third game, we returned to Cape Town, where in the ODI in 2006 they thrashed us 7–289 to 93 all out. This time they didn't beat us quite that emphatically, but they were still clearly

---

Australia v South Africa One-Day Internationals 2009

First ODI, at Durban (April 3): Australia 7–286 (50 overs: BJ Haddin 53, MEK Hussey 83) defeated South Africa 145 (33.1 overs: GC Smith 52; NM Hauritz 4–29) by 141 runs

Second ODI, at Centurion (April 5): Australia 131 (40.2 overs: CJ Ferguson 50; DW Steyn 4–27, WD Parnell 4–25) lost to South Africa 3–132 (26.2 overs: GC Smith 40) by seven wickets

Third ODI, at Cape Town (April 9): South Africa 6–289 (50 overs: JH Kallis 70, AB de Villiers 80; MG Johnson 4–34) defeated Australia 7–264 (50 overs: CJ Ferguson 63, JR Hopes 63*; RE van der Merwe 3–37) by 25 runs

Fourth ODI, at Port Elizabeth (April 13): South Africa 6–317 (50 overs: HH Gibbs 110, AB de Villiers 84, JP Duminy 40) defeated Australia 256 (45.5 overs: BJ Haddin 78, MJ Clarke 50, RT Ponting 53; DW Steyn 4–44, RE van der Merwe 3–46) by 61 runs

Fifth ODI, at Johannesburg (April 17): Australia 7–303 (50 overs: BJ Haddin 62, MJ Clarke 66, RT Ponting 40, CJ Ferguson 41, MEK Hussey 49; JP Duminy 3–48) defeated South Africa 256 (45.5 overs: HH Gibbs 82, JH Kallis 64; MG Johnson 3–58) by 47 runs

---

the better side, overcoming an outstanding bowling performance by Mitchell Johnson to win by 25 runs. At Port Elizabeth, where we had to win to stay in the series, they were even more dominant, building a huge innings total on the back of a Herschelle Gibbs century and then cruising to victory courtesy of some excellent overs from Steyn and Roelof van der Merwe. At Newlands, our top-order batting was pretty terrible; it was as if everyone was waiting for someone else to do the job. In game four, Brad Haddin, Michael Clarke and I all made good starts, but none of us went on to the big score that might have kept us in the contest.

So we'd lost the series, which I guess meant the South Africans had reaffirmed their status as the No. 1 one-day team. However, I didn't come away from these games dreading the idea of playing them in an important Champions Trophy or World Cup match. The fact we were able to win game five confirmed this feeling — we talked about the need to end the tour on a good note, rediscovered that winning feeling, and we came out and delivered on the back of a good all-round batting effort.

I guess I could quibble about the fact no-one made a big score — and I am concerned about our inability to make hundreds in recent one-dayers (I haven't got one in any of my past 20 ODI innings, which isn't good enough for the No. 3) — but every member of the top five did make it to 40 which allowed us to post a winning total. The bowling and fielding performance that followed was very professional, with Ben Laughlin's catch on the mid-wicket boundary that dismissed Albie Morkel a highlight, and we knocked them over in the 46th over.

It was finally time for the Australian cricket caravan to move on to Dubai, though for me, the 2008–09 season is over. Next stop: England. The Ashes 2009 is fast approaching.

Through this photo section are images of the 22 men who played Test cricket for Australia between October 2008 and August 2009.

TOP LEFT: Cameron White after taking his first Test wicket in Bangalore.

TOP RIGHT: Jason Krejza during his 12-wicket Test debut in Nagpur.

MIDDLE: Andrew Symonds at the Gabba.

LEFT: Doug Bollinger (left) and Andrew McDonald (right) at a media conference before the two guys made their Test debut in the New Year's Test in Sydney.

ABOVE: Matthew Hayden (right) with the great Glenn McGrath at a promotion for
Jane McGrath Day — the third day of what proved to be Haydos' final Test, the
Sydney match against South Africa.

BELOW: Keeper Brad Haddin and I acknowledge our support staff after Graeme
Smith was caught behind for a duck in Mitchell Johnson's first over in Johannesburg.
We were keen to have Mitch attacking Smith straightaway, to test his recently healed
broken finger, and the plan worked beautifully.

ABOVE LEFT: Phillip Hughes brings up his maiden Test century with a six on the first day in Durban.

ABOVE RIGHT: Bryce McGain during his unlucky debut in Cape Town.

BELOW: Mitchell Johnson on the way to his first Test hundred later in the same game.

ABOVE LEFT: Brett Lee knocks over Vikram Solanki during our warm-up game against the England Lions at Worcester a week before the first Ashes Test.

ABOVE RIGHT: Peter Siddle has Paul Collingwood caught in the gully on the dramatic final day at Sophia Gardens in Cardiff.

BELOW: Ben Hilfenhaus takes the first wicket of the Ashes series: Alastair Cook caught by Mike Hussey in the gully.

Above: Simon Katich became the first man to score an Ashes century in Wales.

Below: Marcus North, having already scored a century on his Ashes debut, congratulates the bare-headed Brad Haddin on doing the same.

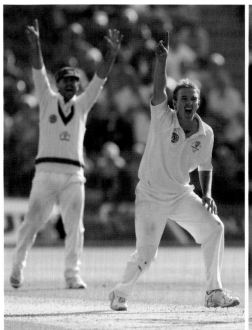

ABOVE LEFT: Nathan Hauritz at Cardiff, trying to spin us to victory on the final day.

ABOVE RIGHT: Shane Watson on his way to a first-up fifty at Edgbaston.

BELOW: Michael Clarke blazes through the covers during his magnificent century at Lord's.

ABOVE: Nathan Hauritz (far left), Mike Hussey (in sunglasses) and Ben Hilfenhaus (far right) share Graham Manou's joy as the South Australian wicketkeeper dons his first baggy green during a brief ceremony that took place before the start of day two of the third Test.

BELOW LEFT: Stuart Clark is congratulated by Simon Katich (with Ben Hilfenhaus moving in) after dismissing Stuart Broad at Headingley.

BELOW RIGHT: Mike Hussey acknowledges the crowd at The Oval after he'd battled his way to a hundred on what proved to be the final day of the series.

Our Test squad is backed up by a strong support team, which includes physio Alex Kountouris (seen here with me after I was struck on the wrist at training in the lead-up to the ICC World Twenty20) and coach Tim Nielsen (running a catching drill at Cardiff, two days before the first Ashes Test).

The Ashes touring party at Lord's before the fourth day's play of the second Test. Back (from left): Frank Dimasi (security manager), Trevor Barsby (development coach), Alex Kountouris (physiotherapist), Stuart Karppinen (strength and conditioning coach), Troy Cooley (pace bowling coach), Michael Marshall (performance analyst), Christian Binder (massage therapist), Philip Pope (media manager). Standing: Brad Haddin, Graham Manou, Nathan Hauritz, Ben Hilfenhaus, Stuart Clark, Andrew McDonald, Peter Siddle, Phillip Hughes, Marcus North, Shane Watson. Front: Simon Katich, Mitchell Johnson, Tim Nielsen (coach), Michael Clarke (vice-captain), Ricky Ponting (captain), Steve Bernard (manager), Brett Lee, Mike Hussey.

Extended Leave

After our loss in the third one-dayer at Cape Town, it was announced that a few familiar names would be rejoining the Australian set-up.

With Brett Geeves returning home because of a fracture in his left foot, Stuart Clark was called up as his replacement. Now recovered from his elbow problem, Stuey landed in Johannesburg on the day of game four, but would only have played in the last match of the series if any of the other bowlers in our squad had been unavailable.

A few days before Stuey arrived in South Africa, he, Brett Lee, Andrew Symonds, Shaun Marsh, Shane Watson and Ben Hilfenhaus were all included in the squad to go to Dubai to face Pakistan. After their big effort in the Tests, Ben and Peter Siddle were rested for the one-dayers in South Africa, and Pete will also miss the Pakistan games.

We first caught up with Bing when we arrived in Port Elizabeth, where he has been training with his IPL side, Kings XI Punjab. He looked in good nick and told us that his battle to regain full fitness was going extremely well. Unfortunately, he then had a bit of a setback, which ruled him out of the first part of the trip to the UAE, but he was obviously close to being ready to go.

One high-profile name missing when the squad for the Pakistan games was announced was mine. Cricket Australia offered me the chance to miss the trip so I could rest up before the World Twenty20 and after discussions with the leadership group I decided it was a good idea. This means that rather than just having a short respite during that period when I wouldn't be playing IPL, I can now have a really good break. Mitchell Johnson and Mike Hussey are doing the same thing. Michael Clarke will captain the side.

Sunday, May 10

AUSTRALIA V PAKISTAN, 2009

First ODI, Australia v Pakistan, at Dubai (April 22): Australia 168 (38.5 overs: BJ Haddin 40, SR Watson 40, JR Hopes 48; Shahid Afridi 6–38) lost to **Pakistan** 6–171 (44.1 overs: Kamran Akmal 48) by four wickets

Second ODI, Australia v Pakistan, at Dubai (April 24): Pakistan 207 (46.2 overs: Salman Butt 57, Shahid Afridi 41; NM Hauritz 3–41) lost to **Australia** 4–208 (45.1 overs: JR Hopes 48, A Symonds 58) by six wickets

Third ODI, Australia v Pakistan, at Abu Dhabi (April 27): Australia 7–198 (50 overs: MJ Clarke 66, CJ Ferguson 41; Umar Gul 3–38) defeated **Pakistan** 171 (47.1 overs: Salman Butt 48, Ahmed Shehzad 40) by 27 runs

Fourth ODI, Australia v Pakistan, at Abu Dhabi (May 1): Pakistan 197 (48.4 overs: Ahmed Shehzad 43, Shahid Afridi 40; DE Bollinger 5–35) lost to **Australia** 2–202 (44.2 overs: SR Watson 85*, MJ Clarke 100*) by eight wickets

Fifth ODI, Australia v Pakistan, at Abu Dhabi (May 3): Australia 4–250 (50 overs: SR Watson 116*, CJ Ferguson 41*) lost to **Pakistan** 3–254 (47 overs: Kamran Akmal 116*, Misbah-ul-Haq 76*) by seven wickets

Twenty20 International, Australia v Pakistan at Dubai (May 7): Australia 108 (19.5 overs: SR Watson 33; Umar Gul 4–8, Shahid Afridi 3–14) lost to **Pakistan** 3–109 (16.2 overs: Kamran Akmal 59*)

***

IN LATE MARCH, NOT long after the third Test in South Africa, it was announced that because of the fragile security situation on the Indian subcontinent — specifically the reality that the Indian police could not provide security for both big-time cricket and the national elections, which would be held at the same time — the IPL would be moved 'off shore' for a season. South Africa was chosen as the alternative host, and for the three or four weeks between that announcement and the start of the competition you could feel the interest growing among South African cricket fans. There seemed little doubt that the games would attract decent crowds to the grounds (and generate huge TV ratings back in India), but it was inevitable — because of the venue change — that this year's 'sophomore season' of IPL would never match the frenzy of excitement that was a feature of the inaugural tournament in 2008.

We left South Africa just as the IPL was starting. For the past three weeks, I have seen a few of the games on TV, mostly Knight Riders matches, but for the most part I have tried to 'get away' from cricket. I did, however, closely study the Australia-Pakistan games from Dubai and Abu Dhabi, and I enjoyed most of what I saw.

To tell you the truth, I don't think Michael Clarke and the boys have received enough credit for the way they earned their victory — how they came from 1–0 down to take an unbeatable 3–1 series lead. There were a number of excellent performances, from guys like Shane Watson, James Hopes, Nathan Hauritz and Dougie Bollinger. Watto's effort in scoring 85 not out in game four and then 116 not out in game five was particularly outstanding, but even that was not enough to win the player-of-the-series award. That went deservedly to Pup, who produced match-winning feats in games three and four. First, he top-scored with 66 and took 3–15 as Pakistan crashed from 0–95 to 171 all out chasing 199; then he hit an unbeaten century in the commanding eight-wicket victory that sealed the series.

Also encouraging was the form of Andrew Symonds in game two, when he scored an important 58, and the return of Brett Lee in the Twenty20 international that ended the tour two days back. Bing opened the bowling and with his first competitive delivery in more than four months he found the edge of Pakistan opener Salman Butt's bat and saw the nick fly to Marcus North at first slip. It was a hot chance first up — the delivery was timed at 149kmph — and it sped through Northy's hands to the third-man boundary. Bing finished with 1–22 from his four overs, a nice return, but otherwise the boys played as if their minds were elsewhere. From being 0–42 after four overs, they stumbled to a seven-wicket loss.

'It looked like we didn't bring our game at all and we had half a foot on the plane,' said Brad Haddin straight after the game. Twelve hours later they were in the air, heading for home.

Meanwhile, in England, Phillip Hughes has been putting together a run of big scores at the start of a short stint with Middlesex, a performance that has some people in the UK (including their chairman of selectors) complaining that he is being handed an unnecessary (from their perspective) advantage in the lead-up to the Ashes. This might be true, but I would have thought the Poms could be using the situation to help themselves, by getting a good look at Huey before the Ashes tour begins.

My only fear is that the little bloke might be scoring his runs a little early — I hope he's able to keep a few up his sleeve for when we need them in July and August. Having seen first-hand how good he is, I'm sure he will. A week from now, Huey's name will be among those chosen for England. Five days after that, we're at Coolum on Queensland's Sunshine Coast for a pre-tour camp. On the Wednesday we leave Australia for the World Twenty20.

It's all getting very close now.

PART SEVEN

THE ICC WORLD
TWENTY20, 2009

Wednesday, June 10

ICC World Twenty20 warm-up match, at Nottingham (June 1): Australia 6–219 (20 overs: SR Watson 52, BJ Haddin 47, MJ Clarke 35; Mahmudullah 4–37) defeated **Bangladesh** 7–181 (20 overs: Shakib Al Hasan 54, Mahmudullah 31*; MG Johnson 3–21) by 38 runs

ICC World Twenty20 warm-up match, at The Oval (June 2): New Zealand 147 (19.5 overs: SB Styris 42, PD McGlashan 49; MG Johnson 4–20) lost to **Australia** 3–151 (19.2 overs: RT Ponting 56, MJ Clarke 49*) by seven wickets

ICC World Twenty20 Group C match, at The Oval (June 6): Australia 7–169 (20 overs: DA Warner 63) lost to **West Indies** 3–172 (15.5 overs: CH Gayle 88, ADS Fletcher 53) by seven wickets

ICC World Twenty20 Group C match, at Nottingham (June 8): Australia 9–159 (20 overs: SL Malinga 3–36, BAW Mendis 3–20) lost to **Sri Lanka** 4–160 (19 overs: TM Dilshan 53, KC Sangakkara 55*) by six wickets

***

AS I'M SURE YOU can imagine, I was always hoping this section of the book — dealing with the ICC World Twenty20 — would be longer than it's turned out to be. I'm a bit stunned at the moment, though the nature of the draw and Twenty20 cricket itself always meant that we were no certainties to make the second stage of the tournament. We were pitted in the same group as Sri Lanka and the West Indies, with only two to go through, and they are two dangerous teams featuring great attacking cricketers such as Chris Gayle, Ajantha Mendis and Kumar Sangakkara. I was confident we'd beat at least one of them, but it wasn't to be. Now, I reckon either team could go on and win the entire tournament — especially the Windies, because if Gayle gets going he's just about unstoppable. Meanwhile, we're heading to Leicester, to lick our proverbial wounds and get ready for the Ashes.

***

AS HAS BEEN WELL-DOCUMENTED, our lead-up to the tournament was dominated by the Andrew Symonds affair. For me, it was just so unfortunate, something I wish had never happened, but from my perspective and the team's perspective nothing about the decision we made in relation to Symmo was too difficult. You never like cutting a bloke, especially a good bloke like Symmo, and we all hate seeing these sort of stories in the papers — and I really hate having to sit in a media conference answering questions about such stories — but this was one of those situations where the team had to come first.

Back in early April, Symmo had been included in a 30-man preliminary squad for the World Twenty20. Then he played in the one-dayers against Pakistan and contributed to the boys' 3–2 victory, before heading to South Africa to help Adam Gilchrist's Deccan Chargers win the IPL. I was looking forward to playing with him again — as I said on the eve of the Ashes team announcement, 'He's a great guy to have around a team, there is no doubt about that' — but once we landed in England I quickly got the feeling that he wasn't all that excited about being here. It was nothing in particular, just that his mood wasn't right, and then came the events of June 2–3 that led to him being axed from our squad.

What happened is pretty much as has been reported. Back home, the first State of Origin rugby league game was played a week ago today, June 3, the day after our second warm-up game, a comfortable win against New Zealand, three days before our first fair-dinkum game of the World Twenty20. The 8pm kickoff at the footy in Australia meant an 11am start in England, and Symmo (a big league fan) and a few others in our squad were determined to watch the game live. Unfortunately, while the other guys who saw the Queensland victory left the bar that was showing the game at full-time, Symmo opted to stay for a little longer. By having a drink, he contravened an undertaking that he would not do so away from the dressing room or the team hotel. None of this, or his actions after the New Zealand game when he left the hotel without advising where he was going (a minor misdemeanour, but our security needs to know where we are at all times in case of a terrorist threat), or a missed recovery session the morning of the Origin, or a couple of other minor breaches of team protocols in previous days that were in themselves not too serious but combined they said pretty clearly to the team hierarchy that he wanted to be somewhere else.

I must stress that in none of these instances was Symmo reported to have behaved badly. But he was contradicting team rules and, more importantly, contradicting commitments he made to himself, his team-mates and Cricket Australia. Later comments I read from people in Australia who are close to him suggested that he no longer felt comfortable in the team environment that's evolved in the past two or three years, and if that is true it's a great shame. There is no doubt that we are a much more professional group today than we were even five seasons ago, let alone 15 years ago when I started (and we were ahead of the game back then), but I don't think we ask too much of the guys. Maybe Symmo has just fallen out of love with the game a bit; if that's true, there might still be a chance he'll come back. Otherwise, as Cricket Australia Chief Executive James Sutherland said, 'We've probably come to the end of the line.'

Our leadership group — me, vice-captain Michael Clarke, coach Tim Nielsen and manager Steve Bernard — met on the Thursday morning and we voted unanimously to send Symonds home. The Cricket Australia board met later in the day and endorsed the decision. So Symmo flew back to Australia and Cameron White was called into the squad as his replacement. It was the right decision to let Symmo go, for him, for us, for everyone, but I still wish it could have worked out differently.

I didn't want to go into too much detail when the media started asking questions as to what had gone on. I do feel let down, but I'm not going to crucify the bloke — he's been a friend for a long time and I'll never forget the good times we've enjoyed playing cricket for Australia. The reporters wanted to know if some grievous crime had been committed, but none had. 'Had he broken curfew?' one bloke asked.

'There's no such thing as a curfew in the Australian cricket team,' I responded quickly. 'You don't need curfews around good teams. That's what being part of the team is all about, having respect for yourself and having respect for your team-mates and not ever disrespecting the opportunity you've got as an Australian player.'

The way I'd decided to cope with this interrogation was to play it down a little, and to focus on the task at hand: the World Twenty20. If that sounded uncaring or impersonal, that was too bad.

'What's the general feeling among your team-mates?' was the last question on the subject.

'To tell you the truth, we are all a little bit disappointed with the events of the last 24 hours,' I said. 'On the eve of a very big tournament for us, losing one of our better players and one of the better performed Twenty20 players in the world right now is far from ideal, but we have to move on from it as quickly as possible.'

∗∗∗

IT HAD ONLY BEEN a week and a half earlier that I'd been writing in the *Australian*, 'It's all starting again and I couldn't be more excited. We've got a new squad and the challenge of the Twenty20 World Cup and the Ashes ahead ...'

At that time, I really was fired up, probably as keen as I've been for quite a while. It's not that I'm not keen now but, gee, I was in a good mood in the days before we left for the UK. The memory of our Test series win in South Africa was still strong, yet nothing beats an Ashes series for an Aussie cricketer. And I was coming off a nice break, where I'd spent some really good time with Rianna and Emmy, hit a few golf balls, and sort of blended back into 'normal' life. I felt as if no one was trying to find me, which was good for a change; there were times when I'd be walking down the street or sitting in a café enjoying a coffee when someone would say, 'What are you doing here? I thought you were in Dubai playing Pakistan.' I liked that, just for a few days.

Emmy had learned to crawl while I was in South Africa, and this added a new dimension to my time back home. She can move pretty quick, and I found myself bending down to stop her charging off in the wrong direction so often that I began to think that a day in the field is less taxing on the body. But her smile is as cheeky as ever, and I love spending time with her — fatherhood is even better than I thought it could be. For two weeks I didn't pick up a bat, and when I finally did it felt as if we were on the verge of a new season.

The squad for the Ashes series was announced on May 20. There were no major surprises, though Dougie Bollinger was unlucky to miss out because Brett Lee and Stuart Clark are back, and Shane Watson and Andrew McDonald edged out Symmo for the all-rounder positions. The day before, I had launched *Run Ricky Run*, a project that brings together two of my passions: cricket and children's cancer charities. And then it was off to Coolum for the pre-tour camp, which involved some sessions in the nets and gym, a bit of team bonding, and a fair amount of 'admin' — contract negotiations and other meetings with Cricket Australia staff where they explained the sort of off-field events we'll be involved in on tour and outlined their expectations in regard to our codes of behaviour, drug policies and so on. Our wives and partners also 'came north', and it was a bit disappointing to see their presence at the camp beaten up in the media, as if the girls had been summoned for a tutorial on how they are expected to behave while they travel with the team. It was nothing of the sort; instead, it was a case of Cricket Australia offering support for what can be a very difficult and stressful role. For me, it is always good to have the girls along, because as has been demonstrated many times over the past 10 years, the team usually functions better when we players have our loved ones with us. It's rarely easy being a cricketer's partner, and as Rianna and I are now learning, it's even tougher when you're travelling with young kids. The ability to share information — whether it be about lessons learned from past experiences or Cricket Australia outlining some of the things that will happen on this tour — has to be a good thing.

***

Run Ricky Run

The launch of *Run Ricky Run* on Tuesday, May 19, marked the beginning of one of the most exciting personal initiatives I've been involved in. The concept is simple: every run I score during the upcoming Ashes series will raise money for the Ponting Foundation, which Rianna and I set up to support some of Australia's leading children's cancer charities.

My ambition for the Tests against the Poms is, of course, to score as many runs as I possibly can. I'm not going to say that *Run Ricky Run* adds an extra incentive, because I was already as fired up as possible to have a big series, but I'm still genuinely pumped by the idea that any runs I score will count for a very good cause. At the launch, the example I gave involved someone who pledged 25 cents a run — if I can make 500 runs in the series that will add up to a $125 donation to the Ponting Foundation. I managed to hit 576 runs in the last Ashes series in Australia, so hopefully I can do something similar this time. I guess it's a bit like the old walkathons or readathons we used to have in school. (And which I'm sure they still have in schools!)

'Every run I score in the Ashes Tests will trigger a donation from the Foundation to one of its beneficiary charities and 100 per cent of the proceeds raised will be distributed to beneficiaries,' I explained. 'There's a fair bit riding on me getting runs in England, which I wouldn't have any other way.

'*Run Ricky Run* provides a direct link between the willingness of the Australian public to donate money to a fantastic cause and my ability to make runs for Australia.'

It'll be great if, during the Ashes Tests, as adults and kids watch me bat or wake up in the morning, they'll think not just about what impact my runs might be having on the fate of the series, but also how much money is being raised for a worthy cause. Having people thinking about cricket and charity at the same time has to be a good thing.

OUR ARRIVAL IN BIRMINGHAM, about lunchtime on May 28 after a flight from Brisbane via Dubai, was way more low-key than it had been in 2005, when there had been a real fervour for the Ashes from the moment we made it through customs. Only 10 members of our Ashes squad were involved in the World Twenty20, but it was the same in 2005, when the one-day squad arrived in England before the Test specialists. Back then, the media was all over us from the moment we arrived. Maybe the fact that this time Manchester United had lost to Barcelona in the

The Squads

'There's one thing on my cricketing resume that hasn't been achieved yet, and that's being captain of a winning Ashes series in England,' I said at the announcement of Australia's squad for the Ashes Tests. 'That's something very dear to my heart, and something I'll certainly be speaking to the players about when we arrive — making sure we get over that hurdle.'

I am one of six guys in the team who were part of the 2005 experience, though only Michael Clarke, Simon Katich and Brett Lee played alongside me in the Tests (Brad Haddin was Adam Gilchrist's understudy and Stuart Clark was called in as cover when Glenn McGrath was injured). The full squad is: Ricky Ponting (captain), Michael Clarke (vice-captain), Stuart Clark, Brad Haddin, Nathan Hauritz, Ben Hilfenhaus, Phillip Hughes, Mike Hussey, Mitchell Johnson, Simon Katich, Brett Lee, Andrew McDonald, Graham Manou, Marcus North, Peter Siddle, Shane Watson.

For the World Twenty20, Nathan Bracken, James Hopes, David Hussey, Andrew Symonds and David Warner were selected instead of Clark, Hughes, Katich, McDonald, Manou and North.

Champions League final the previous night had something to do with the relative lack of attention. We arrived to news that Andrew Flintoff had been ruled out for the next couple of weeks because of a right-knee injury, but that he is still hopeful of being okay for the first Test, even though one newspaper reported that 64 per cent of respondents to a internet poll had decided that he shouldn't be chosen for the series opener.

I sensed quickly that Flintoff's injury worries might be an ongoing saga throughout this English summer. The first time I met their media, at Trent Bridge the day after we landed, I was immediately asked what I thought of his situation, as if I had some inside information. 'Flintoff is very important to their make-up and set-up,' I answered. 'Maybe, as we saw in 2006–07, if he is not 100-per-cent fit then that sort of impact he can have around the team is not there. The Flintoff we saw in 2005 and the one we saw in Australia two years later when we won 5–0 are two completely different players. That had a lot to do with the level of fitness he had under his belt leading into both series.'

This chat was supposed to be about the World Twenty20, and at the start the tournament trophy was positioned so close to me that I had to move it so I could get a look at who I was talking to. As it turned out, that was kind of symbolic, because the press boys didn't really want to talk about the short game, rather just to focus on the Tests.

I was asked to compare my preparation for the Ashes series with that of Flintoff and England's other key man, Kevin Pietersen, who apparently damaged an Achilles tendon during the Indian Premier League. 'For me, it was simple,' I said. 'It (missing the IPL) was a good opportunity to have a couple of weeks off cricket to make sure when I got here I was in the best mental and physical shape I could be, not just for the World Twenty20 but for the Ashes as well.'

The journos nodded their heads as one, as though I'd espoused some great wisdom. Clearly they didn't approve of Freddie and KP's recent sojourn to South Africa. There didn't seem any harm in underlining the point.

'I don't know how much cricket Flintoff and Pietersen played in the lead up to the IPL. There was obviously a great incentive for them with the amount of money they went for,' I continued. 'I'm refreshed and raring to go.'

Five days later, I was facing the media again, but I was in a much more sombre mood. This time I was talking about my recently departed team-mate.

***

WE DIDN'T TAKE THE World Twenty20 lightly. We wanted to win, and if you'd asked me before the first game how our preparation had gone I would have told you that aside from the drama with Symmo we were very comfortable with where we were. Maybe the fact the competition came just before an Ashes series meant that in the back of our minds we'd downplayed things just a little, but I didn't feel that way beforehand so it would be wrong to use that as an alibi now. Fact is, we were outplayed by two teams who right at this moment are a little bit more proficient at Twenty20 than we are. The nature of the game — where one explosive innings or one fantastic bowling spell can prove crucial — means that the gap between the top and bottom teams is smaller than with Test matches (England's loss in the tournament opener to Holland is proof of that), but for Australia this just adds to the challenge. I'll be very disappointed if we don't learn plenty from this experience.

Furthermore, we have to accept that we haven't been brilliant at Twenty20 international cricket from its inception in 2005.

Our record now, after these two losses, is played 23, won 11, which is hardly in keeping with our record in Tests and ODIs over the past few years. We've got a lot of thinking to do.

Some critics have been saying that we didn't take our lead-up seriously enough, and they point to the fact that quite a few of us didn't play in the T20 game against Pakistan in Dubai last month as proof of that. But given all the cricket in front of us we had to take a break at some point, and if you look back to the T20 internationals we played in South Africa, when we made a point of

---

Ouch!

Our first training session in Nottingham nearly ended in disaster for me when, while I was having a hit, I made the mistake of bending down to pick up a ball at precisely the moment another ball firmly driven by Mike Hussey slammed into the adjoining net to mine and struck me on the same wrist I had surgically repaired last year. Just for a second, I thought I was in serious trouble — the blow immediately ended my net session — but our physio, Alex Kountouris, put the wrist in ice and quickly determined that there was no need for an X-ray.

First indications were that I wouldn't even miss our first Twenty20 warm-up game against Bangladesh, and that proved to be the case. We won that game by 38 runs, with Shane Watson hitting a quickfire 52 from 23 deliveries. The next day, in a second dress rehearsal, Mitchell Johnson and Brett Lee starred in a seven-wicket victory over New Zealand, taking 5–29 between them. I was happy to make a half century and in the process confirm that the wrist was in perfect working order. It was just a pity we couldn't take our form in the practice matches into the tournament itself.

flying over guys like Dave Warner and Shane Harwood just for those two games, I reckon that showed how fair dinkum we are about the new game. It would have been easy to just use on the guys from the one-day squad for those matches, but we didn't do that.

No doubt, Symmo's departure hurt us. I was hoping the flexibility in our squad would be enough to cover for his loss, but he was coming off some dynamic performances for the Deccan Chargers in the IPL and could have been the 'wild card' we needed to counter guys like Gayle, Mendis and Sangakkara. I'm still a believer that the finest cricketers in the world are the best, whatever the form of the game, but in T20 the guys who can hit at two runs a ball for a few overs or can come on and immediately take a couple of wickets, these blokes are mood-changers and as such are priceless. Symmo was our man; now that he's gone we have to find a substitute for Australia's future T20 adventures, and find him quickly.

Maybe the most frustrating thing about the impact Symmo's absence had on our results is that in the past we've usually been able to cope when some of our better players have been out of the side. I think quickly of when Shane Warne dropped out of the 2003 World Cup, when I missed the Tests in India in 2004, or when Damien Martyn retired in the middle of the 2006–07 Ashes series. But over the past few days we haven't been good enough to do that. Sure, when you lose someone of his calibre out of your Twenty20 team, it leaves a big hole, but in the days following Symmo's departure I didn't hear any talk about him not being around so I'd like to think it didn't play on the guys' minds. But we missed Symmo's ability to take the short game by the scruff of the neck and change the mood. We tried our best, but that wasn't enough.

Our loss to the West Indies looks bad on paper — by seven wickets with 25 balls to spare — but while I knew we were about

15 or 20 runs short with the bat I still thought we were a chance if we could get past Gayle. However, the Windies' skipper was at his bludgeoning best, taking to Brett Lee with relish and making the end result inevitable. He and his opening partner, Andre Fletcher, blazed at 12 runs an over, and Gayle finished with 83 from 50 balls, with six fours and six sixes. As captain, you feel helpless when a bloke like Gayle is killing everyone, and almost guilty when you ask one of your bowlers to try his best. I wonder how cricket historians will rate Chris Gayle — a very good Test cricketer, terrific in ODIs and exceptional in T20. A fabulous one-day player like Michael Bevan is marked down by the people who try to rate the game's greatest players because he rarely excelled in Tests; but if someone like Gayle is great in one-dayers *and* 20-over games, should that put him ahead of a guy like Justin Langer, for example, who was a great Test batsman but hardly played any one-day cricket?

One of the cricket writers in the *Guardian* said we were 'eviscerated', and while I'm not completely certain what that means it sure sounds right. Bing's first three overs went for 51, 43 of them to Gayle, and one of his sixes was so colossal it landed on the roof of the Bedser Stand, next to the old pavilion. That's no mean feat at a ground as big as The Oval. At the other end, Mitchell Johnson conceded 'only' 19 from his first two overs, and I couldn't help but think back to our poor beginning — which started with an almost comical opening over from Jerome Taylor that included three wides, one a head-high beamer, two wickets (Shane Watson caught at mid-off and me lbw) and no runs off the bat. What makes things worse is that we talked about getting the first over of each innings right, because momentum is so important in these games right from the jump. When Michael Clarke was dismissed in the fourth over we were 3–15 and though Dave Warner pulled the very next ball

Wallybies

I would have been disappointed if the British papers didn't get excited about our quick exit from the World Twenty20, and they didn't let me down. The headline on the *Sun's* website was 'SEE YA, SHEILAS', and the accompanying story by their cricket correspondent John Etheridge began, 'Australia failed their make-or-break exam last night and now we can all merrily mock them for the next month.' Elsewhere, after the Irish knocked out Bangladesh, the paper chortled, 'Even Ireland make the Super 8s but Ricky's boys crashed out as wallybies.'

'What do you call an Aussie at the Twenty20?' asked the *Daily Mirror*. 'A spectator!' it responded excitedly.

The *Daily Express* wondered how we are going to spend our time, and kindly suggested we try the London Eye when we go to the British capital this weekend. After all, the paper continued, 'there is only so much net practice and thumb-twiddling a team can do.' Meanwhile, back at the *Sun*, their writers warmed to the fact we have some spare hours on our hands.

'The Aussies now have two weeks to fill before the Ashes tour begins. So throw another shrimp on the barbie, Ricky!' they giggled.

Based on some of the things written about the English team on my early tours, they were actually being pretty kind to us. I remember in 1997, when our captain Mark Taylor was struggling for runs, they tried to present him with a metre-wide bat. And in 2001, when we were going really well, they changed tack, rated a few of our blokes by their looks instead of their cricket ability and came to the conclusion that Steve Waugh was 'no spring chicken' and that Adam Gilchrist was 'not exactly pin-up material'. Occasionally, the tabloids go too far but often their coverage is good fun, even if there are times when you have to shake your head and wonder if they've been watching the same game you've been playing in.

over mid-wicket for six, we never really recovered. The Windies are usually better when they're in front, and this game was no exception.

After the loss, I was asked about the consequences of us losing our second game to Sri Lanka, and I made the mistake of trying to be funny. 'We'll have two weeks in Leicester if we have an early exit here (and) that won't be good for anybody,' I said, which, of course, didn't go down well with people in the midlands. I hope no offence was taken — I've actually been to Leicester a few times, with a Young Australia team in 1995 and then on the 1997 and 2005 Ashes tours, and I made a hundred the last time we played there — because I actually have no bad memories of the place. It's just that the alternative was still being involved in the World Twenty20, and that's where I'd much rather be.

England came back from their loss to the Dutch to beat Pakistan on the back of a rousing display from a less than fully fit Kevin Pietersen. We needed a similar effort to get past Sri Lanka, but none of us made a decent score against their spinners and then we couldn't dismiss Sangakkara or Tillekaratne Dilshan, who made the two big scores of the match. I was impressed by the way our spinners, Nathan Hauritz and Michael Clarke, tried to keep us in the game, but a few overs before the end I was resigned to the fact we needed a miracle for us to sneak through. It didn't happen. We'd been outplayed two games straight.

At the media conference straight after the Sri Lanka game, the last thing I said was, 'Now we have to move on as quickly as possible and focus on the Ashes.' This all sounded good, but then I realised that our failure to make the second stage had created something of a problem, in that while the guys who won't be involved in the Ashes Tests are leaving, the men who'll be replacing them aren't scheduled to join up with the rest of us until tomorrow week. Ideally, it would be nice to work as a group immediately, and to arrange a practice match of some kind for the coming weekend, but we'll be short of personnel. I know a lot of phone calls are being made, and the likelihood is that we'll be training with a full squad sooner than we'd originally anticipated but whatever happens the key is that we make the most of the next couple of weeks. I'm sure the coach will give us a bit of a flogging, to remind us we've got an urn to retain. We deserve nothing less.

My first reflex is to try to forget about the T20, and focus instead on the positive things we achieved in the recent Tests against South Africa. That won't be easy, but as I said to the reporters, 'The excitement and atmosphere for the start of the Ashes is going to be tremendous and if we can get caught up a little bit in that, I'm sure there won't be any negatives from the last few days hanging around.'

As for the tournament itself, already, even though it is not even half over, most people over here are calling it a big success, and every indication is that the buzz that has been created will be sustained all the way to the final at Lord's in 11 days time. Meanwhile, we'll be in Leicester, disappointed that we're no longer involved but working our butts off to get ourselves ready for the Ashes. Maybe the break can work to our advantage.

Monday, June 22

One of the things we often heard or read about in the days after we were knocked out of the World Twenty20 was that the selectors had got the team all wrong. Straight after our loss to Sri Lanka, I read one former Australian player turned commentator who described the squad we chose as 'pretty experienced, conservative'. He then went on to explain how he liked the approach of the Indian and South African selectors, who had chosen teams that were, in his view, specifically designed for T20 because they featured players who had gone well in domestic T20 leagues and the IPL.

Maybe we could have done a few things differently, but what this bloke thought when both India and South Africa were eliminated from the tournament, India after three straight defeats and South Africa following a narrow loss to eventual champions Pakistan in a semi-final, was not recorded. For me, these results (especially India's decline) just demonstrated what I've believed for a while — that in this abbreviated form of the game all the countries are brought closer together, which means that on any given day or night just about any team can beat any other team. Zimbabwe can beat Australia, as happened in 2007; Holland can beat England. It might not always be this way, as teams get more experienced and more scientific in their approach, but for the moment we're all learning as we go.

After Pakistan lost their first match to England, their captain Younis Khan was quoted as saying, 'It will be sad if we don't make it to the Super Eights but it won't be a disaster. Twenty20 cricket is fun cricket. It's more for entertainment even if it is international cricket.' As it turned out, Pakistan didn't just get through to the second stage, they went on to win the final and from what I saw they fully deserved their championship, while the team they beat in the final, Sri Lanka, were responsible for some of the best cricket played in the 16 days from first game to last. The results of all the games played were as follows:

GROUP MATCHES
June 5, at Lord's: **England** 5–162 lost to **Netherlands** 6–163 by four wickets
June 6, at The Oval: **Scotland** 4–89 lost to **New Zealand** 3–90 by seven wickets
June 6, at The Oval: **Australia** 7–169 lost to **West Indies** 3–172 by seven wickets
June 6, at Nottingham: **India** 5–180 defeated **Bangladesh** 8–155 by 25 runs
June 7, at The Oval: **South Africa** 5–211 defeated **Scotland** 81 by 130 runs
June 7, at The Oval: **England** 5–185 defeated **Pakistan** 7–137 by 48 runs
June 8, at Nottingham: **Bangladesh** 8–137 lost to **Ireland** 4–138 by six wickets
June 8, at Nottingham: **Australia** 9–159 lost to **Sri Lanka** 4–160 by six wickets
June 9, at Lord's: **Pakistan** 5–175 defeated **Netherlands** 93 by 82 runs
June 9, at Lord's: **South Africa** 7–128 defeated **New Zealand** 5–127 by one run
June 10, at Nottingham: **Sri Lanka** 5–192 defeated **West Indies** 5–177 by 15 runs
June 10, at Nottingham: **Ireland** 8–112 lost to **India** 2–113 by eight wickets

SUPER EIGHTS
June 11, at Nottingham: **New Zealand** 5–198 defeated **Ireland** 115 by 83 runs
June 11, at Nottingham: **England** 111 lost to **South Africa** 3–114 by seven wickets
June 12, at Lord's: **Sri Lanka** 7–150 defeated **Pakistan** 9–131 by 19 runs
June 12, at Lord's: **India** 7–153 lost to **West Indies** 3–156 by seven wickets
June 13, at The Oval: **South Africa** 7–183 defeated **West Indies** 9–163 by 20 runs
June 13, at The Oval: **New Zealand** 99 lost to **Pakistan** 4–100 by six wickets
June 14, at Lord's: **Sri Lanka** 9–144 defeated **Ireland** 7–135 by nine runs
June 14, at Lord's: **England** 7–153 defeated **India** 5–150 by three runs
June 15, at The Oval: **Pakistan** 5–159 defeated **Ireland** 9–120 by 39 runs
June 15, at The Oval: **England** 6–161 lost to **West Indies** 5–82 by five wickets (D/L method)
June 16, at Nottingham: **Sri Lanka** 5–158 defeated **New Zealand** 110 by 48 runs
June 16, at Nottingham: **South Africa** 5–130 defeated **India** 8–118 by 12 runs

SEMI-FINALS
June 18, at Nottingham: **Pakistan** 4–149 defeated **South Africa** 5–142 by seven runs
June 19, at The Oval: **Sri Lanka** 5–158 defeated **West Indies** 101 by 57 runs

FINAL
June 21, at Lord's: **Sri Lanka** 6–138 lost to **Pakistan** 2–139 by eight wickets

✳✳✳

THIS WILL BE MY fourth Ashes tour, which is something that hasn't been done very often and reflects the fact that I've been around for quite a while now. It's possible none of the English players we'll be facing in this fast-approaching series appeared in an Ashes Test before 2005, so hopefully I'll be able to use my experience in Australia-England cricket, which dates back to 1997, to our advantage.

Before the first World War, when Australian teams often toured England every three years, a number of cricketers made four or more tours, and one — Syd Gregory, the captain of the 1912 side — actually made eight. Among these players are some of the most famous names in early Australian cricket history, such as Jack Blackham, Joe Darling, George Giffen, Clem Hill, Billy Murdoch, MA Noble, Fred Spofforth, Hugh Trumble and the legendary Victor Trumper.

Three champions whose careers started before World War I and continued afterwards — Warwick Armstrong, Warren Bardsley and Charlie Macartney — also experienced four tours, but from then until Shane Warne went on his fourth Ashes tour in 2005, the only Australians to make four tours were Bert Oldfield (1921–1934), Sir Donald Bradman (1930–1948), Neil Harvey (1948–1961), Doug Walters (1968–1977), Rod Marsh (1972–1981), Allan Border (1981–1993) and Steve Waugh (1989–2001). So I'm in elite company, and very proud of my achievement …

2009 ICC World Twenty20 Tables

GROUP A

Teams	T20s	Won	Lost	Tied	NR	Points	Run-rate
India	2	2	0	0	0	4	1.23
Ireland	2	1	1	0	0	2	-0.16
Bangladesh	2	0	2	0	0	0	-1.00

GROUP B

Teams	T20s	Won	Lost	Tied	NR	Points	Run-rate
England	2	1	1	0	0	2	1.18
Pakistan	2	1	1	0	0	2	0.85
Netherlands	2	1	1	0	0	2	-2.03

GROUP C

Teams	T20s	Won	Lost	Tied	NR	Points	Run-rate
Sri Lanka	2	2	0	0	0	4	0.63
West Indies	2	1	1	0	0	2	0.72
Australia	2	0	2	0	0	0	-1.33

GROUP D

Teams	T20s	Won	Lost	Tied	NR	Points	Run-rate
South Africa	2	2	0	0	0	4	3.28
New Zealand	2	1	1	0	0	2	0.31
Scotland	2	0	2	0	0	0	-5.28

GROUP E (Super Eights)

Teams	T20s	Won	Lost	Tied	NR	Points	Run-rate
South Africa	3	3	0	0	0	6	0.79
West Indies	3	2	1	0	0	4	0.06
England	3	1	2	0	0	2	-0.41
India	3	0	3	0	0	0	-0.47

GROUP F (Super Eights)

Teams	T20s	Won	Lost	Tied	NR	Points	Run-rate
Sri Lanka	3	3	0	0	0	6	1.27
Pakistan	3	2	1	0	0	4	1.19
New Zealand	3	1	2	0	0	2	-0.23
Ireland	3	0	3	0	0	0	-2.18

Notes

1. NR indicates No Result; Run-rate is the net run-rate, calculated by dividing a team's achieved run-rate by the run-rate it conceded, the higher the net run-rate the better.
2. The top two teams in each group during the first stage qualified for the Super Eights; the top two teams in Groups E and F qualified for the semi-finals.

PART EIGHT

THE ASHES 2009

Tuesday, June 23

You could almost feel the country move into Ashes mode yesterday, following the conclusion of the World Twenty20. Suddenly, we're the centre of attention again when it comes to matters cricket, and while I think I would have found that a bit wearing if it had happened straight after our T20 losses to the West Indies and Sri Lanka, now I don't mind at all. I feel like the tour has commenced again after a false start, and we're eagerly counting the days to the first Test. Right at the moment, it's 16 days to go.

Our first tour match, against Sussex at Hove, commences tomorrow. It's 12-a-side, a concession we sought so we could give an extra player a chance to get some match time. As far as the likely makeup of our XI for the first Test is concerned, apart from Mitchell Johnson I don't think any bowler is certain of a starting spot. I feel a certain loyalty to the guys who did so well in South Africa, but at the same time we have two quicks — Brett Lee and Stuart Clark — who are proven Test performers but who were unavailable for that series due to injury. From what I've seen from Bing so far I have to say he's jumping out of his skin, genuinely fired up to have a big tour. Over the past couple of weeks, he has trained harder than I have ever seen him train before, in the nets and at the gym, but it's still important for him, for all our bowlers really, to take whatever opportunities come their way in our next two games. We've read plenty of suggestions that the wicket in

Turning up the 'Heat'

At the *Run Ricky Run* launch back on May 19, I was asked for my thoughts on England captain Andrew Strauss.

'Being captain, as we all know the Australian team tries to target the captain a little bit and put the captain of opposition teams under a bit more pressure,' I replied. 'If you can do that, you can generally take another couple of the guys down with him.

'That is what we'll be trying to do. We had the better of him out here in Australia last time, we had him under a lot of pressure here and it is important that we start the series off the same way over there.

'Since he has been captain he has played very, very well; I think he had his best series against the West Indies over there in his first as captain. He has played well and led the team well in these last two matches against the West Indies as well. He is an important player for them.'

That all sounded pretty fair and diplomatic, I thought to myself. It was true that Strauss had performed very well in England's two recent Test victories over the Windies, at Lord's and in Durham, and it was also natural that we'd be paying him a lot of attention, in the way we've always focused on our opponents' key players, especially their leader. I didn't realise, though, until I picked up the next day's paper that I had, in the words of one reporter, 'turned the heat up' on the England captain and 'publicly dared rival skipper Andrew Strauss to stand up to an onslaught of pressure coming his way'. I had, according to this writer, 'begun a merciless psychological campaign'.

And it was still six weeks until the first Test.

Cardiff will be a turner, and if it is Nathan Hauritz will play, a contrast with South Africa where Marcus North was our frontline spinner in the two Tests that we won. With Shane Watson struggling with a knee injury, I think the top six is almost certainly going to be Katich, Hughes, Ponting, Hussey, Clarke and North. Brad Haddin will be the keeper.

I think Watto's knee will be okay, but we did have a brief chat about it this afternoon, about whether we should get someone else into our squad as cover. He's missed two days of training, and Alex Kountouris has organised to get some scans done on the knee, just to be sure there's no major damage. I'd say he's going to be right, but if he's out for a while longer we probably do need an extra bat, because as things stand at the moment Shane is our only 'spare' batter.

We're hopeful the cricket we play before the series opener will provide a good guide to where our pace bowlers are at. All the reports are that Brett went pretty well in the IPL, and while I'm yet to be convinced that Twenty20 cricket is an adequate measure for Test matches, Bing didn't take 300-plus Test wickets by accident. As for Stuey Clark, I've thought since just about the first time I saw him bowl that he'd be a beauty in English conditions and his record in county cricket supports that theory. A little part of me would like to play four quicks, but then over-rates might become an issue; and I'm a big fan of having a balanced attack and if Cardiff is going to turn we'd be crazy to leave Horrie out.

It's funny how we keep hearing about the big advantage England have in the spin-bowling department. I'm not sure I agree with that. Apparently, they're thinking of using both the off-spinner, Graeme Swann, and the left-armer, Monty Panesar, though I reckon they could only do that if they have Andrew Flintoff fit and batting at No. 6. Freddie has said publicly he'll be right to play, and we've heard nothing to refute that. It is true that we don't have

Shane Warne any more, but from what I've heard about and seen of Swann, I think he and Horrie are pretty similar, and beyond that I reckon our 'part-timers' — Clarke, North and Katich — can all do a job for us. As I responded to one media enquiry a few days ago: 'Are England more of a (spinning) threat this time? I suppose they had (Ashley) Giles last time, so maybe they are.'

It's amazing how people like to denigrate our bowling attack, keep harping on the fact we've got no McGrath or Warne, but I think, as a group, from first man to fifth, this is the best group of fast men I've toured with. And Horrie will surprise people, I'm sure of that. I like the way he's improved as he's become more settled in the squad, and while we haven't had a lot of success in ODIs or T20s in recent months, he's never let us down while bowling some economical spells. It's true, he's not a big wicket-taker — he's never taken more than four wickets in a first-class innings, never more than six in a first-class match — but I think that's become a mental hurdle for him. Once he does nab a five-for, a bit like a batter who takes ages to get his first hundred, I reckon there will be a few more for him just around the corner.

I also feel more comfortable having Troy Cooley sitting in our dressing room, instead of where he was four years ago, working with the English. There is no doubt the English bowlers were more proficient at reverse swing in '05 than we were, but I doubt that will be the case this time. I believe we can match anyone when the ball is swinging these days, whether batting or bowling. Look at the recent Tests in Johannesburg and Durban, when the ball swung and we outplayed the South Africans.

***

WE WERE REALLY HAPPY with the way the people in Leicester looked after us. The practice wickets at Leicestershire's home

Out of Form?

I could sense after the World Twenty20 that Mike Hussey's form was going to come under scrutiny in the lead-up to the first Test. Huss's Test batting average has 'slumped' to the mid 50s after the games against South Africa, and he hasn't scored a lot of runs in ODIs or T20 games of late, but I'm not too concerned.

As often as not, when you're batting in the middle order in the shorter forms of the game you can be on something of a hiding to nothing — you don't always get a chance to build an innings and you've often got to swing the bat and suffer a few 'cheap' outs for the team, which means the stats mightn't reflect the fact that you've done a good job. Take, for example, the World T20 game against the West Indies, when he came in at No. 7 and hit 28 not out from 15 balls — that's not a big enough knock to prove you're back in form or pump your average up, but it's still a pretty fair effort. We still all know how good a player Huss is and has been for Australia over the past few years and I'm confident he'll play an important part during our Test campaign.

The thing I like most about Huss is that no one works harder on their game. There's absolutely no doubt he'll be giving himself every opportunity to enjoy a productive Ashes series.

ground of Grace Road are outstanding, and there was no shortage of willing locals eager to bowl at us in the nets or to help us get to know the place. Our training was pretty intense, a lot of physical work, but at other times I managed to enjoy a round or two of golf, while a few of the lads went to the races. All in all, we had a good time until we had to leave last Tuesday, to join up with the 'Test-only' guys — Stuart Clark, Phillip Hughes,

Simon Katich, Andrew McDonald, Marcus North and Graham Manou — in London ahead of our tour matches against Sussex at Hove and then the 'England Lions' (essentially an England A team) at Worcester.

Even though we weren't the centre of attention, just about every day in Leicester it seemed as if there was news breaking about the upcoming series. One day, Kevin Pietersen's nagging Achilles tendon injury was the main story; the next, it was how much the Cardiff pitch was going to turn and how the groundsman there was advising the local selectors to choose two spinners; then Shane Warne was sledging Ravi Bopara, who after his three hundreds against the West Indies will most likely be batting three for England during the Ashes series. 'I think he's got all the talent in the world but I just don't think he's got the temperament,' Warney was quoted as saying of Bopara. 'He can be put off his game too easily, and he's too worried about how he looks. Let's hope England aren't relying on Bopara because they could be in trouble.' Then, yesterday, the day after the World T20 final, came the biggest story to date so far as the home team is concerned, when Michael Vaughan and Steve Harmison were left out of England's Ashes squad.

It wouldn't have surprised me if Vaughan and Harmison had been included. A couple of months ago, I thought they were certainties, but my gut feeling changed after we arrived in the UK, as people kept telling me that most likely they'd stick with the players who thrashed the West Indies in a two-Test series last month. And that's what has happened. The England selectors have named 16 players for a training camp they'll apparently be holding next weekend, and their side for the first Test will be chosen from that group, which doesn't feature their former captain or former No. 1 fast bowler. This doesn't mean we won't be seeing either man during the series — Harmison has been included in the England Lions team that we'll meet at Worcester — but that scenario has got to be less likely than we'd thought before this squad was announced.

Frankly, I'm happy the Poms have gone this way — even though he's battled injury and hasn't scored a lot of runs of late, I've still got a lot of respect for Vaughan's ability and his cricket nous, while Harmison is a bowler who can have a real impact if he's in form, and I reckon their team would look stronger if they were included. I don't want to denigrate the blokes who've been picked ahead of him, especially the quicks, but Harmy is the sort of bowler we'd talk about more in pre-game meetings. I still have vivid memories of his opening spell in the 2005 series, most notably that riser that speared through the grille of my helmet and cut me on the cheek. There was a stage three or four years back when he was just about the best fast bowler in the world.

I know, though, that there is no point me buying into the media debate about who the Poms have picked and who they've left out, and they did go very well in their two recent home Tests against the West Indies without either Vaughan or Harmison, so maybe they know what they're doing. I know that if I start saying who should or shouldn't have been included, there's a good chance I'll be revving up the blokes who have been chosen, the players we'll be facing. And I don't want to be giving either Vaughan or Harmison too many big wraps either, in case we come up against them later in the series. So I played a straight bat when I was asked for a reaction.

'I think it (the England squad) pretty much picked itself,' I said flatly.

Their full squad is: Andrew Strauss (Middlesex, captain), Jimmy Anderson (Lancashire), Ian Bell (Warwickshire), Ravi Bopara (Essex), Tim Bresnan (Yorkshire), Stuart Broad (Nottinghamshire), Paul Collingwood (Durham), Alastair Cook

The Dukes

One advantage that came from our extra time in Leicester is that it gave our bowling coach, Troy Cooley, an earlier-than-expected chance to introduce our bowlers to the red Duke cricket balls we'll be using during the Test matches. The Dukes do behave differently to the Kookaburra balls we use at home, in that they have more lacquer on them when they're new, which means they often behave differently early in an innings to later on, as the lacquer gets worn away. That's when the Dukes start swinging.

Guys who've played a lot of county cricket have often seen matches where the ball hasn't started moving about until about the 30-over mark, to the point that some teams don't give their best pace bowlers the new ball, preferring to keep them for when the ball begins to bend. Furthermore, we've all heard stories of county bowlers using mints and the like as they work on the ball between deliveries, to get one side shinier than the other, to help it swing. We don't want to get obsessed by the change of balls (or by any other contrasts between English and Australian conditions), but we do need to know how these balls behave in different circumstances.

I think it's fair to say that in 2005 the Poms had a better understanding than us as to what the Dukes could do, and Troy (who was their bowling coach back then) played a big part in that. We won't be at the same disadvantage this time.

(Essex), Andrew Flintoff (Lancashire), Graham Onions (Durham), Monty Panesar (Northamptonshire), Kevin Pietersen (Hampshire), Matt Prior (Sussex), Adil Rashid (Yorkshire), Ryan Sidebottom (Nottinghamshire) and Graeme Swann (Nottinghamshire).

Meanwhile, our XII for the Sussex game will be as follows: Phillip Hughes, Simon Katich, Ricky Ponting, Mike Hussey,

Michael Clarke, Marcus North, Brad Haddin, Brett Lee, Nathan Hauritz, Peter Siddle, Stuart Clark and Ben Hilfenhaus. After Mitchell Johnson's good performances in the World Twenty20 we're comfortable with resting him, to make sure he's 100 per cent for the back-to-back Cardiff and Lord's Tests, but I'm disappointed we couldn't find room for Andrew McDonald. Ronnie did a great job for us in South Africa, but someone had to miss out and unfortunately he was the guy. I know it's a bit clichéd, but if we can leave a bloke like him out of our strongest side, then I reckon we're going okay.

Sunday, June 28

Tour game, Australians v Sussex, at Hove (June 24–27): Australians 7–349 dec (BJ Haddin 69, NM Hauritz 65*) and 7–379 dec (PJ Hughes 78, RT Ponting 71, MJ Clarke 75*) drew with **Sussex** 311 and 7–373 (MH Yardy 67, CD Hopkinson 115)

***

ON PAPER, THE RESULT against Sussex doesn't look that encouraging, but we've come away from the game feeling pretty good about where we're at with our preparation. In fact, I'd go as far to say that in four Ashes tours, this is the best lead-in we've had to a Test series in England. Part of this is a result of the glorious weather England has enjoyed over the past couple of weeks, which has allowed us to train outdoors day after day; as well it was good straight after our elimination from the World Twenty20 that we weren't the centre of attention, so we could 'get away' and prepare as a group. The days in London after the new guys arrived were terrific, as it usually is when fresh blood comes into a group, and then while we didn't get a result in Hove only Marcus North of our top six didn't spend some quality time in the middle, and as a first-up run from a spell I thought our bowlers went all right.

I also thought most (but not all) of our fielding was encouragingly sharp, and in the second half of our first innings and through the second we put together some decent

What the Ashes Means to Us

One interesting exercise we've started in the past few days, since we came together as a 'Test group' in London, has been to have team members standing up in front of their mates to explain why the Ashes is special to them. I started the process by briefly saying that reputations and legends are generally made during the bigger Test series and there is no bigger series than the Ashes. Since then, a couple of guys have offered their thoughts on this subject each day, and a constant theme has been that memories of past Ashes battles have been recalled. There are more presentations to come and it's become something we're all looking forward to each day. We've already had speeches that were much rehearsed, speeches off-the-cuff, poetry, there's rumours of a soon-to-be-released Powerpoint presentation. There hasn't been a bad one yet.

More than once, a younger guy in the squad has recalled nights as a kid staying up late to watch Ashes Tests on the TV. Only trouble for me is that I was playing in some of those games! A favourite memory for many of us is of Michael Slater making his first Test century at Lord's in 1993, especially how he kissed the Aussie emblem on his helmet when he reached three figures. I have some vague images in the back of my mind of 'Botham's Ashes' in 1981, when I was six years old; stronger recollections of 1985, when Australia lost again; but vivid memories of the 1989 triumph, when Allan Border's team won 4–0 and guys like AB, Terry Alderman, Steve Waugh, David Boon, Mark Taylor, Dean Jones and company were in fantastic form. Mum and Dad could never get me to bed during that series.

I can clearly remember thinking during that (Australian) winter how I'd like to be involved in something similar. Hopefully this time we can inspire the next generation of Aussie cricketers to chase their own Ashes dreams.

partnerships — two areas of our game that we weren't very good at in 2005. Similarly, our training sessions have been much more intense than they were early in '05. The way we prepared for the Tests in South Africa has become our blueprint and so far on this tour we've stuck pretty closely to that script. Right at the moment, there'll be no excuses if we're not fully primed for the first Test when it begins in Cardiff in 10 days time.

Lord Sheffield's Shield

Our game in Hove drew good crowds and during the match the fans had a chance to take in an exhibition that is celebrating the links between Sussex and Australia, with the No. 1 attraction being the Sheffield Shield, Australian domestic cricket's biggest prize, which has been flown over from Australia. Apparently, it is only the second time the Shield has left Australia since it was first played for in 1892, to be fought for at that time by New South Wales, Victoria and South Australia, and later by Queensland, Western Australia and Tasmania, too.

Later in the summer the Shield will be on display at Lord's, and today it was at Sheffield Park, the site of the third Earl of Sheffield's old property in East Sussex, where a game between 'Old England' and 'Old Australia' was played to commemorate the Earl's memory. Though I wouldn't call myself a huge student of cricket history, I always enjoy seeing the game's early heroes being celebrated, and in this instance I liked the fact that while the Shield was originally created using a £150 donation from Lord Sheffield, for this trip it's insured for exactly 1000 times that amount. That level of inflation suggests that the administrators were right on the money when they introduced the Shield to Australian cricket all those years ago.

The biggest glitch on our fielding effort against Sussex came on the last day, when their century–maker, Carl Hopkinson, was on 69 and facing Nathan Hauritz. Hopkinson went to sweep, but only succeeded in top-edging a gentle catch in my direction at mid-wicket. It was one those ones that is usually easier to catch than drop, but down it went, to the delight of the locals who gave me the razzing I fully deserved. I felt so sorry for Horrie, who needed a couple of wickets to boost his confidence a little. He didn't need me to let him down.

There were some other downsides in our performance, primarily the number of no-balls we bowled during the game and the way our top order struggled on the opening day. Phillip Hughes's first appearance as an Aussie cricketer in England was brief but entertaining, as he immediately belted three fours to the point boundary but then had his middle stump knocked out of the ground by the spectacularly named Pepler Sacto Emiano Sandri, who we learned later is a 26-year-old South African who travels on an Italian passport and who was making his Sussex debut. I was caught behind for only 8, but then Mike Hussey and Simon Katich got us back on track until we lost three wickets for the addition of a solitary run. After that, though, the game settled down on a good batting wicket, with Brad Haddin batting particularly well on the first afternoon and a few of us getting some quality time in the middle during our second innings.

Brett Lee and Pete Siddle were the pick of our bowlers. Bing struggled a bit early, as he seemed a bit put off by the slope of the ground, which is considerable from one sightscreen to the other, and which saw him bowl four no-balls in his first five overs. However, when I switched him to the other end, uphill if you like, he bowled much better and quickly got into a groove. Sidds pretty much locked up his place in our first Test line-up, while

Stuey Clark also had his moments, taking three wickets in Sussex's first innings and hitting their No. 7, Andrew Hodd, on the throat. Off the field, though, we learned that Shane Watson's 'knee' injury is actual a minor strain of one of his quadriceps muscles, and while Alex Kountouris is confident the injury will be right in a few days there is now no chance of Watto playing in the first Test.

Late today I started getting calls seeking comment on Michael Vaughan's impending retirement. It seems he's going to make an announcement in regards to his future during the week, maybe as early as Tuesday. If the reports are right, it'll be a shame he won't be playing against us — you always like to test yourself against the toughest opposition and at his best Vaughan was as tough and smart as they come.

Tuesday, June 30

NO SOONER HAD WE arrived in Worcester and the run of good weather broke, which meant that Shane Watson was unable to enjoy what would have been his first net session since he hurt his leg. We already knew he wasn't going to be available for the game against England Lions, which starts here tomorrow, but it still would have been nice to see him in action, to get a handle on exactly where his recovery is at.

On the climate front, it was kind of funny seeing some drizzle after all the sunny days. Things had been so 'brutal' in Hove the ground announcer was even telling the fans to make sure they drank plenty of fluids, so they didn't melt in the 23-degree heat! We all had a bit of a chuckle at that one.

With our batting line-up pretty much sorted for the first Test, much of the scrutiny in this upcoming encounter will fall on the guys fighting it out for the remaining bowling positions. Much of the advanced info we'd been getting about the Sophia Gardens ground at Cardiff was that it will turn, or at least that it won't suit the quicks too much, so on that basis we've been thinking that Nathan Hauritz is a big chance to play. However, I was handed a bunch of statistics last night about games played there this season and last, and they showed that the spinners actually haven't had that much success there in first-class matches. What to do? The race for the 'final' pace bowling spot behind Mitch and Sidds is wide open, and a compelling performance from Brett Lee or

Stuart Clark in tomorrow's game might be enough to get them into the first Test. That said, we still have strong memories of the way Ben Hilfenhaus bowled in South Africa, and while I've had any number of people telling me how well the English conditions will suit Sarf, I'm confident Hilfy will enjoy them, too.

Maybe we should play four quicks. Should we go back to the formula from South Africa, where Andrew McDonald batted at No. 8 and Marcus North bowled a few overs? All the debate about what Cardiff will or won't do is really confusing the issue. It's been renowned as one of the driest wickets in Britain, and much has been made of the fact that the wicket there turned a lot

In the Trenches

In 2001, the Australian team visited Gallipoli on the way to England for that year's Ashes tour. Four years later, we travelled to Villers-Bretonneux in northern France, to see where some of the worst battles of World War I were fought and to honour the soldiers who lost their lives there. This time, there was no such journey on our itinerary, but I did see where the members of the England squad have just returned from a trip to Ypres in Belgium, where they honoured the men who lost their lives in the trenches there during the Great War.

It was a little weird seeing the English players mimicking what we had done on past tours, but I know from our experiences that such visits are extraordinarily moving, a real case of putting things in perspective, so I would never knock them for doing so. Unfortunately, they hit a bit of a hurdle when Andrew Flintoff missed the team bus for some reason and he has subsequently been reprimanded, but I doubt even the negative press that comes from that will diminish the value of the exercise for the remainder of their squad.

during a 50-over match between Glamorgan and Essex in May, to the point that the ECB penalised Glamorgan for staging that game on a sub-standard pitch. George Sharp was an umpire in that game, and he also officiated in our tour game at Hove. He told me that Danish Kaneria, the Pakistani leggie who plays for Essex, was unplayable at Sophia Gardens. He was, in George's words, 'turning them square'. But maybe, as the county officials argued, that was a one-off. A lot of work was done on the playing surface during the last off-season, a new groundsman was brought in, and I really doubt — especially given this is their first Test match — that they'll produce anything other than a first-class deck. It might be slow, but I really doubt it will turn square. Or will it? They know we haven't got Warney anymore, and whether it's true or not I'm sure they think they've got a big advantage in the spin-bowling department. We're thinking of sending team manager Steve Bernard or maybe Troy Cooley there in the next couple of days to have a look at exactly where the pitch preparation is at, but I think until we all get there next week we've got to keep a reasonably open mind.

At a media conference this afternoon, I sensed that as I gave a series of non-committal responses to questions about our likely first-Test team, many people were sure I was just playing some sort of mind game, but the truth is that right at this moment we're just not sure which way to go. One bloke prefaced his question with the statement, 'With Ben Hilfenhaus ruled out …' which immediately had me thinking to myself, *Where did you get that from?* Right at this moment, Hilfy remains a big chance to make his Ashes debut.

Then, out of the blue, someone asked, 'Ricky, have you ruled out coming back to England in 2013 for a fifth Ashes tour?'

'Mate,' I replied with a bit of a grin, 'I think I'd need a wheelchair if I'm still playing then!'

Sunday, July 5

Tour game, Australians v England Lions, at Worcester (July 1–4):
Australians 358 (SM Katich 95, MEK Hussey 150; SJ Harmison 4–80) and
4–438 dec (MJ North 191*, MJ Clarke 80, MEK Hussey 62) drew with
England Lions 352 (JL Denly 66, SC Moore 120, SM Davies 53, AU Rashid
66; B Lee 6–76) and 4–162

***

FROM OUR PERSPECTIVE, the biggest story to come out of
our tour game against the England Lions was the form of Brett
Lee, who performed beautifully in their first innings and backed
it up with another good display on the final afternoon. The way
he got the Duke ball to reverse swing was magic, and he
outclassed a few of their batters — most notably Ian Bell,
Vikram Solanki and Eoin Morgan — while taking 5–21 from 40
deliveries on day two. Before the contest, we spoke about how
we needed to look after the ball on such a slow wicket so it
would reverse after 30 or 40 overs, and if this match is any guide
we might be getting this aspect of modern cricket right. However,
as quickly as we all got excited by Bing's bowling, we learned
that he has damaged an abdominal muscle and is now 100 to 1
to play in the first Test. While we headed for Cardiff, Bing went
to London to get scans done on the injury, and unless there is a
miracle cure found in the next 48 hours unfortunately he'll be
out of the first Test and maybe the second as well.

Another major talking point to come out of the game just completed was the clash of Steve Harmison, fighting to revive his Test career, and Phillip Hughes, all of 20 years old, seeking to further his already glowing reputation. First ball of the game, Phillip ducked into a bouncer and then, soon after, another vicious delivery speared into the glove and he was caught in the gully. It wasn't quite as dramatic as his first spell in the 2005 series, but Harmison did finish with 1–6 from his first six overs, and he came back later in the innings to claim another three wickets. In the second innings, it was more of the same as the big

Welcome Back, Pigeon

Last Wednesday night, we had a terrific meeting at our hotel in Worcester, where we were joined by Glenn McGrath, who went through how he would be approaching the coming series if he was still playing. Glenn, who is one of a number of prominent past Australian players in England for the start of the Ashes series, had made contact with Troy Cooley to say he was nearby. 'Do you think it would be a good idea for me to come up and say something to the boys?' he asked, and Troy quickly replied, 'When's a good time for you?'

The meeting was basically a get-together for our bowlers, and the great man went through his thoughts about how to bowl to the English batsmen. 'Pigeon' had a fair bit of success against Andrew Strauss, Alastair Cook, Ian Bell, Kevin Pietersen and Andrew Flintoff in 2005 (when England won the two Tests he did not play) and 2006–07, so his advice is always welcome. It's not for me to reveal what Pidge told us, but one thing he did say afterwards was that he really enjoyed getting to experience the team environment again. 'It's all right, though, mate' he added, 'I don't want to play any more.'

quick worked our young opener over, and we all know now that Huey will be copping plenty of short stuff when we get to Cardiff. Most likely, Andrew Flintoff will be leading that charge.

If there were any doubts about what Phillip will be up against, Harmison quickly put them to rest. 'I've seen him on television, he is 20, averaging 60 in Test cricket for Australia. He is no mug,' the fast man said at stumps on day one. 'England have got to be wary of him but if what happened today has unearthed an area where England can bowl at him, then great. If you put the short ball in the right area, he will belt it. But he is susceptible to any ball coming anywhere around his hip and armpit area ... we have got some tall bowlers in the England team and they might target that area.'

Phillip wasn't the only one to struggle with the bat. I managed to score 1 and 15 in our two innings, and on the first day we collapsed from 2–165 (Simon Katich 95) to 6–197 before Mike Hussey and Mitchell Johnson got things back in the order, but in our second dig, Marcus North, Michael Clarke and Huss again all had plenty of time out in the middle, so most of our batters will go into the first Test in pretty good touch. Huss's hundred on the first day was his 50th first-class hundred but his first three-figure score in nine months, and in the second innings he looked very solid as he made 62, his innings only ending when he retired 'hurt' to give Brad Haddin half an hour at the crease.

The bowling, Bing apart, was not quite so productive, though it must be said that the Worcester wicket was very placid. Everyone worked hard, but Joe Denly and Stephen Moore, two guys we most likely won't see during the Tests, batted very well at the start of their first innings and then the match petered out on the final day. There was, though, time for Nathan Hauritz to have Bell caught at short leg, while Stuart Clark sent down eight overs for 11 runs.

The match ended in slightly bizarre circumstances just after 5 o'clock, when umpire Jeff Evans collapsed during the 48th over of the Lions' second innings. It looked ugly for a moment, and first Alex Kountouris and then paramedics and a doctor rushed on to the field, but it turned out that he was suffering from heat stress — more evidence that things are a bit warmer than usual in the UK at present — and was able to get up and walk off the field. My understanding is that he has already made a full recovery. Meanwhile, I was asked if I was comfortable with our preparation, and I said that I was.

'I've been really happy with the way things have gone for the past month,' I said. 'And we got a lot out of this game. Almost everyone did something … except me!'

***

WHILE WE WERE FACING the England Lions at Worcester, over at Edgbaston in Birmingham an XI that is ostensibly the English Test team was playing a three-day match against Warwickshire. I didn't pay too much attention to the action there (leaving that job to others), but I did check out the match scores and saw that Alastair Cook and Ravi Bopara scored hundreds. However Kevin Pietersen was caught at second slip for 1, and apparently didn't look too good when he was out there. Maybe his Achilles tendon is troubling him. The bowlers clearly had a good day, knocking over Warwickshire for just 102, with Jimmy Anderson taking 5–34.

One interested observer at Edgbaston was our former coach John Buchanan, who has taken on some form of consultancy role with the ECB. I find it a bit weird that Buck has chosen to take on this role in an Ashes summer but I understand that he is a professional coach who is always on the lookout for new

Poker Face

It's happened every so often during the first few weeks of this tour. I'll be doing an interview and the subject will turn to spin bowling and how we've struggled a bit in this department ever since Shane Warne retired. There might be a little banter about how you can't replace a legend and then it comes ... *Is there any truth to the rumour that Warne might be getting a late call-up to the Australian team?*

It happened again yesterday while I was being interviewed by Simon Briggs from the *Telegraph*. This time I mentioned that Warney was the guy responsible for giving me my nickname of 'Punter', because I liked the occasional bet on the greyhounds. 'So what of the rumours that England's greatest nemesis could make a last-minute comeback?' Simon enquired.

'Two months ago, I asked Shane whether he could come to a charity function the night before the Lord's Test,' I answered. 'He replied, "I'm part of the world poker tour. I'm not even sure I'll be in London at that time." So if he's playing poker, he's got no chance.'

challenges. Recently, Buck was sacked as coach of my IPL team, the Kolkata Knight Riders, which I thought was a shame but I sensed it was going to happen after two unsuccessful seasons. I'm not sure if Buck's duty statement will extend to a hands-on role with the England Test team, but even if it does, I don't know if there is too much he can tell them about our team that they don't already know. His time as Aussie coach ended two years ago, and much has changed with our set-up since then.

Buck, of course, was somewhat notorious for occasionally slipping books, notes or documents under the doors of his players' hotel rooms, to help with our build-up to a game or series. It might have been a newspaper clipping, a 'secret' dossier on our opponents, or a copy of Sun Tzu's *The Art of War*. Recently I read an interview with our current coach Tim Nielsen, where he was asked what he might push under the door.

'I'm not sure,' Vin responded. 'Maybe the footy scores.'

✳✳✳

SO NOW WE'RE OFF to Cardiff for the first Test. It's a place that holds a special cricket memory for me, going back to my first tour in 1997. I wasn't in the Test team for the first three Tests — Greg Blewett was at No. 3 and Michael Bevan at No. 6, with the Waugh twins in between — but when Bevo struggled against the England pace bowlers, I realised there might be an opening, if only I could make a big score in the tour game versus Glamorgan.

Sure enough, I scored 126 not out, which was enough to get me into the team for the fourth Test at Headingley. And my first innings there remains one of favourite achievements in Ashes cricket. We were 4–50 and in a heap of trouble, but Matthew Elliott played one of the finest knocks I've ever seen, going all the way to 199, and I managed to make my first Test hundred as we went on to win by an innings. Had I not made those runs against Glamorgan I might not have got that opportunity, so I'll always remember the ground at Sophia Gardens in Cardiff with affection. Hopefully, after the Test that starts in just three days time, I'll love it even more.

Tuesday, July 7

Of all the things I still have to do as a cricketer, the ambition that sits at the top of my list is captaining a winning Australian team in a Test series in England. Part of this motivation comes from the fact we lost in 2005; most of it, however, comes back to the simple reality that the Ashes is the ultimate in cricket for me — always has been, always will be. It's a way of thinking that was hammered into me when I was the young bloke in the squad, sharing a dressing room with hardened cricketers such as Mark Taylor and Ian Healy, Steve and Mark Waugh, who loved thrashing the Poms. Ashes glory crowned those guys' careers; nothing else — not even beating the once mighty West Indies in the West Indies — came close.

These days, I'm part of a different squad — 21st century cricketers with iPods, Twitter accounts but the same mindsets we had in the 'good old days'. Even with the rise in our rivalries with India and South Africa, the Ashes remains No. 1 in these young punks' minds. Occasionally, someone will ask me if the Border-Gavaskar Trophy has replaced the Ashes as the biggest prize we play for, but for us it's still not even close. The cricket on the field might be just as competitive, but there is too much history and tradition associated with the Ashes for anything else to rival it. This time, our squad is full of cricketers who are playing their first Test series in England, so it will be a different experience for me — but a special one, especially if we can retain that urn.

Some of the guys weren't even playing first-class cricket when we lost in 2005. Phillip Hughes was still at school. Back in '97, he was all of eight; I was 22, and Ashes tours were different. We arrived in England in mid May and left in late August, having played six Tests and 21 other tour games. In the process, we'd crisscrossed the country, spending many an hour on the team bus, playing cards, watching movies, putting up with Michael Slater's guitar, telling (or, in my case, listening to) stories. They might at times have been long and wearying, but those bus trips were a terrific bonding experience and I treasure the memory of them. It was different on tours to other countries, which were quicker, and more likely to involve hours in airport terminals before short flights from one city to the next, or in the Caribbean from one island to the next. The county grounds offered something different, and the locals are always welcoming and they love their cricket. The history and cricket ambience in England is something you don't experience anywhere else; we don't see as much of it these days because the tour is shorter, but I still love it.

Still, cricket moves very rapidly these days. *Will you miss Warne?* I've been constantly asked since I arrived here. *Will you miss McGrath?* they wonder. *Gilchrist? Hayden? Langer?* To tell you the truth — and I mean no disrespect to those champions — I haven't had time to miss them so far and I doubt that will change before this tour is through. To lead this team on this trip is a special experience; I would dearly love to help guide them to an Ashes triumph in England. And when I look at the team I'm leading I can't help thinking we're being underrated.

For me, the most impressive thing about each man in this group is that they have a determination to do well for themselves and their mates that is as good as I have ever seen. That is an exciting thing for me. And their talent is considerable. Simon Katich has

Amazing

I knew before we had our team meeting this morning that I wanted to make my speech a good one. I really wanted to hammer home the point that legends can be made in Ashes series, and to do that I went back through my Ashes story, from the time when my uncle, Greg Campbell, was selected for the 1989 Ashes tour — I remember getting the word that his touring kit had arrived, so I rushed down to his house and went through that bag, and touched his baggy green cap, his jumper, playing shirts, blazer. It was magic. I got to touch the clothes *and* the baggy green. My Ashes dream got a big kick-a-long that day.

On I went to my first tour in 1997, how we fought back from being 1–0 down after two Tests to win three straight. I remembered Tubby Taylor's 100 at Edgbaston that saved his career, Glenn McGrath's eight-for at Lord's, Steve Waugh's hundreds in each innings at Old Trafford, the celebrations after we retained the Ashes at Nottingham. In 2001, we'd won the series by the third Test, the first time that had been done in 80 years. There was the disappointment of 2005, but also the joy of the 2006–07 clean sweep, especially the comeback in Adelaide when Warney spun us to a famous victory.

I'm not saying by the end I had them eating out of my hand, but I did get very emotional about what the Ashes means to me. I sensed a genuine excitement around the room. I ended by going back just a few weeks, reminding the boys of the work we did in South Africa and the results it brought us — not just the series victory but also the great camaraderie we enjoyed.

'My great hope is that over the next couple of months we can surprise some people,' I concluded. 'That's what I want to see from you guys. I know what you can do. What I want to see from you in the next couple of months are some things that everyone will be amazed by.'

been one of the best openers in the game over the past 12 months, while Phillip Hughes has done things in his short Test career that only very special players can do. The guys in the middle order all have excellent Test batting averages, and if Brad Haddin is not Gilly, he's still a reliable keeper and a No. 7 batsman capable of scoring big hundreds. Mitchell Johnson is one of the best pace bowlers in the world, and left-handed, too, which is a rare combination, while Brett Lee has taken 300 Test wickets, Stuart Clark was man of the series in 2006–07 and Peter Siddle and Ben Hilfenhaus were brilliant in South Africa. It's only in spin bowling that we've declined, but I really feel that statements along such lines are not so much a sledge on Nathan Hauritz as an acknowledgment of Warney's unique ability. Replacing him was always going to be difficult, like finding an alternative to Bradman. Now that these guys have enjoyed a winning experience, as they did in South Africa, I expect them to power on.

***

I'M NOT SURE IF the England XI that opposes us this time is as good as the 2005 side, but we could end up looking at them in a similar light. Inevitably, a lot will depend on Andrew Flintoff, who was the heart and soul of their team four years ago. They will miss Michael Vaughan and Simon Jones, who bowled some important overs of reverse swing, but Kevin Pietersen is a better player than he was then and I think that is true of Andrew Strauss, too. Jimmy Anderson and Paul Collingwood, who we saw in Australia in 2006–07, have become important Test cricketers in the past couple of years, while a group of players we haven't faced — Ravi Bopara, Matt Prior, Stuart Broad, Graeme Swann and Graham Onions — have a chance to start building their Ashes reputations. It is possible that one or more of these 'rookies' could have the same sort of impact on this series that Strauss, Jones and Steve Harmison had in 2005.

From a runs perspective, though, Pietersen holds the key to England's chances. In my *Captain's Diary* for 2006 I wrote that I thought he could develop into the 'next superstar of world cricket'. I guess he hasn't quite reached such heights, but he remains a rare talent and a constant threat when he's out in the middle. His approach to batting is so positive, he can take the game away from you quickly, and he has played well against Australia in the past. He averages 50.49 in all Test cricket, but 53.50 against Australia; not a big difference, I hear you say, but to me it still suggests he is the kind of cricketer who gets up for the big occasion.

There have been times in the past two series when we have attempted to exploit Pietersen's ego, tried to get him to play the big shot at the wrong time, but you have to be careful how you do this sort of thing. He was too good for us at The Oval in '05; we returned the favour more than once in Australia 18 months later. Some guys love to interact with their opponents, and KP is one of those. Say too much, or get into his face at the wrong moment, and he can make you pay. What this underlines for me is that we have to know our opponents' individual personalities, try to discover what makes them tick. Cricket Australia is keen for us to play to the spirit of the game (though they haven't, as some have reported, issued us with a 'no sledging' edict), and so are we, but if we can find a way to get under an opponent's skin without resorting to unfair or unsporting methods of course we will do so. England will try to do the same to us.

***

INITIALLY, IT DID FEEL A bit weird being in Wales for the start of an Ashes series, but we're used to the concept now. The mood here is so positive I'm happy to go with it. But this is a big break in tradition, and while it was never customary for the opening Test to be at Lord's (I'm told the only times Lord's has been the first Test of a five-match or six-match Ashes series was 1977 and 2005), there was something special about the opener being there in '05, and I still wouldn't have minded if that schedule had been repeated this time. At the same time, it is clear that the Welsh have put a lot of work into the staging of tomorrow's Test; the facilities are first-class and while the wicket does look like it'll be a slow one, my first impressions on seeing it are that it's hardly going to be the raging turner some people have predicted. The Test will almost certainly go five days; my fear is that the pitch could be a little too kind for the batsmen, and that we might be going to Lord's for the second Test still tied at 0–0.

I have no doubt they'll play two spinners, we've thought that for a long time, and we are sure to include Nathan Hauritz. The question we have to resolve is which quick to leave out, and our thinking at this stage is we should play Ben Hilfenhaus, mainly because of the contrast he offers to Peter Siddle and Stuart Clark. Ben is more likely to get the ball to swing, especially if the cloud cover of recent days hangs around, while Sidds and Sarf would both be looking for movement off the pitch. Maybe, on this type of deck, they'd be too much of the same thing. Leaving Sarf out for Hilfy will surprise a few people, but I've got a lot of faith in my Tassie team-mate. He won't let anyone down.

We've been happy with the way things have gone over the past few days, even if things were a little difficult yesterday because of the rain. It got very heavy at times, especially in the morning, to the point that when someone asked Pup if he'd seen the pitch our vice-captain responded: 'Mate, we haven't been able to see much at all today.'

We left the ground before the weather improved, but when the rain slowed to a drizzle I was able to marvel at all the changes from the quaint little ground I remember from 1997, even from the slightly updated venue where we were beaten by Bangladesh in a ODI in 2005. My understanding is that all up the renovations have cost something like £14 or £15 million and most of the work has been done in the past 18 months. Today, the sky was much clearer and the ground and pitch seem to be drying quickly; unless there's more rain — and none is forecast — I don't think there'll be a lot of moisture in the Test strip on day one. For tomorrow, the pre-match festivities will have a definite Welsh feel, with Katherine Jenkins, a popular mezzo-soprano from Neath, singing the Welsh national anthem, *Hen Wlad Fy Nhadau* ('Land of My Fathers'), followed by *Advance Australia Fair, God Save the Queen* and *Jerusalem*. (For those that don't know, a mezzo-soprano is 'a type of a classical female singing voice whose range lies between the soprano and the contralto singing voices, usually extending from the A below middle C to the A two octaves above' — I looked it up on *Wikipedia*.) It's funny talking to the locals — they're all very keen to tell you they're supporting England but at the same time they never stop saying that they're *really* Welsh. The flags fluttering at the stadium reflect this mixed loyalty. Most of them look pretty Welsh to me, with many a scarlet dragon to be seen, but it's the Flag of St George that flies from the main pavilion.

There'll definitely be a full house on all five days, I like the atmosphere that keeps building, and it sure feels like an Ashes series is about to begin. We're really looking forward to tomorrow, and I'll be going to bed tonight dreaming of Andrew Strauss tossing that coin ... me calling 'heads' as usual ... and it lands our way. That, and a big contribution from the Aussie No. 3, would be the ideal start.

Monday, July 13

FIRST ASHES TEST
England v Australia at Cardiff (July 8–12): England 435 (KP Pietersen 69, PD Collingwood 64, MJ Prior 56) and 9–252 (PD Collingwood 74) drew with **Australia** 6–674 dec (SM Katich 122, RT Ponting 150, MJ Clarke 83, MJ North 125*, BJ Haddin 121)

***

THIS WAS ONE OF those games where, at the end of it, you're not quite sure what to think. We could so easily have won, and given that on the final day England slumped to 5–70 before lunch we probably should have, but the wicket was flat and their lower order resisted very well.

I prefer to think about the fact that, having lost the toss and then conceded 435, it was a superb effort getting into a position where by early on the fourth day we were the only team that could win. We had good performances from Ben Hilfenhaus and Nathan Hauritz with the ball, and from just about all our batsmen, most notably Simon Katich, Marcus North and Brad Haddin, who all made hundreds, and Michael Clarke, who scored a polished 83. I also managed to make a hundred, and it was one of my most enjoyable, while I took great satisfaction from the way we handled Andrew Flintoff and Kevin Pietersen, their two 'big guns'. If the wicket suited anyone it was the spinners, which was supposed to be England's strong suit, but we

Ashes Experience

We knew when we made the hard call to leave out Stuart Clark that we'd be going into the Test with our leading four bowlers all devoid of Ashes experience. This is a very rare but not unprecedented situation. In 1986–87, Australia's first four bowlers used — Bruce Reid, Merv Hughes, Chris Matthews and Steve Waugh — were all making their Ashes debuts, while that team's spinner, Greg Matthews, had appeared in just one previous Ashes Test. In 1978–79, during the World Series Cricket upheaval, none of the Australian bowlers in that season's first Ashes Test had any Ashes Test experience, though two, Alan Hurst and Jim Higgs, had toured England with Ian Chappell's Australians in 1975.

Before that, you have to go back to the opening Test of 1946–47, the first Ashes Test for more than eight years because of World War II, to find an Australian attack against England that went into the game without any Ashes experience. Before that, it's back to 1884–85, when the entire Australian team from the first Test refused to play in the second because of a dispute over money, and nine Australians made their Ashes debut in the same game. However, in that second Test, one of the two 'experienced' men, Sammy Jones, bowled fifth change and took 4–47 from 25.2 overs. And before that, you have to go back to the very first Test match, at the MCG in March 1877, to find an Australian attack with the same lack of pre-match Australia v England experience as we had for this Test.

I'm never one to underrate experience, but I was happy with the attack we chose for this game because they all do things differently. Hilfy moves the ball away from right-handers, Sidds comes into the right hander more often than not and Mitch is a left-armer. Once we saw how much the wicket had dried out after the rain earlier in the week, we knew we had to play a spinner, so Stuey was the unlucky odd man out.

clearly had the better of the game. We just couldn't get that crucial final wicket.

No one could quibble with the effort we put in on the final day. I thought it was tremendous. But the pitch was a tough one to bowl on. On the previous day, the Saturday, Marcus North and Brad Haddin batted for much of the day without looking like getting out. Twenty-four hours later, we took seven wickets and created plenty of chances — and we're supposed to be a fast-bowling team. I was thrilled by the way our new blokes, especially Hilfy and Horrie, responded to the challenge of Ashes cricket. Before the last day's play, I told Nathan that he didn't need to try to take a wicket with every ball, that he'd find enough 'natural variation' from the wicket. Afterwards, he was a bit dirty on himself that he couldn't get us over the line, but I tried to pick him up. I was very proud of him — he'd bowled 37 overs in the day and given his all.

Unfortunately, it got a little messy in the end, after they took a small lead. We'd bowled enough overs in the day so time mattered, and with just a few minutes to go their last pair, Jimmy Anderson and Monty Panesar, were looking for anything that would save a few seconds. That was okay; I had no problem with their actions. But when someone in the England dressing room sent the 12th man out to change batting gloves two overs in a row and then their physio jogged out even though no one was injured — I thought that was pushing things too far. We complained to the umpires and tried to hurry the intruders off, and in the end it made no difference to the result, but I still think it looked bad — for the people who sent those people out there and for the game itself.

It was a bizarre finish, with the result going to be either an exciting draw, with honours supposedly even, or a win by an innings, which you always think of as an emphatic victory. Yet if you'd walked into Sophia Gardens with just a few overs of the

Test remaining and without knowing the score, you might have sensed that you were about to witness a great English triumph, so raucous and jubilant was the crowd. Good luck to them, it was, as I said, a brave rearguard action on the part of their lower-order, inspired by Paul Collingwood, who defended superbly. But as I sat up last night trying to analyse the game as a whole I kept wondering if the finish might camouflage the reality that we were the dominant team — will England go to Lord's for the second Test as the team on the up ... or will we?

***

COMPARED TO MOST GROUNDS, the dressing rooms at Sophia Gardens in Cardiff are a long way from the actual playing area. They are perched at the top of a grandstand, and to get out onto the field we had to walk down a long hallway, then down

---

Heads or Series Logo?

It wasn't just Cardiff or our bowling attack that was new to Ashes cricket on the first morning of the Test. Rather than using any old piece of local coin for the toss, Andrew Strauss was handed a gold medal specially produced by the Royal Mint, one of a limited edition of 150 we were told, that can be bought for a cool £1595 each (though numbers one through five, the medals to be used for the five tosses in this series, will be auctioned to raise money for charity).

The medal features a batsman who looks like he's playing a defensive shot on one side, and an npower Ashes series logo on the other, which meant that initially we were all a little confused as to what was heads and what was tails. In the end, I called 'heads' as usual, the npower logo came up and Andrew decided to bat. We'd have done the same thing.

Hughes v Flintoff

The duel between Andrew Flintoff and Phillip Hughes was one of the most talked about confrontations of the Test. There's no doubt Flintoff targeted him, tried to intimidate him, went round the wicket and had a word or two to say between deliveries, but I thought Phillip stood up to him pretty well. If the short ones got in at his ribs, Huey looked unconventional and uncomfortable, but if they gave him any width he hit them for four.

Flintoff got him in the end, caught behind for 36 off an inside edge (Freddie's only wicket of the Test), but by then Huey had knocked all the England bowlers bar Flintoff off their stride. It was important innings, because with Simon Katich he established the foundation on which our huge total was built. I know the Poms are looking forward to bowling at him on a quicker wicket, but I reckon he'll keep surprising them.

a few flights of stairs to get to the stand itself, and then another 40 steps or so to get down to the turf. Whether you got up to go out to bat a little earlier than usual, or you got out onto the ground a fraction late, it felt a little rushed, going out to bat. Apparently, I copped a few boos when I finally touched the grass — I guess from those fans who heckle the opposition captain out of habit, as if that will put him off. Once I got out to the middle, though, at 1–60 at the end of the 15th over after Phillip Hughes was dismissed, I quickly felt at home. Flintoff was charging in, but once Kato saw him off we felt as if we were in control, as we gradually built a sizeable partnership. England's big first-innings score suddenly seemed reasonable at best.

This was the second day of the series, but already so much had happened. As expected, England had chosen a team that featured two spinners — Swann and Panesar — a move that looked pretty smart when Andrew Strauss called correctly at the toss and chose to bat. However, Hilfy immediately set about justifying his selection with a debut Ashes spell of 1–10 from seven overs (Alastair Cook, spectacularly caught in the gully by Huss, being his wicket), Sidds hit Ravi Bopara up near the throat with a nasty riser, Mitch knocked over Strauss and Bopara, and England were 3–97 at lunch. In the middle session, Pietersen and Collingwood batted sensibly, and I had fears that Pietersen was going to cut loose, but after tea we bowled really well at him, Horrie in particular, and that set up his peculiar dismissal.

After Collingwood hit Siddle over mid-wicket for four at the start of the 32nd over there wasn't another boundary for 20-plus overs, at which point there were suddenly three in seven balls. When Collingwood was caught behind, the fourth-wicket stand was worth 138 runs, and then straight after Pietersen was dropped at short extra cover. He seemed to be limping a little, and then I brought Horrie back to bowl the 71st over. Matthew Prior was facing, the first three balls were scoreless, he swept a single from the fourth, and then it happened ... Pietersen shaped to sweep even before the bowler let go of the delivery, Horrie aimed it well outside the off-stump, almost a wide, and still Pietersen went through with his shot. He was off-balance as if he was trying to play a snooker shot he couldn't reach without a rest, and the ball took the top edge, brushed his helmet and spooned up aimlessly, an easy catch for Kato at short leg. We could hardly believe it, Cardiff went very, very quiet, and almost immediately I began pondering how the manner of his demise might impact on him and the series: *If the press gets into him, how will he handle it?* At the same time, I can't be too critical of him for the shot. It's the way he plays, a major reason why he has dominated so many international bowling attacks over the past four years.

***

PRIOR AND FLINTOFF BATTED beautifully from this point until close to stumps, but we nailed them both before stumps and I was absolutely thrilled to have them seven down at stumps on such a good wicket. Unfortunately, we didn't come up on the second morning and they smashed another 99 runs for the last three wickets on the second morning. When we batted, Phillip Hughes rushed to 28 from 30 balls, but then came his dramatic skirmish with Flintoff which was thrilling to watch, tough to play. When I made that long walk out there, Freddie was certainly fired up and Kato did me the favour of facing every ball of his next two overs (not through design, I should add, but I wasn't complaining). At this point, Strauss took his spearhead off after a dynamic six-over spell, I settled in against Stuart Broad, Jimmy Anderson and then Graeme Swann, and we were on our way. Neither of their spinners got as much out of the wicket as Horrie had, Flintoff was unable to reproduce the fire of his first spell and through the final session Kato and I were able to enjoy that rare Test-match experience of being in total control.

By stumps the total was 1–249 and we were both past our hundreds, though me only just, as I reached three figures minutes before the close, rushing for a quick single that was tighter than I thought it was going to be when the ball left my bat. I think my celebrations when I made it betrayed the fact that the century meant a lot to me, and there was quite a bit of relief, too, to get there just before the close. I know it is important that I, as captain and No. 3, set an example, and to do so at the earliest opportunity was very satisfying. I learned later that this was the 11th time in my career I'd scored a hundred in the opening Test of a series, the sixth time in the past four years, and the third time against England (after 2002–03 and 2006–07). Further, it was important that we rebounded after what the England

Milestones

The second day was a good one for me statistically, and not just because I managed to score my 38th Test hundred, eighth against England and 18th as Australian captain. I also scored my 11,000th Test run and my 2000th run in Ashes Tests. I'm not sure if any one of these records stands out from another — they've all come about because I've played a lot of Test cricket, and that, really, is what I'm most proud about. I really admire those people in any professional sport who have the durability and persistence to keep going, so the fact I'm still chugging along 13-and-a-half years after I played my first Test, 12 years after my Ashes debut, that's what I think about first when people ask if one landmark is more important to me than any other.

tailenders did at the start of the day, and to have two top-order batters established and past their hundreds going into day three was a good comeback.

While I was very happy with my performance, I'm sure Kato's was even better. One on-drive off Flintoff, not long after I'd joined him in the middle, was a stunning blow — whatever happens between now and the fifth Test, it might stay the shot of the summer. I think the English critics who remembered him from 2005, when he struggled a little, were stunned by the way he batted here, but we who have seen him going so well and so consistently over the past 13 months — a period in which he has now scored six centuries in 15 Tests — weren't surprised at all.

Our first task on the third day was to get through to the second new ball and then, if we managed that, to go on to build a good first-innings lead. Often, if you're well set, the best time to bat is when that second new ball is introduced because the hardness of the ball means that it comes on to and pings off the bat just a little bit better than the old one. On this occasion, though, we lost three wickets in the 15 overs after the new ball was called for — Katich (122) and Hussey (3) to Anderson; me (150) to Panesar. I was really disappointed to get out, just when I was thinking about making a really big score, but Monty deceived me as I tried to cut a ball that was too full and just a little too close to the line of off-stump. At 4–331 just before lunch the game was in the balance once more, but from this point on we made all the running.

***

IT WASN'T A HUNDRED, but Michael Clarke's effort was, in my view, one of his very best. His feet were moving beautifully and it was one of those innings where the bat looked wider than it's supposed to be. At the other end, Marcus North was a terrific ally and it looked for a while, as the weather closed in, that they'd bat through to stumps. Play was suspended at 4.10pm, just after tea, when Pup was on 74 and Northy on 51 and our lead was 28, and it seemed as though that might be it. However, the playing regulations for this tour allow for play under lights, if the umpires think the conditions are okay for the batters, so back out they went two hours later, and Pup was caught behind down the leg-side in the gloom during the six overs of play that were deemed possible. I think the umpires were unlucky, in that the light probably was okay when they went back out, but it deteriorated pretty much as soon as they got out there. I can just imagine them thinking, *Well, we can't go off now seeing as we've just come out … let's give it an over or two.*

Day four was one for the statisticians, as Northy and Brad Haddin both went on to three figures. In doing so, they became the first players to make a century in their debut Ashes Test since Adam Gilchrist and Damien Martyn did so at Edgbaston in 2001. For Marcus, there was the added honour of becoming the first man to score a century on his Ashes debut, having already scored a century on his Test debut in a previous Test. I like Geoff Boycott's comment about him: 'He's been brought up properly.' There's no doubt that as well as being talented, he is a shrewd cricketer endowed with a great deal of commonsense. Hadds is the fourth Aussie keeper to make an Ashes hundred, after Rod Marsh, Ian Healy and Adam Gilchrist, and his 121 is the fourth highest score made by an Australian keeper in an Ashes Tests. He also scored his 1000th Test-match run, while their 200-run partnership is the fifth highest fifth-wicket stand for Australia in Ashes Tests. The stats kept coming. This was the fifth occasion there have been two 200-run partnerships in the same innings of an Ashes Test — three times by England and now two by Australia. Our total of 6–674 declared is the fifth highest in Ashes Tests, and fourth highest by Australia. When the sixth wicket fell at 674, it was the highest score at the fall of the sixth wicket in an Australian innings in Ashes Tests.

Someone told me that back in Australia on SBS's Ashes coverage the former Australian fast bowler Rodney Hogg had confidently stated before the second day's play that 'no one will score a hundred in this Test'. He's a good bloke, Hoggy, but he was a little out on this occasion. This was the first time four Australians have each scored centuries in the same innings of an Ashes Test. It was also the first time five bowlers have each conceded a century in the same innings of an Ashes Test.

And yet, after all this run-scoring, following our declaration England quickly lost two wickets before tea — Cook lbw to Johnson; Bopara lbw to Hilfenhaus. Unfortunately, as had been predicted, the rain returned during the interval and play was eventually abandoned for the day, with the home team 2–20.

***

AS WELL AS HAVING a dramatic and unusual finish, the final day also had a quite bizarre start, when Kevin Pietersen and Mitchell Johnson had a animated conversation after the two came together during warm-ups. It was all pretty trivial, really, though it did reflect the stress levels that were rising through the game, as we built our hefty advantage.

KP is a man under pressure. He was still copping criticism for his errant sweep shot on the first day, while it is clear that he is struggling with that much-discussed Achilles; we've all had injuries at different times and when they prevent you from playing at top-speed you can get cranky and frustrated. His body language throughout the Test has suggested he's not enjoying himself as much as I've seen in the past.

Getting Lucky

There were a number of lbw shouts that were turned down during this Test that we felt at the time were at least very close — and TV replays supported such a view. Two of the most discussed not-out verdicts concerned Kevin Pietersen, who was given the benefit of the doubt when he was on 61 in England's first innings, and Simon Katich, who survived a confident appeal from Graeme Swann when he was 56.

I guess you could say in both cases the batters were a bit fortunate. But only one of the pair took advantage of their luck to go on and make a big total. Pietersen was out for 69, whereas Kato scored 122. It's one of the keys to being a 'lucky' batsman — you need the skill and temperament to take advantage of the days when things are going your way and in this match Kato had these traits working for him big time.

The clash with Mitch occurred after he hit a tennis ball into our group as we were preparing for the start of play. It was one of those things that can happen, and someone told him to be more careful as Mitch just kicked the ball away, figuring that if KP wanted the ball back he could fetch it himself. Pietersen didn't like that, and said so ... Mitch didn't like that attitude and told him so ... and eventually Stuey Clark had to walk over and tell them both to calm down. It was the proverbial storm in a tea cup, though I certainly didn't mind Mitch standing up to him.

There were a couple of other clashes between players when things got tight later in the day, most notably when Stuart Broad and Peter Siddle went shoulder to shoulder just before Broad was dismissed. Again, I had no problem with what transpired, and neither did the umpires. Frankly, I would have been more concerned if there was no emotion on display.

***

WE'D GONE INTO THIS last day expecting it to be a grind, and I was fearful that Pietersen might react to the criticism of his first-innings dismissal by playing like he did at The Oval in 2005, when his 158 saved the Ashes for England. Instead, Ben Hilfenhaus bowled beautifully at him, and in his second over of the day there was an lbw shout, an uppish drive, and then the dangerman was bowled, letting the ball go. His two dismissals in this Test were a crazy contrast — caught trying to sweep a near off-side wide in the first dig; then bowled not offering a shot at all to ball that took his off-stump out. It was beautiful bowling, a real highlight of Hilfy's career so far. Our strategy of placing two men in catching positions on the leg-side — one between short mid-wicket and short mid-on, the other where a left-hand quick would follow through — seemed to have an impact.

Nathan Hauritz took the other two wickets to fall before lunch: Strauss with a quicker one that turned and took the outside edge; Prior with one that bit and jumped and forced a catch to slip. At this point, with a minimum 78.3 overs still to be bowled, I thought we'd win, but the Cardiff pitch was holding up really well and we knew from our innings that it was a beauty to bat on. Collingwood was their salvation; he made his second half-century of the match and fought with the same grit he showed in Adelaide in 2006–07, when he batted for nearly 12 hours over the course of two innings. Broad was lbw to Horrie in the 67th over, putting them seven down with a minimum 38.2 overs still to go, and I still thought we'd be okay. But Graeme Swann gave Collingwood great support as the tension grew.

Almost immediately, Sidds was at the new batter — one short ball crunched into Swann's fingers; another two balls later collected the elbow; the next rattled his helmet. Words sniped between the two, then there was almost a catch, then more chat. Swann decided to attack a little, as if England's best chance was to clear their first-innings deficit, while I took the new ball as soon as we could, in the hope that the quicks would be more dangerous with it in their hands and if that didn't work, Horrie would have a harder ball to work with at the death. Unfortunately, Mitch was way off line in this crucial spell and I had to ask Horrie for one more effort sooner than I'd intended.

With 19 overs to go, Hilfy trapped Swann in front, as the batter went for an ambitious pull shot. Three overs later, there was a big shout for lbw against Collingwood off Horrie, while I grabbed the ball at silly point and appealed for the catch. I've copped a bit of stick for this appeal this morning, but I really thought this was out at the time, the ball going from pitch to pad to bat to me, though I've been told the replays suggest otherwise. First ball of the next over, Collingwood wanted a single to get back on strike, Anderson

'I Caught It, Mate'

There was an episode in the middle session of the final day when things could have got testy, but in my view the moment was handled in the correct manner and no negative headlines were created. Having crashed to 5–70, Paul Collingwood and Andrew Flintoff were mounting the sort of fight that we'd expected from their top order, and they took the score to 102 at lunch and then continued after the interval, resisting stoutly for 11 excellent overs from Hilfenhaus and Johnson.

At this point I brought Hauritz back on and after he bowled a maiden to Flintoff, Collingwood took a single off Mitch and then Flintoff edged a catch to me at second slip. I took it clean, with the ball pressing my fingers against the turf, and immediately claimed the catch. The batsman hesitated, as if he was going to stay, but then he turned and looked at me, as if to ask, *Did you catch it?*

'I caught it, mate,' I quickly affirmed. 'I caught it.'

And with that, Freddie walked off, no fuss no controversy.

---

sent him back and there would have been a run out if the throw had hit the stumps. The crowd was right into the game by this stage, and they kept at it for the rest of the day, adding considerably to the drama. The last hour started with a minimum 15 overs remaining, England 8–225 (trailing by 14), Collingwood on 74, Anderson 2. Then, with them still six runs behind and a minimum 11-and-a-half overs to go, Collingwood tried to push a ball from Sidds through the offside but only succeeded in steering a catch into the gully, where Huss took the chance at the second attempt. Was I pumped when this catch was taken!

Monty Panesar is not a very good batter, but only when he needs to score a run or two. His defence is actually not that bad;

a bit like Glenn McGrath, you have to get him out. Apparently, Collingwood has been helping him, in the same way Steve Waugh used to help Pidge. Straightaway, though, Horrie beat his outside edge twice, and then there was an appeal for lbw, but he survived. It struck me that this was a situation a little like Old Trafford in 2005, when Brett Lee and Pidge had to see out the final four overs to save that day, but whereas England could attack relentlessly back then, we had the added dilemma of them getting closer to making us bat again. That finally happened with seven-and-a-bit overs to go, when Anderson hit two fours in a row, which meant we had to factor in the two overs lost in the change of innings in calculating our fading chances of a win. Countering this negative slightly was the realisation that because we'd been getting through our overs rapidly, we might be able to bowl more than the minimum before stumps.

Sidds bowled the 100th over of the innings without success, Horrie then went for a single off the 101st, and then I made a decision that I know has caused some controversy. England led by seven runs. If we got the last wicket immediately there'd be three, maybe four overs for us to bat, depending on the umpires' calculations of time remaining. I decided to bring on Marcus North, my logic being that he'd get through his overs quicker and maybe, if he did get the last out, give us an extra over to get the runs we'd need. I could have brought Hilfy back, but he'd take more time and time was an issue. Maybe I should have worked on the principle that one good over was better than two or three rushed ones, but if Northy had come through and then we'd won in the extra over I'd have looked very clever. It was, remember, a spinner's wicket. It was one of those calls that is a lot easier with hindsight.

Before Marcus bowled a ball was the moment the England 12th man made his first appearance. He was, as I said at the start of this diary entry, probably entitled to come out with a message as to how long there was to go. Throughout these last few overs the crowd was making an amazing amount of noise, which reached its peak, I think, when Monty hit Northy's second ball for four. The over cost five runs, and then the 12th man came out again with some more batting gloves; then the physio appeared, too, and it got a little embarrassing. It was a pity, in a way, for Anderson and Panesar, because they played really sensibly, and deserved every bit of the applause they got for keeping the series level.

***

ALMOST IMMEDIATELY AFTER THE last ball was bowled I was being interviewed on the field, and the question was quite a reasonable one: 'Did you let England off the hook?'

'I'm not sure if you could say we let them off the hook, because I think we did most things in our power today to get those last five wickets,' I replied, 'There wasn't much in that wicket at all right through the game, and as you saw yesterday we batted pretty much a whole day without even looking like losing a wicket, really. For us to have done what we did today and create a few chances and take the seven wickets that we took was, I think, a reasonable effort from everyone.'

I was then asked about the 12th man and the physio coming out at the end, and part of my reply went this way: 'As far as I'm concerned it was pretty ordinary, actually. They can play whatever way they want to play. We'll do everything we can to play by the rules and the spirit of the game. It's up to them to do what they want to do ... We just had to try and get them off as quick as we could and try to get another couple of overs' play in. That's all we could do.'

Maybe, straight after the battle, I should have deflected this question, not said anything. If some comments I heard last night and read in today's papers are any indication, the fact I used those two phrases — *play by the rules* and *spirit of the game* — is now going to be being used against me, as if I'm some kind of hypocrite. I really don't think that's fair. We wouldn't have done what the England team did in those last few overs, but it seems very few people outside our group believe me.

'The game had been played in pretty good spirits for the last four-and-three-quarter days,' I was then asked. 'You were obviously pretty unhappy with what went on out there?'

'Yeah, I was unhappy with it, but it lasted for a couple of minutes, we got them off the ground. I don't want to make that big a deal about it … it's not the reason we didn't win … It's better off just leaving it at that and moving on.'

Unfortunately, by replying honestly to the earlier question I had, in my critics' eyes, made a big deal out of it. There was no way now the media would just 'leave it at that'.

The subject matter finally changed. 'How do you get them back up again for Thursday after the letdown?' I was asked.

Unbeaten Runs

Although we didn't win the Test, we did extend a couple of significant Ashes sequences. First, by not losing the opening Test of the series, Australia have now not lost the first Test of an Ashes series since 1997, and have only lost once since being beaten at the Gabba in 1986–87.

And secondly, we took our latest undefeated run in Ashes Tests to seven (a draw in the fifth Test of 2005, a clean sweep in 2006–07, and a draw here). This equals the sixth best unbeaten run in Ashes history.

'It depends how you look at it,' I responded. 'I'm not looking at this game as being a letdown. I'm disappointed that we didn't win, but I'm not let down by the way we played over five days. From pretty much the time we started batting I felt there was only one team that was going to be able to win the game and that was us. We had done everything in our power to give ourselves a great chance of winning. With probably an hour left in today's play everybody here probably thought we were going to achieve that. We didn't and I'm disappointed about that. But we've got to look at the positives and the things that we did well in the game, and there are so many of those. So we'll focus on those over the next couple of days and make sure Thursday morning we are spot on and ready to go again and ready to play at this level of cricket again for the next five days.'

And that, really, is the key. We're a young team, learning as we go. Judging by some of the faces I saw in the rooms after the game and in the hotel last night, the guys are finding it difficult to acknowledge just how well we have played. We are naturally disappointed that we didn't win, but as a batting group we delivered and our bowlers toiled away and worked exceptionally hard on a surface that offered them nothing.

We have proved to ourselves as a group that no matter what happens with the toss, or whatever conditions we are confronted with, we can play an exceptionally high standard of Test-match cricket. We have more guys coming out of this game feeling good about themselves than they do. As I keep saying, it's a bit hard working out exactly what to think. We gave ourselves a great opportunity and we cannot let our disappointment choke us for too long. We've got another Test to play in just three days' time and we have to be up for it.

Tuesday, July 14

Aside from the actual cricket, last night was one of the biggest occasions of this entire tour for me, because the Ponting Foundation staged an 'Ashes to Ashes' dinner at the 'Room by the River' on London's South Bank. This was the first major fund-raiser the Foundation has staged, so we were a bit brave taking it offshore, but such is the interest in the Ashes at the moment we were able to sell the night out and raise a considerable amount of money. Rianna and I owe plenty to all the people who worked so hard to help make the night a success, and also to the many prominent figures and former star cricketers who took time out from their own busy schedules to come along and support us.

The night was organised as a celebration of Ashes cricket through the eras, so it was terrific that we had some of the best players of recent times, from the '70s to today, in attendance. A highlight of the night came when I was interviewed on-stage by the great Sir Michael Parkinson. I really enjoyed it and I sensed Michael did, too, while the reaction from the audience was fantastic.

Michael started by asking how I felt about not winning in Cardiff, but it was when we moved on to talk about the Foundation, how Rianna and I are so committed to trying to help kids with cancer and their families, that I sensed that our conversation moved from being just another cricket chat to something much more moving. I talked about how I first came to be involved with childhood cancer charities, the impact our first visit to the Sydney Children's Hospital at Randwick had on us, and how inspiring I have found meeting and getting to know brave young kids and their families while they fight their disease.

The Ultimate Cricket Print

There were some fantastic items up for auction at the Ashes to Ashes dinner, but maybe the pick of them was an original oil painting, measuring 2.15 metres by 1.75 metres, by Sacha Jafri, which he had produced especially for the night as a celebration of Ashes cricket. The painting featured original handprints and signatures from 25 great cricketers and I was given the honour of adding my handprint and autograph on the night. The frame was constructed from 10 original cricket bats hand-signed by 10 champion Ashes batsmen, including — Ian Chappell, Kevin Pietersen, Allan Border, and Andrew Flintoff.

Quoting from the menu card, 'Sacha is a world-renowned artist who has produced commissions for the likes of David Beckham, George Clooney and Bill Gates and accordingly his originals have sold for healthy six-figure sums. However, as a result of having recently been commissioned to paint the official 2012 London Olympics painting and by Barack Obama, Prince Charles and King Abdullah of Jordan to paint the 21 most influential living Muslims (including Muhammad Ali, Zinedine Zidane, Omar Sharif and HH Sheikh Mohammed), Christie's chairman recently stated in the May 2009 edition of the Art Newspaper that "… his work is set to soar".'

On the night, Sacha's Ashes tribute sold for £70,000. Everyone agreed that the successful bidder had got himself or herself a bargain.

I talked about the joy of hearing about instances where the kids have beaten cancer, and the distress we feel when we see children and their families suffer. Throughout our conversation, I was grateful for the shrewd and compassionate way Sir Michael approached his role as interviewer, and at the end I knew that we had struck a chord.

Rianna and I have been determined for quite a while to make the Ponting Foundation as big a success as it can be. But now I feel as if I've been hit with an even stronger resolve to get it right. Not least, I was thinking, *If we can do this in London, what will we be able to do back home?* It was such a magnificent night; I am very, very happy that my name and our Foundation were associated with it.

✳✳✳

AMONG THE AUCTION ITEMS at the dinner were the actual racing gloves Australian Formula One driver Mark Webber wore when he won the German Grand Prix ... two days ago. That's right — the day before the dinner!

For me, the story of how Mark came to be at our function started late last year, after Mark hurt himself while he was competing in his own charity event, the 'Mark Webber Pure Tasmania Challenge', a 250km test involving mountain bikes, kayaks and trekking across Tassie. Unfortunately, he was struck by a car while riding a bike near Port Arthur and badly broke his leg.

After spending some time in Royal Hobart Hospital, Mark moved to Melbourne to continue his rehabilitation. While he was there, I had a discussion with a good friend of mine, Trevor O'Hoy, the former boss of Foster's who is on the board of the Ponting Foundation, and the end result of that was that Trevor approached Mark to see if it would be okay for me to pay him a visit, to give him a kick along as he worked back to full fitness. Trevor has long been one of Mark's biggest supporters.

I'd met Mark a few times in the past, but on this occasion, within a few minutes, I felt I was talking to a kindred spirit. Our lives are similar in many ways — plenty of nights in hotel rooms, often under close scrutiny, subject to heavy criticism when things go wrong, a lot of fitness work and planning to be done away from the cameras to ensure we're ready to perform 'when the flag drops'. Further, I feel as if we both have the same fierce desire to succeed at the highest level, and we both love sport and representing Australia. Mark mightn't have a baggy green cap to wear when he drives for the Red Bull team in F1, but he does race with the Australian coat of arms on the back of his helmet. He is good mates with Brad Haddin, with whom he played some junior cricket when they were growing up together in Queanbeyan, near Canberra, and he retains a real love for our game.

The first time I got to catch up with Mark on this trip was at Worcester, when he came up for a day while we were preparing for our tour game against the England Lions. He was happy to talk to the guys and offer the inside word on why some of the traditionally powerful teams like Ferrari and McLaren are struggling, but there was no way he was going to have a hit against Test fast bowlers — when I lobbed some pads at him and suggested he put them on, he just laughed and threw them right back at me.

Quite a few of our lads were enthusiastic about having an F1 driver in our midst, but I think Mitchell Johnson, Nathan Bracken and Michael Clarke were the three most excited — they're the petrol heads in our group! While Mark was there I asked if he was still a chance to come to the Ashes to Ashes dinner and he said absolutely, and while I was sure he meant it I wouldn't have been surprised if he'd been a last-minute scratching — because it was just 24 hours earlier that he'd scored his Grand Prix victory at the Nurburgring. It was a result that must have meant the absolute world to him, and I would have fully understood if in the excitement he had to cross our function off his list. But sure enough he was there and he stayed for most of the night.

As an indication of just how much Mark loves cricket, I read an interesting quote in the *Telegraph* this morning in a column penned by the great Scottish driver David Coulthard, who is now a consultant for the Red Bull team. 'I'm absolutely thrilled for Mark Webber, whose day would only marginally have improved had his close buddy, Ricky Ponting, got the job done in Cardiff.'

Similarly (I guess), the disappointment I felt when we couldn't close out the first Test was softened slightly when I heard about his triumph, and I was quick to send him a text congratulating him on his achievement. There were stories about (largely on Indian websites) that Mark was crediting his victory on some advice I gave him, which was a nice yarn but it wasn't true.

The extraordinary global popularity of Formula One was illustrated at the dinner by the size of the paparazzi pack that waited outside to get a photograph of the sport's latest champion as he arrived. Mark had already donated an opportunity for two people to be his VIP guests at next year's British Grand Prix and now he handed over his gloves, which was a wonderful gesture. Last I saw him, he was on his way out to do some interviews with breakfast radio shows back in Australia, but before he left I made sure he was still coming to the first day's play at Lord's.

'Mate, I'll be there for sure,' he said. 'I wouldn't miss it.'

Wednesday, July 15

The lead-up to the Lord's Test has been as intense a prelude to a big game as I can remember. My past three days have involved handling the fallout from the first Test, the Ashes to Ashes dinner last Monday, and also — most importantly — trying to get the most out of our preparation for tomorrow's Test match. Lord's is always a special occasion for Aussie cricketers and this year is no different, but the past couple of days have been among the most hectic I can remember. On past Ashes tours, when Lord's was the second Test, there was always at least a week and a half between the first and second Test. In 2005, when Lord's was the opening Test, there were nine days between the last of that summer's ODIs and the start of the Test series. This time, there are just as many people looking for tickets, just as many media and sponsor commitments, but so little time because of the tight itinerary. I know it's always awkward to get schedules right, but because an Ashes Test at Lord's is such a special event I believe the authorities should have re-jigged things so there was more time between the Cardiff Test and this one.

Mind you, back-to-back Tests are hard whatever the circumstances, especially if you haven't done well in the first of them. The feeling I'm getting from the group is that we've gained a lot of confidence from the way we played at Sophia Gardens. There is an eagerness among the group for the Lord's experience to get under way — for all but Kato, Pup and me this is the first

Lord's Hoodoos

Lord's was the fifth Ashes venue, and third in England after The Oval and Old Trafford. The 2009 Test was its 34th Ashes Test — the previous 33, from 1884 to 2005, resulted in 14 Australia wins, five English wins and 14 draws.

That doesn't sound too good for England, but in fact their record in the past 100-plus years has been even worse. The home team went into the '09 Test having not beaten Australia at Lord's since 1934. Their other wins all occurred in the 19th century: in 1884, 1886, 1890 and 1896. Australia's record at Lord's since losing in 1934 is 18 Tests, nine wins, nine draws, no losses. We talked about the record at our team meeting yesterday, and I was left with the strong impression that the pressure of sustaining won't act as a bridle; rather, we take great comfort from the fact Australian teams always go well here and are looking forward to producing more of the same.

We've kept hearing from the commentators about Lord's being a terrible ground for England, but I've also had plenty of interviewers asking me about my ordinary Test record at the ground: four innings, 69 runs, highest score 42, average 17.25. Hopefully, England won't be able to overcome their hoodoo, but I'll be able to do something about mine.

time the guys have played a Test at the 'Home of Cricket'; I could hear the excitement in their voices and see an almost glazed look in their eyes when they first looked out over the ground they've dreamt about playing a Test on since they first thought about playing for Australia.

I haven't had much personal success in two Tests at Lord's, and bar for a hundred I made there against England in 2005 I haven't had much luck in ODIs at the ground either. At the same time, though, I've never been on the losing side in a Test or ODI, so I can't say the place has been bad for me. It is amazing how, when you arrive at a venue where you've enjoyed some success, you immediately feel comfortable, and that's how I felt here. I love the Long Room and the thought of it being packed for the first session on Thursday, the honour boards that list all those who've scored Test hundreds and five-fors ... how I'd love to get my name up there ... the knowledge the Ashes urn itself sits in pride of place in the Lord's Museum and that we'll be playing on a good cricket wicket, the way the field drops so starkly from one side to the other. Even the lunch menus are magnificent.

I think that slope will suit Peter Siddle's bowling best of all. Sidds bowls a bit like Glenn McGrath, who played three Tests at the venue and never failed to take a five-for. I was watching him when we walked onto the ground yesterday, and it seemed like he wanted to mark out his run from the Pavilion end straightaway; he was that keen to go. Before that, though, I actually had to show Sidds how to get out onto the ground. He got lost, went down too many flights of stairs and found himself at the bottom of the pavilion.

'Out through that door, mate,' I said to him. 'Then through that Long Room there.'

I felt like a parent shuffling their kid off to his or her first day at school.

Hilfy should be good from the other end, too, while we're hoping the faster wicket will suit Mitch better than the slow surface at Cardiff. There's no doubt he can bowl better than we saw last week. I think the problem was that he was trying to swing the ball all the time, and he bowled a lot more slower balls than he normally does. Something wasn't quite right. Even so, he still got a couple to jump at their batters, most notably when he surprised Andrew Strauss on the opening day, and our expectation is that'll he'll be better for the run.

We believe England will make just the one change, leaving a spinner out — probably Monty Panesar — and playing a quick, most likely Graham Onions. There is a bit of a push around for Steve Harmison, but even though he had a big impact on the Lord's Test four years ago and he bowled pretty well for the England Lions against us at Worcester I don't think they'll go with him here.

✳✳✳

I'VE COPPED A LOT in the past few days, in the wake of the comments I made straight after the first Test about the way England tried to save time in the final few minutes of the game. It was inevitable that usual suspects like Simon Barnes from *The Times* and the former England coach Duncan Fletcher would be in to me — a few people don't like me and I guess they never will — but I was a bit surprised at how brutal much of the coverage was. I was especially disappointed England coach Andy Flower claimed that 'I'd made a meal of it', when I'm sure I didn't (a point made pretty firmly by ex-England player Derek Pringle, for one, in the *Telegraph*) while a few reporters have used the incident to basically call me a cheat, as if I was the one wasting a few seconds in those dramatic final overs. I did cop a few boos from the spectators in Cardiff; now, it's as if they're geeing up the Lord's crowd to have a go at me.

'I don't think I have ever been pulled up for anything outside of playing within the spirit of the game,' I said yesterday when I was asked about all the criticism in the papers. 'We have always had the finger pointed at us about that sort of stuff, but we never seem to get in too much trouble from the authorities about the spirit of the game.'

One of the Australian reporters asked me what I thought of Fletcher's criticism in particular and I said what I think: 'He is an irrelevant person in my world and probably in the cricketing world right at the moment.'

'Was I that bad after the game?' I asked when the press boys went back to the matter again today. 'That was a one- or two-minute thing that has been made into a five-day thing.'

'But Ricky, that's what your comments encouraged,' one of the journos replied with a bit of a grin. 'They were a gift from heaven.'

'I'll know better next time, won't I?' I responded.

The Honour Boards

A lot is made of the honour boards at Lord's, as they show the names of all the men who have scored a Test century or taken five wickets in a Test innings at the ground. Many of Australia's greatest cricket names are on those boards — batsman such as Victor Trumper, Clem Hill, Don Bradman, Bill Brown, Greg Chappell, Allan Border, Mark Taylor, Steve and Mark Waugh; bowlers such as Clarrie Grimmett, Ray Lindwall, Graham McKenzie, Alan Davidson, Terry Alderman and Jason Gillespie. CTB Turner, better known as 'the Terror', makes it three times (5–27 and 5–36 in 1888, 6–67 in 1893), as does Glenn McGrath (8–38 in 1997, 5–54 in 2001, 5–53 in 2005). Keith Miller is there as a batsman (109 in 1953) and a bowler (5–72 and 5–80 in 1956). Bob Massie is there, too, for taking 8–83 and 8–53 during his remarkable Test debut in 1972.

Another reflection of the inexperience of this Australian squad I'm leading is that none of us have our names up on the boards as yet. Hopefully, that will change in the coming days. In contrast, only Stuart Broad and Graeme Swann among the likely England starting team have *not* made a Test 100 or taken a Test five-for at Lord's.

AT TODAY'S MEDIA CONFERENCE, I was keen to talk up the way we played at Cardiff, how we dominated large chunks of the play. Not surprisingly, Andrew Strauss was also eager to point out the positives England took out of the game.

'As captain, I was very happy with the fight we showed,' he said, when asked about the way England's lower order batted on the last day. 'That is a huge attribute to have as a side, probably more important than any other attribute you have ... we have got a nice little bit of momentum from that fifth day, which we are really looking to build on.'

'It's hard to tell where the momentum is,' was my response when asked the same question. 'It depends, I think, on how many individuals you have who perform well in a game and we had a lot of individuals who performed very well last week. We didn't get the result we were after, but the individuals who came out of the game are very happy with the shape their games are in.'

I was asked if we were likely to bring Stuart Clark in, and while I played a straight bat my expectation is that we'll have an unchanged line-up.

'It looks like a particularly good wicket,' I said. 'It's got a little bit of grass on it but it's hard underneath.'

Inevitably, someone asked me about 2005, this time referring specifically to the dramatic start to that series, when we were bowled out for 190 but then had them 7–97 by stumps.

'We didn't bat very well early on,' I replied, as I quickly thought back to that amazing day. 'Hopefully if we get the chance to bat first again it will be a slightly different result.'

I still have a slight mark on my right cheek as a memento of the fierce riser from Steve Harmison that speared through the grille of my helmet and cut my cheek.

'If you ever look at that scar, Ricky — when you shave, for example — does it have you thinking about last time?' I was asked.

'I guess marks like that are the battle scars you end up with after playing a sport like this for as long as I have,' I replied. 'I've got a few others as well. My fingers are not that straight. It's part of what we do.'

I've said many times that this series is not about revenge for '05, just simply about playing as well as we can. For some of us — especially the guys who played in that series — it's also about a bit of redemption, just as 2006–07 was, but that's all. That's why I played down that memory.

✳✳✳

THERE WERE REPORTS THAT Andrew Flintoff hadn't pulled up too well after Cardiff, that his knee was bugging him, but we would have been astonished if he hadn't been included in their squad for the second Test. What I never saw coming, not at this stage of the series anyway, was that he would announce his retirement from Test cricket, effective straight after the fifth Test.

His decision was confirmed earlier today, after word got out yesterday. We'd actually heard a whisper along these lines during the first Test, but dismissed it as gossip. I guess, when I first heard news of his impending media conference this morning, which meant the story was on the money (you don't call a media conference to announce you're playing on), I was supposed to think about a great player he has been and how much Test cricket will miss him. Both those things are true — he might not quite have the statistics of the greatest all-rounders in the game's history but his dynamic talent and rare ability to change a game have been exceptional — but the first thing I thought was, *I'm not sure that's a smart thing for him to do; it could create a major distraction for the England team.*

I think that response came out of our experience in 2003, when Steve Waugh announced he was going to retire. We still had a series against India to play, but we all felt that our preparation going into each Test was compromised, as the media and the public celebrated Steve's imminent departure. I'm sure our captain had no idea his retirement was going to be treated in this way, as one long farewell, but that's what happened and we were a little below our best for most of that series.

I think the great affection the Australian public has for Steve is pretty similar to how the English feel for Freddie, so I think the comparison is valid. Freddie said today that announcing his impending retirement now is a 'weight off my shoulders', but as his fans crave a grandstand finish the pressure on him and the England team to play out of their skin could build until it becomes hard to handle. All the attention will be on him, and there'll be plenty of people demanding that his team-mates give him an appropriate send-off. We have to be ready for him to produce a big performance here at Lord's; I think after that it'll get harder for him, especially if that knee keeps aching.

I had no problem with discussing this potential problem publicly. 'Knowing the stature he has in the game in England, I can see it turning into that,' I replied when I was asked if his retirement could evolve into a 'circus'. 'You can see that the fans here are very passionate about watching Andrew Flintoff play. If they know that it's his last chance to play here and at Edgbaston and Headingley, then I'm sure there'll be a bit of a circus around it. If that is the case, it will create some distractions, but that's not for us to worry about.'

Flintoff has performed very well against Australia in recent years and in 2005, of course, he was phenomenal. Test cricket will miss him, and I'll miss playing against him. It was fun trying to take the fight to him, though at times we were just trying to resist him. He's such a competitor; we always know we're in a battle when he comes up against us. You could see that early in our first innings in the first Test; when he came on for his opening spell the atmosphere around the ground changed, as if the scale of the fight had gone up a cog or two. In the circumstances, I thought we played him really well — Kato was brilliant — but it was still a strong reminder of what he's still capable of doing, though maybe not for quite as long as he did in his heyday.

I wonder if the sheer pride Freddie takes in his performance was a factor in his decision — the injuries he's suffered in recent years must have shackled him, stopped him from playing at his best, yet at least some of those injuries must have come about because he never wants to ease off, never wants to give anything other than his best. He's always kept charging in, even when his body was telling him to stop. It's so tough in 21st-century cricket for men to be true all-rounders, because of the amount of top-class cricket we are asked to play and the way itineraries are getting more and more compressed. Fans see us playing Test matches on the television but they don't see all the work we put in before the Test begins. A Test is almost an eight-day event for us now: everyone does a lot of work just to get ready, and an all-rounder has to do twice as much as the rest.

For Freddie to survive for so long is in itself a notable effort. That he was the most influential and important player in the English game for a fair part of his career is a fantastic achievement.

Tuesday, July 21

SECOND ASHES TEST
England v Australia at Lord's (July 16–20): England 425 (AJ Strauss 161, AN Cook 95; BW Hilfenhaus 4–103) and 6–311 dec (PD Collingwood 54, MJ Prior 61) defeated **Australia** 215 (MEK Hussey 51; JM Anderson 4–55) and 406 (MJ Clarke 136, BJ Haddin 80, MG Johnson 63; A Flintoff 5–92, GP Swann 4–87) by 115 runs

***

The atmosphere at the start of an Ashes Test at Lord's is one of the most special things in our game. The sense of anticipation around the ground is intense in the period between the toss and the moment the players walk out of the pavilion, through the gate and on to the ground. Before that, though, having lost the toss on this occasion, we had to wait in our dressing room until we got the call, and then we walked down the stairs and through the crowded Long Room, vigorous applause ringing in our ears. No sooner were we on the field, and we could hear behind us a much bigger cheer, which meant the English opening batsmen were walking through the members. I quickly looked around to see Andrew Strauss and Alastair Cook appear, and then we all merged into a huddle, for one last pep talk. Then Ben Hilfenhaus was checking his run, we all moved to the fielding positions we'd discussed before the start, and then there was a hush ... as everyone waited for the first ball.

Part of the Job

I knew I'd get a bit of stick from the locals, but I was surprised by the intensity of some of the heckling, especially as we were at Lord's, which is the one place in England where you don't expect to receive such treatment. I'm now the 'bad guy', which I'll cop — I can remember back in the 1980s in Australia how our home crowds used to get into blokes like Richard Hadlee and Ian Botham, so it would be a bit rich for me to complain about it now.

I suppose I've been targeted for a few reasons. I'm the Australian captain, so it's natural that I'll come under more scrutiny than anyone else in our team. There's also a sense that the papers needed a villain and my comments after Cardiff were enough for me to get the job. Like I said before the Test: 'I'll know better next time.'

A few people seem keen to egg the story on. I couldn't help but notice how on the third day they kept replaying the catch I muffed on the big screen, but 24 hours later there weren't too many replays of Andrew Strauss' controversial slip catch. And it was interesting, in the post-match interviews, how former England cricketers-turned commentators kept asking questions designed to give me the chance to bag the umpires, in the hope that I'd bite and thus create another controversy. There was a touch of smug about that. You can bet they would have objected if a journo had done that to them back in their day, but I guess things are different now.

After five overs, three of them Hilfy maidens, England were 0–7. And from there it all went wrong.

I don't know why we bowled so badly on that first morning. There just wasn't any intensity among the group, we bowled too many bad balls and before we could correct our lethargy Cook and Strauss were away and gone. We talked before the game about how neither of the England opening bats is particularly strong when you force him to hit into the offside off the front foot, and that in those circumstances there is always a chance that we'll find the outside edge. Here, though, especially in the first two hours, we gave them plenty of chances to blaze away off the back foot, and both of them love doing that. Twenty-two fours were hit in the first session as they raced to 0–126, and though we fought back okay to have them 6–364 at stumps, we'd got ourselves in a position where if we made one more mistake the Test was over. Unfortunately, our top-order then buckled against some excellent pace bowling from Jimmy Anderson, and the end result of that was that on days four and five we were chasing more than 500 to win.

Someone will get that many to win a Test one day, but not in this game, and though Michael Clarke and Brad Haddin put on a tremendous show to give us a fleeting chance, Andrew Flintoff came out on the final morning to show again just how good a strike bowler he can be. There have been a couple of times in this series — right at the start at Cardiff and now on the last day here — where he has been as dangerous and magnificent with the ball as at any time in his career. He carried the Lord's crowd with him, the hoodoo is over, and we've now a got a real fight on our hands if we want to retain the Ashes.

***

INEVITABLY, GIVEN THAT THE opening day of an Ashes Test at Lord's is such a great occasion, a lot has been made about our below-par performance at the start, but in my view the batting effort on day two was where we really lost the Test. I think 400 was about par on this course, and even with the partnerships of Strauss and Cook (196, the second highest opening stand in an

Ashes Test at Lord's) and Jimmy Anderson and Graham Onions (47, an English record for the last wicket in an Ashes Test at Lord's), we managed to hold them to 425, which reflects the fact that we didn't bowl too badly for the second half of day one. But in reply, after Simon Katich and Mike Hussey took us from 2–10 to 2–103, we lost six wickets for just 49 runs, which simply isn't good enough. Four of our top six were dismissed for less than five. Yes, they bowled well — Anderson was superb — and maybe we were a little unlucky in that there was cloud cover that made conditions more receptive to traditional swing bowling, but this is Test cricket and we batters can't always expect to have conditions to suit. We needed to fight much harder; instead, wickets fell all too easily. A great tradition for Aussie excellence at Lord's was forgotten.

The only alibi we could have clung to was the umpiring, which provoked a fair amount of comment during the Test, but while it is true that we got the worst of it there is no way we can blame it for such a heavy defeat. We probably would have got closer, though, if a bit of luck had gone our way — in our second innings, three of the first four dismissals had a tinge of controversy about them — replays show that Simon Katich was dismissed by an Andrew Flintoff no-ball, Phillip Hughes fell to a contentious catch and Mike Hussey was ruled out, caught at slip, when the ball diverted off a crack on the wicket, not the outside edge. I must say, that with everything that was made of these and other incidents, I reckon the players on both sides did a fine job just getting on with the game.

I was at the centre of the first of the major umpiring controversies, and involved in two others. Right at the start of our first innings, as we began our pursuit of their 425, I tried to on-drive an inswinger from Jimmy Anderson but struck my boot as the ball clipped my pad. From my pad, the ball deflected to

Playing for Keeps

A few people have asked me why Brad Haddin won't be playing in our next tour game, at Northampton, after his troubles with the gloves in the second Test (he conceded 31 byes over the two English innings), but in my view he should not be marked down too much. Hadds has been magnificent with the bat, and is unlucky not to have two centuries to his name after making a hundred on his Ashes debut at Cardiff and then scoring 80 in the second innings at Lord's.

I think his problems behind the stumps have been caused by the general difficulties keepers can have adapting to the conditions over here. I've found that on many grounds anywhere behind the wicket can be an awkward place to field, whether you're the keeper or in the slips. With certain styles of bowlers, the ball can actually swing after it has pitched than it did before it hit the wicket. Peter Siddle is a good example of this type of bowler — more than once he has had Hadds diving left and right as the ball deviates considerably after it goes past the batsman.

Andrew Strauss at first slip. Anderson's first instinct was to appeal for lbw; those behind the wicket were shouting for the catch; I was sure I hadn't hit it and pretty sure the delivery had been missing my leg-stump, so my reflex was 'not out'.

However, umpire Rudi Koertzen opted to go the third umpire. From that moment, I knew I was in trouble because you can't check lbw decisions in this way. He clearly thought I had hit the ball onto my pad. Simon Katich, who was batting with me, told me he thought Strauss had caught the ball just above the turf, so I found myself in the weird situation of firmly believing that I wasn't out yet knowing that I was almost certainly about to be sent on my way. Sure enough, the verdict came and all I could do was confirm what I already knew.

'How am I out,' I asked Rudi after he signalled I was gone.

'Caught,' he replied.

Some commentators have tried to rationalise the decision by saying that I was lbw anyway — and I know that on the TV coverage the 'Hawkeye' technology gave me out — but at the time I thought the ball was dipping off line and I've yet to see a replay that convinces me otherwise.

The second controversy occurred on day three, as we were

Hilfy and Horrie

In the eyes of some people outside our touring party Ben Hilfenhaus and Nathan Hauritz were surprise selections for the first Test, but not to me, and I think both guys have more than justified their selections over the course of the first two Tests.

Hilfy was excellent in Cardiff and in the process set himself to have a great series, but we always thought he'd be well-suited to English conditions — that's why he was picked in the first place. It is true that Horrie owed his selection in the first Test to the turning wicket, but he did some good things there and backed that performance up with another solid effort at Lord's, dismissing the top three in the England batting order during their second innings. His performance was especially impressive given that he bowled for much of the game with a dislocated finger, after he bent the middle digit of his bowling hand trying to take a hot caught-and-bowled chance off Andrew Strauss on the first day. He showed us a lot of character to come out and want to bowl again.

After two Tests, the two share the title of leading wicket-taker in the series, with nine wickets apiece.

endeavouring to get back into the game. Ravi Bopara chipped a chance towards mid-on, where Nathan Hauritz ran in and appeared to take the good catch at ground level. Horrie had no doubt he'd grabbed it, but Bopara stood his ground and the umps opted to go the third umpire, despite my strong argument that there was no need to do so.

I knew as soon as they went 'upstairs' the batsman was going to get the benefit of the doubt — they always do in these situations because the replays hardly ever unequivocally show that the ball hasn't nipped the grass. When I became a Test captain five years ago, I argued that we should always take the fielder's word for it in these situations, but other international skippers disagree and I've had to cop that. So Bopara survived, but we were left with a sour taste in our mouths, because the batsman and the umpires had essentially said that Horrie's word isn't good enough. I wasn't happy and having Kevin Pietersen offer me his two bob's worth didn't alter my mood.

The next day, as Phillip Hughes was battling to survive against Andrew Flintoff, he edged a low chance to first slip, where Andrew Strauss claimed the catch. I have no doubt that the England captain genuinely believes he caught it, but I was at the non-striker's end and it looked line-ball to me (an opinion reinforced by the replays I watched that night). If they'd accepted Horrie's word the previous day I'd have been happy for the same thing to happen here, but now I expected them to go the video replay again. Instead, the umpires consulted and the man at square-leg, Billy Doctrove, said it had carried. Huey had to go.

Of course, we all want the umpires to be right as often as possible. After that, the thing we crave most is consistency. I cannot understand why the two appeals were treated differently.

***

OF COURSE, THE UMPIRES weren't the only ones making mistakes in this Test match, and none of their errors was as bad as my blooper. I don't know if I have ever felt worse on a cricket field than when I dropped Bopara during England's second innings. The moment came at a time when the mood was getting pretty tense, as the home fans wondered if their team was about to waste a big first-innings lead. The run-rate had slowed. Cook and Strauss, the first innings heroes, had just been dismissed. Then, in the space of an over, I managed to bungle a clear-cut chance to run out Kevin Pietersen and then spill a sitter of a chance at second slip.

The missed run out was a weird one. Pietersen was off his game and it seemed his Achilles was bugging him again. Then he drove at Hilfy, there might have been an inside edge, the ball dribbled off his pad to me in the slip cordon. Crazily, just as I gathered the ball, KP shuffled down the wicket as if there was a chance of a single, so all I had to do was hit the stumps from short range. But the whole situation was so bizarre, I rushed my throw when I should have taken my time and when I really needed my aim to be sweet it was awry. Pietersen returned sheepishly to his crease, and then he tried to pretend it was all part of the plan. You could tell, though, that he knew he'd almost goosed himself. I felt like I'd missed a two-metre putt to win the Open.

First ball of the following over from Peter Siddle, Bopara edged a straightforward catch in my direction. I went to take it with my fingers pointing up, as if it was chest or head high, but the ball died on me and I found myself with my hands in completely the wrong position, fingers at knee level, my wrists angled up as I tried to create a cup for the ball to nestle in. It's very hard to catch a ball in such a situation ... and sure enough it bounced out. There are few bigger joys in cricket than taking a great catch, but at the other end of the spectrum there are few worse feelings than the anguish

A Welcome Guest

Mark Webber did make it to the first day of this Lord's Test, and I was pleased that James Sutherland and Jack Clarke from Cricket Australia were able to arrange a seat for Mark in the Cricket Australia box. Mark came to the cricket on the Tube — no flash hire cars for this modest hero — and later on my manager James Henderson told me about a conversation he and Mark had around tea time.

'James, will they want me in the room,' the German Grand Prix winner said. 'Or will I be in the way?'

Mark was concerned, because we were having a tough day in the field, that the last thing we'd want is for a 'hanger on' to be around looking for cheerful conversation. But James knew that we'd be very happy to see him, that such a visit would be a big boost for us.

So Mark did come in, I was very pleased to see him, and we talked for a long time — a little about the cricket, mostly just two mates yarning about a whole variety of things. And then he bid us farewell, and walked back up to St John's Wood station to catch the Tube home.

that comes with dropping a 'gimme'. I know it sounds a bit clichéd but I really did want the ground at Lord's to swallow me up and get me out of there. The crowd was into me, but that didn't matter. We've all dropped catches … and you never mean to spill them … but you still feel like you've let your mates down when you bugger up a regulation one. The guilt nags at you. It's ugly.

If we'd got both dismissals, England would have been 4–88, a lead of 298. The tension would have tightened right up, we'd have been right back in the game. Instead, Bopara and Pietersen scratched around until after tea, and then after they were dismissed Collingwood, Flintoff and especially Prior put the foot to the floor and rattled along at a run a ball until stumps. They belted 181 runs after tea, in 31.2 overs, and our only bright spot was the dismissal of Prior, run out by a direct hit by Marcus North from the backward-point boundary.

***

Meeting the Queen

One of the traditions of the Lord's Test is that the Queen meets the two sides out on the field, in front of the Pavilion. This year, this occurred on the second day, during the lunch break, and it was my job to introduce our players and support staff to Her Majesty, while Michael Clarke did the same for the Duke of Edinburgh. There are certain protocols you have to stick to, but I tried to be as cheerful as I could. For example, rather than just introduce Simon Katich by name I referred to him as 'one of the real veterans of the team', which got a bit of a laugh from everyone, including Her Majesty. She then stopped and chatted with Kat for a moment.

Much funnier was Michael's effort when he went to introduce our security manager Frank Dimasi to the Duke. In the heat of the moment, Pup just couldn't remember Frank's last name. He was batting at the time and I'm sure he was more focused on the task at hand than these formalities; I must confess I was still stewing at my dismissal and it took a stack of concentration on my part to get to the end of the line.

This isn't the first time this sort of thing has happened. Before the 1999 World Cup final, our captain Steve Waugh had the job of introducing the team to the Duke, but when he went along the line he completely missed Damien Fleming. On the next Ashes tour, two years later, as we were introduced to the Queen at Buckingham Palace, Flem was looking hard at the skipper and kept mouthing his name as Steve approached him.

I WAS INTRIGUED BY some of the criticism of Andrew Strauss for not enforcing the follow on. I would have been delighted if he'd asked us to bat again, as I believe that would have given us a chance to get back into the game. It is very much the modern way not to send a team back in, in part because rates of scoring in Test cricket these days are such that you are usually making this decision on the third day, often, as in this instance, early on the third day. Further, in these days of back-to-back Test matches, you can put a lot of pressure on your bowlers if you ask them to bowl in two innings straight, and thirdly, wickets tend not to deteriorate so much these days, a fact demonstrated by the number of large fourth-innings totals made in 21st-century Tests. Indeed, this Lord's track proved to be another good example of this.

And there might have been a fourth factor in this case: the cloud cover. If it had been cloudy on the third morning, I wondered whether Strauss might have bowled, given how his quicks had moved the ball around on the second day. But the sky was much brighter and by batting again Strauss ensured his batters got the best of the conditions. This, surely, was a sensible move.

Despite all this, there were a number of critics queuing up to have a shot at Strauss, including former England captains such as Mike Brearley, Bob Willis and Ian Botham. Of course, they are entitled to their opinion, but to me it's old-school thinking. I'm not saying that these days you automatically bat again, few things in cricket are ever that clear-cut, but I think your first reflex should always be to send your own opening bats out there. A tougher call for Strauss to make was when to declare his second innings — it says something else about modern cricket and the way pitches hold up nowadays that before play on day four he clearly wasn't sure if a 521-run lead was enough. As we were getting organised to have our team photograph taken before play that morning, the whisper from the home dressing room was that he was going to bat on for a little while, to further extend his advantage, but then a shower of rain blew over Lord's just before the scheduled start of play and he decided to close. When we slumped to 5–128 that decision looked like an inspired one, but Michael Clarke and Brad Haddin started building their big partnership and by stumps on day four we needed another 209 to win, with five wickets still in hand.

Before we started our innings, I told the boys that there was no reason, apart from history, why we couldn't make the runs. The plan, I said, was to break the chase into two days of 250 runs each. Ideally, I would have liked to be only two or three wickets down at stumps, but runs-wise at least we were on track.

Pup batted beautifully. It was one of his very best hundreds, one of those digs special players can produce where they never look like getting out. He was brilliant the way he kept forcing and stroking the ball through the covers, as he raced to 50 from just 58 balls, and though he slowed on his way to 100 he was always in command. With hindsight, it was such a pity that he and Hadds had to come off 12 overs early on the fourth evening, because they'd handled the second new ball with aplomb, making the England quicks look ordinary. They might have knocked another 40 or 50 runs off the target if the weather had been kinder. The contrast with earlier in the game, when Anderson and Flintoff had been so dangerous (Anderson in our first innings; Freddie especially when he charged in at Phillip Hughes in our second), was remarkable. Strauss was so concerned when he took the second new ball he called his men together for a team talk, an action that had me thinking we might really be in with a chance. But it wasn't to be.

✳✳✳

The Missing 'X Factor'

Meanwhile, a lot as had been made of Mitchell Johnson's performance at Lord's, and there's no getting around the fact that he isn't bowling very well. It started when he went for eight runs off his third over of the Test and 11 off his fourth, on the way to conceding 10 fours in the opening session.

Who'd have thought, after all the superb overs Mitch has bowled in international cricket over the past nine months, that the media is suggesting he might be dropped for the third Test. At the start of the series, I thought that he would play a huge part in this series — he was the 'X factor' that would set us apart from our opponents. I still believe that if he gets back to his best we'll win the series, and I was encouraged by the way he improved as the game went on, so there's no way we'll be leaving him out for Edgbaston. One delivery — the inswinger that bowled Matt Prior late on the first day — was a reminder of his great ability. Hopefully, it was a forerunner for the way he'll bowl throughout the rest of the summer.

The thing with Mitch is that his slinging action can work for him or against him. If he's got his rhythm right then he has that element of surprise where he can stun a batter by the surprising pace and lift he generates. But his action is so unusual, if something's out of sync — it might only be a little thing — then it can throw everything out, like a minor mechanical fault can stuff up a finely tuned race car. In my view, the thing we have to do with Mitch is not do too much. He told me that when he was running into bowl at Lord's there were times when he was obsessing about his wrist position and how he had to get his follow-through right. I think I'd rather he was just running in and bowling fast, and letting everything else look after itself.

Most of all, we need him to regain his self belief, get his confidence back. Hopefully we'll see the start of his renaissance at Northampton, and things will get better from there.

BECAUSE OF FREDDIE'S BUNG knee we never quite know these days just how lethal he might be when he begins a spell. He'd been at his fearsome best when he worked Huey over in our second innings, but couldn't get out of second gear later in the day. Then, on the final morning, when England really needed him, he put on a show. The great ones can do that.

First to go was Haddin, without adding to his overnight score, caught by Collingwood in the slip cordon off his fourth ball of the day, from a ball that kicked up off a length to hit the outside edge up near the splice of the bat. With that dismissal, the full house could relax knowing that the unlikely victory was now just about impossible, while Flintoff could deliver what became — for all the good work of Graeme Swann at the other end — a one-man show. Throughout his 10-over spell, easily his longest so far in the series, Freddie's pace never dropped as he found a fire in the wicket that we thought had disappeared. Hauritz was bowled without offering a shot and Sidds knocked over by one that kept a little low, as the local hero completed his first Test five-for in four years, milking each wicket for all it was worth for his subjects in the stands. He was down on one knee after Horrie's wicket, as if he was waiting for a knighthood; maybe he will become 'Sir Fred' if he regains the Ashes.

More than his celebrations or the fans' reactions or the bowling figures, though, it was the menace he brought to his work that stood out for me. No one was safe while he had the ball in his hand and he dominated the morning so considerably it was no surprise he was named man of the match during the post-match party. There's no doubt the passion and excitement he brought to yesterday morning's action played a part in that decision, and no one argued with it, but when I thought about it later it probably wasn't the right call — Andrew Strauss had played magnificently when he batted right through the first day for 161 not out. I'm not saying Freddie wasn't a good choice, but Strauss would have been my pick.

Pup's great innings had come to an end when he was bowled by Swann, which left Mitchell Johnson to swing his way to a half-century and take us to 406, Australia's highest ever fourth-innings total in an Ashes Test. Not that achieving that record was any consolation and all I was left with was the dubious task of getting through the media interviews without creating a headline — a task I managed so effectively I've had some writers commenting on my good sportsmanship in this morning's papers. I sense a few people were a bit unnerved by the scale of the booing that accompanied my walk to the wicket in both innings. When I tried to crack a joke at the post-match presentation the crowd laughed along and they even gave me some applause when I said that the umpiring had been 'irrelevant'. When I commented later that was the first time I'd been cheered by the England supporters for quite a while, no one disagreed with me.

✳✳✳

AS I PONDERED OUR position over coffee this morning I couldn't help thinking that the 10-day break before the third Test will be good for us. The momentum is with England now, and we have to work out a way to get it back. Fortunately, we can step away from the spotlight for a little, and head up to Northampton and focus on getting things back on track. I really think we're in need of some fine-tuning rather than an overhaul, though there is no doubt that for a few of our guys — notably Shane Watson and Stuart Clark — there is the chance in the three-day game against Northants that starts on Friday to really push hard for a place in our XI for the third Test. At least a couple of blokes are under pressure to hold their spots, but that said, I'm not expecting too many changes for Edgbaston.

As I've said many times over the past few months, winning the big moments is the key to us winning Test matches — we showed that when we lost in India, and when we lost to and defeated South Africa — and I think we have the personnel in our squad to achieve that. The crucial times in this Lord's Test were the opening session on day one, when Strauss and Cook won the battle against our bowlers, and then at the start of our first innings, when Anderson was too good for us. That was two strikes against us. And then there was that first hour of day five, when if Pup and Hadds had survived then maybe we could have given 500 a shake.

Instead, Freddie Flintoff delivered strike three and now we find ourselves one-down with three to play.

Tuesday, August 4

Tour game, Australians v Northamptonshire, at Northampton (July 24–26): Australians 8–308 dec (SR Watson 84, MEK Hussey 75) and 3–270 dec (PJ Hughes 68, AB McDonald 75, SR Watson 50, GA Manou 59*) defeated **Northamptonshire** 7–226 dec (AG Wakely 62, MH Wessels 50) and 217 (NJ O'Brien 58; AB McDonald 4–15) by 135 runs

THIRD ASHES TEST
England v Australia at Birmingham (July 30–August 3): Australia 263 (SR Watson 62; JM Anderson 5–80, G Onions 4–58) and 5–375 (SR Watson 53, MEK Hussey 64, MJ Clarke 103*, MJ North 96) drew with **England** 376 (AJ Strauss 69, IR Bell 53, A Flintoff 74, SCJ Broad 55; BW Hilfenhaus 4–109)

✳✳✳

IT'S BEEN EXACTLY TWO weeks since my last diary entry, and in that time we've been through quite a bit — yet the series score remains the same: we're still one-down. Our situation, though, after our draw at Edgbaston, is even more perilous. Just two more Tests to play. As my co-author has revealed to me, there have been only two instances in Ashes history, I've been informed, of a team coming back from being down after three Tests to retain the Ashes, and both those instances occurred in Australia. In 1936–37, Australia trailed 2–0 after two Tests but came back on the back of three big innings from captain Don Bradman to win 3–2. In 1965–66, Bob Simpson's Australians trailed 1–0 after three Tests, but recovered to square the series.

A Fairway From Lord's

The day after the Lord's Test, while some of the lads spent the day playing tourist with their families in and around London, I found myself in Buckinghamshire, at Stoke Park Golf Club, where a number of players who'd been rivals just 24 hours earlier, plus a few former stars such as John Emburey, Jason Gillespie, Dean Jones, Barry Richards and Shane Warne, competed in an event that was tagged the 'Ashes Golf Challenge'. Our host was Sir Michael Parkinson and our aim was to raise awareness and money for a cause close to Sir Michael's heart: the Child Bereavement Charity.

It was good to support such a worthy endeavour, and good, too, to be able to get on such a superb layout and relax a little away from the cricket spotlight. And the Aussies came out on top on this occasion, which didn't make up in any way for the Test result the previous day, but it was nice to win something.

I had first been introduced to Sir Michael and Lady Parkinson during the past Australian summer, when Rianna and I went out to dinner with them and we talked not just about cricket but also about many of the causes that we both believe in. It was then that he agreed to come to the Ashes to Ashes dinner and I committed to this golf event, and I'm glad I did because it turned out to be a terrific day. After the round, we adjourned to the clubhouse, where Sir Michael interviewed Andrew Strauss and me, and I was grateful for the way he didn't talk too gleefully about the previous day's result.

One thing I did notice was just how enthusiastic people were when they walked up to Andrew, Alastair Cook and Jimmy Anderson to congratulate them on the Test win. The Ashes means plenty to a lot of people over here, and while that passion can be a burden if England are struggling, now that they're in front I'm sure it will act as a spur.

I'm being reminded too often at the moment that I'm in with a chance of becoming only the second Australian captain to lose two Ashes series in England, after Billy Murdoch, who lost in 1884 and 1890. That is true, though maybe I can point to the fact that Murdoch, one of the greatest of all the early Australian batsmen, was also captain in 1880, when Australia lost the first ever Test played in England, so maybe he'll still be ahead of me even if we lose this series. But that was the only Test of that tour, so I guess it doesn't constitute a 'series'. And it came before the famous Test of 1882, which Australia (led by Murdoch) won by seven runs and led to the birth of the Ashes legend, so strictly speaking 1880 wasn't an 'Ashes tour' either.

In my defence, can I point out that only seven men have led Australia on two or more Test tours of England. I'm a member of a small club, which also includes Murdoch (lost the only Test in 1880, won the only Test in 1882, lost in 1884, lost in 1890), Joe Darling (won in 1899 and 1902, lost in 1905), Bill Woodfull (won in 1930 and 1934), Don Bradman (drew in 1938, won in 1948), Ian Chappell (drew in 1972, won in 1975) and Allan Border (lost in 1985, won in 1989 and 1993).

A fact that doesn't appear to have been picked up is that, if we don't manage to fight back from our current situation, I'll become the first Australian captain to lose the Ashes twice (as distinct from just losing an Ashes series). It's never been done (by a captain from either team), a fact that surprises me and certainly doesn't thrill me. But again we're talking about a small sample size.

Australia have lost the Ashes on 11 occasions — six times in England, in 1893 (with Jack Blackham as captain), 1926 (Herbert Collins), 1953 (Lindsay Hassett), 1977 (Greg Chappell), 1985 (Allan Border) and 2005 (me); and five times in Australia, in 1882–83 (Billy Murdoch), 1903–04 (Monty Noble), 1911–12 (Clem Hill), 1932–33 (Bill Woodfull) and 1970–71 (Bill Lawry).

So, if we go down in 2009, I will become the first Australian captain to lose the Ashes on two occasions (not just on two occasions in England). However, of those 11 captains who lost the Ashes, less than half — Noble, Woodfull, Chappell, Border and me — were able to win the Ashes back. And of those five — only Noble, Border and now me — led Australia in another series after regaining the Ashes after losing them.

That I'm in such elite company doesn't mean I'll be happy to get such a notorious mark on my cricket CV. But at least these facts give the 'achievement' (if it happens) a little perspective. When you're captain for a while, it is almost inevitable that there'll be some tough times to go with the good. The key, always, is to learn from your setbacks, and I must confess that after our wins in South Africa I really thought we were on the road back. We still might be — the way we batted in our second innings at Edgbaston was encouraging. But we've got to find our best form immediately; one more sub-par effort and the Ashes are gone, and I'd much rather be with Sir Donald Bradman as the only Aussie captain to successfully come back from one-down after three Tests to win an Ashes series than be the only Aussie captain to lose the famous urn twice.

✳✳✳

BEFORE EDGBASTON, WE HAD a three-day game at Northampton, a match that took on greater importance given the fact that a few places in our Test XI were undecided. The end result was a win for the good guys, a result that was especially heartening for Mike Hussey, our stand-in captain (Pup and I both had the game off), because he made some runs in our first innings and because it was his first win as an Australian skipper. But as happy as Huss was, the bloke who probably got the most

Lang Goes Past The Don

I was very happy to see my old mate Justin Langer become the highest-scoring Australian batsman in first-class cricket.

I've spoken to Lang, who is currently captain at Somerset, a few times during our time over here, and he has been helping us with little titbits of information about how the England players are going, especially those blokes with whom we're not too familiar. On July 23, while playing against Worcestershire, he finally overhauled Sir Donald Bradman's career total of 28,067 first-class runs. Admittedly, he took 615 innings to get there, compared to The Don's 338, but it is still a magnificent achievement and I'm very happy for him.

Lang told me how after he broke the record, one of his Somerset team-mates asked him how much cash it would take for him to play for Australia again. 'Mate, I'd play in the third Test for nothing,' he replied.

Unfortunately, that line made it into the public arena and soon word was about that Lang wanted to make a comeback. This meant that he had to contact Cricket Australia to confirm that he had been joking and that he had total faith in the guys in the Australian team.

out of the match was Shane Watson, who made 84 and 50, batting three. He reached his half-century in the second dig in just 28 balls, with 11 fours, and was so impressive we decided to pick him for the Test match … as an opening bat. Didn't that move create a storm!

We knew some observers would interpret this as a panic move, but the truth is that we've looked at Watto as a potential opener for quite a while now. Back in September 2006, when I was commenting on a DLF Cup one-day match we played against India in Kuala Lumpur, I wrote in *Captain's Diary 2007*,

'Watto has a good technique for batting against the new ball and, as he showed against the Indians, he can play good and aggressive strokes when the ball is new and field is up. One day he might even open the batting for Australia in a Test match. He's got the talent to do that.'

When we considered the form Watto showed at Northampton and compared that to the way Phillip Hughes struggled against a county attack that bounced him incessantly, and also when we thought back to the first two Tests and how Flintoff had really tested our young opener's technique, we had no choice but to think about whether Watto was the better bet for Edgbaston. The fact Shane can bowl a few overs didn't hurt his credentials, though it didn't really play that much of a part in what was a very difficult decision.

Still No Bing

Unfortunately, Brett Lee was not able to make his much-anticipated return in the Northants game. He was close, but not quite right and once we realised that he was not going to be available for the third Test we opted to play safe, in the hope that he might be right for the fourth Test at Headingley.

The problem is that Bing's injury is to a part of his body, his side, that is so much a part of his bowling action. If he comes back too early, he could re-tear the muscle and be out for another eight or 10 weeks, which won't help anyone. And if we get him back, we want him back as the strike bowler we came to rely on in 2007–08, when he led our attack so brilliantly. The memory of his spell against the England Lions before the first Test is still strong, but at the same time we've also got Stuart Clark in reserve, so we've still got some attractive alternatives on offer even if he remains on the sideline.

ABOVE: Preparing for the ICC World Twenty20 soon after our arrival in England.

LEFT: Andrew Strauss tosses the specially minted limited-edition medal and the Ashes series is finally underway.

BELOW: Simon Katich and I during our big partnership at Cardiff, leaving the field at stumps on day two.

ABOVE: Kevin Pietersen tries to play the unlikely sweep off Nathan Hauritz that led to his dismissal on the opening day of the Ashes series.

BELOW LEFT: Pietersen's second-innings dismissal at Cardiff — bowled by Ben Hilfenhaus without offering a shot.

BELOW RIGHT: Congratulations for Jimmy Anderson after he and Monty Panesar had batted through the final overs to save the first Test for England.

TOP: The confused scene near the end of the first Test, with England's 12th man Bilal Shafayat at far right, and their physio, Steve McCaig, jogging out to the middle.

MIDDLE: **Jimmy Anderson appeals for lbw against me at Lord's.**

BOTTOM: **A couple of minutes later, after the video umpire had been consulted, I was given out caught at slip, even though replays showed I didn't hit the ball.**

ABOVE: **Alone with my thoughts, but with the whole world watching, after dropping Ravi Bopara during the second Test.**

MIDDLE: **The MCC President, former England spinner Derek Underwood, introduces me to the Queen at Lord's.**

BOTTOM: **Moments later, it was Michael Clarke's job to introduce our security manager Frank Dimasi to the Duke of Edinburgh, but for what seemed like an eternity poor Pup couldn't remember Frank's surname.**

TOP: The drive through mid-wicket at Edgbaston that brought me my 11,175th run in Test cricket, breaking Allan Border's Australian Test run-scoring record.

MIDDLE: Bowled through the gate by Graeme Swann in the second innings of the same game.

BELOW: Simon Katich (fielder in helmet), Mitchell Johnson and Peter Siddle (far right) celebrate after Mitch bowled Graham Onions to end the fourth Test.

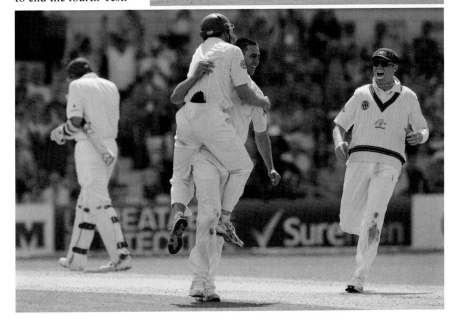

LEFT: **A pull shot during my first-day 78 at Headingley.**

BELOW: **With Emmy on the ground after the fourth Test.**

BOTTOM: **A proud family after we'd taken a little more than seven sessions to level the Ashes series.**

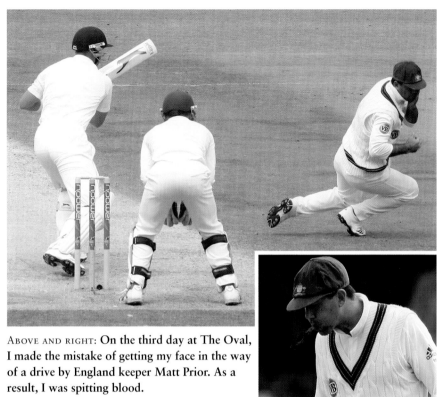

ABOVE AND RIGHT: On the third day at The Oval, I made the mistake of getting my face in the way of a drive by England keeper Matt Prior. As a result, I was spitting blood.

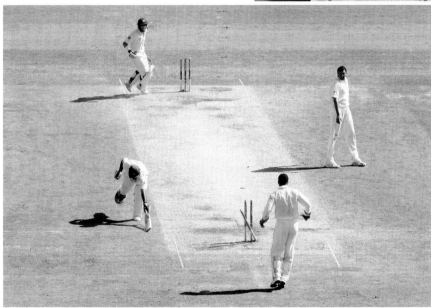

The run out. Just as it was beginning to look as if we might make more than 500 to save the Ashes, I was a fraction late taking off for a sharp single, Andrew Flintoff picked up the ball at mid-on and flung it at the stumps ... and my series was over.

Three of the venues — one new, two hallowed — from the 2009 Ashes. Top: The scene at Sophia Gardens during the first day of the series. Middle: The Lord's Pavilion, as the hero of the fifth day, Andrew Flintoff, goes down on one knee after dismissing Peter Siddle. Bottom: The shell of the old gasometer next to The Oval looks down as hometown celebrations begin following the fall of the final wicket of the series: Mike Hussey, caught Cook bowled Swann. England have regained the Ashes.

More and more, I'd been impressed with how positive Shane had become, once he got over the injury worries that stifled him earlier on the tour. He is a very confident cricketer. The fact that his previous experience as an opener in first class cricket (for Queensland a couple of seasons ago) wasn't successful hasn't fazed him. He averages more than 50 as an opener in one-day international cricket.

As soon as the news became public (see 'Not So Tweet' breakout), Phillip's supporters began pointing to the fact that only four Tests ago he scored a hundred in each innings against South Africa, but I was batting with him at Durban and I know he's definitely not in the same sort of form now as he was back then. Ever since Steve Harmison bowled short and at his body at Worcester he's looked shaky, and we have to acknowledge that. Even then, after Harmison got him out in both innings, I took him to one side and said, 'Mate, we've got to go and do some work.' Which we did, but it wasn't enough. It's also true that three of our four selectors were opening batsmen, while the fourth was an expert at getting the ball into a batter's ribs — you have to respect that sort of experience and cricket know-how. One thing they all agree on is there is no escape, at least in the short term, once a bowler or a group of bowlers have the better of an opening batter. You have to give a lot of credit to the England bowlers for the way they've put Phillip under so much pressure, and in doing so, they've put our entire batting order under pressure. The South Africans had plenty of opportunity earlier this year to do something similar, but all they did was concede a lot of runs.

In the end, it was almost a gut call — there were strong arguments to retain him (his recent success in South Africa, his precocious talent, give youth a chance) but also reasons to leave him out (Watto looked so good at Northampton, Flintoff might have a hold over him) — and in these situations your instinct is sometimes the right thing to trust. It was the selectors who finally made the decision, but I was okay with it. It was definitely one of the toughest selection calls of my time as captain.

I've heard suggestions that we've done Phillip's confidence a lot of damage by dropping him, but we could also argue that if we stuck with him, for Flintoff (and maybe Harmison, too, if he comes back into their team) to keep pounding him, doing that would cause more harm. I've got no doubt Huey will make a lot of runs in Test cricket, but we had to make a judgment call as to what line-up would give us the best chance to win the third Test match, and that is what we did.

What Phillip has to do now is get over his disappointment — which I know isn't easy; I remember clearly the pain in the guts I felt when I first got dropped from the Test XI, when I was about to turn 22. He's got to listen to the right people and focus on getting his game back to the level that excited us all so much just a few short months ago. Having toured with him to South Africa and now here, and seen what sort of character he is, I'm sure he'll be back, sooner rather than later.

***

THE FIRST BIG STORY related to the Ashes to break after the second Test was the news on July 22 of Kevin Pietersen's withdrawal from the rest of the series, because of that Achilles tendon problem. Surgery was required to get the injury right, and while it's not absolutely certain he's out for the season, we'll be astonished if we see him on the field again. It's been suggested he might make it back for the one-dayers that follow the Tests, but I doubt it. It's one of those injuries that he's tried to battle through without success — now, I'm sure his thinking will be, *However long it takes to get it right, that's how long I'll give it.*

Introducing Gary Manou

Graham Manou made his Australian debut in the game against Northants and had the misfortunate to make a golden duck in his maiden innings. He did keep really well throughout the game, however, but apparently did not do enough to catch the eye of the ground announcer, who originally introduced him to the crowd as 'Gary Manou' when he came out to bat at No. 4 in our second innings.

Graham's first run in Australian colours was a nervous push into the covers, but from there he batted nicely, finishing on 59 not out when Huss closed the innings. That he made a decent score is not surprising, as he's averaged about 40 with the bat in the past two Australian first-class seasons, and finished 11th on the Australian first-class aggregates in 2008–09.

There's no doubt England are weakened considerably by Pietersen's absence. He's a great player, and even though he was a long way from his best in the first two Tests (a credit, in my view, to Ben Hilfenhaus in particular, who bowled beautifully at him), there is no doubt their batting order looks a lot less intimidating without his name in the line-up. I don't think there is another batter in international cricket today who can so consistently score at a rapid rate and put the bowlers on the back foot like he can. Ideally, I'd like to beat their strongest team but we can't worry about things we can't control, and as soon as we heard the news we started developing plans for Ian Bell, Pietersen's logical replacement, who we knew well from the 2005 and 2006–07 Ashes series. As it turned out, Bell did okay in the third Test, but he never threatened to blow the game apart as Pietersen can do.

***

Calling Matty Hayden

First thing Mike Hussey was going to do straight after the game at Northampton, he explained to anyone who was listening, was get on the phone to Matthew Hayden.

'Why Haydos?' someone asked.

'Remember New Zealand two years ago,' he explained, recalling the Chappell-Hadlee tour the team did just before the 2007 World Cup. Gilly, Pup and I missed that trip, so Huss was in charge and they lost 3–0. 'Haydos was vice-captain. I've been trying to blame him for the losses ever since but he wouldn't have a bar of it. I want him to know I'm now on the winner's board.'

PIETERSEN'S DEPARTURE WAS THE headline story for 24 hours; speculation about the state of the Edgbaston pitch continued right up until the day the third Test started. A few weeks earlier, we'd heard all sorts of speculation as to how the Cardiff pitch would play and most of those predictions proved a fair way off the mark. This time, as we kept hearing the latest from Birmingham, I couldn't help but think back further than Cardiff, to four years ago, in the lead-up to that year's second Test, at Edgbaston, and how we kept getting told that the pitch was going to be a minefield. It turned out to be nothing of the sort.

So when we heard reports while we were at Northampton that the Edgbaston groundsman had said his wicket was 'a bit like jelly' because of all the rain that had been falling in the midlands in the days before the Test, we opted to wait until we saw the square for ourselves before we made any decisions about what we might do if we won the toss. Four years ago, I made the now almost notorious call to bowl first — a decision that was certainly influenced by what we'd heard from the groundstaff about the pitch's preparation — and then got belted for 407 on the first day. I'm more experienced now and won't ever again get carried away by what I've heard, while playing down what I can actually see.

A few days after I read about the pitch being like jelly, I saw the groundsman's name in the papers again, this time offering his opinion on my decision to send in England in '05.

'I still think Ponting was probably in the right to bowl first,' he said. 'There was a lot of moisture underneath it (the pitch). The fact that they didn't bowl well, nobody says anything about that. Knowing what I know what was underneath and being a bowler, I would have bowled first anyway.'

Suddenly, I liked the guy. I've always felt I've copped more stick than I deserved for that decision. Maybe it was wrong, and I've certainly been less keen to bowl first in the four years since, but there was some logic to the way we went. And it's not as if we were flogged in that game. As was talked about and written about and shown repeatedly on television in the days before this third Test, we were beaten by a solitary run in a thrilling match, a game that some people called the 'Test of the Century'. Without changing too much we might have won fairly comfortably — even though we lost our bowling spearhead, Glenn McGrath, just minutes before the start.

A day or two after I read about the groundsman's view on my call in '05, I saw him quoted in the papers a third time, and this time he was advising us not to play a spinner. 'With the conditions like this, Nathan Hauritz could be a waste,' he reckoned. 'Australia should play four seamers, I would think.'

Maybe Sarf has got in his ear, I thought to myself.

The groundsman clarified his original appraisal of his pitch by saying that when he said the pitch was like jelly he actually meant the outfield, not the wicket. When we finally got to have a look at the deck for ourselves we were surprised how dry it was. It was all getting a bit confusing.

***

IN THE LEAD-UP TO the Test, the media was keen to write Mitchell Johnson off, and even managed to get our coach a little agitated during an interview (which is not easy to do), as they badgered him about our fast man's future. I wondered if the critics had paid enough attention to his final spell against Northants, which I thought was easily his best spell of the game, and I knew they hadn't faced him in the nets like I had during our time in Northampton, because he was quick and dangerous and got through me a few times. I spoke to Kato after one of his net sessions and he had been similarly impressed (and bruised) by a couple of Mitch's quicker ones.

I know that Troy Cooley was convinced, going into the third Test, that Mitchell was on the way back. Stuart Clark and Andrew McDonald were much more economical against Northants, but deciding to stick with Mitch wasn't that hard a call because he is such a fantastic strike bowler when he's right. To me, it was a bit like England continuing to choose Andrew Flintoff even though he is clearly not 100 per cent fit. In this instance, I didn't blame the commentators who criticised our decision, because they were right when they said that it must have been very hard to leave a bowler as good as Sarf out, but what I did find somewhat amusing was Kevin Pietersen's opinion that it would be to England's advantage if Mitch played. That was very brave, KP saying that, given that he was out of the series and wouldn't have to face him.

Ironically, especially given Pietersen's comments, I thought just about the best appraisal of the situation came from a member of the England team. 'If I'd have had 18 months like he had, then two bad games, I would not expect to get dropped for the next game,' Jimmy Anderson said. 'As a bowler, you do go through varying bits of forms. The last 18 months he's been the best bowler by a country mile for Australia and all their success has pretty much centred around him. For him to have a couple of bad Tests and for people to be getting on his back is a bit harsh. He's just going through a bit of a dodgy patch, and I think he's a good enough bowler to come through the other side.'

As it turned out, Mitch did perform better in the Test, though he was still a fair way below the form he showed against South Africa. Taking the new ball off him seemed to help, and he hurled down some pretty quick deliveries, but he bowled a few too many loose ones, too. His fight for form is a continuing reminder for me that one of the tasks I've had to do over the past couple of years is get to know team-mates with whom I'd never

Happy Birthday

Though I wasn't playing, I spent most of the three days of the Northants game at the ground. I guess I could have gone away for two or three days, as a couple of the blokes who were resting did, but given our situation and where some of the guys' games are at, I felt a strong obligation to be available to help in any way I could.

However, I did get away for an hour on the final day of the game, to spend some time with our daughter Emmy. It was her very first birthday, and I was so glad that I was able to have a little party to help her celebrate. I love having my family with me on tour — I can't imagine what it would have been like for the cricketers of old to be apart from their loved ones for months at a time.

or rarely played before. An important part of a leader's role is to try to identify and understand different blokes' personalities as well as you can, to know which guys you need to rev up, which ones you need to cajole. It's very hard to communicate properly with guys unless you understand them and know them inside out, and with so many guys coming into the team in recent times that has sometimes been difficult. Peter Siddle, for example, is a

Not So Tweet

As I said, the decision to leave Phillip Hughes out of the third Test was a very difficult one, and after it was confirmed Jamie Cox, the selector on duty, went off to tell our young opener about his demotion. I know some of the guys would prefer to hear about these things from me as captain, but it was decided a couple of years back that it was a selector's job so that was the way it was.

What was disappointing was the way the decision got out into the public domain earlier than it should have, though we know that wasn't Huey's fault. It was his manager, who is currently based in India, who put the story on Phillip's Twitter page a number of hours before the Test was due to start, apparently because he got his time zones wrong. At the time, I had other things to worry about, and now, after the Test, I can't see too much value in revisiting what occurred. Hopefully, more care will be taken in future.

I'm not saying it was going to give us a big advantage keeping the news of our team change to ourselves until as late as possible, though Graeme Swann did say at stumps on day one: 'We had good plans against Hughes, so we were hoping he'd be there, and we knew a bit less about Watson.' Certainly, there was nothing to be gained for us by leaking the information early.

bloke who can cop a bit of stick, who actually needs a blast occasionally to get him back on track. As recently as the Lord's Test, I ran all the way from second slip before the start of an over to tell him to 'pull his finger out' and very next ball he dismissed Pietersen. With Mitchell, in contrast, I'm always looking for a chance to pat him on the back, to remind him I believe in him.

The funny thing with some people is that when they're down they think no one has ever felt that way, and that the road back is a million miles away. But everyone I've ever played with has gone through periods when they don't feel they're on top of things. At the moment it's Mitch's turn, and it's my job as captain to help get his mindset back to where it was earlier in the year.

I really believe in all the members of our bowling attack, though sometimes it was very frustrating trying to convince them to believe in themselves. There were a couple of times at Lord's, when one or more of them wasn't bowling well, when I felt a strong obligation to give them another over, because I knew I had to give them the opportunity to get it right. As long as the effort is there, I figure, it is worth giving them the chance to get the wicket that might suddenly put a new spring in their step.

My main concern, always, is that the effort is there. Of course, they can't keep going for boundaries, but it's when they're not running in hard or not hitting the crease hard, that's when I drag them real quick.

***

THERE WAS THE WICKET, there was Mitch, there was Phillip Hughes and there was our 'aura'. They were the things the press kept asking me about between Lord's and Edgbaston, and to tell you the truth it was the cracks about our aura, as it became more and more fashionable to claim we'd lost it, that bugged me the most. The last time I formally met the media before the third Test I went there determined to be happy and friendly and not to say anything that might encourage the 'boo-boys' at the Test, and I was doing great until they kept going on about our 'aura' or lack thereof.

The trouble was that Andrew Strauss had just said that he did not think we had an aura about us anymore, that playing against this Australian team was not the same as it had been against the Australian teams of old. Of course, he'd been responding to a question, but now I was expected to comment, too.

'It is okay for Andrew to say that now,' I responded when told of the England captain's remarks. 'I am not sure he was saying that after Cardiff. I think we had it well and truly over most of their batsmen down there.

'Aura is built up over a period of time and we have some fresh faces who are just starting to find their feet at international level. The aura of a side changes and comes about with performances. If we put in a performance here, then England may be thinking slightly differently at the end of the game.'

I guess, after this game, that England will be thinking pretty much the same as they did before the toss. Though they'll probably be disappointed they couldn't put us away ...

**

I'VE PLAYED A LOT of Test matches — 134 including this one — but never one that had a start quite like this. First, there was the Twitter, which got me cranky. Then there was the weather, which was so frustrating, because we never knew if or when we were going to get underway. Finally, just when we were starting to think there'd be no play for the day, the umpires said we'd be starting at 5pm. All day, I'd been saying to the match officials, 'If we are going to play today, please give us time to do our warm-ups.' But when they did decide to get going, there was hardly time to get ready for the toss. The special coin rolled my way for the first time in the series and we were batting. Then, as I began to get ready, as No. 3, for the start of our innings, there was suddenly a commotion in the room, and someone shouted that something was wrong. *Why*, I thought to myself, *won't they just let me play?* Out on the ground, Brad Haddin was in trouble and it quickly became apparent that he had just busted a finger — he had been trying to get his warm-up done when he took a ball on the end of the left ring finger. There was no time, yet I had to focus on my task at hand, so our manager Steve Bernard went to Jeff Crowe, the match referee, to see what our options were.

Hadds wanted a few minutes to see if he could keep with the broken joint, but there was no time for that. We needed to make a change, if we could. But strictly speaking, because the team sheets had been exchanged at the toss, it was too late for that. Steve put it to the officials that because the toss and the warm-ups had been so rushed, these were special circumstances and they accepted that argument, but we still needed Andrew Strauss to agree. Which, to his credit, he immediately did, so Hadds was out and Graham Manou was in. There wasn't time to officially present Graham with his baggy green; that had to wait for before the start of play on day two.

A lot was made of the England camp agreeing to us making the switch, as if it was one of the great gestures in cricket history, but to tell you the truth I don't think it was that big a deal. We would certainly have done the same thing if the roles had been reversed, and most likely if Strauss had knocked us back it would have created a bitterness that would have come back to bite them in the end. Hadds is such a tough bloke, if they'd made him play he would have gone all right, I'm sure of that, though Graham did an excellent job with the gloves, fitting in as though he'd been playing Test cricket for years. Ironically, 'Choc' took a blow on the gloves when he batted on the final day and judging by the way they were looking at his mitt afterwards it wouldn't surprise me if his hand is broken, too.

Given all that was going on around him, Shane Watson batted beautifully on that first afternoon. We went to stumps at 1–126 after 30 overs, with ambitions of going on to a match-winning score, and Watto was 62 not out. I was at the other end on 17, just eight away from breaking Allan Border's Australian Test run-scoring record, and the only wicket to fall had been Simon Katich, who was lbw to the off-spin of Graeme Swann. Their quicks had hardly offered a threat.

On the second morning, however, everything changed. I remember being a bit surprised that Strauss gave Graham Onions the opening over, but then Watto was lbw to the first ball of the day and Mike Hussey was bowled by the second. There was cloud cover, and we were well aware that the Duke balls have a reputation for swinging from about the 20-over or 30-over mark, but you could never have believed that this was the same game as the one we'd been playing the evening before. I was caught behind trying to hook an Onions bouncer that got 'big' on me, and in all we lost seven wickets before lunch in 23.5 overs, a terrible duplication of our batting failure at Lord's, and though we played pretty well for the rest of what proved to be a rain-interrupted match, comfortably batting out the final day to ensure a draw, the memory of that batting collapse is what stays with me. It wasn't easy on that second morning, Anderson and Onions were excellent, but if we'd fought through that tough period — that big moment — we could have set up the game to our advantage. Instead, at stumps on day two England were 2–116 in reply to our 263. We spent the rest of the game just trying to survive.

***

ALL IN ALL, I thought we bowled pretty well, at least until Andrew Flintoff and Stuart Broad hit half-centuries on the fourth day and gave them a lead of 113. It's been a feature of the first three Tests how the England 'tail' has scored nearly as many as their top six. At Cardiff, they were 5–241 and 5–70 but made 435 and 9–252 respectively, and at Lord's, after they lost 6–147 to go from 0–196 to 6–333, they managed to total 425. Here, we couldn't quite shatter their middle order, but things might have been different if Ian Bell had been given out lbw to Mitchell Johnson on the second afternoon when we thought he was plumb. Bell was 18 at the time and the wicket would have given Mitch the lift he was looking for, but Rudi Koertzen turned our appeal down and the batsman was able to go on to scratch out an unconvincing innings of 53.

Mitch hadn't looked half as out when he was fired for a first-ball duck in our first innings, and his frustration boiled over on day three, when he found himself going face-to-face with both Flintoff and Broad. I thought the umpires handled these confrontations (and also a later verbal stoush between Jimmy Anderson and Shane Watson) really well — there was no harm done, just tough competitors seeking an edge in the heat of battle, so they stayed out of it and quickly everyone got on with the game. Broad, who has had a fairly mediocre series to date — though I shouldn't forget that he did knock me over in the second innings at Lord's — seemed to revel in the attention we gave him, but I was also pleased to see Mitch really get into it. We've talked often, in South Africa and here, about how we have to let our opponents know we're out there, always ready and willing for the battle. It's about not letting them get too comfortable in the middle, the way we let Strauss and Cook settle in on the first morning at Lord's.

England's first innings lasted more than 48 hours, because the third day was washed out completely. I know some people have suggested the rain saved us, but by the time the game ended we were leading by more than 250, with five wickets still in hand — maybe, if the rain hadn't come, we might have seen England chasing 350 or more in the fourth innings, which could have been interesting. It is true, after Kat and I were dismissed early in our second innings (me to a superb off-break from Swann that spun sharply out of Mitch's footmarks and knocked back my middle stump), that England were right on top. But the mood has changed a little since then.

In a way, the situation is reversed from what occurred at and after Cardiff, where England batted out the last day and seemed to gain some encouragement from that achievement, while as a bowling and fielding group we might have been flattened a little by having to work so hard for no reward. I know the feeling in our camp is pretty positive now after the way Shane Watson, Mike Hussey and especially Michael Clarke and Marcus North batted in our second innings. Pup scored his 12th Test century, and also marked his 50th Test appearance by taking his Test batting average over 50, while Marcus missed out by just four runs on scoring his third Test hundred in his first five Tests and their 185-run stand was a record for the fifth wicket in an Ashes Test at Edgbaston.

Flintoff, on the other hand, failed to wicket during the Test. He fell heavily while bowling on the last day and didn't take the second new ball, and after the game Andrew Strauss couldn't confirm that he'll be available for the fourth Test which starts at Headingley on Thursday. You've got to wonder, even if he does play, just how sharp he will be after being on the field at Edgbaston for much of the last two days of the Test.

I haven't felt as if we've had a lot of luck during the first three Tests. Maybe things are changing now.

THERE WAS AN INTERESTING sequel to the third Test, which occurred at a team meeting when manager Steve Bernard suddenly stood up and said, 'Hang on Punter, we've got something else here that has just come in from the Warwickshire County Cricket Club.'

My first reflex was to think it might be some sort of presentation relating to me breaking AB's record, but then Steve explained that it an invoice for 'damages rendered to a toilet door'.

What could I do? I was guilty as charged. After I was bowled in our second innings of the third Test by that big off-break from

No. 411

Graham Manou, who made his first Test dismissal off the third ball of England's innings (Alastair Cook, caught off Peter Siddle), is the 411th Australian Test cricketer, the 30th Australian to be chosen for Australia as the designated wicketkeeper, and the 24th man to make his Test debut during my time as Test captain (that's 63 Tests, from my Test captaincy debut in 2004 to this game and including the four times Adam Gilchrist led Australia in my absence). By way of comparison, seven men made their Test debut during Steve Waugh's time as captain (59 Tests) and 21 men made their Test debut under Mark Taylor (50 Tests).

Graham is the third man to keep for Australia in a Test in which I was captain, after Gilly and Brad Haddin. Steve had two Test keepers (Ian Healy and Gilly) and so did Mark Taylor (Heals and Phil Emery). Allan Border had five in 93 Tests between 1984 and 1994: Steve Rixon, Wayne Phillips, Tim Zoehrer, Greg Dyer and Heals.

Graeme Swann, I walked off the field slowly. I had set myself to play a match-saving innings, but had come up well short. The Edgbaston crowd, as they'd been throughout the match, was in to me, even worse than the hecklers at Lord's, and one bloke in

Bittersweet

I might have only made 38 in our first innings but I still managed to pass a couple of notable landmarks. On the first evening I scored my 20,000th run in first-class cricket and then the next morning a push for two between mid-wicket and mid-on took me to 11,175 Test runs, one more than Allan Border's record. Straight away, Pup came down the wicket, shook my hand and said, 'Congratulations, I'm very proud of you.'

'Thanks mate,' I replied. 'But we've got a job to do.'

I did stop momentarily to acknowledge the crowd's applause, but I was much more concerned with going on to get a big score, and when I didn't manage to do that, it made the moment a bittersweet one for me. I can assure you that for the rest of the day I was stewing about my failure with the bat, not savouring my new record.

Still, I think that after I retire, when I look back on my career, this is the sort of record I'll treasure most. Like playing 100 Tests or making four Ashes tours, the personal achievements I rate highest are the ones that show that I've been able to succeed at the highest level for a long period of time. You need to be tough and durable and have a certain grit to be able to keep playing this game, so I reckon I'm entitled to be proud of the fact that my Test career is still going, 13-and-a-half years and counting.

After the Test, the boys presented me with a bottle of Grange with a message congratulating me on breaking the record engraved in the glass.

particular got a bit too close as I walked off the ground and gave me a real gobful. If there was one place in the entire ground where a security bloke should have been, it was right there but at that moment there was no law enforcement to be seen (I learnt later that the 'gentleman' was thrown out of the ground but I don't know whether that was for the abuse he hurled at me or for something else).

They are doing a lot of building work at the ground and the area around our change rooms was part of that. When I walked in after getting out I put my bat down and then went to open a toilet door, but it was jammed. I was in a furious mood, I gave it a shove, nothing, gave it another, bigger shove ... and it just came off at the hinges. What could I do? I'm no carpenter, I wouldn't have known how to put it back together, so I just picked it up and quietly but purposefully placed the door behind a nearby refrigerator.

Later in the day, I was back in the room and I overheard Brad Haddin talking to Andrew McDonald. 'Wasn't there a door over there?' Hadds asked. 'I'm sure we've been walking through it all week.'

'Nah, there's never been a door there' Ronnie replied. 'You're dreaming.'

'There it is, boys,' I chipped in. 'Over there, behind the fridge.'

I'd offered to fix things up, but the people at the ground told me not worry. Now, though, there was this bill from the club, which was for something like £200. However, just as I was starting to contemplate whether I was going to pay cash or cheque, our manager added that he had talked to some Warwickshire officials and they had said that as part of all the work going on they had no intention of replacing the door. I'd been conned; the bill was a mock-up. I'd actually helped them with their renovations.

Wednesday, August 5

I NEVER THOUGHT I'D be a football club owner. Well, I'm still not really, but I am now the proud owner of 500 shares in Altrincham FC, who play in the Blue Square Premier, the competition that is a step below the English Second Division (which was the old Division Four when I was a kid). Altrincham is located a few kilometres south of the City of Manchester.

Last night, while a few of the lads represented the team at a function in Leeds, I went to Moss Lane, Altrincham's home ground, with Stuey Clark, Shane Watson, Mike Hussey and Pete Siddle to see my new team take on a Manchester United XI. We were guests of the club chairman, Geoff Goodwin, who owns the company that provides the team bus for our tour and also happens to be our driver. It's a job Geoff has carried out brilliantly on past tours, too, and it has led to him building firm friendships with a number of players and team officials. I know Adam Gilchrist and Jason Gillespie have shares in the club, as does Steve Bernard.

Geoff's bus-driving job can be a tough one — I'll never forget the look on his face when he got hit with a £120 ticket for parking illegally outside Lord's on the final day of the second Test (in his defence, he told us the ECB had given him a dispensation certificate and he was fully entitled to park where he did, but the traffic warden didn't want to know about that) — and we are always grateful for the work he does for us. In response, we are always happy to help out if he needs some

Ins and Outs

We were initially fearful that Brad Haddin's Ashes series was over after he broke that finger during the warm-ups immediately before the third Test. But he's one tough cookie, and instead of heading back home he had the wicketkeeper's gloves back on by last Monday, a good sign that he'll be right to play tomorrow.

There was a stage when we thought Brett Lee might be right to play. I know Brett thinks he's ready to go (and so does Mike Hussey, after he was hit on the head by a short one from Bing in the nets a couple of days back), but we are thinking more cautiously — that while his body might be okay he's still not match fit and that consequently it would be too big a risk to rush him back in such an important match. This created a minor controversy yesterday when Shane Watson was asked about Brett's fitness and echoed our belief that he's not quite right, and Brett then came out and said the opposite. Bing didn't think it was Watto's job to be commenting on his fitness, and said so, but I really couldn't see how any major damage was done.

Unless something changes between now and tomorrow morning, we'll be playing four quicks and leaving Nathan Hauritz out, but it will be Stuart Clark who comes into the XI.

---

cricket memorabilia to auction at club fundraisers. It was funny when he tried to hand me a certificate that detailed my new shareholding in his club — the first one had my address wrong (it claimed I resided at Cronulla in Tasmania) and the second designated the shares to some fellow named *Richard* Thomas Ponting. So a third certificate had to be drawn up.

On the night, we were introduced to the crowd, watched the game from the directors' box, had a quick kick-around on the pitch and I was introduced to a few notable football identities, including Ole Gunnar Solskjaer, the former Man Utd striker who now coaches their reserves team, Jack Crompton, who was the 'Red Devils' goalkeeper in the 1948 FA Cup Final, and Ian Watmore, the Football Association Chief Executive, who also happens to be an Altrincham fan. Geoff told us that he'd never seen so many cameramen and photographers at the ground and the game drew what the local paper described as a 'bumper' attendance of 1772. The final result was Altrincham 0, Man Utd 2, but I thought we gave a good account of ourselves.

It was especially interesting talking to Solskjaer, a player good enough to win 67 caps for Norway and play 235 first-team games for Man U. I asked him about Cristiano Ronaldo, the FIFA World Footballer of the Year who had just been transferred to Real Madrid, and he spoke well of him, saying that even though everyone knew Ronaldo wanted to go to play in Spain he never stopped putting in while he was wearing a United shirt. And Solskjaer was also very positive about the way the club looked after him when he had to stop playing because of injury. It wasn't as if they just cast him aside; instead, after he told the great manager, Sir Alex Ferguson, that he was going to quit, they quickly found a coaching role for him.

'Alty' is a really nice friendly club and I'm proud to be associated with them — I'll be following their results closely and if I ever get the chance to come back to see them play again I'll certainly do so.

Thursday, August 6

IT WAS NICE, WHEN we were at Altrincham, that the crowd there gave me a cheer when I was introduced. I've been heckled most other places I've gone to on this tour. In fact, the manner in which the English crowds have been into me has become a big story here, to the point that Giles Clarke, the head of the England and Wales Cricket Board (ECB), has actually written a message in the match program for the upcoming fourth Test in which he asks the spectators to give me a break.

When I first started getting booed, I took it in my stride, as if it was a sort of back-handed compliment. Most of the chants are good-humoured anyway. More recently, some of the stuff I've had to deal with has been pretty unpleasant — but it still hasn't been hard to acknowledge that the vast majority of the fans are really good; it's only a small minority who are out of line. I will always remember the standing ovation I got from the Edgbaston crowd when I broke Allan Border's Test run-scoring record and, more broadly, I'll never grow tired of playing Ashes cricket in England because the atmosphere that is created at the grounds is always terrific. I've enjoyed every minute.

I'm a fan of the Barmy Army; they've got to be among the best sports fans in the world. Their jibes and songs and chants are always delivered in the right spirit, and the only knock I can put on them is that they are always at their loudest when England are winning. The times I most need my supporters behind me are when I'm struggling. At Edgbaston, with England on top, the crowd was incredibly boisterous, especially when I walked out to bat in our second innings, on the fourth afternoon. I was expecting a 'warm' reception — I can remember, as I got up to go out there after Simon Katich was dismissed, thinking, *Okay, let's get the booing out of the way ... and then I can get on with my innings.* They didn't let me down.

I don't believe anything the ECB will say or write is going to change the reality that I'll be copping more of the same this week, and I've got no problem with that. I do fear, though, that if the authorities try too hard to clamp down on the banter then some of the fun and some of the atmosphere might be lost.

My main job at the moment is to focus on the task at hand. I've been asked if it matters if we only draw the series, because that result will be enough for us to retain the Ashes. My response is simple: we aim to win every game and we came here to win the series. But if the best we can do is a draw that would still be pretty sweet. People also want to know if I'm worried about losing our No. 1 status. Apparently, we'll farewell the top spot if we draw the series and would slip to No. 4 if we lose. It would annoy me if we slipped down the rankings, but the fact it could happen hasn't changed the way we've been approaching things, because, again, we aim to win every game we play, whatever may hinge on the result. For the moment, our main concern is winning the Test that starts tomorrow.

Headingley is a ground that has been very kind to me — I made a hundred there on my Ashes debut in 1997 and another ton when my place in the side was in jeopardy four years later. The scorecards from the past 10 or more years strongly suggest it's a result venue, and of course we need a win. Right now, with the series on the line, rowdy spectators or not, Leeds is just the place I want to be.

Monday, August 10

FOURTH ASHES TEST

England v Australia at Leeds (August 7–9): England 102 (PM Siddle 5–21) and 263 (SCJ Broad 61, GP Swann 62; BW Hilfenhaus 4–60, MG Johnson 5–69) lost to **Australia** 445 (SR Watson 51, RT Ponting 78, MJ Clarke 93, MJ North 110; SCJ Broad 6–91) by an innings and 80 runs

∗∗∗

This was an astonishing match from start to early finish. We won easily, probably should have won by even more, and if momentum means anything in this series then we'll be going into the final Test at full speed. Yet such has been the ebb and flow of this series, I'm not going to allow the scale of our victory to impinge on the way we prepare for The Oval. This game was great, but we go into the Ashes decider square at one-all. There is still everything to play for.

More than anything else, what this fourth Test has shown me is that we definitely have the talent and the right attitude within the group to continue to be a genuinely strong force in world cricket. I felt that after the Tests in South Africa and I believe it again now. What we have now that we lacked just a short couple of weeks ago is more guys who are in form and who believe in themselves and their team-mates. You can sense a new confidence around the squad. We've put in a lot of hard work since the setback we suffered at Lord's and the three days at

Headingley have demonstrated the value of that effort. I don't think we're over the line yet, none of us do, but I do like where we're at — both in terms of the upcoming Test and in the longer term, too.

The lead-up to the Test was a bit crazy. First, we learnt on the Thursday night, on the eve of the game, that Andrew Flintoff was going to be ruled out because his knee was too sore. When we got to the ground the next morning there was a whisper about that he had been keen to play, had been omitted anyway, and was not happy. At the same time, we were told about the fire alarm that had woken the England players at around 5am, and it was hard not to think that they'd be a little distracted by that. We'd resolved our selection dilemmas the day before, so we could focus on our warm-ups, but over in the England camp they suddenly had another problem, when Matt Prior's back seized up while they were playing a game of football. Then Mark Saxby, their massage therapist, was hit in the head (but fortunately not badly hurt) by an errant high ball from one of our fielding warm-ups. Their coach, Andy Flower, approached Tim Nielsen to ask if the toss could be delayed by 10 minutes, which we had no problem with, while their medical staff tried to assess Prior's fitness and their leadership contemplated going into the game with Paul Collingwood as their keeper, or whether they'd make an emergency call to Warwickshire's Tim Ambrose, who was playing in Birmingham, about an hour and a half away. Someone suggested that maybe their keeping coach Bruce French, who'd played for England in the late 1980s, could fill in for an hour or so if England did field first, but I think that would have been pushing the friendship a little far, and then we were told that Prior was going to play. Finally, we tossed ... tails again ... Andrew Strauss said he'd bat (I would have done the same), and a few minutes later we were out there, and first ball from Ben

Hilfenhaus we had a confident lbw shout against the England captain. But Billy Bowden said no, and it was only then that the home team and their supporters could have a bit of a breather.

***

WE BOWLED BRILLIANTLY ON that first morning. Strauss might have survived the opening delivery, but last ball of the fourth over he sparred at one from Peter Siddle and Marcus North took a terrific catch at third slip. At the other end, Ben Hilfenhaus was bowling beautifully and it was he who had Ravi Bopara caught in the gully. Alastair Cook and Ian Bell made it through to drinks, when the score was 2–38 from 14 overs.

At this point, Stuart Clark had bowled one over: a maiden. Second over after play resumed, Bell was caught behind off Mitchell Johnson, and then Stuey took over, producing a pre-lunch spell of 6.5 overs, three maidens, three wickets for seven, as England crashed to 6–72. The wicket was lively and I'm sure the England players have batted better, but our blokes bowled really well. After lunch, Peter Siddle cleaned up the tail to finish with his best Test figures of 5–21, and the home team were all out for just 102. But though Pete was outstanding we all had no doubt who the chief destroyer was.

As Sidds said, 'It's always nice having Sarf up one end bowling so tight and consistently, it frees up the other end. I was lucky enough to be at the other end.'

The wicket had some pace and bounce in it, and the ball was moving sideways a bit, which are conditions tailor-made for Stuey. I know now, after this display, that we'll be criticised for not picking him earlier in the series, but I'm not sure if the conditions at Cardiff, Lord's or Edgbaston would have suited him as much as here. Still, it was a joy to see him attack the outside edge so consistently. None of our bowlers went too hard, which meant they were much more consistent, bowled to the plans that we'd developed for each of the batters, and put pressure on our opponents in a way that had been missing too often in the first three Tests. The first five outs were all catches behind the wicket, and the sixth, Stuart Broad right on lunch, was a classic — we pushed Simon Katich back a bit at short leg so he was about five or six metres from the bat, Sarf got one up around Broad's ribcage, and just as we hoped he half-pushed, half-fended it away and Kato caught it near his bootlaces.

I was surprised later to learn that Sidds' effort was only the second five-for taken by an Australian in a Test match this year, after his 5–59 in the New Year's Test against South Africa at the SCG. He took his last four wickets in this innings for three runs in 14 balls. At the end, we were all a bit stunned. To get through the English innings so quickly was fantastic, but we knew we still had to bat on what was clearly a wicket with something in it for the bowlers.

***

WITH FLINTOFF OUT, STEVE Harmison had come into the England team and after Shane Watson took 10 from the first over of the innings, from Jimmy Anderson, with the fourth ball of his first over Harmison got one up around chest height to Kato, who could do no more than jab it around the corner to Bopara. I hadn't banked on being in this early, but I knew from having fielded through the England innings that it wasn't going to be easy and I soon discovered that it was actually a lot harder than that.

My plan was to attack at every opportunity, but straightaway Harmison made me look foolish as, first ball, he nearly cut me in half and, second ball, I sort of pulled at one well wide of the off-stump but didn't go close to making contact. Watto assured me it was easier at the other end, and he handled Anderson with aplomb, turning the fifth ball down to fine leg for his third boundary. But then Harmison was into me again, and immediately I betrayed my nervousness by starting for a quick single that wasn't on. Watto quickly sent me back. Next ball was kinder, a long hop outside off-stump that I cracked through point for four, and I got through the rest of the over without incident. I noticed, though, how Harmison stopped to study the way I lunged far forward as I let the fourth ball go through outside the off-stump. I sensed he wanted me on the back foot; that he had two ways of getting me out in his mind — either through the steep lift he was getting out of the wicket or caught in the slip cordon as I half-pushed at fuller-length deliveries. I was relieved he wasn't attacking the top of my off-stump. *That*, I thought, *is what I don't want him to aim.*

Watto took another six runs off Anderson's next over, giving him 20 from his first 18 balls. In the post-game analysis very few people mentioned this innings, but in the context of the match it was crucial. After five overs of our reply to England's 102, we were 1–29, nearly a third of the way to a first-innings lead, and Watto had forced Anderson — reputedly England's ace in the absence of Flintoff — out of the attack. Next over, Harmison went short nearly every delivery, and I got him away for two fours, a two and a single off the last ball, which meant I was on strike when Graham Onions replaced Anderson.

I sensed that right here was a chance to take the game right away from our opponents. Maybe because they were defending such a small score, it seemed England were looking for a wicket off nearly every ball. Or maybe they were just excited by the extra bounce. Either way, I took the punt on meeting fire with fire, and when Onions pitched short first ball I smashed it away over mid-wicket for six. Next ball, he got his line wrong and I helped it on its way to fine leg, to bring up the Australian fifty in 6.2 overs. The fifth ball was short again and it, too, went off to the mid-wicket boundary. Another single and I was 32 from 20 balls, with five fours and a six. The bowlers and fielders were quiet, the crowd was hushed, there wasn't a boo to be heard. It was the best counterattack of my life.

From there, it was as if all the fire went out of the wicket, but in truth it was more that the life went out of the bowlers. They reverted to trying to stem the run-rate, by bowling a lot outside off-stump, and we were able to let go a lot of deliveries. I was very impressed by how organised Watto was, how he knew which balls to leave and which to play, and it took us until the 23rd over to pass England's score. The 100 partnership was

Round the World in Seven Days

We lost one member of our touring party during this Test, when Andrew McDonald flew home to be with his wife for the birth of their first child. The plan is that Andrew will return to England in time for our two-day game against the England Lions at Canterbury that begins this Saturday. I'm not sure he'll be playing in that match, but my understanding is that he's going to try to get back in time anyway.

A player leaving a tour like this would never have been considered a few years ago, but times have changed and if it's possible to put family first then I reckon that should happen. Managing jet lag has become something of a science for our medical staff in recent times and because we now know how to look after ourselves on a flight, travelling long distances doesn't have the same negative impact it once did.

reached in the following over (Watson 44, Ponting 63), Harmison's first of his second spell, which included three fours to my partner, two pulls and a slashing cut, and I was beginning to have visions of a stand like the one Kato and I put together in Cardiff. But then, out of the blue, Watto missed a straight one from Onions and was given out lbw, and in the following over from Stuart Broad I did the same thing and was gone as well. My 78 had taken 101 deliveries, and I was dirty on having missed out on the hundred, because it would have been one I treasured. Still, I was happy to have put us in the situation we were now in, if only the rest of the batting order could back us up.

Broad had bowled a nice little spell to me. The frustrating this was that I could see his plan — he was bowling mostly full and wide of the off-stump, with two slips, gully, deep point, cover, but I knew that sooner or later he'd go wide of the crease and bowl one at the stumps, hoping it would either swing away or hold its line. He did just as I suspected, the ball stayed straight, and I missed it and was gone, leg before.

I'd got out this way first ball against the West Indies in the World Twenty20 and against Jimmy Anderson at Lord's, I don't think I've worked harder on any aspect of my game than making sure my balance is right, here I was in terrific form, but Broad still got me. The trouble happens, I've concluded, only when the ball is swinging, and I reckon I'll have it fixed real soon. I'm very conscious of guarding against the ones that duck away, but sometimes that leaves my balance just slightly crooked, with my weight going a little too much towards the offside. My first reflex is to look for it to swing … and but when it holds its line as this one did, I'm sometimes a fraction late with my shot and the delivery can sneak through. If the ball's not swinging, however, and someone like Broad or Anderson bowls that sort of line and length, I hit him for four just about every time.

Unfortunately, Mike Hussey soon followed Watto and me back to the pavilion, but from there Michael Clarke and Marcus North saw us safely through to stumps with just the odd piece of drama. Pup was struck on the helmet by Harmison, and there was a big caught behind appeal against him that might have been glove, more likely was on the arm, above the wrist, but they survived the last 17 overs of the evening session to be 4–196 at the close. It had been quite a day — 14 wickets for 298 runs! — one of the most memorable of my career.

***

THE SECOND DAY WASN'T QUITE as chaotic and exciting as the first, but it was another beauty for us and by the close we were on the threshold of a colossal victory. Before play, we resolved to stay aggressive throughout the day, and we stuck to that mantra brilliantly. The batting early on was superb, and in the last hour Mitchell Johnson roared back to his best form, taking three wickets for a single run in 14 balls and unluckily missing a fourth scalp off the last ball of the day.

England, I'm sure, would have talked about getting away to a bright start, to diminish the memory of their ugly first day, and I'm sure Anderson and Harmison were determined to charge in from the jump. But Clarke and North were too good for them, scoring 23 runs from the first four overs of the day, and 49 from the first eight, and the tone for the day was set. Seventy-two runs came in the first hour, and it wasn't until about 10 minutes before lunch that a wicket fell, when Pup was lbw to Onions for 93. He'd gone so close to joining an elite club of batters (which features names such as Don Bradman, Jack Hobbs, Wally Hammond, Herbert Sutcliffe, Charlie Macartney, Arthur Morris, David Boon and Stuart Broad's father Chris) who have scored hundreds in three straight Tests in the same Ashes series, and fully deserved to be included in such company.

After the break, the party continued, as Northy went on to his third Test hundred, reaching three figures with a six over mid-wicket off Graeme Swann. This gave him three centuries and a ninety in his first six Tests. Our lead on the first innings was 343, which I figured must have been close to a record until someone told me Australia had led by 453 in 1993, when Allan Border scored 200 not out and David Boon and Steve Waugh made hundreds. At the end, Stuart Clark clobbered 32 from 22 balls and our overall run-rate of 4.27 was the third highest achieved in a completed innings of an Ashes Test at Leeds, after Australia's 4.46 (447 all out) in 2001 and Australia's 4.36 (407 all out) in 1921, which was a stat I was very proud of — we'd

The Langer Dossier

The big news story on what proved to be the final day of the fourth Test was the leaking of the 'Langer Dossier', as it was grandly called in the Sunday papers. Justin had written some notes for Tim Nielsen before the first Test, in which he outlined his views on some of the England players and the culture of English cricket. He didn't hold back in some of his criticisms, and now the document has been leaked to the *Telegraph*.

My first reaction when I read the story was disappointment — Lang's notes were given to Tim in confidence, Tim showed them to the team in confidence, but somehow they've found their way into the media. I have no idea how they were leaked; for all I know, they might have just been left lying around and the wrong person picked them up. I do know Tim hasn't got a clue how the story broke, but is very upset and feels that he's let Lang down.

set ourselves to be positive on a wicket that had something in it for the bowlers and we'd sure achieved that. By taking the life out of the England bowlers and fielders we'd taken the life out of the pitch.

There were 32 overs left in the day when Strauss and Cook went out to start their second innings, and my hope was that we could get two or three wickets before stumps. They started well, and when their stand reached 50 I began to reassess my ambition — maybe one wicket would do. But then Hilfy went bang! bang! — Strauss lbw for 33 and Bopara lbw first ball — and we were right on top again. At the other end, I'd just brought Johnson on to bowl and you could see from his opening over that he was much closer to his best. The plan was straightforward: soften Bell up with a couple of short ones, like the one he got out to in the first dig, and then come back to that off-stump line. Sure enough, he edged a catch to me at second slip. Then Collingwood was plumb lbw and Cook caught behind, and they'd lost 5–20 in about 40 minutes. Last ball of the day, Prior sliced a hot chance off Mitch to Northy at third slip, but it went down. It would have been the perfect exclamation point for a sensational day, but it was hard to complain. England were 5–82 at stumps, still trailing by 263 runs. I can't remember ever sleeping better after two days of a Test match.

✳✳✳

DAY THREE STARTED JUST about perfectly for us: dot ball; four; Anderson, caught Ponting bowled Hilfenhaus 0. From there, though, the England tail resisted strongly, with Stuart Broad following up his best Test bowling figures (6–91) he'd achieved the previous day by belting 61 at much better than a run-a-ball. He became just the seventh Englishman to make a half-century and take a six-for in the same Ashes Test. Graeme Swann hit 62, one short of his highest Test score, and the innings continued on until beyond the lunch interval. Our final winning margin was still considerable — for the third time in the past four Ashes Tests at Headingley we won by an innings, this time an innings and 80 runs — and Mitchell Johnson took the last two wickets to give him five for the innings. When the last wicket fell, I ran down to the third-man boundary to rescue the ball, and made sure it found its way into Mitch's possession, as a memento. If he keeps improving as he'd done over the last four England innings in this series he'll be right back to his very best at The Oval.

'We're looking forward to the rest of the tour now,' I said after the game. 'Everything's heading in the right direction.'

***

THE CONSENSUS IN THE local papers is that only Flintoff can save them now. Some writers are suggesting that 39-year-old Mark Ramprakash should be recalled, which I enjoyed reading, not because I don't rate Ramprakash as a player but if the papers are going to be full of speculation about who might be in and out of the England side, then that will take the attention away from us, which can only be a good thing.

It's not for me to tell England what to do, but I'm sure it's not the time for them to panic — in my view, England's ordinary performance here was a one-off, a bit like our effort on the first two days at Lord's. We weren't on our game at the start of that second Test and similarly circumstances conspired here to put the home team behind the eight ball from the start of this game. Sure, it will be hard for them to come back, but mostly because a big loss like the one they've just suffered can be so deflating. It will be a big challenge for the leadership group to rebuild the team's confidence, but if they can get away to a good start in the series decider then we've still got a huge battle on our hands if we want to retain the Ashes.

For the next couple of days, though, we've got some unexpected free time, and the boys are taking advantage in different ways. Marcus North, for example, has headed north, to Newcastle, to catch up with his in-laws, while Ben Hilfenhaus is

Time Off

While I'm keen to play the tour game at Canterbury, it was nice to hear from Cricket Australia that they are okay with me returning home after the fifth Test, to spend some time with Rianna and Emmy in the comfort of my own home. Consequently, I will be missing the ODI against Scotland, the two T20 Internationals against England and the first two or three games in the ODI series against England.

If I didn't get a break somewhere in the next few weeks I may not have had one for six months or more, so packed is our schedule. I must say that Cricket Australia has been terrific in the past couple of years in the way they've let me miss a game or two, always with the bigger picture in mind. The recent experiences of Kevin Pietersen and Andrew Flintoff spring to mind when I think about how important it is to manage the programs of the game's leading players, and in this regard I believe Cricket Australia is leading the way.

I am sure there will be some criticism of me going home, especially if we are beaten at The Oval, but I also have no doubt that there will be moments during our upcoming ODI campaign at the Champions Trophy and in India when I am going to be very grateful for the time off I was given after the Ashes Tests. It's a balancing act, getting my program right, and in this instance I'm confident we're doing the appropriate thing.

already on the train to Paris and Michael Clarke is going to London, where he can rest a slight stomach muscle strain he's been carrying since Edgbaston. I'm happy to stay here in Leeds, and just spend as much time as possible with Rianna and Emmy.

As for the next week, in the main, I'm keen for most of our guys to keep 'ticking over', and Mitchell Johnson and Peter Siddle are two guys who I want to see play in the tour game, the two-dayer at Canterbury, that starts on the weekend. I'll play in that game as well, and so will Brett Lee, to give him a real chance to prove he is back to full fitness. After the way the four quicks went here, I doubt there will be room for him in our team for the final Test, but Bing is still the best proponent of reverse swing in our squad and we shouldn't forget that. Strangely, after what happened in 2005, reverse swing hasn't been a factor in this series, but the conditions at The Oval might be different, and if they are Brett could become a 'wild card' for us.

The make-up of the two sides for the series decider, especially the England side, is just one of many storylines that will appear time and again over the next week. After four Tests of fluctuating fortunes the series is heading for a big climax. There's a real buzz in our group, while I'm sure England will relish the return of Andrew Flintoff, will be more comfortable as underdogs, and will also feel good about the fact that they are heading to The Oval, where they have an imposing record in Ashes Tests. Australia have only won six Tests at the ground, from 34 starts, and only three times (1948, 1972 and 2001) since World War II.

I can't be too concerned with what has happened in the past, but I'm mightily focused on the present. I've always said that the reason I play cricket is for the big occasions — well, as far as I'm concerned, they don't come any bigger than what's ahead of us. I can hardly wait.

Wednesday, August 19

Tour game, Australians v England Lions, at Canterbury (August 15–16):
Australians 9–340 dec (81 overs: SR Watson 95, RT Ponting 45,
MEK Hussey 65) defeated **England Lions** 237 (80.4 overs: JWM Dalrymple
58) by 103 runs (one-innings match)

∗∗∗

IT WAS A GOOD hit-out we had last weekend. We batted first
and Shane Watson had another productive innings, hitting 15
fours and a six in 85 balls on his way to 95, including 92 before
lunch on the first day, while Huss looked all right while scoring
65 and I had a lot of fun making 45 with nine fours.

It was almost relaxing batting in the actual game, because
before play on the first day I had a net and our quicks seemed to
be queuing up to bowl at me. It was pretty gruelling … and
fantastic. Strangely (or so it seemed), I was applauded when I
walked out to bat in the match and then again as I left the field;
somehow, without setting out to change perceptions, I've turned
a lot of people around. Whereas earlier in the tour I was getting
quite a bit of negative press, now a lot of commentators seem to
be going out of their way to write nice things about me, and the
way many in the crowd are treating me reflects this turnaround.

We had one new face in our team for the game. Queensland
wicketkeeper Chris Hartley, who had been playing for Chorley in
the Northern Premier League in Lancashire, was called up at the
last minute when it was determined that Graham Manou's hand

injury still wasn't right. There was no way Brad Haddin was going to play, as we need him for The Oval Test and we couldn't risk him doing any further damage to his broken finger, and Chris responded by taking four catches and looking right at home, but on the second day the selectors announced that Tim Paine, who is coming over the T20 and one-day games that follow the Tests, will act as cover for Hadds in the lead-up to the fifth Test.

Drafting someone from league cricket onto an Ashes tour is not unprecedented. I know Mike Whitney was playing in the Lancashire League when he was called up for the last two Tests in 1981, while on my first Ashes tour, in 1997, Shane Lee and Shaun Young were drafted into the touring party for our last tour game, which coincidentally was also at Canterbury, because Jason Gillespie, Brendon Julian and Paul Reiffel were all unavailable. Like Whit 16 years earlier, Shane came to us from the Lancashire League, while Shaun (who went on to make his Test debut in the sixth Test of that tour) had been playing for Gloucestershire.

We ended up winning this game by 103 runs, on the basis that because it was a two-day game a result could be determined on the first innings. Given the score, that seemed pretty fair to me. On day two, Nathan Hauritz bowled pretty well, sending down 16 straight overs that brought him two wickets (in consecutive balls). Marcus North and Simon Katich both picked up a wicket, while Brett Lee looked good as he took three wickets, including both openers, from 16 overs,

A funny moment came near the end when a bird flew in — in the way you sometimes see crows make off with golf balls or seagulls take chips at the beach — to steal a bail, after Bing bowled Liam Plunkett. It was quite a bold effort, though we weren't quite sure what the thief was going to do with the bail once he got it home. All the umps could do was call for a replacement so we could complete our victory.

We left Canterbury that night, bound for London, and had our first look at The Oval on the Monday.

**

FOR US, THE MAIN story has been the selection quandary created by our fantastic performance at Headingley. As a general rule, I would rather not play four quicks in a five-day game—because I usually prefer to have a more balanced attack. I had no problem with having a pace quartet in the fourth Test, because we realised the wicket had something in it for the fast men and that Stuart Clark could do some damage for us. As we ponder what to do at The Oval, we know that if we leave Stuey out and then get beaten we'll be heavily criticised, but we can't let the prospect of criticism affect our thinking. Mind you, if we do leave Horrie out again and the wicket's a turner then we'll probably get bagged for that decision, too. Same as if we leave Brett Lee and the Poms start getting the ball to reverse swing. More often than not, with

---

Aussie Cricket Goes Dutch

On August 12, the Australian selectors named our squad for the two Twenty20 games to be played in the gap between the fifth Ashes Test and the seven-game ODI series in September. There were a few surprises, chief of whom, I guess, was Victorian paceman Dirk Nannes, who had played for the Netherlands in the recent World Twenty20.

Nannes joins Dave Warner, Adam Voges and Callum Ferguson in a team that will be led by Michael Clarke. Tasmanian wicketkeeper Tim Paine will don the gloves in place of Brad Haddin and Graham Manou, who were not considered because of the injuries they are carrying.

---

the tough selections all you can do is back your best judgment and then cop the knocks if things go wrong.

There are many things to consider. Recent first-class games at The Oval have seen a lot of runs and not too many wickets, and on what I've seen in the last three days the Test strip looks hard and true. There is a suggestion about that it might dry out a bit in the coming days, especially if the weather is hot, but whether that means it will so suit the spinners we're not so sure. My past Ashes Tests at The Oval have included a couple of games where the spinners have gone pretty well — England's left-arm spinner Phil Tufnell took 11 wickets in 1997 and Shane Warne took 11 in 2001 and 12 in 2005 (though on each occasion they cost him more than 200 runs), but from what we understand there has been nothing in the first-class games played at the ground this season to suggest it will turn appreciably. Rather, it's been a batters' deck.

We do expect England to be aggressive, because they can't sit back and wait for us to throw it away, which is a reason to stick with Sarf, because he can keep it tight whatever the conditions. I'm sure they'll try to produce a 'result wicket', because a draw is no good to them, but remember how we dominated at Cardiff, after they did play two spinners, while we've had our moments against their quicks during this series, especially at Lord's and the first innings at Edgbaston. England did call Monty Panesar into their squad last week, but they've since announced that he won't be playing, that they'll be going into the game with just one spinner: Graeme Swann. That they've made this call already strongly suggests they don't expect the wicket to be, as they like to say over here, a 'Bunsen' (as in Bunsen burner).

Horrie was struggling a little today at training because of a minor heel injury, while Brett was charging in. Clearly, Bing is back to full fitness, and there's no doubt in anyone's mind that he's still good enough, but it sure would be a bold move to pick him instead of one of the four fast bowlers who did so well for us just a week and a bit ago.

Bing would have played at Cardiff but for injury, but the only way he'll play in the fifth Test is if we believe that reverse swing will play a big role. For that to happen, we'd have had to experience a series of hot, dry days, but that hasn't really happened. Back in 2005, reverse swing was a key factor in the series — we have to admit that the England bowlers, coached as they were then by Troy Cooley, mastered this art better than we did. But it hasn't been as hot or as dry this English summer, and that has meant that when the ball has really swung — such as on the second day at Lord's and Edgbaston — it has been conventional swing. The Oval is the one ground where that may change and we have to be aware of that. I do know Bing is jumping out of his skin to get involved.

It's hard to forget how well Stuey went on the first day in Leeds, and there is also that the fact that, as captain, to have an extra pace-bowler option means I'm much less likely to be forced to bowl one of the other quicks for extra-long spells. Instead, we can fashion the right bowling partnerships and create match-ups we want, with certain bowlers against certain batters. Sarf, for example, has a great record against Paul Collingwood, while Mitch has dismissed Ian Bell in each innings of this series since Bell came back into the England XI.

I'm sure you can sense that we've been going one way, then the other, over the past few days. The bottom line is we've got more thinking to do between now and the toss tomorrow.

***

WE HAD BEEN EXPECTING to get our first look at Warwickshire's Jonathan Trott in the game at Canterbury, but

Fired Again

There was a weird sequel to the 'fire alarm' controversy from Leeds that saw the England team forced out of their hotel at 5am on the morning of the fourth Test. Initial reports suggested the incident had been caused by a prank by Australian fans, and I was pretty filthy about that, but we later heard that the hotel believed the most likely cause was a smoke detector going off after some clothes were left too close to a hair dryer.

While we were staying in Canterbury, we had a similar drama, when last Wednesday morning we found ourselves out on the footpath in the rain after a fire alarm came to life. At first, we thought it might be a revenge attack by the Barmy Army, but quickly it was determined that the alarm was faulty and we were allowed back into our rooms.

the England selectors withdrew him from the England Lions XI at the last minute, which meant we'd have to wait until The Oval to see first-hand what he can do.

You've got to say there is a sense of desperation in their decision to pick Trott for so big a game. Two months ago he wasn't in the England Lions team (a virtual England A team) that played us at Worcester, but now — on the back of some nice scores and a big batting average in county cricket — he'll be in their Test top order. No doubt at all, he'll be under a lot of pressure, or at least he will be if we bowl well at him. What we mustn't do is give him any cheap early runs. We've done plenty of research on him, studied some film, and the Aussies on the county circuit we've spoken to have told us that he's a very sensible player who is in excellent form. But I can't help thinking, *if I've played 135 Tests and I'm feeling the pressure, how must he be coping?*

I'm also thinking about this upcoming Test as being one of the biggest moments of my career, so it was almost bizarre that, for the first week of the lead-up at least, really until a couple of days ago, I was able to stay out of the media spotlight to a large degree. This wasn't by design on our part, more a reflection of the massive debate in the media about the make-up of the England team. First up, almost straight after Headingley, Andrew Flintoff was cleared to play. For a few days there was a lot of conjecture about whether Ramprakash might be recalled, or that Trott (who had been on the edge of the England squad for the fourth Test) or Kent's Robert Key would be called up. Would Ravi Bopara be dropped and maybe Ian Bell, too? We

Hilfy's Handicap

There are a number of blokes in our squad who like to attack the golf course, and of course I'm always keen on a round if I can find the time. Throughout this tour, we have had a bit of running joke going that revolves around Ben Hilfenhaus and his handicap, which he claims is seven but should be, by our reckoning, more like 15. Hilfy insists he's off single figures, which means that if you draw him as your partner it's pretty much guaranteed you can't win.

The early finish to the Leeds Test gave us a chance to have one final hit before the end of the tour. Up to this point, I'd managed to avoid having Hilfy as my partner, but on this occasion, just before we got organised to head to the first tee, I had to duck off for a minute and when I came back I was quickly told that the draw had been made and, who'd have thought it, I was playing with my fellow Tasmanian. Hilfy didn't realise the ballot had been rigged, but I knew. Sure enough, I ended up hitting the ball very nicely, thank you, but it didn't matter — we were still buying first drinks when we got back to the clubhouse.

Going by the Book

Last night, I was told that a story is going to be published on *Cricinfo* concerning an incident that occurred back in July, after the Lord's Test. Back then, one of our players was approached at our team hotel by a bloke who we suspected might have links to bookmakers. We didn't know that for sure, but as is regularly explained to us at pre-tour camps the protocol is that you report any worries to team management and they then take the matter to the ICC.

That's basically the story. None of us is under suspicion, there was no money offered, just a strange bloke hanging around the hotel and maybe trying to steer the conversation in the wrong direction. I have no idea where the ICC investigation has gone, but because the story will mention terms like 'match fixing' and 'illegal bookie' it will generate headlines. That's inevitable, given what happened in our game in the 1990s, but I really don't think this is the start of a new controversy. All we could do was go by the book, which we did, and worry about the games to come. The fact the story is out now makes no difference to us; all our focus is on The Oval. We'll let others look after the things we can't control.

learned that Kevin Pietersen had experienced a setback in his recovery from his Achilles tendon surgery, which ruled out any chance of KP making a miracle comeback. Apparently, he suffered an infection of some kind, and now he won't be playing in the ODI series that follows the Ashes Tests or in the Champions Trophy in South Africa that starts in late September. Then Panesar was called into their squad. Late Friday, I think, word got out that it was Trott who was going play, with Bopara out and Bell moving up to three. With the two-spinners option having been ruled out, their final dilemma is whether to play

Graham Onions or Steve Harmison and apparently they won't decide on that until tomorrow.

The major distraction for them last week revolved around Flintoff, who is apparently still disappointed at the decision to leave him out of the fourth Test, because he clearly wanted to play and felt fit enough to play. I made sure not to offer any opinion on whether they were right to leave him out, just enjoyed the lack of attention the story bought us for a few days. Like a lot of things in cricket, there are two sides to this debate. Sure, they missed him, no doubt about it, but they were leading the series 1–0 with two to play and there was logic in resting in him, to give him every chance of being as fit as possible for The Oval. Had they played him and he'd broken down and been forced out of this Test, the press would have slaughtered Andrew Strauss and their

Always in the Right Spirit

At my chat with the media I was asked for my thoughts on Andrew Flintoff as he goes into his farewell Test. This is what I said:

'He'll want to have a good game in his last Test match, so whether or not that frees him up or whether or not that puts more pressure on him I'm not sure. Having not been in that situation of playing my last game, I don't know what it's like but what we do know is, whenever he plays for England, the crowd gets a lot more involved in the games.

'Whenever he's bowling, the whole ground lifts a little bit and the difference between the first three games and Headingley was they just didn't have him to turn to and the crowd didn't get involved in the game. It will be sad to see such a big figure in the game of Test cricket move on.

'He's been a great opponent of ours over the years and someone who's always played the game in the right spirit ...'

selectors for being so reckless with such an asset. On the other hand, after their heavy defeat at Leeds there is now a hell of a lot of expectation on Flintoff's shoulders. He'll give everyone in their set-up a lift just by being there and he'll pick the crowd up, but how will he play? The fans will want another last day at Lord's, another revival of 2005, but that won't be easy.

***

THROUGHOUT THE TOUR, I'VE tried to play down comparisons with '05, but over the past few days in my own mind that's been getting more and more difficult to do.

I have played a lot of cricket but maybe even including The Oval four years ago I'm not sure I've ever played in a Test as huge as this one. For me, there is nothing bigger than playing in the deciding game of an Ashes series, and now, as I get closer to my 35th birthday, I keep telling myself that I have to grab moments like these, make the most of them, because I may never experience their like again. What this scenario has done is create a tangle of different thoughts through my brain, as the experienced pro in me battles some of my more impulsive instincts. I know this will probably be my last crack as winning an Ashes series over here, yet I have to try to forget that and just prepare as if it's any other game. At the same time, I don't remember being this excited about a cricket match and on occasions I'm struggling to disguise that reality. This morning, I was up at 6.30am wanting to get to breakfast, to have our morning team meeting, get to practice. You can tell from the extra zip in my training that I'm really fired up. Yet I'm supposed to exude a feeling of calmness. We probably got overtaken by the occasion at Lord's and I don't want that to happen again.

I keep telling myself not to think about 2005, yet too often that's what I find myself doing. I think what frustrates me most about the final Test in '05, when England achieved the draw they needed to win the series, is that we were off the field because of bad light when we lost the Ashes. We never had a chance to have a crack at chasing down a target. Of course, that wasn't just the weather's fault — Kevin Pietersen played a great innings to keep us at bay and Ashley Giles gave him terrific support, but it was still a dud feeling not being able to have one last shot at it. I remember how, after I sought out Michael Vaughan to shake his hand and congratulate him on his team's deserved win, I made sure I stayed outside to watch the presentation, the crowd reaction, the ticker tape, the popping of champagne corks and the fireworks. That memory fired us up a little in 2006–07; hopefully it can do the same for me this time. But not, I have to keep reminding myself, too much.

Of course, the Ashes are at stake again and we're the holders and England the challengers, but the situation is still a little different this time. In 2005, we were the team with selection problems — players struggling for form or carrying injuries; England had a settled line-up. We have just won the fourth Test; in '05, England went to The Oval having won the preceding game. Back then, we needed to win, we had to make all the running; England just needed to draw. This time, that situation is reversed and I'm happy about that.

This game, this series, is not about seeking revenge for that defeat four years ago. That time is gone; you can't change history. We've played more than 40 Tests since then, won an Ashes series in Australia, I've seen most of my team-mates from '05 retire. The lesson learned was that you can't ease off in your preparation, not even a little, and expect to win. Working hard doesn't guarantee you victory but it gives you every chance and that has been our philosophy for the past four years. Our preparation these past few days has been terrific.

Just one more sleep to go …

Thursday, August 27

FIFTH ASHES TEST

England v Australia at The Oval (August 20–23): England 332 (AJ Strauss
55, IR Bell 72; PM Siddle 4–75) and 9–373 (AJ Strauss 75, IJL Trott 119,
GP Swann 63; MJ North 4–98) defeated **Australia** 160 (SM Katich 50;
GP Swann 4–38, SCJ Broad 5–37) and 348 (RT Ponting 69, MEK Hussey
121; GP Swann 4–120) by 197 runs

***

After all the drama of the Edgbaston and Headingley starts, I
was ready for just about anything on the first morning at The
Oval, but by this series' standards the hour before the first ball
was pretty tame. Most attention was placed on the make-up of
the two sides, but in the end both teams went as most people
expected: we went with the same XI from the fourth Test;
England brought in Flintoff and Trott for Bopara and Onions.
There were a number of people predicting that the pitch would
break-up, but strangely (given the way the wicket played) most
of those who saw the pitch immediately before the toss were of
the view that it was a good, hard track.

Within a few minutes, though, as deliveries started to cut
through the surface, I knew that we'd misread the pitch. I'm sure,
if England could have changed their line-up after half an hour's
play, they would have brought in Monty Panesar to work with
Graeme Swann. In the same circumstances, we'd have definitely
gone with Nathan Hauritz. But this, of course, is with hindsight.

With hindsight, I would have called tails, too. For the fourth time in the series, I got it wrong at the toss and Andrew Strauss chose to bat. What followed was good, tough Test-match cricket as England sought to exploit their advantage in winning the toss, and our quicks tried to contain them. We got an early wicket — Cook, caught Ponting bowled Siddle in the sixth over — but after that there were times when it felt like they might be about to get away. This was especially true just before we dismissed Paul Collingwood about half an hour before tea. But we kept fighting, Mitchell Johnson came back to dismiss Matt Prior and Andrew Flintoff, and when Simon Katich produced a brilliant piece of reflex fielding at short leg to run out the new boy Trott, we were even on top. Had we got another wicket at that point, and cleaned up the tail before stumps, we would have gone into the second day on a real high.

Instead, Stuart Broad and Graeme Swann added 39 in the last 11 overs of the day. It was a crucial little stand, and there was a further minor frustration the next morning when Broad and Harmison put on 24 for the last wicket. However, we seemed to be back on song when Kato and Shane Watson started our reply in confident fashion. Just before lunch, though, it started to rain and with four balls left of the 21st over, the players came off early. We were 0–61. As I sat on our balcony, I was staggered to see how slowly the groundstaff were moving to get the covers on the wicket. For a while, it seemed as if they hadn't realised that this wasn't just the lunch interval, this was a break caused by rain and they had to get out there. I yelled at Tim Nielsen and Steve Bernard to ask someone to get them moving, but it still took what to me seemed like an eternity before the pitch was covered.

When the weather cleared it was announced that play would resume at 2.30pm. Swann finished his over, Strauss brought Flintoff back and then Broad was given his first over of the innings. The first five balls, from round the wicket, went for seven and then, back over the wicket for the last ball of the over, Watto was lbw, the beginning of just about the most disappointing batting collapse I have ever been involved in.

***

FIRST UP, I HAVE to say that Stuart Broad bowled magnificently. For the first Test and a half of this series, he looked out of sorts, as if he didn't really belong in Ashes cricket. Knocking me over in the second innings at Lord's probably helped, and looking back we probably did him a big favour at Edgbaston when we got in his face during his innings there. I guess by doing that we said we rated him (which we do), so maybe we should have just kept quiet and left him to battle with his lack of confidence. His effort in a losing cause at Headingley, taking his best figures in Test cricket and then smashing an impressive 61 on the final day, was excellent, but he was even better here.

The other thing is, we didn't bat well. There were too many loose shots and with the Ashes on the line that was just unacceptable. It wasn't easy and the bowling was good, but we had to battle through that and on the day we weren't up to the challenge. But I can't help thinking about that water that got on the wicket during the lunch break. That shouldn't have happened.

I was the second wicket to fall, playing on to Broad in similar fashion to how I was dismissed at Lord's. It was a poor shot, I should have let the delivery go, but he had seamed a couple into me and I found myself in two minds, not quite knowing where my off-stump was. Four runs later, Mike Hussey was lbw and four runs after that Michael Clarke pushed a ball to short cover, where Trott took a sharp catch. Wickets kept falling at regular intervals

— in 80 minutes we lost our first seven wickets for 38 runs — and our eventual first-innings deficit was 172.

In the middle session of the first day, England lost 2–72. In the middle session of the second day, we lost 8–72.

***

WE ACTUALLY STARTED THEIR second innings pretty well, getting three wickets before the close. Then, first ball of the third day, we thought Sidds had Trott caught behind but replays showed that umpire Asad Rauf had made a brilliant call, as the delivery just missed the outside edge but then brushed the thigh pad. The next ball hit the leading edge of Trott's bat and ballooned up into open territory on the offside for a single. It was incredibly tense cricket, and Strauss, the cagey veteran, and Trott, playing in his first game but looking just as composed, were brave and excellent. Later in the day, as the life went out of the wicket, things got a lot easier for the batters, but early on it was tough and I thought we really tested them. Strauss scored 75, and became the leading run-scorer in the series from either side, while Trott went all the way to a debut ton, a magnificent achievement. He became just the 18th man to score a century on his Test debut for England, and the seventh to do so in a Test against Australia — after WG Grace (in 1880), KS Ranjitsinhji (1896), RE Foster (1903–04), George Gunn (1907–08), Nawab of Pataudi Snr (1932–33) and Graham Thorpe (1993). Amazingly, four members of this current England team scored centuries on their Test debut: Strauss, Cook, Prior and now Trott.

Probably most impressive of all, Trott is the first man to score a century on debut in a Test that would decide the fate of the Ashes. That is quite a feat. He handled the pressure with aplomb and I was

Damn that Medal!

Earlier in this book, I highlighted my ordinary luck with the toss in Test matches. Having done that, I then went on a bit of run, winning six tosses in a row — the three Tests at home and the three away against South Africa.

Unfortunately, here in England I've been back to my old ways — winning one out of five. Over three Ashes series, I've won five tosses out of 15, and all up I've won 26 out of 61. I've been told WG Grace once refused to let Australian captain Jack Blackham use a 'lucky' penny at a Test-match toss, instead insisting on doing so himself. An Aussie captain, Joe Darling, lost all five tosses during the 1905 Ashes series and proposed wrestling for choice of innings, figuring he might have more luck that way. I'm not sure what to do, except maybe suggesting that we use any old coin next time rather than a beautiful specially minted medallion.

Maybe Stuart Clark is right. He ribs me about the toss every time I lose one. 'Punter,' he says, 'you've got to change. If you call "heads" every time you're probably going to win about 50 per cent of them. The only way you can win every toss is if you call different every time.'

'It's also the only way you lose every toss,' I counter.

That doesn't stop him.

taken by the television images I saw later of his mum as he reached three figures. She was clearly very, very proud, and rightly so.

Strauss chose to declare 20 overs before stumps, with a lead of 545 and the wicket playing better than it looked. There were instances when the ball broke the surface, dust and dirt sprayed everywhere, and some of the fast bowlers were really getting into the pitch on their follow-throughs, yet as a number of batters demonstrated during the Test, if you got in and you played smart you could make runs. I think a great spinner like Warney or Murali would have had a field day on this track, but while some balls did bite and kick and turn, a spinner still had to be good and clever to get wickets. Graeme Swann showed this during the Test and so did Marcus North.

To win, we needed to break all sorts of records for big fourth-innings run pursuits — the Test record for a successful fourth-innings chase is 7–418 by the West Indies against us in Antigua in 2003; the first-class record is 9–513 by Central Province against Southern Province at Kandy in 2003–04; win lose or

Stats Can Lie

There was quite a battle going on through the fifth Test to claim the title of the series' leading wicket-taker. Going into the game, Ben Hilfenhaus led the way with 18 wickets, clear from Peter Siddle and Mitchell Johnson, both on 16, with Stuart Broad and Jimmy Anderson the best of the Englishmen on 12.

By stumps on day one, Sidds had moved into the lead, on 20, with Hilfy on 19 and Mitch on 18, but then Hilfy took the last two wickets of the England innings and Broad took five in our first innings. After England's second innings, Hilfy was on 22, with Sidds and Mitch on 20, and Broad could only take one more wicket to leave my Tassie mate on top. This is quite an achievement for a bloke who probably would not have been selected for the first Test if Brett Lee had been fit.

So we finished with the leading wicket-takers for the series, and we also dominated in the century department. We scored eight in the series, to England's two. But sometimes it's not how many you score but when you make them that matters.

draw, there have only been 13 instances of a first-class team scoring 500 or more in the fourth innings, only four instances of a team scoring more than 546. But Watto and Kato did manage to get us to 0–80 at stumps, and there had been 395 runs scored during the third day, for the loss of six wickets, just a day after 15 wickets fell for 243.

I refused to think of the target as mission impossible, though I knew that if we were going to pull off an Ashes miracle that almost certainly I had to come up with a very big score. That's what I set myself to do.

✳✳✳

THE LAST THING WE needed was to lose early wickets, but that's what happened, with Kato and then Watto lbw in the first five overs. Huss came out to join me with his Test career on the line, but quickly we gelled and though every so often the ball would do something a little peculiar soon I felt like I was 'in'. Back at Edgbaston, Swann had embarrassed me with a superb delivery, but though this wicket was turning a lot, I rarely felt threatened by him.

It wasn't about batting to our target, more just taking it as it comes, an over, then a half-hour, then an hour, then a session at a time. I've always liked batting with Huss, who's great at geeing you up without ever going over the top. We knew this was a wicket that was difficult to bat on early, but if you could get used to the slow pace and variable bounce you could do a lot more than just survive. Occasionally, a ball would do something silly — as Strauss and Trott had done so well the previous day, you just had to put that out of your mind and not let it impinge on your approach to the next ball. Swann is a bowler who can often start to worry if he doesn't get a wicket and though I only scored

16 from my first 40 balls, after I hit him through the offside for consecutive boundaries he began to bowl a little quickly. Perhaps strangely, Strauss bowled Broad and Anderson before Flintoff, so that when the 'people's champion' (as he was being called on the television) came on to bowl I was on 26 and Huss was 25 and we were just about set. He bowled just the last four overs before lunch, and then Broad was back on after the resumption. Maybe the all-rounder's baton was being passed on.

There was one scare, just after I reached my fifty, when Collingwood almost conjured a slip catch off his boot, but other than that we continued on reasonably comfortably. Our hundred partnership came up in the 56th over, Broad was warned for running on the pitch, and then Strauss finally gave Harmison a bowl, for the first time all day. The bowler to come off was Swann, who had bowled all day pretty much without a break but taken only one wicket. There was precious little talk among the England players, the big crowd had gone quiet and Harmison started with a maiden. Then Huss reached his fifty after a poor piece of fielding and the crowd groaned.

First two balls of Harmison's third over were no-balls, and then off the second legitimate delivery I pushed him through the offside for two, no three, because Bell wasn't chasing hard. You couldn't help notice how ragged they were getting, and some of the spectators were into them. Three balls went scoreless, the third a real good yorker that Huss had to dig out. One ball left in the over ...

We were coming up to the drinks break, maybe another over, still only two wickets down. The refreshment would be just another signpost reached, and then we would set our sights on tea. Harmison was bowling, just lumbering in, and Huss got one a little short of a length and pushed it towards Andrew Flintoff at mid-on. My reflex, as the ball left the bat, was that there wasn't a run there, but Huss called, 'Yes!'

I was caught ball-watching, only for one stride, but a critical stride, and then I went with the call. If I'd gone immediately I might have been a chance but after that initial moment of hesitation I realised halfway down, maybe even earlier, that I was in trouble … I looked back once or twice, maybe hoping for a misfield, but that didn't slow me down and as I reached the striker's end the stumps exploded.

I knew immediately I was gone.

It's one of the cruel twists about the video replay. I was only a few inches out, maybe less than that, but I was definitely out. Even so, I had to stay there … to wait for a death sentence I knew was inevitable. It had to be Flintoff, too. This was his moment. After his throw ripped the off-stump out of the ground, he stood there with his arms outstretched just as he'd done at Lord's, and the crowd roared with him and for him. Then, when the out verdict came up on the big screen, they roared some more. I walked off in a daze, scarcely believing what had just happened to me. I was playing by the over, never getting ahead of myself, and I was playing well, so in control of my game. I had set myself to just bat and bat and bat and bat, be there at the finish, either to celebrate a remarkable victory or to be the last man out. But it wasn't to be. I've been in that state of mind when batting, been 'in the zone' as they say, a few times and the only occasions I can recall when it hasn't led to a big score was at Sydney in 2006–07, when I made 45 without playing a false stroke, and now here. I was run out both times. Cricket can be a cruel game.

So Pup had to get his runs and some of mine as well. Five balls after I was out, he drove a ball into Cook at short leg and took a stride or two down the wicket while the ball rebounded to Strauss at close-in backward square, just a couple of metres from the wicket. Strauss underarmed the ball into the stumps as Pup got back, and then umpire Bowden, as is his way, decided to wait a few unnecessary moments to call for the third umpire. I hadn't seen the run out 'live', because I was still coming to terms with my demise, but I found a TV and watched the replays and straightaway there didn't seem to be a problem, because there was nothing panicky about the way Pup reclaimed his ground. But then they showed another angle, and suddenly we realised he was in serious trouble. He looked out and it was clear the video umpire was seeking an angle that might tell a different story. None of them did. Two run outs … it just didn't seem fair.

Only then, as Pup walked off, did they call the drinks on to the field. Ten minutes earlier, you could almost hear the crowd starting to do their sums, as they realised if we could get to stumps with only three or four wickets down, we'd need less than 200 to win. Instead, we were 4–220. We still had batting to come, Huss was going well, but the mood had changed. You don't want to say it because you've got to have faith in your mates, but sometimes you can just sense these things. We were just about done.

✳✳✳

TO THIS POINT IN the series there hadn't been even one stumping, but when Northy was on 10 he went for a sweep, missed, and Prior took off the bails. Umpire Bowden didn't even need the video umpire. Maybe Hadds could repeat his Lord's heroics, though we needed more than 80 from him, even more than the 100 he made in Cardiff, which now seemed so long ago. Typical of the bloke, he went on the attack while Huss continued on to his hundred, his first since the Test in Bangalore back in October, the first Test covered in this book. He reached three figures from 219 balls, batting with a sense of calm and confidence that we hadn't seen all series. Back in '05, Matthew Hayden got a century at The Oval, which he used as a springboard to kickstart three more highly successful years in the baggy green. I'd love Huss to do the same.

The end came quickly. When Hadds miscued Swann to Strauss at mid-wicket we were 6–327, and then Mitch was caught in the slips off Harmison in the very next over. The same crowd that had once been dreading the ultimate Australian comeback was now in overdrive at the thought of actually witnessing the final wicket for themselves. All we could hope was

Blood Sport

I love fielding close to the wicket on the offside when the spinners are bowling, especially when there is something in the wicket for them. You're always in the game, you can look into the batter's eyes, and often see how he's thinking, there's a chance of a catch, straight off the bat or bat-pad, or maybe a run out if the batter thinks the ball has got by you, but it hasn't. And unlike fielding at short leg, there isn't much chance of being injured — maybe the ball hit hard into your shins, or your knee, but rarely anywhere near your head. There's no need for a helmet.

Usually! During England's second innings, as we searched for a wicket just before lunch on the third day, I went into silly mid-off to try to make something happen. Last ball of the over, Prior went for a big cover drive and slammed it straight into the ground. From there it flew into my face, catching me on the side of the mouth and I went to the interval spitting blood. It did hurt a bit, but not half as much as the scoreboard: England were 4–157, a lead of 329.

that somehow we could survive to stumps and then torrential rain that wasn't forecast would arrive overnight, but Sidds edged a catch to Flintoff and then Sarf was caught at short leg to put Harmison on a hat-trick. And 15 balls later, Huss's brave stand finally ended when he went bat-pad to Swann. He deserved better than to be the last wicket, the one they keep showing on the highlights reel, but like I said cricket can be cruel. Meanwhile, there was close to bedlam in the stands. England had regained the Ashes.

Inevitably, Andrew Flintoff was the focus of the crowd's joy and chants of 'Fred-dee! Fred-dee!' rang out time and again. The Barmy Army's trumpeter, who had been banned at Headingley, made up for lost time, but I must say that the England fans were very generous to us. I was grateful for the way I was clapped and cheered to and from the wicket, and there was none of the rubbish I'd been subjected to earlier in the tour. Freddie even asked if I'd hired a PR company to manage the crowd, such was their applause. The presentation seemed to go on forever, though I'm sure it was actually no longer than any other, and same as 2005 I was obliged to stay there and watch the ticker tape, the popping of champagne corks and the fireworks. Before this series, I would have bet 1000–1 about me coming back in four years time. As I stood there, though, I kept saying to myself, *I need to do this again, to get it right, to beat them on their turf.* And as I looked around The Oval, this great and famous venue where the Ashes legend was born, I was thinking, *It would be nice to have some good memories from this ground.*

I'll be 38 in 2013, maybe too old, but I won't rule it out, not if I've still got the desire. It's not 1000–1 anymore.

***

Goodbye to Fred

Andrew Flintoff's final Test might have been a bit of an anti-climax from his personal point of view if it hadn't been for the run out. He made only 7 in their first innings, had a couple of reasonable lbw shouts against Shane Watson, got the final wicket of our first innings (Ben Hilfenhaus), had some fun when he batted on the third day, took a catch near the end. That was it.

When he batted the second time, I made a point of shaking his hand. Then I brought in two short legs, to goad him into having a go. Which, of course, he did, slog-sweeping his second ball for four. He got to 22 from 17 deliveries and then aimed an almighty swing at Marcus North, and most fans' eyes went instinctively to a spot in the stands, maybe 20 rows back, as if that was the most likely place for it to go. However, he didn't quite get it and Peter Siddle took a comfortable catch about 10 metres in from the boundary rope.

He hardly scored a run and took just the one wicket, but he got the run out and he got it in spectacular style. As Kevin Garside wrote in the *Telegraph*, years from now there'll be plenty of Poms who'll remember exactly where they were and what they were doing when Freddie ran out Ponting, as if the Test and the Ashes were won and lost in that single moment, as if he did it all on his own. He was a special kind of cricketer, almost always with a smile on his face, a real stand-out in the current England set up. Test cricket won't be the same without him.

WHEN YOU WIN, YOU don't really want to go to the post-game media conference because you'd rather be with your mates, part of the celebrations. And who wants to talk about losing? It started, who'd have guessed, with a question about how this one compared to 2005.

'I don't remember exactly how I felt that night (in 2005). I know now that this defeat is hard to swallow. For me, the leader, the captain, the most experienced player, it's difficult for me to accept. Just as difficult for the rest of the guys.

'We had opportunities in this series. In Cardiff and Leeds we were exceptional, but a couple of really bad sessions have cost us the series. That is where we have come up a little bit short.'

I've talked a lot about the key moments over the past couple of years, how we have to win them if we want to win the big games. As it turned out, the key moments for us in this series came in those sessions when the ball started moving around and the England bowlers exploited the conditions superbly. Our first innings totals in the series reflect this: 6–674 declared, 215, 263, 445 and 160. When things started to go against us, we were unable to limit the damage; instead, we crashed and fell too many lengths behind. We just didn't show enough skill in those crucial passages of play. Our young players, many of whom with no Ashes experience before the series, have now learned that one hour, one ball, can determine a whole series.

I was asked if I thought there would be calls for my head …

'Leaders are always looked upon on their results. Unfortunately for me and the rest of the guys we haven't got the results we would have liked.

'You always have questions to answer when you lose a game like this. That is part of the job. It is what leaders are expected to do, whether in sport or business, and I have never doubted myself when I have the baggy green cap on. I always accept challenges head on.'

What about the future?

> 'There couldn't be a better example for the young guys than the last couple of months. They all should be a lot better off for being part of it.
>
> 'We're definitely heading in the right direction and I'm really proud of the guys. I think there are a lot of Test wins in this group of players ...
>
> '(But) we haven't been good enough. England won the big moments and they deserve to win the series.'

∗∗∗

By the time I got back to the room the boys had already had a couple of beers as they sat around having a chat about it all. I noticed Freddie was down one end, talking to Brett Lee, so I went over and joined them, congratulated him again on his career and asked him about his knee, about what would happen next. It was probably the longest chat I've ever had with him. He seemed very emotional, as if the occasion and the way the fans had cheered him had really got to him, brought out a side of him I'd never seen before, but before too long we all headed over to the home dressing room and we ended up staying there for a few hours. It was the first time the two teams had got together like this during the series. I had a couple of beers with Andrew Strauss, talking about the battles we'd just come through, how tough and competitive Ashes cricket is, about Twenty20 and how it might affect our futures, and about golf, something we're both pretty keen on. We talked about family, too — about how difficult it is to leave the ones we love and about the amount of time we are away from them. It was until close to midnight that we Aussies left the ground to go back to our hotel, where we —

A Day-Three Pitch

I don't think anyone who saw the pitch before the start of play would have thought in their wildest dreams that it would break up as badly as it did. Before the game, it had a good hard feel to it, and we believed it would turn later in the game. However, once the game started we realised quickly that by Test-match standards it wasn't a good wicket. Yet it produced a good Test match. The wicket didn't affect the result. Ironically, we batted better on the wicket when it was at its worst, in our second innings, than when it was close to its best, during our first innings. When you were batting, the occasional ball did surprise you, stop, keep low or kick up at you, but very few batters over the four days got out to deliveries made unplayable by the wicket.

Maybe Ian Bell got it right when he said, after making 72 on the first day, that it felt like 'a day-three pitch'. That being the case, by the end it was always going to worn and dusty.

the team and wives and partners — had a drink together at the hotel bar.

Next day, we had a sleep in and then Rianna and I found a nice restaurant where we had lunch together. I caught up with the coaches and a few of the boys at a pub later that afternoon and we had a bit of an informal 'debrief' on the series, dinner was had back at our room, and then we began the job of packing for the flight home. Throughout the 24 hours after the final wicket fell, I sensed that most of the guys felt pretty much the same as me about the loss of the Ashes, but I don't think anyone was hurting any more. I don't think anyone could.

***

I AM VERY GRATEFUL for the support Cricket Australia CEO James Sutherland gave me and the team straight after The Oval Test.

The day after the game, James responded to the inevitable calls from some quarters for players, coaches, selectors and the captain to be sacked by explaining that, while Cricket Australia would be conducting a comprehensive review of the series, he did not expect sweeping changes. He thought suggestions I should be given the boot were 'completely unfair' and acknowledged that I had been under 'incredible pressure'. He also stated that he didn't think the selectors were to blame for the loss of the Ashes. I don't think that either.

'At the end of the day, the players go out and do the business on the field,' James said. 'It was only six or seven months ago that we had a fantastic series in South Africa where we beat the No. 1 team in the world with a pretty similar line-up and the selectors were hailed for their selection and in some way the perceived risks that they took in backing young talent.'

As to all the criticism over Nathan Hauritz being left out of the final Test, maybe James nailed it best of all.

'We've lost the game by 200 runs which is a pretty significant defeat,' he said. 'Having a spinner in the side wouldn't have helped us in the first innings when we were bowled out for 160 and effectively lost the game.

'I don't think we're under any illusions as to where this team's at,' he continued. 'We're definitely in a rebuilding phase after losing some of the best players to ever play cricket for Australia. What you get with a young and relatively inexperienced team is some ebbs and flows in performance.

'Our best cricket was very, very good and our not-so-good cricket, perhaps in a couple of critical moments, were perhaps why we let the Ashes slip.'

I'll leave it to others to agree or disagree with James' views. I know, though, that he could have waited a few days, to see how the mood was shifting, before passing comment. He didn't do that. As I said, I am grateful for his backing, and the fact he gave it so strongly and immediately. There were a number of good things to come out of the past 12 months of cricket, even though we lost as often as we won. The growth in the relationship between the Australian team and Cricket Australia is one of them.

***

SO THIS MORNING, RIANNA, Emmy and I found ourselves at Heathrow, waiting to board our plane for home. I know that on the flight I will think a lot about the past seven weeks, and the last 12 months. It is a year to the day since I gave the Bradman Oration in Sydney, yet it seems so much longer than that.

I've already thought about the things they'll ask me after we land in Sydney. It'll be the future, specifically my future. What I'll tell them is that I think I've still got a lot to offer the team as a batsman and leader. I've got no intention of retiring, and I'll keep playing whether I've got a 'c' next to my name or not, but at the moment I feel I'm the best person to take the team forward. I am thinking about how to find more time to rest away from cricket, but how I achieve that for the moment I'm not quite sure.

If it ever gets to the point that I don't think I'm the best person to lead the team then I'll step aside, and if that happens, the way I feel at the moment, I'll keep playing. I love the game and I love wearing the baggy green cap. I also think I can get better — as a batter and a leader — and while that desire to improve is still in me I'd be mad to even contemplate giving it away. After we won in South Africa, and the way we won, I really thought we were on the right track and I still think that now, even though we've lost the Ashes. Our younger players can only be better for the experience.

I can't mask my disappointment at the Ashes result, yet there is so much to like about our future. Michael Clarke is now clearly one of the best batters in the world. I think our pace attack, that mixture of youth (Johnson, Hilfenhaus and Siddle) and experience (Lee and Clark) has the potential to be exceptional. After a frustrating few years battling injuries, Shane Watson looked every bit an international player — he can be the all-rounder we need to add balance to our side. Ideally, I'd like to see him in our middle-order, playing a true all-rounder's role, with Phillip Hughes coming back into the side. Despite being dropped after two Tests in this series, there is no doubt that Huey has a very bright future. You don't make 10 first-class centuries before your 21st birthday, and a hundred in each innings of just your second Test, unless you have something special.

Sure, he has work to do on his game, we all do — but I have no doubt he can come back a better player for his Ashes experience. Many of us have been dropped from the side and then come back to make a very significant contribution to the future of Australian cricket.

Huey's ups and down reflect the fact that right at the moment we're working through a difficult transition period, and I think we're going to be on a roller-coaster ride for a while yet. But the thought that has nagged at me over the past three days, since the last ball of the series was bowled, is that this current collection of Australian cricketers is a good group and they're going to get better. I really want to be part of that journey back to No. 1.

Epilogue

I GUESS, GIVEN THE way we dominated the seven-game NatWest series, I could write about how we got our 'revenge' on Andrew Strauss and England, how we 'set the record straight' and 'proved our critics wrong'. But it wasn't like that. It was good to win, it always is, but I would gladly swap all of our six victories for an Ashes win. I'd do that in a heartbeat.

I was in Australia while the boys thrashed Scotland in Edinburgh, had the weather ruin their two-match T20 series against England, and then won the first two one-dayers, at The Oval and Lord's. The day after the second game, I hopped on a plane to return to the tour, and you wouldn't believe how much fresher I felt after the 10 days at home. I really needed to free my mind of the Ashes and the time I spent with Rianna and Emmy sure did that. For game three, at the Rose Bowl in Southampton,

---

Australia v Scotland
One-Day International 2009

Only ODI, at Edinburgh (August 28): Australia 345 (50 overs: SR Watson 68, DJ Hussey 111, AC Voges 72; G Goudie 5–73) defeated Scotland 156 (39.3 overs: SR Watson 3–30)

I was in the dressing room as Cameron White (who was later named player of the series) and Michael Clarke guided us to a sensational victory. And then I came back for game four, if not feeling quite like a new man then at least feeling much, much brighter than the old bloke who'd been so mentally spent at the end of the final Ashes Test.

I was thrilled to see how the new blood — guys like Cameron, Callum Ferguson and Tim Paine — had revitalised the entire group, and with the break I'd enjoyed it was easy and exciting to fit in. First up, I hit a nice 48 as we cruised to victory at Lord's on the back of a brilliant bowling effort spearheaded by Brett Lee and Nathan Hauritz. Then I smashed my first ODI hundred since February 2008, a really fun innings of 126 from 109 balls which included a big six off the left-arm quick Ryan Sidebottom that landed up near the Trent Bridge press box beyond the long-on boundary. At the presentation afterwards I described it as 'the furthest I've ever hit one in my life' and I'm pretty sure that's right. Our winning margin this time was only four wickets, but considering we scored 6–302 to win, only the second time an Australian team had scored 300 in a ODI against England and the first time against England on their home turf, it was quite a

Binga's Back

After we announced our team for the fifth Ashes Test, I assured Brett Lee that just because he wasn't going to play in that crucial game, it didn't mean his Test career was over. 'Mate, for the moment, you've just got to focus on the shorter forms of the game,' I said. 'But if you get yourself back bowling well, don't worry, there'll be opportunities to get back into the Test team.'

Fact is, if Brett bowls as well as he can bowl and as fast as he can bowl, then there would be a place for him in any team around the world. I've got no doubt he can get back into our Test side if he puts the work in.

Bing is obviously disappointed he didn't get to play in the Tests, but he acknowledges that this happened because of bad luck rather than because the selectors took a set against him. He is a fast man who needs plenty of bowling under his belt, and it would have been asking a lot — in our view too much — to expect him to be going at full tilt in the fifth Test so soon after returning from a long spell. He finished as the leading wicket-taker in this NatWest series and his performance in game four, when he took the ninth five-for of his ODI career, was magnificent.

We'll always wonder what might have been if Bing had been available for the Tests, but of course England can think the same about Kevin Pietersen, and also, to a lesser degree, about Andrew Flintoff, who was missing when they lost the fourth Test.

polished effort. Two days later at the same venue, I only made six as we won by 111 runs on the back of some brilliant batting from Tim Paine and Mike Hussey and a swashbuckling all-round effort from James Hopes. But I came back in game seven to make another fifty, which hopefully will springboard me into a successful Champions Trophy campaign. I also had a good time in the field, averaging a run out a game, two of them direct hits from mid-wicket.

The only downer was that we were unable to complete a clean sweep. Because we lost, the final match of the series at Chester-le-Street wasn't a particularly memorable one for us, but it did have one unique feature — when Tim, Ben Hilfenhaus and I walked onto the field together, it was the first time three Tasmanians had featured in the same Australian side for an international match (Test, ODI or T20 game).

Tim kept wicket and opened the batting for us throughout the series, with his highlight being the terrific century he scored at Nottingham. He became the third Aussie keeper to score a ODI hundred, after Gilchrist and Brad Haddin (coincidentally, all these hundreds have been made as an opening batsman) and he'll continue as our keeper for the upcoming Champions Trophy, to give Hadds all the time he needs to fix that finger he broke a few minutes before the start of the third Test.

It's amazing to think, as I write this, that it's less than two months since that frantic start at Edgbaston, when the toss was rushed, Hadds broke his finger, Shane Watson opened the batting for Australia for the first time and Graham Manou made his Test debut. That all seemed to happen a long time ago. Our first match in South Africa is against the West Indies in Johannesburg on September 26. The final, if we make it, is on October 5. Then we go to India for seven one-dayers, then we're back home for another summer of cricket, this time against the West Indies and Pakistan. The cricket caravan rarely stops, and when it does, it's never for long.

✳✳✳

IT WAS MOSTLY BECAUSE of this never-ending schedule that I made the decision, before I returned to England after my short break, to retire from international Twenty20 cricket. I'm keen to continue my relationship with the Kolkata Knight Riders and where possible play for Tasmania in the domestic T20 competition in the coming seasons, but as far as Australian representation is concerned, I'm going to focus on Tests and ODIs.

It was a tough decision, made because I need to best manage my overall schedule. It's not as if I've set myself to continue until any specific date, but I have been thinking, *If I want to keep going for a few more years, something has to give.* Test cricket is especially dear to my heart, I've still got my sights firmly on the 2011 World Cup, so that something had to be the T20s. One thing that has been nagging at me is the reality that in recent years I have been at my best at the start of series. As I've already documented in this book, the hundred I made at Cardiff was the 11th time I scored a hundred in the opening Test of the series and the sixth time in the last four years. In contrast, while I've scored a century in the last Test of a series on nine occasions, it's never happened in a series involving more than three matches. It could be just coincidence, but I have to accept that maybe mental fatigue is a factor.

I remain very passionate about and committed to being the best player I can be for Australia for as long as possible. Retiring from T20 international cricket means I will now have set periods of rest throughout the Australian summer and while touring, which I feel will be very beneficial. By my maths, I could get an extra four weeks of rest over the next 12 months, which I'm sure will prolong my life as a Test and ODI cricketer.

Whether it'll give me the chance to have one more crack at the Ashes in England, though, we'll just have to wait and see.

NatWest Series: Australia v England One-Day Internationals 2009

First ODI, at The Oval (September 4): Australia 5–260 (50 overs: SR Watson 46, CK White 53, MJ Clarke 45, CJ Ferguson 71*) defeated England 8–256 (50 overs: RS Bopara 49, OA Shah 40; MG Johnson 3–24) by four runs

Second ODI, at Lord's (September 6): Australia 8–249 (50 overs: CL White 42, CJ Ferguson 55, MG Johnson 43*) defeated England 210 (46.1 overs: AJ Strauss 47, PD Collingwood 56) by 39 runs

Third ODI, at Southampton (September 9): England 9–228 (50 overs: AJ Strauss 63, EJG Morgan 43; SR Watson 3–36) lost to Australia 4–230 (48.3 overs: CL White 105, MJ Clarke 52) by six wickets

Fourth ODI, at Lord's (September 12): England 220 (46.3 overs: AJ Strauss 63; B Lee 5–49) lost to Australia 3–221 (43.4 overs: TD Paine 51, RT Ponting 48, MJ Clarke 62*) by seven wickets

Fifth ODI, at Nottingham (September 15): England 299 (50 overs: JL Denly 45, EJG Morgan 58) lost to Australia 6–302 (48.2 overs: RT Ponting 126, MJ Clarke 52) by four wickets

Sixth ODI, at Nottingham (September 17): Australia 8–296 (50 overs: TD Paine 111, MEK Hussey 65; JM Anderson 4–55) defeated England 185 (JR Hopes 3–32) by 111 runs

Seventh ODI, at Chester-le-Street (September 20): Australia 176 (45.5 overs: RT Ponting 53, MEK Hussey 49; GP Swann 5–28) lost to England 6–177 (40 overs: AJ Strauss 47, JL Denly 53) by four wickets

TEST SCORES AND AVERAGES

AUSTRALIA'S MATCHES
AUGUST 2008–SEPTEMBER 2009

Date	Match	Opponent	Venue	Result
Aug 30	First ODI	Bangladesh	Darwin	won by 180 runs
Sep 3	Second ODI	Bangladesh	Darwin	won by 8 wickets
Sep 6	Third ODI	Bangladesh	Darwin	won by 73 runs
Sep 27–28	Tour game	RCA Centre of Excellence	Jaipur	drawn
Oct 2–5	Tour game	Indian Board President's XI	Hyderabad	drawn
Oct 9–13	First Test	India	Bangalore	drawn
Oct 17–21	Second Test	India	Mohali	lost by 320 runs
Oct 29–Nov 2	Third Test	India	Delhi	drawn
Nov 6–10	Fourth Test	India	Nagpur	lost by 172 runs
Nov 20–23	First Test	New Zealand	Brisbane	won by 149 runs
Nov 28–Dec 1	Second Test	New Zealand	Adelaide	won by innings & 62 runs
Dec 17–21	First Test	South Africa	Perth	lost by 6 wickets
Dec 26–30	Second Test	South Africa	Melbourne	lost by 9 wickets
Jan 3–7	Third Test	South Africa	Sydney	won by 103 runs
Jan 11	First T20I	South Africa	Melbourne	won by 52 runs
Jan 13	Second T20I	South Africa	Brisbane	won by 6 wickets
Jan 16	First ODI	South Africa	Melbourne	lost by 3 wickets
Jan 18	Second ODI	South Africa	Hobart	won by 5 runs
Jan 23	Third ODI	South Africa	Sydney	lost by 3 wickets
Jan 26	Fourth ODI	South Africa	Adelaide	lost by 8 wickets
Jan 30	Fifth ODI	South Africa	Perth	lost by 39 runs
Feb 1	First ODI	New Zealand	Perth	lost by 2 wickets
Feb 6	Second ODI	New Zealand	Melbourne	lost by 6 wickets
Feb 8	Third ODI	New Zealand	Sydney	won by 32 runs
Feb 10	Fourth ODI	New Zealand	Adelaide	won by 6 wickets
Feb 13	Fifth ODI	New Zealand	Brisbane	no result
Feb 15	T20I	New Zealand	Sydney	won by 1 run
Feb 20–22	Tour game	SA Board President's XI	Potchefstroom	drawn
Feb 26–Mar 2	First Test	South Africa	Johannesburg	won by 162 runs
Mar 6–10	Second Test	South Africa	Durban	won by 175 runs
Mar 19–22	Third Test	South Africa	Cape Town	lost by innings & 20 runs
Mar 27	First T20I	South Africa	Johannesburg	lost by 4 wickets
Mar 29	Second T20I	South Africa	Centurion	lost by 17 runs
Apr 3	First ODI	South Africa	Durban	won by 141 runs
Apr 5	Second ODI	South Africa	Centurion	lost by 7 wickets
Apr 9	Third ODI	South Africa	Cape Town	lost by 25 runs
Apr 13	Fourth ODI	South Africa	Port Elizabeth	lost by 61 runs
Apr 17	Fifth ODI	South Africa	Johannesburg	won by 47 runs
Apr 22	First ODI	Pakistan	Dubai	lost by 4 wickets
Apr 24	Second ODI	Pakistan	Dubai	won by 6 wickets
Apr 27	Third ODI	Pakistan	Abu Dhabi	won by 27 runs
May 1	Fourth ODI	Pakistan	Abu Dhabi	won by 8 wickets
May 3	Fifth ODI	Pakistan	Abu Dhabi	lost by 7 wickets
May 7	T20I	Pakistan	Dubai	lost by 7 wickets
Jun 1	T20 warm–up	Bangladesh	Nottingham	won by 38 runs
Jun 2	T20 warm–up	New Zealand	The Oval	won by 7 wickets

Date	Match	Opponent	Venue	Result
Jun 6	World T20I	West Indies	The Oval	lost by 7 wickets
Jun 8	World T20I	Sri Lanka	Nottingham	lost by 6 wickets
Jun 24–27	Tour game	Sussex	Hove	drawn
Jul 1–4	Tour game	England Lions	Worcester	drawn
Jul 8–12	First Test	England	Cardiff	drawn
Jul 16–20	Second Test	England	Lord's	lost by 115 runs
Jul 24–26	Tour game	Northamptonshire	Northampton	won by 135 runs
Jul 30–Aug 3	Third Test	England	Birmingham	drawn
Aug 7–9	Fourth Test	England	Leeds	won by innings & 80 runs
Aug 15–16	Tour game	England Lions	Canterbury	won by 103 runs
Aug 20–23	Fifth Test	England	The Oval	lost by 197 runs
Aug 28	ODI	Scotland	Edinburgh	won by 189 runs
Aug 30	First T20I	England	Manchester	no result
Sep 1	Second T20I	England	Manchester	abandoned
Sep 4	First ODI	England	The Oval	won by 4 runs
Sep 6	Second ODI	England	Lord's	won by 39 runs
Sep 9	Third ODI	England	Southampton	won by 6 wickets
Sep 12	Fourth ODI	England	Lord's	won by 7 wickets
Sep 15	Fifth ODI	England	Nottingham	won by 4 wickets
Sep 17	Sixth ODI	England	Nottingham	won by 111 runs
Sep 20	Seventh ODI	England	Chester–le–Street	lost by 4 wickets

SUMMARY

TESTS

Opponent	Tests	Won	Lost	Drawn
India	4	–	2	2
New Zealand	2	2	–	–
South Africa	6	3	3	–
England	5	1	2	2
Total	17	6	7	4

ONE-DAY INTERNATIONALS

Opponent	ODIs	Won	Lost	No Result
Bangladesh	3	3	–	–
New Zealand	5	2	2	1
South Africa	10	3	7	–
Pakistan	5	3	2	–
Scotland	1	1	–	–
England	7	6	1	–
Total	31	18	12	1

TWENTY20 INTERNATIONALS

Opponent	T20Is	Won	Lost	No Result
South Africa	4	2	2	–
New Zealand	1	1	–	–
Pakistan	1	–	1	–
West Indies	1	–	1	–
Sri Lanka	1	–	1	–
England	1	–	–	1
Total	9	3	5	1

First Test, Australia v India at Bangalore

9–13 October 2008 • TOSS: Australia
UMPIRES: Asad Rauf (Pakistan) and Rudi Koertzen (South Africa)
MATCH REFEREE: Chris Broad (England)
PLAYER OF THE MATCH: Zaheer Khan (India)

Australia first innings

ML Hayden	c Dhoni b Khan	0
SM Katich	c Dhoni b Sharma	66
RT Ponting	lbw Harbhajan Singh	123
MEK Hussey	b Khan	146
MJ Clarke	lbw Khan	11
SR Watson	b Sharma	2
BJ Haddin	c Laxman b Sharma	33
CL White	c Harbhajan Singh b Sharma	6
B Lee	b Khan	27
MG Johnson	b Khan	1
SR Clark	not out	0
Extras	(lb 11, w 1, nb 3)	15
Total	(all out; 149.5 overs)	430

FALL OF WICKETS: 1–0 (Hayden, 0.3 ov), 2–166 (Katich, 54.4 ov), 3–226 (Ponting, 78.4 ov), 4–254 (Clarke, 89.2 ov), 5–259 (Watson, 92.3 ov), 6–350 (Haddin, 122.6 ov), 7–362 (White, 126.5 ov), 8–421 (Lee, 147.5 ov), 9–429 (Johnson, 149.1 ov), 10–430 (Hussey, 149.5 ov)

BOWLING: Khan 29.5–4–91–5; Sharma 30–7–77–4; Harbhajan Singh 41–8–103–1; Kumble 43–6–129–0; Sehwag 6–0–19–0

India first innings

G Gambhir	lbw Lee	21
V Sehwag	c Hayden b Johnson	45
R Dravid	lbw Watson	51
SR Tendulkar	c White b Johnson	13
VVS Laxman	c Haddin b Johnson	0
SC Ganguly	lbw Johnson	47
MS Dhoni	b Clarke	9
Harbhajan Singh	c Haddin b Watson	54
Z Khan	not out	57
A Kumble	lbw Watson	5
I Sharma	b Clarke	6
Extras	(b 23, lb 23, nb 6)	52
Total	(all out; 119 overs)	360

FALL OF WICKETS: 1–70 (Gambhir, 19.2 ov), 2–76 (Sehwag, 22.6 ov), 3–94 (Tendulkar, 28.4 ov), 4–106 (Laxman, 32.6 ov), 5–155 (Dravid, 49.5 ov), 6–195 (Dhoni, 65.4 ov), 7–232 (Ganguly, 77.3 ov), 8–312 (Harbhajan Singh, 99.3 ov), 9–343 (Kumble, 111.6 ov), 10–360 (Sharma, 118.6 ov)

BOWLING: Lee 26–6–64–1; Clark 17–3–58–0; Johnson 27–4–70–4; Watson 19–4–45–3; White 13–2–39–0; Clarke 17–3–38–2

Australia second innings

ML Hayden	lbw Khan	13
SM Katich	c Laxman b Harbhajan Singh	34
RT Ponting	c Laxman b Sharma	17
MEK Hussey	b Harbhajan Singh	31
MJ Clarke	c Sehwag b Sharma	6
SR Watson	b Sharma	41
BJ Haddin	not out	35
CL White	not out	18
Extras	(b 13, lb 10, w 6, nb 4)	33
Total	(6 wickets dec; 73 overs)	228

FALL OF WICKETS: 1–21 (Hayden, 12.2 ov), 2–49 (Ponting, 22.2 ov), 3–99 (Katich, 44.3 ov), 4–115 (Clarke, 47.5 ov), 5–128 (Hussey, 50.5 ov), 6–203 (Watson, 69.2 ov)

BOWLING: Khan 17–4–46–1; Sharma 14–3–40–3; Harbhajan Singh 27–5–76–2; Sehwag 7–1–12–0; Kumble 8–0–31–0

India second innings (target: 299 runs)

G Gambhir	b Johnson	29
V Sehwag	c Hayden b Clark	6
R Dravid	c Ponting b Lee	5
SR Tendulkar	c Clarke b White	49
VVS Laxman	not out	42
SC Ganguly	not out	26
Extras	(b 16, lb 3, nb 1)	20
Total	(4 wickets; 73 overs)	177

FALL OF WICKETS: 1–16 (Sehwag, 5.1 ov), 2–24 (Dravid, 8.3 ov), 3–77 (Gambhir, 26.4 ov), 4–138 (Tendulkar, 52.2 ov)

BOWLING: Lee 11–3–26–1; Clark 11–6–12–1; Watson 5–2–8–0; Johnson 8–3–23–1; Clarke 20–7–40–0; White 18–4–49–1

Stumps Scores
DAY 1: Australia first innings 4–254 (Hussey 46; 89.2 overs)
DAY 2: India first innings 0–68 (Gambhir 20, Sehwag 43; 18.1 overs)
DAY 3: India first innings 8–313 (Khan 35, Kumble 0; 101 overs)
DAY 4: Australia second innings 5–193 (Watson 32; Haddin 28, 68 overs)

MATCH DRAWN

Second Test, Australia v India at Mohali

17–21 October 2008 • TOSS: India
UMPIRES: Asad Rauf (Pakistan) and Rudi Koertzen (South Africa)
MATCH REFEREE: Chris Broad (England)
PLAYER OF THE MATCH: MS Dhoni (India)

India first innings

G Gambhir	c Haddin b Johnson	67
V Sehwag	c Haddin b Johnson	35
R Dravid	b Lee	39
SR Tendulkar	c Hayden b Siddle	88
VVS Laxman	c Haddin b Johnson	12
SC Ganguly	c Lee b White	102
I Sharma	c Katich b Siddle	9
MS Dhoni	lbw Siddle	92
Harbhajan Singh	b White	1
Z Khan	run out (Lee/Haddin)	2
A Mishra	not out	0
Extras	(b 4, lb 10, w 5, nb 3)	22
Total	(all out; 129 overs)	469

FALL OF WICKETS: 1–70 (Sehwag, 14.2 ov), 2–146 (Dravid, 40.5 ov), 3–146 (Gambhir, 41.1 ov), 4–163 (Laxman, 45.1 ov), 5–305 (Tendulkar, 81.5 ov), 6–326 (Sharma, 89.6 ov), 7–435 (Ganguly, 119.1 ov), 8–442 (Harbhajan Singh, 123.1 ov), 9–469 (Khan, 127.6 ov), 10–469 (Dhoni, 128.6 ov)

BOWLING: Lee 24–5–86–1; Siddle 28–5–114–3; Johnson 27–4–85–3; Watson 24–3–71–0; Clarke 7–0–28–0; White 19–0–71–2

Australia first innings

ML Hayden	b Khan	0
SM Katich	b Mishra	33
RT Ponting	lbw Sharma	5
MEK Hussey	c Dhoni b Sharma	54
MJ Clarke	lbw Mishra	23
SR Watson	lbw Mishra	78
BJ Haddin	b Harbhajan Singh	9
CL White	b Mishra	5
B Lee	c Dravid b Harbhajan Singh	35
MG Johnson	not out	9
PM Siddle	st Dhoni b Mishra	0
Extras	(lb 13, nb 4)	17
Total	(all out; 101.4 overs)	268

FALL OF WICKETS: 1–0 (Hayden, 0.3 ov), 2–17 (Ponting, 7.5 ov), 3–62 (Katich, 21.6 ov), 4–102 (Clarke, 40.5 ov), 5–130 (Hussey, 47.5 ov), 6–146 (Haddin, 55.3 ov), 7–167 (White, 62.2 ov), 8–240 (Lee, 90.1 ov), 9–262 (Watson, 99.2 ov), 10–268 (Siddle, 101.4 ov)

BOWLING: Khan 25–7–56–1; Sharma 21–4–68–2; Harbhajan Singh 29–9–60–2; Mishra 26.4–8–71–5

India second innings

G Gambhir	c Hussey b White	104
V Sehwag	c Haddin b Siddle	90
MS Dhoni	not out	68
SC Ganguly	c Clarke b Lee	27
SR Tendulkar	not out	10
Extras	(b 3, lb 4, w 5, nb 3)	15
Total	(3 wickets dec; 65 overs)	314

FALL OF WICKETS: 1–182 (Sehwag, 39.1 ov), 2–224 (Gambhir, 47.5 ov), 3–290 (Ganguly, 61.6 ov)

BOWLING: Lee 14–0–61–1; Siddle 15–1–62–1; Johnson 14–0–72–0; White 8–0–48–1; Watson 5–0–20–0; Hussey 8–0–38–0; Clarke 1–0–6–0

Australia second innings (target: 516 runs)

ML Hayden	lbw Harbhajan Singh	29
SM Katich	c Tendulkar b Harbhajan Singh	20
RT Ponting	b Sharma	2
MEK Hussey	lbw Harbhajan Singh	1
MJ Clarke	c Sehwag b Mishra	69
SR Watson	lbw Sharma	2
BJ Haddin	b Khan	37
CL White	c Dhoni b Khan	1
B Lee	b Khan	0
MG Johnson	c&b Mishra	26
PM Siddle	not out	0
Extras	(b 4, nb 4)	8
Total	(all out; 64.4 overs)	195

FALL OF WICKETS: 1–49 (Hayden, 7.2 ov), 2–50 (Katich, 7.6 ov), 3–52 (Hussey, 9.5 ov), 4–52 (Ponting, 10.2 ov), 5–58 (Watson, 16.3 ov), 6–142 (Haddin, 46.6 ov), 7–144 (White, 48.2 ov), 8–144 (Lee, 48.3 ov), 9–194 (Johnson, 62.6 ov), 10–195 (Clarke, 64.4 ov)

BOWLING: Khan 15–3–71–3; Sharma 13–4–42–2; Harbhajan Singh 20–3–36–3; Mishra 11.4–2–35–2; Sehwag 5–2–7–0

Stumps scores
DAY 1: India first innings 5–311 (Ganguly 54, Sharma 2; 85 overs)
DAY 2: Australia first innings 4–102 (Hussey 37; 40.5 overs)
DAY 3: India second innings 0–100 (Gambhir 46, Sehwag 53; 23 overs)
DAY 4: Australia second innings 5–141 (Clarke 42, Haddin 37; 46 overs)

INDIA WON BY 320 RUNS

Third Test, Australia v India at Delhi

29 October–2 November 2 2008 • TOSS: India
UMPIRES: Aleem Dar (Pakistan) and Billy Bowden (New Zealand)
MATCH REFEREE: Chris Broad (England)
PLAYER OF THE MATCH: VVS Laxman (India)

India first innings

G Gambhir	b Watson	206
V Sehwag	lbw Lee	1
R Dravid	c Hayden b Johnson	11
SR Tendulkar	c Haddin b Johnson	68
VVS Laxman	not out	200
SC Ganguly	c Ponting b Katich	5
MS Dhoni	c Haddin b Watson	27
A Kumble	lbw Johnson	45
Z Khan	not out	28
Extras	(b 6, lb 8, w 2, nb 6)	22
Total	(7 wickets dec; 161 overs)	613

Did not bat: I Sharma, A Mishra

FALL OF WICKETS: 1–5 (Sehwag, 2.1 ov), 2–27 (Dravid, 10.4 ov), 3–157 (Tendulkar, 51.5 ov), 4–435 (Gambhir, 123.6 ov), 5–444 (Ganguly, 126.2 ov), 6–481 (Dhoni, 133.4 ov), 7–579 (Kumble, 155.4 ov)

BOWLING: Lee 30–2–119–1; Clark 33–9–69–0; Johnson 32–4–142–3; Watson 20–4–66–2; White 15–1–73–0; Clarke 14–0–59–0; Katich 15–3–60–1; Ponting 2–0–11–0

Australia first innings

ML Hayden	lbw Sehwag	83
SM Katich	b Mishra	64
RT Ponting	b Sehwag	87
MEK Hussey	b Sehwag	53
MJ Clarke	c Khan b Mishra	112
SR Watson	b Sehwag	36
BJ Haddin	st Dhoni b Kumble	17
CL White	b Sehwag	44
B Lee	lbw Kumble	8
MG Johnson	c&b Kumble	15
SR Clark	not out	1
Extras	(b 28, lb 17, w 2, nb 10)	57
Total	(all out; 179.3 overs)	577

FALL OF WICKETS: 1–123 (Katich, 34.1 ov), 2–202 (Hayden, 57.2 ov), 3–284 (Ponting, 85.4 ov), 4–326 (Hussey, 101.6 ov), 5–399 (Watson, 122.1 ov), 6–426 (Haddin, 131.5 ov), 7–532 (White, 162.5 ov), 8–555 (Lee, 175.4 ov), 9–567 (Clarke, 178.1 ov), 10–577 (Johnson, 179.3 ov)

BOWLING: Khan 23–5–86–0; Sharma 25–5–84–0; Kumble 43.3–9–112–3; Mishra 47–12–144–2; Sehwag 40–9–104–5; Tendulkar 1–0–2–0

India second innings

G Gambhir	lbw Johnson	36
V Sehwag	b Lee	16
I Sharma	c Ponting b Clark	1
R Dravid	b Lee	11
SR Tendulkar	c Hayden b White	47
VVS Laxman	not out	59
SC Ganguly	not out	32
Extras	(lb 4, w 1, nb 1)	6
Total	(5 wickets dec; 77.3 overs)	208

FALL OF WICKETS: 1–29 (Sehwag, 8.2 ov), 2–34 (Sharma, 9.1 ov), 3–53 (Dravid, 20.4 ov), 4–93 (Gambhir, 36.5 ov), 5–145 (Tendulkar, 57.1 ov)

BOWLING: Lee 17–3–48–2; Clark 12–6–22–1; Clarke 20.3–7–56–0; Katich 1–0–5–0; Johnson 12–0–23–1; White 8–0–23–1; Watson 7–0–27–0

Australia second innings (target: 245 runs)

ML Hayden	not out	16
SM Katich	not out	14
Extras	(lb 1)	1
Total	(0 wickets; 8 overs)	31

BOWLING: Kumble 4–0–14–0; Sehwag 2–0–14–0; Mishra 2–0–2–0

Stumps scores

DAY 1: India first innings 3–296 (Gambhir 149, Laxman 54; 89 overs)
DAY 2: Australia first innings 0–50 (Hayden 16, Katich 29; 15 overs)
DAY 3: Australia first innings 4–338 (Clarke 21, Watson 4; 105 overs)
DAY 4: India second innings 2–43 (Gambhir 21, Dravid 5; 13 overs)

MATCH DRAWN

Fourth Test, Australia v India at Nagpur

6–10 November 2008 • TOSS: India
UMPIRES: Aleem Dar (Pakistan) and Billy Bowden (New Zealand)
MATCH REFEREE: Chris Broad (England) • PLAYER OF THE MATCH: Jason Krejza (Australia)
PLAYER OF THE SERIES: Ishant Sharma (India)

India first innings

V Sehwag	b Krejza	66
M Vijay	c Haddin b Watson	33
R Dravid	c Katich b Krejza	0
SR Tendulkar	lbw Johnson	109
VVS Laxman	c Haddin b Krejza	64
SC Ganguly	c Clarke b Krejza	85
MS Dhoni	b Krejza	56
Harbhajan Singh	not out	18
Z Khan	b Krejza	1
A Mishra	b Krejza	0
I Sharma	c Katich b Krejza	0
Extras	(b 4, lb 2, w 1, nb 2)	9
Total	(all out; 124.5 overs)	441

FALL OF WICKETS: 1–98 (Vijay, 17.5 ov), 2–99 (Dravid, 18.4 ov), 3–116 (Sehwag, 22.3 ov), 4–262 (Laxman, 68.4 ov), 5–303 (Tendulkar, 82.5 ov), 6–422 (Dhoni, 116.4 ov), 7–423 (Ganguly, 116.6 ov), 8–437 (Khan, 122.3 ov), 9–437 (Mishra, 122.4 ov), 10–441 (Sharma, 124.5 ov)

BOWLING: Lee 16–2–62–0; Johnson 32–11–84–1; Watson 20–5–42–1; Krejza 43.5–1–215–8; White 10–1–24–0; Katich 3–0–8–0

India second innings

V Sehwag	c Haddin b Lee	92
M Vijay	lbw Watson	41
R Dravid	c Haddin b Watson	3
SR Tendulkar	run out (White/Haddin)	12
VVS Laxman	b Krejza	4
SC Ganguly	c&b Krejza	0
MS Dhoni	c Hussey b Krejza	55
Harbhajan Singh	b Watson	52
Z Khan	c Haddin b Krejza	6
A Mishra	b Watson	7
I Sharma	not out	1
Extras	(b 6, lb 3, w 6, nb 2, pen 5)	22
Total	(all out; 82.4 overs)	295

FALL OF WICKETS: 1–116 (Vijay, 28.2 ov), 2–132 (Dravid, 32.5 ov), 3–142 (Sehwag, 35.1 ov), 4–163 (Laxman, 47.1 ov), 5–163 (Ganguly, 47.2 ov), 6–166 (Tendulkar, 49.5 ov), 7–274 (Dhoni, 77.1 ov), 8–286 (Khan, 79.2 ov), 9–288 (Harbhajan Singh, 80.1 ov), 10–295 (Mishra, 82.4 ov)

BOWLING: Johnson 14–4–22–0; Lee 10–3–27–1; Krejza 31–3–143–4; Watson 15.4–2–42–4; White 2–0–15–0; Hussey 4–2–3–0; Clarke 6–1–29–0

Australia first innings

ML Hayden	run out (Vijay)	16
SM Katich	lbw Khan	102
RT Ponting	b Harbhajan Singh	24
MEK Hussey	run out (Vijay/Dhoni)	90
MJ Clarke	c Dhoni b Sharma	8
SR Watson	b Harbhajan Singh	2
BJ Haddin	c Dravid b Mishra	28
CL White	c Sehwag b Harbhajan Singh	46
JJ Krejza	lbw Sharma	5
MG Johnson	c Khan b Mishra	5
B Lee	not out	1
Extras	(b 12, lb 3, w 2, nb 6, pen 5)	28
Total	(all out; 134.4 overs)	355

FALL OF WICKETS: 1–32 (Hayden, 6.5 ov), 2–74 (Ponting, 17.1 ov), 3–229 (Katich, 70.6 ov), 4–255 (Clarke, 84.4 ov), 5–265 (Hussey, 89.5 ov), 6–266 (Watson, 91.4 ov), 7–318 (Haddin, 115.5 ov), 8–333 (Krejza, 126.1 ov), 9–352 (White, 133.2 ov), 10–355 (Johnson, 134.4 ov)

BOWLING: Khan 28–8–68–1; Harbhajan Singh 37–7–94–3; Sharma 26–8–64–2; Mishra 23.4–5–58–2; Sehwag 18–2–38–0; Tendulkar 2–0–13–0

Australia second innings (target: 382 runs)

ML Hayden	lbw Harbhajan Singh	77
SM Katich	c Dhoni b Sharma	16
RT Ponting	run out (Mishra)	8
MJ Clarke	c Dhoni b Sharma	22
MEK Hussey	c Dravid b Mishra	19
SR Watson	c Dhoni b Harbhajan Singh	9
BJ Haddin	c Tendulkar b Mishra	4
CL White	not out	26
JJ Krejza	st Dhoni b Mishra	4
B Lee	c Vijay b Harbhajan Singh	0
MG Johnson	lbw Harbhajan Singh	11
Extras	(b 6, lb 1, w 4, nb 2)	13
Total	(all out; 50.2 overs)	209

FALL OF WICKETS: 1–29 (Katich, 5.4 ov), 2–37 (Ponting, 6.6 ov), 3–82 (Clarke, 15.5 ov), 4–150 (Hussey, 28.4 ov), 5–154 (Hayden, 29.2 ov), 6–161 (Haddin, 32.4 ov), 7–178 (Watson, 38.4 ov), 8–190 (Krejza, 43.5 ov), 9–191 (Lee, 44.4 ov), 10–209 (Johnson, 50.2 ov)

BOWLING: Khan 8–0–57–0; Sharma 9–0–31–2; Harbhajan Singh 18.2–2–64–4; Sehwag 4–0–23–0; Mishra 11–2–27–3

Stumps scores

DAY 1: India first innings 5–311 (Ganguly 27, Dhoni 4; 87 overs)
DAY 2: Australia first innings 2–189 (Katich 92, Hussey 45; 49 overs)
DAY 3: India second innings 0–0 (Sehwag 0, Vijay 0; 1 overs)
DAY 4: Australia second innings 0–13 (Hayden 5, Katich 8; 1.3 overs)

INDIA WON BY 172 RUNS

First Test, Australia v New Zealand at Brisbane

20–23 November 2008 • TOSS: New Zealand
UMPIRES: Billy Doctrove (West Indies) and Rudi Koertzen (South Africa)
MATCH REFEREE: Chris Broad (England)
PLAYER OF THE MATCH: Mitchell Johnson (Australia)

Australia first innings

ML Hayden	c Taylor b Southee	8
SM Katich	c McCullum b Southee	10
RT Ponting	c How b Southee	4
MEK Hussey	lbw Martin	35
MJ Clarke	b Ryder	98
A Symonds	c McCullum b O'Brien	26
SR Watson	c McCullum b O'Brien	1
BJ Haddin	c How b Ryder	6
B Lee	c McCullum b Southee	4
MG Johnson	c Taylor b Vettori	5
SR Clark	not out	13
Extras	(lb 2, w 1, nb 1)	4
Total	(all out; 77 overs)	214

FALL OF WICKETS: 1–13 (Hayden, 3.6 ov), 2–22 (Katich, 5.6 ov), 3–23 (Ponting, 7.1 ov), 4–96 (Hussey, 33.4 ov), 5–132 (Symonds, 45.5 ov), 6–139 (Watson, 49.1 ov), 7–152 (Haddin, 54.4 ov), 8–160 (Lee, 59.4 ov), 9–183 (Johnson, 66.3 ov), 10–214 (Clarke, 76.6 ov)

BOWLING: Martin 18–4–42–1; Southee 18–3–63–4; O'Brien 19–6–44–2; Elliott 10–4–29–0; Vettori 8–0–27–1; Ryder 4–1–7–2

Australia second innings

ML Hayden	c McCullum b Martin	0
SM Katich	not out	131
RT Ponting	c Redmond b O'Brien	17
MEK Hussey	c McCullum b O'Brien	0
MJ Clarke	run out (Redmond)	9
A Symonds	c McCullum b Martin	20
SR Watson	lbw Martin	5
BJ Haddin	b Vettori	19
B Lee	b Vettori	7
MG Johnson	c Vettori b Elliott	31
SR Clark	c Vettori b Southee	18
Extras	(lb 10, nb 1)	11
Total	(all out; 81.2 overs)	268

FALL OF WICKETS: 1–0 (Hayden, 0.1 ov), 2–40 (Ponting, 8.2 ov), 3–40 (Hussey, 8.6 ov), 4–53 (Clarke, 14.5 ov), 5–109 (Symonds, 31.5 ov), 6–115 (Watson, 35.2 ov), 7–156 (Haddin, 50.2 ov), 8–186 (Lee, 58.2 ov), 9–239 (Johnson, 77.3 ov), 10–268 (Clark, 81.2 ov)

BOWLING: Martin 21–5–69–3; Southee 16.2–5–62–1; O'Brien 17–1–58–2; Elliott 6–1–15–1; Vettori 19–4–46–2; Ryder 2–0–8–0

New Zealand first innings

AJ Redmond	c Ponting b Clark	3
JM How	b Lee	14
JD Ryder	c Haddin b Watson	30
LRPL Taylor	lbw Lee	40
BB McCullum	c Ponting b Johnson	8
DR Flynn	not out	39
GD Elliott	b Watson	9
DL Vettori	c Symonds b Johnson	2
TG Southee	c Symonds b Johnson	0
IE O'Brien	c Clarke b Johnson	1
CS Martin	b Clark	1
Extras	(lb 3, nb 6)	9
Total	(all out; 50 overs)	156

FALL OF WICKETS: 1–7 (Redmond, 5.1 ov), 2–44 (How, 14.4 ov), 3–64 (Ryder, 19.3 ov), 4–73 (McCullum, 20.6 ov), 5–108 (Taylor, 30.5 ov), 6–127 (Elliott, 41.4 ov), 7–143 (Vettori, 46.2 ov), 8–143 (Southee, 46.6 ov), 9–149 (O'Brien, 48.1 ov), 10–156 (Martin, 49.6 ov)

BOWLING: Lee 16–5–38–2; Clark 15–2–46–2; Watson 10–2–35–2; Johnson 8–3–30–4; Symonds 1–0–4–0

New Zealand second innings (target: 327 runs)

AJ Redmond	c&b Clark	10
JM How	c Ponting b Lee	0
JD Ryder	lbw Johnson	24
LRPL Taylor	c Haddin b Johnson	75
BB McCullum	lbw Clark	3
DR Flynn	b Johnson	29
GD Elliott	b Clark	0
DL Vettori	c Symonds b Johnson	10
TG Southee	not out	12
IE O'Brien	c Clarke b Clark	3
CS Martin	b Johnson	1
Extras	(lb 5, w 2, nb 3)	10
Total	(all out; 54.3 overs)	177

FALL OF WICKETS: 1–1 (How, 0.3 ov), 2–30 (Redmond, 9.6 ov), 3–40 (Ryder, 14.6 ov), 4–49 (McCullum, 17.3 ov), 5–133 (Flynn, 40.4 ov), 6–143 (Elliott, 43.6 ov), 7–160 (Vettori, 50.4 ov), 8–161 (Taylor, 52.1 ov), 9–164 (O'Brien, 53.2 ov), 10–177 (Martin, 54.3 ov)

BOWLING: Lee 9–0–53–1; Clark 17–5–43–4; Johnson 17.3–6–39–5; Watson 5–1–19–0; Symonds –4–0–12–0; Clarke 2–0–6–0

Stumps scores

DAY 1: New Zealand first innings 0–7 (Redmond 3, How 2; 5 overs)
DAY 2: Australia second innings 6–131 (Katich 67, Haddin 6; 38 overs)
DAY 3: New Zealand second innings 6–143 (Taylor 67; 44 overs)

AUSTRALIA WON BY 149 RUNS

Second Test, Australia v New Zealand at Adelaide

28 November–1 December 2008 • TOSS: New Zealand
UMPIRES: Billy Doctrove (West Indies) and Rudi Koertzen (South Africa)
MATCH REFEREE: Chris Broad (England) • PLAYER OF THE MATCH: Brad Haddin (Australia)
PLAYER OF THE SERIES: Michael Clarke (Australia)

New Zealand first innings

AJ Redmond	c Symonds b Hauritz	83
JM How	c Haddin b Johnson	16
JD Ryder	c Clarke b Hauritz	13
LRPL Taylor	lbw Clark	44
PG Fulton	c Katich b Symonds	29
DR Flynn	b Lee	11
BB McCullum	c Haddin b Lee	30
DL Vettori	not out	18
TG Southee	c Katich b Johnson	2
IE O'Brien	c Haddin b Lee	0
CS Martin	b Lee	0
Extras	(b 5, lb 7, w 1, nb 11)	24
Total	(all out; 98.3 overs)	270

FALL OF WICKETS: 1–46 (How, 16.5 ov), 2–101 (Ryder, 27.5 ov), 3–130 (Redmond, 35.2 ov), 4–194 (Fulton, 57.1 ov), 5–200 (Taylor, 60.2 ov), 6–228 (Flynn, 68.5 ov), 7–266 (McCullum, 92.4 ov), 8–269 (Southee, 95.3 ov), 9–270 (O'Brien, 96.4 ov), 10–270 (Martin, 98.3 ov)

BOWLING: Lee 25.3–8–66–4; Clark 20–6–56–1; Johnson 25–5–56–2; Hauritz 16–2–63–2; Symonds 12–2–17–1

New Zealand second innings

AJ Redmond	c Clarke b Lee	19
JM How	c Ponting b Lee	28
JD Ryder	c Symonds b Lee	3
LRPL Taylor	c&b Lee	1
PG Fulton	b Johnson	7
DR Flynn	lbw Johnson	9
BB McCullum	not out	84
DL Vettori	c Hayden b Hauritz	13
TG Southee	c Ponting b Hauritz	11
IE O'Brien	lbw Lee	0
CS Martin	b Johnson	0
Extras	(b 7, lb 8, nb 13)	28
Total	(all out; 74.1 overs)	203

FALL OF WICKETS: 1–39 (Redmond, 9.2 ov), 2–55 (Ryder, 15.1 ov), 3–58 (Taylor, 19.6 ov), 4–63 (How, 21.4 ov), 5–76 (Flynn, 29.5 ov), 6–84 (Fulton, 37.1 ov), 7–105 (Vettori, 46.4 ov), 8–131 (Southee, 58.3 ov), 9–181 (O'Brien, 71.5 ov), 10–203 (Martin, 74.1 ov)

BOWLING: Lee 25–5–105–5; Clark 10–5–22–0; Johnson 15.1–7–29–3; Hauritz 24–11–32–2

Australia first innings

ML Hayden	run out (How/McCullum)	24
SM Katich	c Ryder b Vettori	23
RT Ponting	c Fulton b O'Brien	79
MEK Hussey	c Redmond b Martin	70
MJ Clarke	c Ryder b O'Brien	110
A Symonds	c McCullum b Martin	0
BJ Haddin	c Fulton b Redmond	169
B Lee	c Taylor b O'Brien	19
MG Johnson	c McCullum b Redmond	23
NM Hauritz	b Vettori	1
SR Clark	not out	1
Extras	(b 2, lb 8, w 1, nb 5)	16
Total	(all out; 157.4 overs)	535

FALL OF WICKETS: 1–38 (Hayden, 10.1 ov), 2–49 (Katich, 14.6 ov), 3–155 (Ponting, 51.1 ov), 4–244 (Hussey, 81.1 ov), 5–247 (Symonds, 81.5 ov), 6–428 (Clarke, 131.1 ov), 7–470 (Lee, 145.1 ov), 8–526 (Johnson, 154.4 ov), 9–532 (Haddin, 156.1 ov), 10–535 (Hauritz, 157.4 ov)

BOWLING: Martin 27–4–110–2; Southee –27–1–100–0; Vettori 59.4–20–124–2; O'Brien 31–6–111–3; Ryder 7–1–33–0; Redmond 6–0–47–2

Stumps scores

DAY 1: New Zealand first innings 6–262 (McCullum 30, Vettori 12; 90 overs)
DAY 2: Australia first innings 3–241 (Hussey 69, Clarke 43; 79 overs)
DAY 3: New Zealand second innings 0–35 (Redmond 15, How 13; 9 overs)

AUSTRALIA WON BY AN INNINGS AND 62 RUNS

First Test, Australia v South Africa at Perth

17–21 December 2008 • TOSS: Australia
UMPIRES: Aleem Dar (Pakistan) and Asoka de Silva (Sri Lanka)
MATCH REFEREE: Ranjan Madugalle (Sri Lanka)
PLAYER OF THE MATCH: AB De Villiers (South Africa)

Australia first innings

ML Hayden	c Smith b Ntini	12
SM Katich	lbw Morkel	83
RT Ponting	c de Villiers b Ntini	0
MEK Hussey	c de Villiers b Steyn	0
MJ Clarke	c Smith b Harris	62
A Symonds	c McKenzie b Harris	57
BJ Haddin	c Duminy b Ntini	46
B Lee	c Duminy b Steyn	29
JJ Krejza	not out	30
MG Johnson	lbw Morkel	18
PM Siddle	c Boucher b Ntini	23
Extras	(lb 7, w 3, nb 5)	15
Total	(all out; 98.5 overs)	375

FALL OF WICKETS: 1–14 (Hayden, 2.4 ov), 2–14 (Ponting, 2.5 ov), 3–15 (Hussey, 5.2 ov), 4–164 (Katich, 50.5 ov), 5–166 (Clarke, 51.5 ov), 6–259 (Symonds, 69.5 ov), 7–298 (Haddin, 80.4 ov), 8–303 (Lee, 81.5 ov), 9–341 (Johnson, 88.6 ov), 10–375 (Siddle, 98.5 ov)

BOWLING: Ntini 19.5–1–72–4; Steyn 23–4–81–2; Kallis 15–2–65–0; Morkel 20–1–80–2; Harris 21–2–70–2

Australia second innings

ML Hayden	c&b Steyn	4
SM Katich	c Boucher b Kallis	37
RT Ponting	c Boucher b Harris	32
MEK Hussey	b Ntini	8
MJ Clarke	c Kallis b Steyn	25
A Symonds	c Smith b Harris	37
BJ Haddin	st Boucher b Harris	94
B Lee	c de Villiers b Kallis	5
JJ Krejza	c de Villiers b Kallis	32
MG Johnson	c Kallis b Morkel	21
PM Siddle	not out	4
Extras	(b 4, lb 7, w 2, nb 7)	20
Total	(all out; 97 overs)	319

FALL OF WICKETS: 1–25 (Hayden, 8.3 ov), 2–59 (Katich, 16.1 ov), 3–88 (Ponting, 26.4 ov), 4–88 (Hussey, 27.5 ov), 5–148 (Clarke, 50.6 ov), 6–157 (Symonds, 58.1 ov), 7–162 (Lee, 59.5 ov), 8–241 (Krejza, 79.4 ov), 9–278 (Johnson, 88.3 ov), 10–319 (Haddin, 96.6 ov)

BOWLING: Steyn 19–3–81–2; Ntini 21–2–76–1; Harris 27–3–85–3; Kallis 14–4–24–3; Morkel 16–4–42–1

South Africa first innings

ND McKenzie	c Krejza b Johnson	2
GC Smith	b Johnson	48
HM Amla	b Krejza	47
JH Kallis	c Haddin b Johnson	63
AB de Villiers	c Haddin b Johnson	63
JP Duminy	c Haddin b Johnson	1
MV Boucher	c Katich b Siddle	26
M Morkel	c Krejza b Johnson	1
PL Harris	c Krejza b Johnson	0
DW Steyn	c Haddin b Johnson	8
M Ntini	not out	5
Extras	(lb 5, w 5, nb 7)	17
Total	(all out; 89.5 overs)	281

FALL OF WICKETS: 1–16 (McKenzie, 7.6 ov), 2–106 (Amla, 31.1 ov), 3–110 (Smith, 32.3 ov), 4–234 (de Villiers, 70.4 ov), 5–237 (Kallis, 72.4 ov), 6–238 (Duminy, 74.1 ov), 7–241 (Morkel, 76.3 ov), 8–241 (Harris, 76.6 ov), 9–256 (Steyn, 80.4 ov), 10–281 (Boucher, 89.5 ov)

BOWLING: Lee 21–3–59–0; Johnson 24–4–61–8; Krejza 25–2–102–1; Siddle 16.5–5–44–1; A Symonds 3–1–10–0

South Africa second innings (target: 414 runs)

GC Smith	lbw Johnson	108
ND McKenzie	c Haddin b Johnson	10
HM Amla	c Haddin b Lee	53
JH Kallis	c Hussey b Johnson	57
AB de Villiers	not out	106
JP Duminy	not out	50
Extras	(b 13, lb 9, w 2, nb 6)	30
Total	(4 wickets; 119.2 overs)	414

FALL OF WICKETS: 1–19 (McKenzie, 14.3 ov), 2–172 (Smith, 50.2 ov), 3–179 (Amla, 53.2 ov), 4–303 (Kallis, 85.3 ov)

BOWLING: Lee 27–4–73–1; Johnson 34.2–5–98–3; Siddle 26–2–84–0; Krejza 24–2–102–0; Clarke 8–0–35–0

Stumps scores
DAY 1: Australia first innings 9–341 (Krejza 19; 89 overs)
DAY 2: South Africa first innings 8–243 (Boucher 2, Steyn 1; 78 overs)
DAY 3: Australia second innings 7–228 (Haddin 39, Krejza 28; 75 overs)
DAY 4: South Africa second innings 3–227 (Kallis 33, de Villiers 11; 64 overs)

SOUTH AFRICA WON BY SIX WICKETS

Second Test, Australia v South Africa at Melbourne

26–30 December 2008 • TOSS: Australia
UMPIRES: Aleem Dar (Pakistan) and Billy Doctrove (West Indies)
MATCH REFEREE: Ranjan Madugalle (Sri Lanka)
PLAYER OF THE MATCH: Dale Steyn (South Africa)

Australia first innings

ML Hayden	c Duminy b Ntini	8
SM Katich	b Steyn	54
RT Ponting	c Amla b Harris	101
MEK Hussey	c Boucher b Steyn	0
MJ Clarke	not out	88
A Symonds	c Kallis b Morkel	27
BJ Haddin	c Smith b Ntini	40
B Lee	c Kallis b Steyn	21
MG Johnson	b Steyn	0
NM Hauritz	c Smith b Steyn	12
PM Siddle	c de Villiers b Kallis	19
Extras	(b 5, lb 12, nb 7)	24
Total	(all out; 113.4 overs)	394

FALL OF WICKETS: 1–21 (Hayden, 7.2 ov), 2–128 (Katich, 33.6 ov), 3–143 (Hussey, 37.3 ov), 4–184 (Ponting, 51.2 ov), 5–223 (Symonds, 66.1 ov), 6–277 (Haddin, 88.3 ov), 7–322 (Lee, 95.2 ov), 8–326 (Johnson, 95.5 ov), 9–352 (Hauritz, 101.5 ov), 10–394 (Siddle, 113.4 ov)

BOWLING: Steyn 29–6–87–5; Ntini 27–7–108–2; Kallis 18.4–4–55–1; Morkel 22–3–89–1; Harris 17–3–38–1

Australia second innings

ML Hayden	c Duminy b Steyn	23
SM Katich	c Boucher b Steyn	15
RT Ponting	c Smith b Morkel	99
MEK Hussey	c Amla b Morkel	2
MJ Clarke	c McKenzie b Steyn	29
A Symonds	c Kallis b Steyn	0
BJ Haddin	c Kallis b Ntini	10
B Lee	b Kallis	8
MG Johnson	not out	43
NM Hauritz	b Kallis	3
PM Siddle	c Boucher b Steyn	6
Extras	(b 1, lb 3, nb 5)	9
Total	(all out; 84.2 overs)	247

FALL OF WICKETS: 1–37 (Hayden, 10.4 ov), 2–40 (Katich, 12.2 ov), 3–49 (Hussey, 15.3 ov), 4–145 (Clarke, 43.1 ov), 5–145 (Symonds, 43.6 ov), 6–165 (Haddin, 53.1 ov), 7–180 (Lee, 58.3 ov), 8–212 (Ponting, 71.3 ov), 9–231 (Hauritz, 78.6 ov), 10–247 (Siddle, 84.2 ov)

BOWLING: Steyn 20.2–3–67–5; Ntini 14–1–26–1; Morkel 15–2–46–2; Harris 21–1–47–0; Kallis 14–1–57–2

South Africa first innings

GC Smith	c Haddin b Siddle	62
ND McKenzie	b Siddle	0
HM Amla	c Symonds b Johnson	19
JH Kallis	c Haddin b Hauritz	26
AB de Villiers	b Siddle	7
JP Duminy	c Siddle b Hauritz	166
MV Boucher	c Hussey b Hauritz	3
M Morkel	b Johnson	21
PL Harris	c Johnson b Hussey	39
DW Steyn	b Siddle	76
M Ntini	not out	2
Extras	(b 5, lb 13, nb 15, pen 5)	38
Total	(all out; 153 overs)	459

FALL OF WICKETS: 1–1 (McKenzie, 1.4 ov), 2–39 (Amla, 8.3 ov), 3–102 (Kallis, 26.4 ov), 4–126 (Smith, 37.6 ov), 5–132 (de Villiers, 41.5 ov), 6–141 (Boucher, 46.4 ov), 7–184 (Morkel, 57.1 ov), 8–251 (Harris, 77.5 ov), 9–431 (Steyn, 141.3 ov), 10–459 (Duminy, 152.6 ov)

BOWLING: Lee 13–2–68–0; Siddle 34–9–81–4; Johnson 39–6–127–2; Hauritz 43–13–98–3; Clarke 8–0–26–0; Hussey 5–0–22–1; Symonds 11–3–14–0

South Africa second innings (target: 183 runs)

GC Smith	lbw Hauritz	75
ND McKenzie	not out	59
HM Amla	not out	30
Extras	(lb 9, w 2, nb 8)	19
Total	(1 wicket; 48 overs)	183

FALL OF WICKETS: 1–121 (Smith, 28.5 ov)

BOWLING: Lee 10–0–49–0; Siddle 14–5–34–0; Johnson 11–1–36–0; Hauritz 10–0–41–1; Clarke 3–0–14–0

Stumps scores
DAY 1: Australia first innings 6–280 (Clarke 36, Lee 0; 90 ov)
DAY 2: South Africa first innings 7–198 (Duminy 34, Harris 8; 63 ov)
DAY 3: Australia second innings 0–4 (Hayden 1, Katich 2; 3 overs)
DAY 4: South Africa second innings 0–30 (Smith 25, McKenzie 3; 6 overs)

SOUTH AFRICA WON BY NINE WICKETS

Third Test, Australia v South Africa at Sydney

3–7 January 2009 • TOSS: Australia
UMPIRES: Billy Bowden (New Zealand) and Asoka de Silva (Sri Lanka)
MATCH REFEREE: Ranjan Madugalle (Sri Lanka) • PLAYER OF THE MATCH: Peter Siddle (Australia)
PLAYER OF THE SERIES: Graeme Smith (South Africa)

Australia first innings

ML Hayden	b Steyn	31
SM Katich	c de Villiers b Kallis	47
RT Ponting	c Boucher b Morkel	0
MEK Hussey	c Kallis b Harris	30
MJ Clarke	c&b Duminy	138
AB McDonald	c Boucher b Ntini	15
BJ Haddin	b Steyn	38
MG Johnson	c Smith b Steyn	64
NM Hauritz	c Duminy b Harris	41
PM Siddle	lbw Harris	23
DE Bollinger	not out	0
Extras	(lb 7, w 3, nb 8)	18
Total	(all out; 136.2 overs)	445

FALL OF WICKETS: 1–62 (Katich, 12.6 ov), 2–63 (Ponting, 13.5 ov), 3–109 (Hayden, 33.3 ov), 4–130 (Hussey, 40.6 ov), 5–162 (McDonald, 56.4 ov), 6–237 (Haddin, 81.4 ov), 7–379 (Clarke, 120.4 ov), 8–381 (Johnson, 121.5 ov), 9–440 (Siddle, 134.3 ov), 10–445 (Hauritz, 136.2 ov).

BOWLING: Steyn 27–5–95–3; Ntini 29–5–102–1; Morkel 27–3–89–1; Kallis 20–6–54–1; Harris 29.2–6–84–3; Duminy 4–0–14–1

South Africa first innings

ND McKenzie	lbw Siddle	23
GC Smith	retired hurt	30
HM Amla	lbw McDonald	51
JH Kallis	c Hayden b Johnson	37
AB de Villiers	run out (Johnson)	11
JP Duminy	lbw Johnson	13
MV Boucher	b Siddle	89
M Morkel	b Siddle	40
PL Harris	lbw Siddle	2
DW Steyn	b Siddle	6
M Ntini	not out	0
Extras	(lb 12, w 9, nb 4)	25
Total	(all out; 120.5 overs)	327

FALL OF WICKETS: 0–35 (Smith, retired hurt), 1–76 (McKenzie, 24.3 ov), 2–131 (Kallis, 40.3 ov), 3–161 (de Villiers, 56.5 ov), 4–166 (Amla, 59.2 ov), 5–193 (Duminy, 74.5 ov), 6–308 (Morkel, 114.2 ov), 7–310 (Harris, 116.1 ov), 8–316 (Steyn, 118.5 ov), 9–327 (Boucher, 120.5 ov)

BOWLING: Siddle 27.5–11–59–5; Bollinger 23–4–78–0; Johnson 28–6–69–2; McDonald 22–8–41–1; Hauritz 20–4–68–0

Australia second innings

ML Hayden	b Morkel	39
SM Katich	lbw Steyn	61
RT Ponting	b Morkel	53
MEK Hussey	not out	45
MJ Clarke	c Amla b Harris	41
Extras	(b 8, lb 9, nb 1)	18
Total	(4 wickets dec; 67.3 overs)	257

FALL OF WICKETS: 1–62 (Hayden, 16.5 ov), 2–134 (Ponting, 36.4 ov), 3–181 (Katich, 50.5 ov), 4–257 (Clarke, 67.3 ov)

BOWLING: Steyn 13–1–60–1; Ntini 12–1–66–0; Morkel 12–2–38–2; Kallis 10–5–13–0; Harris 20.3–1–63–1

South Africa second innings (target: 376 runs)

ND McKenzie	c Hussey b Bollinger	27
M Morkel	c Johnson b Bollinger	0
HM Amla	c Katich b Hauritz	59
JH Kallis	c&b McDonald	4
AB de Villiers	b Siddle	56
JP Duminy	lbw Johnson	16
MV Boucher	lbw Siddle	4
PL Harris	lbw Siddle	6
DW Steyn	lbw McDonald	28
M Ntini	not out	28
GC Smith	b Johnson	3
Extras	(b 12, lb 18, w 4, nb 2, pen 5)	41
Total	(all out; 114.2 overs)	272

FALL OF WICKETS: 1–2 (Morkel, 1.2 ov), 2–68 (McKenzie, 30.2 ov), 3–91 (Kallis, 35.3 ov), 4–110 (Amla, 41.1 ov), 5–166 (Duminy, 70.2 ov), 6–172 (Boucher, 76.5 ov), 7–190 (de Villiers, 83.6 ov), 8–202 (Harris, 90.1 ov), 9–257 (Steyn, 107.4 ov), 10–272 (Smith, 114.2 ov)

BOWLING: Siddle 27–12–54–3; Bollinger 21–5–53–2; Johnson 23.2–7–49–2; McDonald 13–6–32–2; Hauritz 28–10–47–1; Clarke 2–1–2–0

Stumps scores
DAY 1: Australia first innings 6–267 (Clarke 73, Johnson 17; 88 overs)
DAY 2: South Africa first innings 1–125 (Amla 30, Kallis 36; 39 overs)
DAY 3: Australia second innings 0–33 (Hayden 18, Katich 9; 6 overs)
DAY 4: South Africa second innings 1–67 (McKenzie 25, Amla 30; 26 overs)

AUSTRALIA WON BY 103 RUNS

First Test, Australia v South Africa at Johannesburg

26 February–2 March 2009 • TOSS: Australia
UMPIRES: Billy Bowden (New Zealand) and Steve Bucknor (West Indies)
MATCH REFEREE: Jeff Crowe (New Zealand)
PLAYER OF THE MATCH: Mitchell Johnson (Australia)

Australia first innings

PJ Hughes	c Boucher b Steyn	0
SM Katich	c McKenzie b Steyn	3
RT Ponting	b Ntini	83
MEK Hussey	c Kallis b Morkel	4
MJ Clarke	c Boucher b Steyn	68
MJ North	st Boucher b Harris	117
BJ Haddin	c Harris b Ntini	63
AB McDonald	c Kallis b Steyn	0
MG Johnson	not out	96
PM Siddle	c Kallis b Morkel	9
BW Hilfenhaus	c de Villiers b Morkel	0
Extras	(b 6, lb 8, w 2, nb 7)	23
Total	(all out; 125.4 overs)	466

FALL OF WICKETS: 1–0 (Hughes, 0.4 ov), 2–18 (Katich, 8.5 ov), 3–38 (Hussey, 14.6 ov), 4–151 (Ponting, 41.2 ov), 5–182 (Clarke, 49.4 ov), 6–295 (Haddin, 83.5 ov), 7–296 (McDonald, 84.4 ov), 8–413 (North, 120.5 ov), 9–466 (Siddle, 125.3 ov), 10–466 (Hilfenhaus, 125.4 ov)

BOWLING: Steyn 30–4–113–4; Ntini 27–6–71–2; Morkel 28.4–3–117–3; Kallis 8–0–33–0; Harris 18–2–64–1; Duminy 14–2–54–0

South Africa first innings

ND McKenzie	lbw Siddle	36
GC Smith	c Haddin b Johnson	0
HM Amla	c Ponting b Hilfenhaus	1
JH Kallis	c Hussey b Siddle	27
AB de Villiers	not out	104
JP Duminy	c Haddin b Johnson	17
MV Boucher	c Haddin b Johnson	0
M Morkel	c&b Siddle	2
PL Harris	lbw North	1
DW Steyn	c North b McDonald	17
M Ntini	b Johnson	1
Extras	(b 4, lb 6, nb 4)	14
Total	(all out; 81.1 overs)	220

FALL OF WICKETS: 1–1 (Smith, 0.5 ov), 2–2 (Amla, 1.2 ov), 3–49 (Kallis, 17.1 ov), 4–93 (McKenzie, 40.5 ov), 5–138 (Duminy, 57.2 ov), 6–138 (Boucher, 57.5 ov), 7–154 (Morkel, 63.5 ov), 8–156 (Harris, 64.6 ov), 9–208 (Steyn, 79.4 ov), 10–220 (Ntini, 81.1 ov)

BOWLING: Johnson 18.1–7–25–4; Hilfenhaus 25–9–58–1; Siddle 21–1–76–3; McDonald 10–4–22–1; North 7–0–29–1

Australia second innings

PJ Hughes	c de Villiers b Harris	75
SM Katich	c Boucher b Morkel	10
RT Ponting	c Amla b Kallis	25
MEK Hussey	c Ntini b Kallis	0
MJ Clarke	c Kallis b Harris	0
MJ North	b Kallis	5
BJ Haddin	c Boucher b Ntini	37
AB McDonald	c Boucher b Ntini	7
MG Johnson	c Kallis b Ntini	1
PM Siddle	not out	22
BW Hilfenhaus	b Steyn	16
Extras	(lb 5, w 1, nb 3)	9
Total	(all out; 53.4 overs)	207

FALL OF WICKETS: 1–38 (Katich, 11.3 ov), 2–99 (Ponting, 26.5 ov), 3–99 (Hussey, 26.6 ov), 4–99 (Clarke, 27.2 ov), 5–104 (North, 28.5 ov), 6–138 (Hughes, 35.3 ov), 7–145 (McDonald, 38.1 ov), 8–147 (Johnson, 40.4 ov), 9–174 (Haddin, 48.2 ov), 10–207 (Hilfenhaus, 53.4 ov)

BOWLING: Steyn 16.4–5–51–1; Ntini 11–3–52–3; Morkel 10–1–41–1; Harris 11–0–36–2; Kallis 5–0–22–3

South Africa second innings (target: 454 runs)

ND McKenzie	c Haddin b Johnson	35
GC Smith	c Johnson b Hilfenhaus	69
HM Amla	c Hughes b Siddle	57
JH Kallis	b Johnson	45
AB de Villiers	lbw McDonald	3
JP Duminy	c Ponting b Siddle	29
MV Boucher	b Hilfenhaus	24
M Morkel	c Hughes b Johnson	2
PL Harris	c Katich b Siddle	8
DW Steyn	b Johnson	6
M Ntini	not out	0
Extras	(b 1, lb 6, w 2, nb 4)	13
Total	(all out; 119.2 overs)	291

FALL OF WICKETS: 1–76 (McKenzie, 27.3 ov), 2–130 (Smith, 41.1 ov), 3–206 (Amla, 69.3 ov), 4–211 (de Villiers, 72.4 ov), 5–229 (Kallis, 82.6 ov), 6–268 (Duminy, 103.6 ov), 7–272 (Morkel, 109.1 ov), 8–284 (Boucher, 114.6 ov), 9–289 (Harris, 118.6 ov), 10–291 (Steyn, 119.2 ov)

BOWLING: Johnson 34.2–2–112–4; Hilfenhaus 31–7–68–2; Siddle 25–8–46–3; McDonald 22–8–31–1; North 7–0–27–0

Stumps scores
DAY 1: Australia first innings 5–254 (North 47, Haddin 37; 68 overs)
DAY 2: South Africa first innings 3–85 (McKenzie 35, de Villiers 13; 37 overs)
DAY 3: Australia second innings 1–51 (Hughes 36, Ponting 1; 16.3 overs)
DAY 4: South Africa second innings 2–178 (Amla 43, Kallis 26; 55 overs)

AUSTRALIA WON BY 162 RUNS

Second Test, Australia v South Africa at Durban

6–10 March 2009 • TOSS: Australia
UMPIRES: Billy Bowden (New Zealand) and Asad Rauf (Pakistan)
MATCH REFEREE: Jeff Crowe (New Zealand)
PLAYER OF THE MATCH: Phillip Hughes (Australia)

Australia first innings

PJ Hughes	c McKenzie b Kallis	115
SM Katich	c Smith b Steyn	108
RT Ponting	c McKenzie b Harris	9
MEK Hussey	b Morkel	50
MJ Clarke	b Harris	3
MJ North	c Steyn b Kallis	38
BJ Haddin	c Amla b Ntini	5
AB McDonald	not out	4
MG Johnson	lbw Ntini	0
PM Siddle	c Boucher b Steyn	0
BW Hilfenhaus	c Smith b Steyn	0
Extras	(b 6, lb 4, w 2, nb 8)	20
Total	(all out; 107.4 overs)	352

FALL OF WICKETS: 1–184 (Hughes, 43.5 ov), 2–208 (Ponting, 51.4 ov), 3–259 (Katich, 67.1 ov), 4–266 (Clarke, 70.1 ov), 5–329 (Hussey, 100.6 ov), 6–348 (North, 104.5 ov), 7–348 (Haddin, 105.3 ov), 8–348 (Johnson, 105.4 ov), 9–352 (Siddle, 107.2 ov), 10–352 (Hilfenhaus, 107.4 ov)

BOWLING: Steyn 25.4–3–83–3; Ntini 19–4–58–2; Morkel 24–4–81–1; Kallis 15–4–49–2; Harris 21–5–66–2; Duminy 3–1–5–0

South Africa first innings

ND McKenzie	c Haddin b Johnson	0
GC Smith	retired hurt	2
HM Amla	lbw Johnson	0
JH Kallis	c Ponting b McDonald	22
AB de Villiers	lbw Hilfenhaus	3
JP Duminy	not out	73
MV Boucher	b Johnson	1
PL Harris	b McDonald	4
M Morkel	b McDonald	2
DW Steyn	c Haddin b Siddle	8
M Ntini	lbw Siddle	0
Extras	(b 10, lb 12, nb 1)	23
Total	(all out; 57.3 overs)	138

FALL OF WICKETS: 1–0 (McKenzie, 0.3 ov), 2–0 (Amla, 0.5 ov), 2–3 (Smith, retired hurt), 3–6 (de Villiers, 5.3 ov), 3–56 (Kallis, retired hurt, 24.5 ov), 4–62 (Boucher, 26.6 ov), 5–104 (Harris, 41.4 ov), 6–104 (Kallis, 41.6 ov), 7–106 (Morkel, 43.3 ov), 8–138 (Steyn, 57.2 ov), 9–138 (Ntini, 57.3 ov)

BOWLING: Johnson 16–5–37–3; Hilfenhaus 11–2–28–1; McDonald 12–4–25–3; Siddle 13.3–6–20–2; North 4–3–6–0; Clarke 1–1–0–0

Australia second innings

PJ Hughes	c Morkel b Ntini	160
SM Katich	c Harris b Kallis	30
RT Ponting	c McKenzie b Morkel	81
MEK Hussey	c Kallis b Duminy	19
MJ Clarke	not out	23
MJ North	c de Villiers b Steyn	0
Extras	(b 12, lb 2, nb 4)	18
Total	(5 wickets dec; 94.4 overs)	331

FALL OF WICKETS: 1–55 (Katich, 15.6 ov), 2–219 (Ponting, 64.3 ov), 3–260 (Hussey, 78.5 ov), 4–330 (Hughes, 93.1 ov), 5–331 (North, 94.4 ov)

BOWLING: Steyn 15.4–1–75–1; Ntini 15–2–55–1; Morkel 14–1–60–1; Kallis 8–0–21–1; Harris 31–8–68–0; Duminy 11 –1–38–1

South Africa second innings (target: 546 runs)

HM Amla	c Ponting b Siddle	43
ND McKenzie	c Haddin b Siddle	31
JH Kallis	c Ponting b Johnson	93
AB de Villiers	c Haddin b Siddle	84
JP Duminy	c Haddin b Hilfenhaus	17
MV Boucher	c&b North	25
PL Harris	c Siddle b Katich	5
M Morkel	c Haddin b Katich	24
DW Steyn	st Haddin b Katich	7
M Ntini	not out	4
GC Smith	absent hurt	–
Extras	(b 13, lb 11, w 3, nb 10)	37
Total	(all out; 132.2 overs)	370

FALL OF WICKETS: 1–63 (McKenzie, 22.2 ov), 2–80 (Amla, 28.5 ov), 3–267 (Kallis, 85.5 ov), 4–279 (de Villiers, 88.6 ov), 5–299 (Duminy, 101.2 ov), 6–307 (Harris, 105.2 ov), 7–345 (Boucher, 125.3 ov), 8–363 (Morkel, 130.5 ov), 9–370 (Steyn, 132.2 ov)

BOWLING: Johnson 33–9–78–1; Hilfenhaus 24–4–79–1; Siddle 28–12–61–3; McDonald 16–3–47–0; North 20–6–36–1; Katich 11.2–1–45–3

Stumps scores

DAY 1: Australia first innings 4–303 (Hussey 37, North 17; 89 overs)
DAY 2: South Africa first innings 7–138 (Duminy 73, Steyn 8; 57 overs)
DAY 3: Australia second innings 3–292 (Hughes 136, Clarke 14; 87 overs)
DAY 4: South Africa second innings 2–244 (Kallis 84, AB de Villiers 68; 80 overs)

AUSTRALIA WON BY 175 RUNS

Third Test, Australia v South Africa at Cape Town

19–22 March 2009 • TOSS: Australia
UMPIRES: Steve Bucknor (West Indies) and Asad Rauf (Pakistan)
MATCH REFEREE: Jeff Crowe (New Zealand) • PLAYER OF THE MATCH: Paul Harris (South Africa)
PLAYER OF THE SERIES: Michell Johnson (Australia)

Australia first innings

PJ Hughes	lbw Harris	33
SM Katich	c Khan b Harris	55
RT Ponting	c Boucher b Morkel	0
MEK Hussey	b Steyn	20
MJ Clarke	b Steyn	0
BJ Haddin	lbw Harris	42
AB McDonald	c Kallis b Ntini	13
MG Johnson	c Prince b Steyn	35
PM Siddle	c de Villiers b Ntini	0
BE McGain	c de Villiers b Steyn	2
BW Hilfenhaus	not out	0
Extras	(lb 6, w 1, nb 2)	9
Total	(all out; 72 overs)	209

FALL OF WICKETS: 1–58 (Hughes, 22.4 ov), 2–59 (Ponting, 23.5 ov), 3–81 (Hussey, 29.4 ov), 4–81 (Clarke, 31.1 ov), 5–152 (Katich, 50.5 ov), 6–158 (Haddin, 54.4 ov), 7–190 (McDonald, 67.3 ov), 8–190 (Siddle, 67.5 ov), 9–209 (Johnson, 71.3 ov), 10–209 (McGain, 71.6 ov)

BOWLING: Steyn 16–5–56–4; Ntini 17–7–38–2; Kallis 10–2–31–0; Morkel 12–3–44–1; Harris 17–5–34–3

Australia second innings

PJ Hughes	c Kallis b Harris	32
SM Katich	c Duminy b Harris	54
RT Ponting	c Boucher b Steyn	12
MEK Hussey	c Duminy b Steyn	39
MJ Clarke	b Steyn	47
BJ Haddin	c Duminy b Harris	18
AB McDonald	c de Villiers b Harris	68
MG Johnson	not out	123
PM Siddle	c de Villiers b Harris	0
BE McGain	run out (sub [Engelbrecht]/Steyn)	0
BW Hilfenhaus	c Prince b Harris	12
Extras	(b 8, lb 2, w 2, nb 5)	17
Total	(all out; 121.5 overs)	422

FALL OF WICKETS: 1–57 (Hughes, 13.3 ov), 2–76 (Ponting, 20.6 ov), 3–138 (Katich, 59.2 ov), 4–146 (Hussey, 68.6 ov), 5–191 (Haddin, 79.2 ov), 6–218 (Clarke, 88.6 ov), 7–381 (McDonald, 115.3 ov), 8–381 (Siddle, 115.4 ov), 9–388 (McGain, 116.4 ov), 10–422 (Hilfenhaus, 121.5 ov)

BOWLING: Steyn 27–5–96–3; Ntini 19–6–66–0; Morkel 20–1–88–0; Harris 42.5–9–127–6; Kallis 10–4–21–0; Duminy 3–1–14–0

South Africa first innings

I Khan	c&b Siddle	20
AG Prince	c Haddin b Hilfenhaus	150
HM Amla	c Haddin b Johnson	46
JH Kallis	c&b Hilfenhaus	102
AB de Villiers	c McDonald b Katich	163
JP Duminy	b Johnson	7
MV Boucher	c Ponting b Johnson	12
JA Morkel	b McDonald	58
PL Harris	c Haddin b Johnson	27
DW Steyn	c Clarke b Katich	0
M Ntini	not out	4
Extras	(b 19, lb 24, w 9, nb 10)	62
Total	(all out; 154.3 overs)	651

FALL OF WICKETS: 1–65 (Khan, 17.4 ov), 2–162 (Amla, 44.6 ov), 3–322 (Prince, 83.1 ov), 4–415 (Kallis, 104.3 ov), 5–443 (Duminy, 113.2 ov), 6–467 (Boucher, 119.6 ov), 7–591 (Morkel, 139.6 ov), 8–637 (de Villiers, 151.2 ov), 9–637 (Steyn, 151.6 ov), 10–651 (Harris, 154.3 ov)

BOWLING: Johnson 37.3–5–148–4; Hilfenhaus 34–4–133–2; Siddle 35–15–67–1; McGain 18–2–149–0; McDonald 27–7–102–1; Katich 3–1–9–2

Stumps scores

DAY 1: South Africa first innings 0–57 (Khan 15, Prince 37; 14 overs)
DAY 2: South Africa first innings 3–404 (Kallis 102, de Villiers 39; 102 overs)
DAY 3: Australia second innings 2–102 (Katich 44, Hussey 13; 36 overs)

SOUTH AFRICA WON BY AN INNINGS AND 20 RUNS

First Ashes Test, Australia v England at Sophia Gardens

8–12 July 2009 • TOSS: England
UMPIRES: Aleem Dar (Pakistan) and Billy Doctrove (West Indies) • MATCH REFEREE: Jeff Crowe (New Zealand)
PLAYER OF THE MATCH: Ricky Ponting (Australia)

England first innings

AJ Strauss	c Clarke b Johnson	30
AN Cook	c Hussey b Hilfenhaus	10
RS Bopara	c Hughes b Johnson	35
KP Pietersen	c Katich b Hauritz	69
PD Collingwood	c Haddin b Hilfenhaus	64
MJ Prior	b Siddle	56
A Flintoff	b Siddle	37
JM Anderson	c Hussey b Hauritz	26
SCJ Broad	b Johnson	19
GP Swann	not out	47
MS Panesar	c Ponting b Hauritz	4
Extras	(b 13, lb 11, w 2, nb 12)	38
Total	(all out; 106.5 overs)	435

FALL OF WICKETS: 1–21 (Cook, 7.6 ov), 2–67 (Strauss, 19.6 ov), 3–90 (Bopara, 24.4 ov), 4–228 (Collingwood, 65.3 ov), 5–241 (Pietersen, 70.5 ov), 6–327 (Flintoff, 86.4 ov), 7–329 (Prior, 88.3 ov), 8–355 (Broad, 93.5 ov), 9–423 (Anderson, 102.4 ov), 10–435 (Panesar, 106.5 ov)

BOWLING: Johnson 22–2–87–3; Hilfenhaus 27–5–77–2; Siddle 27–3–121–2; Hauritz 23.5–1–95–3; Clarke 5–0–20–0; Katich 2–0–11–0

England second innings

AJ Strauss	c Haddin b Hauritz	17
AN Cook	lbw Johnson	6
RS Bopara	lbw Hilfenhaus	1
KP Pietersen	b Hilfenhaus	8
PD Collingwood	c Hussey b Siddle	74
MJ Prior	c Clarke b Hauritz	14
A Flintoff	c Ponting b Johnson	26
SCJ Broad	lbw Hauritz	14
GP Swann	lbw Hilfenhaus	31
JM Anderson	not out	21
MS Panesar	not out	7
Extras	(b 9, lb 11, w 4, nb 9)	33
Total	(9 wickets; 105 overs)	252

FALL OF WICKETS: 1–13 (Cook, 4.3 ov), 2–17 (Bopara, 5.3 ov), 3–31 (Pietersen, 10.4 ov), 4–46 (Strauss, 16.6 ov), 5–70 (Prior, 26.3 ov), 6–127 (Flintoff, 49.4 ov), 7–159 (Broad, 66.4 ov), 8–221 (Swann, 86.1 ov), 9–233 (Collingwood, 93.3 ov)

BOWLING: Johnson 22–4–44–2; Hilfenhaus 15–3–47–3; Siddle 18–2–51–1; Hauritz 37–12–63–3; Clarke 3–0–8–0; North 7–4–14–0; Katich 3–0–7–0

Australia first innings

PJ Hughes	c Prior b Flintoff	36
SM Katich	lbw Anderson	122
RT Ponting	b Panesar	150
MEK Hussey	c Prior b Anderson	3
MJ Clarke	c Prior b Broad	83
MJ North	not out	125
BJ Haddin	c Bopara b Collingwood	121
Extras	(b 9, lb 14, w 4, nb 7)	34
Total	(6 wicket dec; 181 overs)	674

DID NOT BAT: MG Johnson, NM Hauritz, PM Siddle, BW Hilfenhaus

FALL OF WICKETS: 1–60 (Hughes, 14.6 ov), 2–299 (Katich, 84.6 ov), 3–325 (Hussey, 90.1 ov), 4–331 (Ponting, 94.5 ov), 5–474 (Clarke, 136.5 ov), 6–674 (Haddin, 181 overs)

BOWLING: Anderson 32–6–110–2; Broad 32–6–129–1; Swann 38–8–131–0; Flintoff 35–3–128–1; Panesar 35–4–115–1; Collingwood 9–0–38–1

Stumps scores
DAY 1: England first innings 7–336 (Anderson 2, S Broad 4; 90 overs)
DAY 2: Australia first innings 1–249 (Katich 104, Ponting 100; 71 overs)
DAY 3: Australia first innings 5–479 (North 54, Haddin 4; 139 overs)
DAY 4: England second innings 2–20 (Strauss 6, Pietersen 3; 7 overs)

MATCH DRAWN

Second Ashes Test, Australia v England at Lord's

16–20 July 2009; TOSS: England
UMPIRES: Rudi Koertzen (South Africa) and Billy Doctrove (West Indies)
MATCH REFEREE: Jeff Crowe (New Zealand)
PLAYER OF THE MATCH: Andrew Flintoff (England)

England first innings

AJ Strauss	b Hilfenhaus	161
AN Cook	lbw Johnson	95
RS Bopara	lbw Hilfenhaus	18
KP Pietersen	c Haddin b Siddle	32
PD Collingwood	c Siddle b Clarke	16
MJ Prior	b Johnson	8
A Flintoff	c Ponting b Hilfenhaus	4
SCJ Broad	b Hilfenhaus	16
GP Swann	c Ponting b Siddle	4
JM Anderson	c Hussey b Johnson	29
G Onions	not out	17
Extras	(b 15, lb 2, nb 8)	25
Total	(all out; 101.4 overs)	425

FALL OF WICKETS: 1–196 (Cook, 47.5 ov), 2–222 (Bopara, 53.6 ov), 3–267 (Pietersen, 65.1 ov), 4–302 (Collingwood, 76.3 ov), 5–317 (Prior, 79.3 ov), 6–333 (Flintoff, 82.3 ov); 7–364 (Strauss, 90.2 ov), 8–370 (Swann, 91.5 ov), 9–378 (Broad, 92.6 ov), 10–425 (Anderson, 101.4 ov)

BOWLING: Hilfenhaus 31–12–103–4 (3.32); Johnson 21.4–2–132–3 (6.09); Siddle 20–1–76–2 (3.80); Hauritz 8.3–1–26–0 (3.05); North 16.3–2–59–0 (3.57); Clarke 4–1–12–1 (3.00)

Australia first innings

PJ Hughes	c Prior b Anderson	4
SM Katich	c Broad b Onions	48
RT Ponting	c Strauss b Anderson	2
MEK Hussey	b Flintoff	51
MJ Clarke	c Cook b Anderson	1
MJ North	b Anderson	0
BJ Haddin	c Cook b Broad	28
MG Johnson	c Cook b Broad	4
NM Hauritz	c Collingwood b Onions	24
PM Siddle	c Strauss b Onions	35
BW Hilfenhaus	not out	6
Extras	(b 4, lb 6, nb 2)	12
Total	(all out; 63 overs)	215

FALL OF WICKETS: 1–4 (Hughes, 2.3 ov), 2–10 (Ponting, 6.6 ov), 3–103 (Katich, 32.4 ov), 4–111 (Hussey, 35.6 ov), 5–111 (Clarke, 36.3 ov), 6–139 (North, 42.3 ov), 7–148 (Johnson, 45.5 ov), 8–152 (Haddin, 47.5 ov); 9–196 (Hauritz, 58.3 ov), 1–215 (Siddle, 62.6 ov)

BOWLING: Anderson 21–5–55–4 (2.61); Broad 18–1–78–2 (4.33); Swann 1–0–4–0 (4.00); Flintoff 12–4–27–1 (2.25); Onions 11–1–41–3 (3.72)

England second innings

AJ Strauss	c Clarke v Hauritz	32
AN Cook	lbw Hauritz	32
RS Bopara	c Katich b Hauritz	27
KP Pietersen	c Haddin b Siddle	44
PD Collingwood	c Haddin b Siddle	54
MJ Prior	run out (North)	61
A Flintoff	not out	30
Extras	(b 16, lb 9, w 1, nb 5)	31
Total	(6 wickets dec; 71.2 overs)	311

FALL OF WICKETS: 1–61 (Cook, 14.1 ov), 2–74 (Strauss, 16.2 ov), 3–147 (Bopara, 44.4 ov), 4–174 (Pietersen, 51.1 ov), 5–260 (Prior, 63.2 ov), 6–311 (Collingwood, 71.2 ov)

BOWLING: Hilfenhaus 19–5–59–0 (3.10); Johnson 17–2–68–0 (4.00); Siddle 15.2–4–64–2 (4.17); Hauritz 16–1–80–3 (5.00); Clarke 4–0–15–0 (3.75)

Australia second innings (target: 522)

PJ Hughes	c Strauss b Flintoff	17
SM Katich	c Pietersen b Flintoff	6
RT Ponting	b Broad	38
MEK Hussey	c Collingwood b Swann	27
MJ Clarke	b Swann	136
MJ North	b Swann	6
BJ Haddin	c Collingwood b Flintoff	80
MG Johnson	b Swann	63
NM Hauritz	b Flintoff	1
PM Siddle	b Flintoff	7
BW Hilfenhaus	not out	4
Extras	(b 5, lb 8, nb 8)	21
Total	(all out; 107 overs)	406

FALL OF WICKETS: 1–17 (Katich, 3.1 ov), 2–34 (Hughes, 9.2 ov), 3–78 (Ponting, 23.4 ov), 4–120 (Hussey, 32.4 ov), 5–128 (North, 38.4 ov); 6–313 (Haddin, 87.4 ov), 7–356 (Clarke 98.2 ov), 8–363 (Hauritz, 99.4 ov), 9–388 (Siddle, 103.6 ov), 10–406 (Johnson, 106.6 ov)

BOWLING: Anderson 21–4–86–0 (4.09); Flintoff 27–4–92–5 (3.40); Onions 9–0–50–0 (5.55); Broad 16–3–49–1 (3.06); Swann 28–3–87–4 (3.10); Collingwood 6–1–29–0 (4.83)

Stumps scores

DAY 1: England first innings 6–364 (Strauss 161, Broad 7; 90 overs)
DAY 2: Australia first innings 8–156 (Hauritz 3, Siddle 3; 49 overs)
DAY 3: England second innings 6–311 (Flintoff 30; 71.2 overs)
DAY 4: Australia second innings 5–313 (Clarke 125, Haddin 80; 86 overs)

ENGLAND WON BY 115 RUNS

Third Test, Australia v England at Edgbaston

30 July–3 August 2009 ;TOSS: Australia
UMPIRES: Rudi Koertzen (South Africa) and Aleem Dar (Pakistan)
MATCH REFEREE: Jeff Crowe (New Zealand)
PLAYER OF THE MATCH: Michael Clarke (Australia)

Australia first innings

SR Watson	lbw Onions	62
SM Katich	lbw Swann	46
RT Ponting	c Prior b Onions	38
MEK Hussey	b Onions	0
MJ Clarke	lbw Anderson	29
MJ North	c Prior b Anderson	12
GA Manou	b Anderson	8
MG Johnson	lbw Anderson	0
NM Hauritz	not out	20
PM Siddle	c Prior b Anderson	13
BW Hilfenhaus	c Swann b Onions	20
Extras	(b 5, lb 7, w 2, nb 1)	15
Total	(all out; 70.4 overs)	263

FALL OF WICKETS: 1–85 (Katich, 18.6 ov), 2–126 (Watson, 30.1 ov), 3–126 (Hussey, 30.2 ov), 4–163 (Ponting, 38.3 ov), 5–193 (Clarke, 49.4 ov), 6–202 (North, 51.4 ov), 7–202 (Johnson, 51.5 ov), 8–203 (Manou, 53.5 ov), 9–229 (Siddle, 61.5 ov), 10–263 (Hilfenhaus, 70.4 ov)

BOWLING: Anderson 24–7–80–5 (3.33); Flintoff 15–2–58–0 (3.86); Onions 16.4–2–58–4 (3.48); Broad 13–2–51–0 (3.92); Swann 2–0–4–1 (2.00)

England first innings

AJ Strauss	c Manou b Hilfenhaus	69
AN Cook	c Manou b Siddle	0
RS Bopara	b Hilfenhaus	23
IR Bell	lbw Johnson	53
PD Collingwood	c Ponting b Hilfenhaus	13
MJ Prior	c sub (PJ Hughes) b Siddle	41
A Flintoff	c Clarke b Hauritz	74
SCJ Broad	c & b Siddle	55
GP Swann	c North b Johnson	24
JM Anderson	c Manou b Hilfenhaus	1
G Onions	not out	2
Extras	(b 2, lb 4, w 6, nb 9)	21
Total	(all out; 93.3 overs)	376

FALL OF WICKETS: 1–2 (Cook, 1.4 ov), 2–60 (Bopara 19.2 ov), 3–141 (Strauss, 44.1 ov), 4–159 (Collingwood, 50.5 ov), 5–168 (Bell, 55.6 ov), 6–257 (Prior, 71.3 ov), 7–309 (Flintoff, 80.4 ov), 8–348 (Swann, 87.3 ov), 9–355 (Anderson, 88.6 ov), 10–376 (Broad, 93.3 ov)

BOWLING: Hilfenhaus 30–7–109–4 (3.63); Siddle 21.3–3–89–3 (4.13); Hauritz 18–2–57–1 (3.16); Johnson 21–1–92–2 (4.38); Watson 3–0–23–0 (7.67)

Australia second innings

SR Watson	c Prior b Anderson	53
SM Katich	c Prior b Onions	26
RT Ponting	b Swann	5
MEK Hussey	c Prior b Broad	64
MJ Clarke	not out	103
MJ North	c Anderson b Broad	96
GA Manou	not out	13
Extras	(b 4, lb 6, w 2, nb 3)	15
Total	(5 wickets; 112.2 overs)	375

FALL OF WICKETS: 1–47 (Katich, 13.2 ov), 2–52 (Ponting, 14.6 ov), 3–137 (Watson, 43.6 ov), 4–161 (Hussey, 52.6 ov), 5–346 (North, 103.1 ov)

BOWLING: Anderson 21–8–47–1 (2.23); Flintoff 15–0–35–0 (2.33); Onions 19–3–74–1 (3.89); Swann 31–4–119–1 (3.83), Broad 16–2–38–2 (2.37), Bopara 8.2–1–44–0 (5.28); Collingwood 2–0–8–0 (4.00)

Stumps scores

DAY 1: Australia 1–126 (Watson 62, Ponting 17; 30 overs)
DAY 2: England 2–116 (Strauss 64, Bell 26; 36 overs)
DAY 3: No play
DAY 4: Australia 2–88 (Watson 34, Hussey 18; 28 overs)

MATCH DRAWN

Fourth Test, Australia v England at Headingley

August 7–9, 2009; TOSS: England
UMPIRES: Billy Bowden (New Zealand) and Asad Rauf (Pakistan)
MATCH REFEREE: Ranjan Madugalle (Sri Lanka)
PLAYER OF THE MATCH: Marcus North (Australia)

England first innings

AJ Strauss	c North b Siddle	3
AN Cook	c Clarke b Clark	30
RS Bopara	c Hussey b Hilfenhaus	1
IR Bell	c Haddin b Johnson	8
PD Collingwood	c Ponting b Clark	0
MJ Prior	not out	37
SCJ Broad	c Katich b Clark	3
GP Swann	c Clarke b Siddle	0
SJ Harmison	c Haddin b Siddle	0
J Anderson	c Haddin b Siddle	3
G Onions	c Katich b Siddle	0
Extras	(b 5, lb 8, w 1, nb 3)	17
Total	(all out; 33.5 overs)	102

FALL OF WICKETS: 1–11 (Strauss, 3.6 ov), 2–16 (Bopara, 6.4 ov), 3–39 (Bell, 15.3 ov), 4–42 (Collingwood, 18.3 ov), 5–63 (Cook, 22.2 ov), 6–72 (Broad, 24.5 ov), 7–92 (Swann, 29.4 ov), 8–98 (Harmison, 31.4 ov), 9–102 (Anderson, 33.4 ov), 10–102 (Onions, 33.5 ov)

BOWLING: Hilfenhaus 7–0–20–1 (2.85); Siddle 9.5–0–21–5 (2.13); Johnson 7–1–30–1 (4.28); Clark 10–4–18–3 (1.80)

Australia first innings

SR Watson	lbw Onions	51
SM Katich	c Bopara b Harmison	0
RT Ponting	lbw Broad	78
MEK Hussey	lbw Broad	10
MJ Clarke	lbw Onions	93
MJ North	c Anderson b Broad	110
BJ Haddin	c Bell b Harmison	14
MG Johnson	c Bopara b Broad	27
PM Siddle	b Broad	0
SR Clark	b Broad	32
BW Hilfenhaus	not out	0
Extras	(b 9, lb 14, w 4, nb 3)	30
Total	(all out; 104.1 overs)	445

FALL OF WICKETS: 1–14 (Katich, 1.4 ov), 2–133 (Watson, 27.3 ov), 3–140 (Ponting, 28.6 ov), 4–151 (Hussey, 30.3 ov), 5–303 (Clarke, 72.6 ov), 6–323 (Haddin, 80.2 ov), 7–393 (Johnson, 96.3 ov), 8–394 (Siddle, 96.6 ov), 9–440 (Clark, 102.5 ov), 10–445 (North, 104.1 ov)

BOWLING: Anderson 18–3–89–0; Harmison 23–4–98–2; Onions 22–5–80–2; Broad 25.1–6–91–6; Swann 16–4–64–0

England second innings

AJ Strauss	lbw Hilfenhaus	32
AN Cook	c Haddin b Johnson	30
RS Bopara	lbw Hilfenhaus	0
IR Bell	c Ponting b Johnson	3
PD Collingwood	lbw Johnson	4
J Anderson	c Ponting b Hilfenhaus	4
MJ Prior	c Haddin b Hilfenhaus	22
SCJ Broad	c Watson b Siddle	61
GP Swann	c Haddin b Johnson	62
SJ Harmison	not out	19
G Onions	b Johnson	0
Extras	(b 5, lb 5 w 5, nb 11)	26
Total	(all out; 61.3 overs)	263

FALL OF WICKETS: 1–58 (Strauss, 22.4 ov), 2–58 (Bopara, 22.5 ov), 3–67 (Bell, 25.5 ov), 4–74 (Collingwood, 27.6 ov), 5–78 (Cook, 29.6 ov), 6–86 (Anderson, 32.3 ov), 7–120 (Prior, 38.6 ov), 8–228 (Broad, 51.3 ov), 9–259 (Swann, 59.2 ov), 10–263 (Onions, 61.3 ov)

BOWLING: Hilfenhaus 19–2–60–4 (3.15); Siddle 12–2–50–1 (4.16); Clark 11–1–74–0 (6.72); Johnson 19.3–3–69–5 (3.53)

Stumps scores

DAY 1: Australia 4–196 (Clarke 34, North 7; 47 overs)
DAY 2: England 5–82 (Anderson 0, Prior 4; 32 overs)

AUSTRALIA WON BY AN INNINGS AND 80 RUNS

Fifth Ashes Test, Australia v England at the Oval

August 20–24, 2009 • TOSS: England
UMPIRES: Billy Bowden (New Zealand) and Asad Rauf (Pakistan) • MATCH REFEREE: Ranjan Madugalle (Sri Lanka)
PLAYER OF THE MATCH: Stuart Broad (England)
PLAYERS OF THE SERIES: Andrew Strauss (England) and Michael Clarke (Australia)

England first innings

AJ Strauss	c Haddin b Hilfenhaus	55
AN Cook	c Ponting b Siddle	10
IR Bell	b Siddle	72
PD Collingwood	c Hussey b Siddle	24
IJL Trott	run out (Katich)	41
MJ Prior	c Watson b Johnson	18
A Flintoff	c Haddin b Johnson	7
SCJ Broad	c Ponting b Hilfenhaus	37
GP Swann	c Haddin b Siddle	18
JM Anderson	lbw Hilfenhaus	0
SJ Harmison	not out	12
Extras	(b 12, lb 5, w 3, nb 18)	38
Total	(all out; 90.5 overs)	332

FALL OF WICKETS: 1–12 (Cook, 5.3 ov), 2–114 (Strauss, 28.1 ov), 3–176 (Collingwood, 47.5 ov), 4–181 (Bell, 53.5 ov), 5–229 (Prior, 65.3 ov), 6–247 (Flintoff, 69.4 ov), 7–268 (Trott, 74.2 ov), 8–307 (Swann, 85.3 ov), 9–308 (Anderson 86.6 ov), 10–332 (Broad, 90.5 ov)

BOWLING: Hilfenhaus 21.5–5–71–3 (3.25); Siddle 21–6–75–4 (3.57); Clark 14–5–41–0 (2.92); Johnson 15–0–69–2 (4.60); North 14–3–33–0 (2.35); Watson 5–0–26–0 (5.20)

England second innings

AJ Strauss	c Clarke b North	75
AN Cook	c Clarke b North	9
IR Bell	c Katich b Johnson	4
PD Collingwood	c Katich b Johnson	1
IJL Trott	c North b Clark	119
MJ Prior	run out	4
A Flintoff	c Siddle b North	22
SCJ Broad	c Ponting b North	29
GP Swann	c Haddin b Hilfenhaus	63
JM Anderson	not out	15
Extras	(b 1, lb 15, w 7, nb 9)	32
Total	(9 wickets declared; 95 overs)	373

FALL OF WICKETS: 1–27 (Cook, 12.3 ov), 2–34 (Bell, 15.4 ov), 3–39 (Collingwood, 17.3 ov), 4–157 (Strauss, 54.3 ov), 5–168 (Prior, 57.6 ov), 6–200 (Flintoff, 64.1 ov), 7–243 (Broad, 74.2 ov), 8–333 (Swann, 87.4 ov), 9–373 (Trott, 94.6 ov)

BOWLING: Hilfenhaus 11–1–58–1 (5.27); Siddle 17–3–69–0 (4.05); North 30–4–98–4 (3.26); Johnson 17–1–60–2 (3.52); Katich 5–2–9–0 (1.80); Clark 12–2–43–1 (3.58); Clarke 3–0–20–0 (6.67)

Australia first innings

SR Watson	lbw Broad	34
SM Katich	c Cook b Swann	50
RT Ponting	b Broad	8
MEK Hussey	lbw Broad	0
MJ Clarke	c Trott b Broad	3
MJ North	lbw Swann	8
BJ Haddin	b Broad	1
MG Johnson	c Prior b Swann	11
PM Siddle	not out	26
SR Clark	c Cook b Swann	6
BW Hilfenhaus	b Flintoff	6
Extras	(b 1, lb 5, nb 1)	7
Total	(all out; 52.5 overs)	160

FALL OF WICKETS: 1–73 (Watson, 22.6 ov), 2–85 (Ponting, 26.6 ov), 3–89 (Hussey, 28.3 ov), 4–93 (Clarke, 30.2 ov), 5–108 (North, 35.3 ov), 6–109 (Katich, 37.1 ov), 7–111 (Haddin, 38.4 ov), 8–131 (Johnson, 43.5 ov), 9–143 (Clark, 47.3 ov), 10–160 (Hilfenhaus, 52.5 ov)

BOWLING: Anderson 9–3–29–0 (3.22); Flintoff 13.5–4–35–1; Swann 14–3–38–4; Harmison 4–1–15–0; Broad 12–1–37–5

Australia second innings

SR Watson	lbw Broad	40
SM Katich	lbw Swann	43
RT Ponting	run out (Flintoff)	69
MEK Hussey	c Cook b Swann	121
MJ Clarke	run out (Strauss)	0
MJ North	st Prior b Swann	10
BJ Haddin	c Strauss b Swann	34
MG Johnson	c Collingwood b Harmison	0
PM Siddle	c Flintoff b Harmison	10
SR Clark	c Cook b Harmison	0
BW Hilfenhaus	not out	4
Extras	(b 7, lb 7, nb 6)	20
Total	(all out; 102.2 overs)	348

FALL OF WICKETS: 1–86 (Katich, 23.6 ov), 2–90 (Watson, 24.3 ov), 3–217 (Ponting, 63.6 ov), 4–220 (Clarke, 64.5 ov), 5–236 (North, 72.2 ov), 6–327 (Haddin, 94.4 ov), 7–327 (Johnson, 95.5 ov), 8–343 (Siddle, 99.4 ov), 9–343 (Clark, 99.5 ov), 10–348 (Hussey, 102.2 ov)

BOWLING: Anderson 12–2–46–0 (3.83); Flintoff 11–1–42–0; Harmison 16–5–54–3; Swann 40.2–8–120–4; Broad 22–4–71–1; Collingwood 1–0–1–0

Stumps scores
DAY 1: England 8–307 (Broad 26; 85.3 overs)
DAY 2: England 3–58 (Strauss 32, Trott 8; 28 overs)
DAY 3: Australia 0–80 (Watson 31, Katich 42; 20 overs)

ENGLAND WON BY 197 RUNS

ENGLAND WON SERIES 2–1 AND REGAINED THE ASHES

AUSTRALIAN TEST SERIES AVERAGES, OCTOBER 2008–AUGUST 2009

Australia in India 2008

BATTING & FIELDING

Batsman	Tests	Inns	NO	Runs	HS	Ave	SR	100	50	4s	6s	Ct/St
MEK Hussey	4	7	0	394	146	56.28	44.97	1	3	42	1	2
SM Katich	4	8	1	349	102	49.85	48.47	1	2	44	0	3
RT Ponting	4	7	0	266	123	38.00	50.86	1	1	35	0	3
MJ Clarke	4	7	0	251	112	35.85	43.57	1	1	25	1	3
ML Hayden	4	8	1	234	83	33.42	63.58	0	2	33	2	5
CL White	4	7	2	146	46	29.20	44.24	0	0	15	1	1
BJ Haddin	4	7	1	163	37	27.16	37.90	0	0	18	1	13
SR Watson	4	7	0	170	78	24.28	44.50	0	1	24	1	0
B Lee	4	6	1	71	35	14.20	33.49	0	0	10	0	1
MG Johnson	4	6	1	67	26	13.40	50.37	0	0	7	1	0
JJ Krejza	1	2	0	9	5	4.50	23.68	0	0	0	0	1
PM Siddle	1	2	1	0	0*	0.00	0.00	0	0	0	0	0
SR Clark	2	2	2	1	1*	–	33.33	0	0	0	0	0

BOWLING

Bowler	Overs	Mdns	Runs	Wkts	Best	Ave	Econ	SR	5w	10
JJ Krejza	74.5	4	358	12	8–215	29.83	4.78	37.4	1	1
SR Watson	115.4	20	321	10	4–42	32.10	2.77	69.4	0	0
MG Johnson	166.0	30	521	13	4–70	40.07	3.13	76.6	0	0
PM Siddle	43.0	6	176	4	3–114	44.00	4.09	64.5	0	0
B Lee	148.0	24	493	8	2–48	61.62	3.33	111.0	0	0
CL White	93.0	8	342	5	2–71	68.40	3.67	111.6	0	0
SM Katich	19.0	3	73	1	1–60	73.00	3.84	114.0	0	0
SR Clark	73.0	24	161	2	1–12	80.50	2.20	219.0	0	0
MJ Clarke	85.3	18	256	2	2–38	128.00	2.99	256.5	0	0
RT Ponting	2.0	0	11	0	–	–	5.50	–	0	0
MEK Hussey	12.0	2	41	0	–	–	3.41	–	0	0

Australia v New Zealand 2008–09

BATTING & FIELDING

Batsman	Tests	Inns	NO	Runs	HS	Ave	SR	100	50	4s	6s	C/S
SM Katich	2	3	1	164	131*	82.00	53.94	1	0	21	0	2
MJ Clarke	2	3	0	217	110	72.33	46.07	1	1	21	0	4
BJ Haddin	2	3	0	194	169	64.66	68.07	1	0	28	2	5
MEK Hussey	2	3	0	105	70	35.00	39.62	0	1	12	0	0
RT Ponting	2	3	0	100	79	33.33	63.29	0	1	14	0	5
SR Clark	2	3	2	32	18	32.00	57.14	0	0	5	0	0
MG Johnson	2	3	0	59	31	19.66	52.67	0	0	8	1	0
A Symonds	2	3	0	46	26	15.33	54.76	0	0	6	0	5
ML Hayden	2	3	0	32	24	10.66	60.37	0	0	7	0	1
B Lee	2	3	0	30	19	10.00	35.29	0	0	5	1	1
SR Watson	1	2	0	6	5	3.00	33.33	0	0	1	0	0
NM Hauritz	1	1	0	1	1	1.00	8.33	0	0	0	0	0

BOWLING

Bowler	Overs	Mdns	Runs	Wkts	Best	Ave	Econ	SR	5w	10
MG Johnson	65.4	21	154	14	5–39	11.00	2.34	28.1	1	0
B Lee	75.3	18	262	12	5–105	21.83	3.47	37.7	1	0
NM Hauritz	40.0	13	95	4	2–32	23.75	2.37	60.0	0	0
SR Clark	62.0	18	167	7	4–43	23.85	2.69	53.1	0	0
SR Watson	15.0	3	54	2	2–35	27.00	3.60	45.0	0	0
A Symonds	17.0	2	33	1	1–17	33.00	1.94	102.0	0	0
MJ Clarke	2.0	0	6	0	–	–	3.00	–	0	0

Australia v South Africa 2008–09

BATTING & FIELDING

Batsman	Tests	Inns	NO	Runs	HS	Ave	SR	100	50	4s	6s	C/S
MJ Clarke	3	6	1	383	138	76.60	47.87	1	2	36	1	0
JJ Krejza	1	2	1	62	32	62.00	57.40	0	0	8	0	3
SM Katich	3	6	0	297	83	49.50	54.69	0	3	30	1	2
RT Ponting	3	6	0	285	101	47.50	69.68	1	2	30	1	0
BJ Haddin	3	5	0	228	94	45.60	58.61	0	1	20	8	8
MG Johnson	3	5	1	146	64	36.50	53.87	0	1	20	0	2
A Symonds	2	4	0	121	57	30.25	53.77	0	1	11	1	1
ML Hayden	3	6	0	117	39	19.50	52.94	0	0	19	0	1
PM Siddle	3	5	1	75	23	18.75	48.38	0	0	7	0	1
NM Hauritz	2	3	0	56	41	18.66	60.86	0	0	9	0	0
MEK Hussey	3	6	1	85	45*	17.00	33.73	0	0	8	1	3
B Lee	2	4	0	63	29	15.75	67.02	0	0	11	0	0
AB McDonald	1	1	0	15	15	15.00	27.77	0	0	1	0	1
DE Bollinger	1	1	1	0	0*	–	0.00	0	0	0	0	0

BOWLING

Bowler	Overs	Mdns	Runs	Wkts	Best	Ave	Econ	SR	5w	10
MEK Hussey	5.0	0	22	1	1–22	22.00	4.40	30.0	0	0
AB McDonald	35.0	14	73	3	2–32	24.33	2.08	70.0	0	0
MG Johnson	159.4	29	440	17	8–61	25.88	2.75	56.3	1	1
PM Siddle	145.4	44	356	13	5–59	27.38	2.44	67.2	1	0
NM Hauritz	101.0	27	254	5	3–98	50.80	2.51	121.2	0	0
DE Bollinger	44.0	9	131	2	2–53	65.50	2.97	132.0	0	0
JJ Krejza	49.0	4	204	1	1–102	204.00	4.16	294.0	0	0
B Lee	71.0	9	249	1	1–73	249.00	3.50	426.0	0	0
A Symonds	14.0	4	24	0	–	–	1.71	–	0	0
MJ Clarke	21.0	1	77	0	–	–	3.66	–	0	0

Australia in South Africa 2009

BATTING & FIELDING

Batsman	Tests	Inns	NO	Runs	HS	Ave	SR	100	50	4s	6s	C/S
MG Johnson	3	5	2	255	123*	85.00	84.71	1	1	27	10	1
PJ Hughes	3	6	0	415	160	69.16	58.53	2	1	53	6	2
SM Katich	3	6	0	260	108	43.33	43.11	1	2	32	2	1
MJ North	2	4	0	160	117	40.00	44.32	1	0	18	0	2
RT Ponting	3	6	0	210	83	35.00	62.87	0	2	29	1	6
BJ Haddin	3	5	0	165	63	33.00	62.73	0	1	21	2	13/1
MJ Clarke	3	6	1	141	68	28.20	56.17	0	1	19	0	1
AB McDonald	3	5	1	92	68	23.00	56.44	0	1	10	0	1
MEK Hussey	3	6	0	132	50	22.00	33.93	0	1	21	0	1
PM Siddle	3	5	1	31	22*	7.75	53.44	0	0	4	1	3
BW Hilfenhaus	3	5	1	28	16	7.00	82.35	0	0	3	0	1
BE McGain	1	2	0	2	2	1.00	12.50	0	0	0	0	0

BOWLING

Bowler	Overs	Mdns	Runs	Wkts	Best	Ave	Econ	SR	5w	10
SM Katich	14.2	2	54	5	3–45	10.80	3.76	17.2	0	0
PM Siddle	122.3	42	270	12	3–46	22.50	2.20	61.2	0	0
MG Johnson	139.0	28	400	16	4–25	25.00	2.87	52.1	0	0
AB McDonald	87.0	26	227	6	3–25	37.83	2.60	87.0	0	0
MJ North	38.0	9	98	2	1–29	49.00	2.57	114.0	0	0
BW Hilfenhaus	125.0	26	366	7	2–68	52.28	2.92	107.1	0	0
MJ Clarke	1.0	1	0	0	–	–	0.00	–	0	0
BE McGain	18.0	2	149	0	–	–	8.27	–	0	0

The Ashes 2009

BATTING & FIELDING

Batsman	Tests	Inns	NO	Runs	HS	Ave	SR	100	50	4s	6s	C/S
MJ Clarke	5	8	1	448	136	64.00	57.43	2	2	54	1	8
MJ North	5	8	1	367	125*	52.42	49.86	2	1	46	1	3
RT Ponting	5	8	0	385	150	48.12	66.26	1	2	48	2	11
SR Watson	3	5	0	240	62	48.00	54.91	0	3	41	0	2
BJ Haddin	4	6	0	278	121	46.33	69.50	1	1	31	3	15
SM Katich	5	8	0	341	122	42.62	53.87	1	1	44	0	6
MEK Hussey	5	8	0	276	121	34.50	47.83	1	2	40	0	6
NM Hauritz	3	3	1	45	24	22.50	49.45	0	0	5	0	0
GA Manou	1	2	1	21	13*	21.00	53.84	0	0	3	0	3
BW Hilfenhaus	5	6	4	40	20	20.00	49.38	0	0	7	0	0
PJ Hughes	2	3	0	57	36	19.00	58.76	0	0	8	0	1
PM Siddle	5	6	1	91	35	18.20	65.46	0	0	14	0	3
MG Johnson	5	6	0	105	63	17.50	62.13	0	1	17	0	0
SR Clark	2	3	0	38	32	12.66	122.58	0	0	2	3	0

BOWLING

Bowler	Overs	Mdns	Runs	Wkts	Best	Ave	Econ	SR	5w	10
BW Hilfenhaus	180.5	40	604	22	4–60	27.45	3.34	49.3	0	0
PM Siddle	161.4	24	616	20	5–21	30.80	3.81	48.5	1	0
NM Hauritz	103.2	17	321	10	3–63	32.10	3.10	62.0	0	0
MG Johnson	162.1	15	651	20	5–69	32.55	4.01	48.6	1	0
SR Clark	47.0	12	176	4	3–18	44.00	3.74	70.5	0	0
MJ North	67.3	13	204	4	4–98	51.00	3.02	101.2	0	0
MJ Clarke	19.0	1	75	1	1–12	75.00	3.94	114.0	0	0
SM Katich	10.0	2	27	0	–	–	2.70	–	0	0
SR Watson	8.0	0	49	0	–	–	6.12	–	0	0

Test Centuries

Batsman	Runs	BF	4s	6s	Opposition	Venue
RT Ponting	123	243	13	0	India	Bangalore
MEK Hussey	146	276	15	1	India	Bangalore
MJ Clarke	112	253	6	1	India	Delhi
SM Katich	102	189	9	0	India	Nagpur
SM Katich	131*	245	16	0	New Zealand	Brisbane
MJ Clarke	110	239	11	0	New Zealand	Adelaide
BJ Haddin	169	222	24	2	New Zealand	Adelaide
RT Ponting	101	126	10	1	South Africa	Melbourne
MJ Clarke	138	250	17	0	South Africa	Sydney
MJ North	117	233	12	0	South Africa	Johannesburg
PJ Hughes	160	323	15	3	South Africa	Durban
SM Katich	108	190	16	0	South Africa	Durban
PJ Hughes	115	151	19	2	South Africa	Durban
MG Johnson	123*	103	11	5	South Africa	Cape Town
SM Katich	122	261	12	0	England	Cardiff
RT Ponting	150	224	14	1	England	Cardiff
MJ North	125*	242	13	0	England	Cardiff
BJ Haddin	121	151	11	3	England	Cardiff
MJ Clarke	136	227	14	0	England	Lord's
MJ Clarke	103*	192	14	0	England	Birmingham
MJ North	110	206	13	1	England	Leeds
MEK Hussey	121	263	14	0	England	The Oval

Five Wickets in a Test Innings

Bowler	Overs	Mdns	Runs	Wkts	Opposition	Venue
JJ Krejza	43.5	1	215	8	India	Nagpur
MG Johnson	17.3	6	39	5	New Zealand	Brisbane
B Lee	25.0	5	105	5	New Zealand	Adelaide
MG Johnson	24.0	4	61	8	South Africa	Perth
PM Siddle	27.5	11	59	5	South Africa	Sydney
PM Siddle	9.5	0	21	5	England	Leeds
MG Johnson	19.3	3	69	5	England	Leeds

Note: Krejza (12–358 at Nagpur) and Johnson (11–159 at Perth) took 10 wickets in a Test.

PHOTOGRAPHS

All the images that appear in the photo sections of *Captain's Diary 2009* come from the fantastic resources of Getty Images and AFP. Our thanks go to everyone at Getty, especially Philippa Hutson and their outstanding photographers who follow the Australian team around the cricket world.

The photographers whose work appears in the book include Hamish Blair, Lucas Dawson, Stu Forster, Paul Gilham, Robert Gray, Laurence Griffiths, Richard Heathcote, Mike Hewitt, Bradley Kanaris, Matt King, Ian Kington, Mark Kolbe, Christopher Lee, Matthew Lewis, Robert Prezioso, Clive Rose, Dibyangshu Sarkar, Tom Shaw, Prakash Singh, Michael Steele, Brendon Thorne, Manan Vatsyayana, William West and Andrew Yates.

Getty Images: Section One — page 1 (top), page 2 (both), page 3 (all), page 4 (all), page 5 (all), page 6 (all), page 7 (all), page 8 (top left, bottom left, bottom right); Section Two — page 1 (all), page 2 (both), page 3 (all), page 4 (all), page 6 (all), page 7 (top & bottom left), page 8 (all); Section Three — page 1 (top & bottom right), page 2 (bottom left & right), page 3 (top & middle), page 4 (all), page 5 (all), page 6 (all), page 7 (all), page 8 (all).

AFP/Getty Images: Section One — page 1 (middle & bottom), page 8 (top right); Section Two — page 5 (both), page 7 (bottom right); Section Three — page 1 (bottom left), page 2 (top), page 3 (bottom).

Chapter Openers

Page 1: Ricky Ponting celebrates his century in the first Test at Bangalore, October 2008 (Getty Images).

Page 59: Brett Lee, Andrew Symonds and Ponting celebrate a New Zealand wicket at the Adelaide Oval, November 2008 (Getty Images).

Page 83: Ponting walks off the MCG after being dismissed for 99 in the Boxing Day Test against South Africa in 2008–09 (Getty Images).

Page 131: Matthew Hayden with his younger son Thomas and Ponting at the media conference where Hayden announced his retirement from international cricket, January 2009 (Getty Images).

Page 141: Joint Allan Border Medallists, Ricky Ponting and Michael Clarke, at the medal presentation, February 2009 (Getty Images).

Page 167: Ponting celebrates Australia's victory in the first Test at Johannesburg, March 2009 (Getty Images).

Page 225: Ponting is bowled by Sri Lanka's Ajantha Mendis during the ICC World Twenty20, June 2009 (Getty Images).

Page 247: Ponting with the Ashes urn the day before the First Test at Cardiff, July 2009 (Getty Images).

Page 405: Ponting during his century in the fifth ODI at Trent Bridge, September 2009 (Getty Images).